Lecture Notes in Computer Science   12778

More information about this subseries at http://www.springer.com/series/7409

Vincent G. Duffy (Ed.)

Digital Human Modeling and Applications in Health, Safety, Ergonomics and Risk Management

AI, Product and Service

12th International Conference, DHM 2021
Held as Part of the 23rd HCI International Conference, HCII 2021
Virtual Event, July 24–29, 2021
Proceedings, Part II

 Springer

Editor
Vincent G. Duffy
Purdue University
West Lafayette, IN, USA

ISSN 0302-9743   ISSN 1611-3349   (electronic)
Lecture Notes in Computer Science
ISBN 978-3-030-77819-4   ISBN 978-3-030-77820-0   (eBook)
https://doi.org/10.1007/978-3-030-77820-0

LNCS Sublibrary: SL3 – Information Systems and Applications, incl. Internet/Web, and HCI

This Springer imprint is published by the registered company Springer Nature Switzerland AG
The registered company address is: Gewerbestrasse 11, 6330 Cham, Switzerland

Foreword

Human-Computer Interaction (HCI) is acquiring an ever-increasing scientific and industrial importance, and having more impact on people's everyday life, as an ever-growing number of human activities are progressively moving from the physical to the digital world. This process, which has been ongoing for some time now, has been dramatically accelerated by the COVID-19 pandemic. The HCI International (HCII) conference series, held yearly, aims to respond to the compelling need to advance the exchange of knowledge and research and development efforts on the human aspects of design and use of computing systems.

The 23rd International Conference on Human-Computer Interaction, HCI International 2021 (HCII 2021), was planned to be held at the Washington Hilton Hotel, Washington DC, USA, during July 24–29, 2021. Due to the COVID-19 pandemic and with everyone's health and safety in mind, HCII 2021 was organized and run as a virtual conference. It incorporated the 21 thematic areas and affiliated conferences listed on the following page.

A total of 5222 individuals from academia, research institutes, industry, and governmental agencies from 81 countries submitted contributions, and 1276 papers and 241 posters were included in the proceedings to appear just before the start of the conference. The contributions thoroughly cover the entire field of HCI, addressing major advances in knowledge and effective use of computers in a variety of application areas. These papers provide academics, researchers, engineers, scientists, practitioners, and students with state-of-the-art information on the most recent advances in HCI. The volumes constituting the set of proceedings to appear before the start of the conference are listed in the following pages.

The HCI International (HCII) conference also offers the option of 'Late Breaking Work' which applies both for papers and posters, and the corresponding volume(s) of the proceedings will appear after the conference. Full papers will be included in the 'HCII 2021 - Late Breaking Papers' volumes of the proceedings to be published in the Springer LNCS series, while 'Poster Extended Abstracts' will be included as short research papers in the 'HCII 2021 - Late Breaking Posters' volumes to be published in the Springer CCIS series.

The present volume contains papers submitted and presented in the context of the 12th International Conference on Digital Human Modeling and Applications in Health, Safety, Ergonomics and Risk Management (DHM 2021), an affiliated conference to HCII 2021. I would like to thank the Chair, Vincent G. Duffy, for his invaluable contribution to its organization and the preparation of the proceedings, as well as the members of the Program Board for their contributions and support. This year, the DHM affiliated conference has focused on topics related to ergonomics, human factors and occupational health, human body and motion modeling, language, communication and behavior modeling, healthcare applications, and digital human models in product and service design, as well as AI applications.

I would also like to thank the Program Board Chairs and the members of the Program Boards of all thematic areas and affiliated conferences for their contribution towards the highest scientific quality and overall success of the HCI International 2021 conference.

This conference would not have been possible without the continuous and unwavering support and advice of Gavriel Salvendy, founder, General Chair Emeritus, and Scientific Advisor. For his outstanding efforts, I would like to express my appreciation to Abbas Moallem, Communications Chair and Editor of HCI International News.

July 2021   Constantine Stephanidis

HCI International 2021 Thematic Areas and Affiliated Conferences

Thematic Areas

- HCI: Human-Computer Interaction
- HIMI: Human Interface and the Management of Information

Affiliated Conferences

- EPCE: 18th International Conference on Engineering Psychology and Cognitive Ergonomics
- UAHCI: 15th International Conference on Universal Access in Human-Computer Interaction
- VAMR: 13th International Conference on Virtual, Augmented and Mixed Reality
- CCD: 13th International Conference on Cross-Cultural Design
- SCSM: 13th International Conference on Social Computing and Social Media
- AC: 15th International Conference on Augmented Cognition
- DHM: 12th International Conference on Digital Human Modeling and Applications in Health, Safety, Ergonomics and Risk Management
- DUXU: 10th International Conference on Design, User Experience, and Usability
- DAPI: 9th International Conference on Distributed, Ambient and Pervasive Interactions
- HCIBGO: 8th International Conference on HCI in Business, Government and Organizations
- LCT: 8th International Conference on Learning and Collaboration Technologies
- ITAP: 7th International Conference on Human Aspects of IT for the Aged Population
- HCI-CPT: 3rd International Conference on HCI for Cybersecurity, Privacy and Trust
- HCI-Games: 3rd International Conference on HCI in Games
- MobiTAS: 3rd International Conference on HCI in Mobility, Transport and Automotive Systems
- AIS: 3rd International Conference on Adaptive Instructional Systems
- C&C: 9th International Conference on Culture and Computing
- MOBILE: 2nd International Conference on Design, Operation and Evaluation of Mobile Communications
- AI-HCI: 2nd International Conference on Artificial Intelligence in HCI

List of Conference Proceedings Volumes Appearing Before the Conference

1. LNCS 12762, Human-Computer Interaction: Theory, Methods and Tools (Part I), edited by Masaaki Kurosu
2. LNCS 12763, Human-Computer Interaction: Interaction Techniques and Novel Applications (Part II), edited by Masaaki Kurosu
3. LNCS 12764, Human-Computer Interaction: Design and User Experience Case Studies (Part III), edited by Masaaki Kurosu
4. LNCS 12765, Human Interface and the Management of Information: Information Presentation and Visualization (Part I), edited by Sakae Yamamoto and Hirohiko Mori
5. LNCS 12766, Human Interface and the Management of Information: Information-rich and Intelligent Environments (Part II), edited by Sakae Yamamoto and Hirohiko Mori
6. LNAI 12767, Engineering Psychology and Cognitive Ergonomics, edited by Don Harris and Wen-Chin Li
7. LNCS 12768, Universal Access in Human-Computer Interaction: Design Methods and User Experience (Part I), edited by Margherita Antona and Constantine Stephanidis
8. LNCS 12769, Universal Access in Human-Computer Interaction: Access to Media, Learning and Assistive Environments (Part II), edited by Margherita Antona and Constantine Stephanidis
9. LNCS 12770, Virtual, Augmented and Mixed Reality, edited by Jessie Y. C. Chen and Gino Fragomeni
10. LNCS 12771, Cross-Cultural Design: Experience and Product Design Across Cultures (Part I), edited by P. L. Patrick Rau
11. LNCS 12772, Cross-Cultural Design: Applications in Arts, Learning, Well-being, and Social Development (Part II), edited by P. L. Patrick Rau
12. LNCS 12773, Cross-Cultural Design: Applications in Cultural Heritage, Tourism, Autonomous Vehicles, and Intelligent Agents (Part III), edited by P. L. Patrick Rau
13. LNCS 12774, Social Computing and Social Media: Experience Design and Social Network Analysis (Part I), edited by Gabriele Meiselwitz
14. LNCS 12775, Social Computing and Social Media: Applications in Marketing, Learning, and Health (Part II), edited by Gabriele Meiselwitz
15. LNAI 12776, Augmented Cognition, edited by Dylan D. Schmorrow and Cali M. Fidopiastis
16. LNCS 12777, Digital Human Modeling and Applications in Health, Safety, Ergonomics and Risk Management: Human Body, Motion and Behavior (Part I), edited by Vincent G. Duffy
17. LNCS 12778, Digital Human Modeling and Applications in Health, Safety, Ergonomics and Risk Management: AI, Product and Service (Part II), edited by Vincent G. Duffy

38. CCIS 1420, HCI International 2021 Posters - Part II, edited by Constantine Stephanidis, Margherita Antona, and Stavroula Ntoa
39. CCIS 1421, HCI International 2021 Posters - Part III, edited by Constantine Stephanidis, Margherita Antona, and Stavroula Ntoa

http://2021.hci.international/proceedings

12th International Conference on Digital Human Modeling and Applications in Health, Safety, Ergonomics and Risk Management (DHM 2021)

Program Board Chair: **Vincent G. Duffy,** *Purdue University, USA*

- Giuseppe Andreoni, Italy
- Mária Babicsné Horváth, Hungary
- Stephen Baek, USA
- Joan Cahill, Ireland
- André Calero Valdez, Germany
- Yaqin Cao, China
- Damien Chablat, France
- H. Onan Demirel, USA
- Martin Fleischer, Germany
- Martin Fränzle, Germany
- Fu Guo, China
- Afzal Godil, USA
- Akihiko Goto, Japan
- Michael Harry, UK
- Sogand Hasanzadeh, USA
- Dan Högberg, Sweden
- Csilla Herendy, Hungary
- Mingcai Hu, China
- Genett Jimenez, Colombia
- Mohamed Fateh Karoui, USA
- Sashidharan Komandur, Norway
- Sebastian Korfmacher, Germany
- Theoni Koukoulaki, Greece
- Noriaki Kuwahara, Japan
- Byung Cheol Lee, USA
- Yi Lu, China
- Alexander Mehler, Germany
- Peter Nickel, Germany
- Thaneswer Patel, India
- Giovanni Pignoni, Norway
- Manikam Pillay, Australia
- Qing-Xing Qu, China
- Fabián R. Narváez, Ecuador
- Caterina Rizzi, Italy
- Joni Salminen, Qatar
- Juan A. Sánchez-Margallo, Spain
- Sebastian Schlund, Austria
- Deep Seth, India
- Meng-Dar Shieh, Taiwan
- Beatriz Sousa Santos, Portugal
- Leonor Teixeira, Portugal
- Renran Tian, USA
- Alexander Trende, Germany
- Dustin Van der Haar, South Africa
- Dakuo Wang, USA
- Anita Woll, Norway
- Kuan Yew Wong, Malaysia
- Shuping Xiong, South Korea
- James Yang, USA

The full list with the Program Board Chairs and the members of the Program Boards of all thematic areas and affiliated conferences is available online at:

http://www.hci.international/board-members-2021.php

HCI International 2022

The 24th International Conference on Human-Computer Interaction, HCI International 2022, will be held jointly with the affiliated conferences at the Gothia Towers Hotel and Swedish Exhibition & Congress Centre, Gothenburg, Sweden, June 26 – July 1, 2022. It will cover a broad spectrum of themes related to Human-Computer Interaction, including theoretical issues, methods, tools, processes, and case studies in HCI design, as well as novel interaction techniques, interfaces, and applications. The proceedings will be published by Springer. More information will be available on the conference website: http://2022.hci.international/:

General Chair
Prof. Constantine Stephanidis
University of Crete and ICS-FORTH
Heraklion, Crete, Greece
Email: general_chair@hcii2022.org

http://2022.hci.international/

Contents – Part II

Artificial Intelligence Applications and Ethical Issues

Digital Human Modeling in Product and Service Design

Contents – Part I

Language, Communication and Behavior Modeling

Rethinking Healthcare

Development and Testing of a Usability Checklist for the Evaluation of Control Interfaces of Electrical Medical Beds

Davide Bacchin[1]([envelope]) [ORCID], Patrik Pluchino[2], Valeria Orso[2], Marcello Sardena[3],
Marino Malvestio[3], and Luciano Gamberini[2]

[1] Department of General Psychology, University of Padova, via Venezia 8, 31121 Padua, Italy
davide.bacchin.2@phd.unipd.it
[2] Human Inspired Technology (HIT) Research Centre, University of Padova,
via Luigi Luzzatti 4, 35121 Padua, Italy
{patrik.pluchino,valeria.orso,luciano.gamberini}@unipd.it
[3] Malvestio S.p.a., via Marconi 12D, 35010 Villanova di Camposampiero, PD, Italy
{sardena.marcello,marino}@malvestio.com

Abstract. The last few decades have seen the hospital environment become more and more technologically advanced with the development of advanced diagnostic and surgical tools. The beds have also undergone a radical transformation, thanks to the integration of electrical and electronic components, that have allowed the birth of the modern widespread electric beds. This work presents a checklist developed to test the usability of the pushbutton panels that control their movements, which could be useful in designing a controller capable of considering the needs of users such as caregivers and patients. The checklist items were created starting from the usability guidelines and then placed within an appropriate Nielsen heuristic. The tool thus designed was tested in a usability expert evaluation session with five experts. The data collected were the responses to the checklist, the experts' comments, the notes collected during the procedure, the time to complete, and the severity and frequency of the problems detected. The results showed that the checklist could detect a substantial series of significant usability problems in a short time, which makes it an easily usable tool in the industrial field for rapid and valuable tests for future interfaces design. The usage of this developed checklist could be useful to design better control panels to facilitate both caregivers' work and patients' stay.

Keywords: Electrical medical beds · Usability checklist · Usability expert evaluation · Push-button panels · HCI

1 Introduction

Healthcare and eldercare facilities are currently struggling to cope with patients' needs all over the world. Among others, the problem of staff shortage is very well known in this field, and caregivers found themselves faced with increasingly high workload and stress levels, characterized by risks, precarious working conditions, long and irregular shifts,

© Springer Nature Switzerland AG 2021
V. G. Duffy (Ed.): HCII 2021, LNCS 12778, pp. 3–19, 2021.
https://doi.org/10.1007/978-3-030-77820-0_1

and emotional pressures [1]. A recent and extensive study carried out in Switzerland in 2018 [2] described a survey with 1840 respondents in the hospital sector showing how the physical, mental, and emotional workload play fundamental roles in developing burnout and intention to leave the profession. The study showed that work stress accounts for 40 to 43% of burnout cases, while for 22–29% of the cases of intention to leave. These data, therefore, show how the health system is greatly affected by the problems deriving from the ageing of the population and the contemporary demographic increment which, combined with the lack of personnel, set hospitals and nursing homes in a difficult condition. Besides, the COVID-19 pandemic and the health crisis have revealed a new set of weaknesses of the sanitary systems, such as the insufficient number of beds in intensive care units [3], and have exacerbated the lack of personnel. Moreover, the large number of patients who needed regular or long-term hospitalization [4] has highlighted the relevance of specific facilities that help caregivers to reduce their workload.

All these issues that in different manner concern both eldercare and healthcare, affect the quality of life and working environment of caregivers, but they also impact the quality of care delivered to guests and patients. Therefore, helping health workers and nurses will allow all categories to improve care quality, given and received. This paper addresses how to help hospital staff work more efficiently without having negative repercussions on work stress. One of the most common solutions and one of the most valuable aids could be the intervention of increasingly sophisticated technologies, capable of making hospital procedures easier or less tiring. These innovations certainly provide proper support, but, at the same time, they can introduce complex tools into the caregivers' work practice, which require to be studied and understood, especially when it comes into contact also with patients. It is crucial to ensure that these technologies are designed according to principles that make them effective, efficient, and satisfying. These characteristics fall within the concept of Usability, defined as "the extent to which a system, product or service can be used by specified users to achieve specified goals with effectiveness, efficiency and satisfaction in a specified context of use" [5]. Given the strong influence that usability exerts on the increase of work well-being, the reduction of time pressure and other aspects of the work of doctors and the rest of the hospital staff [6], the point is, therefore to make more usable the instruments used in these environments.

This work was born from these concepts and from the intention to create an easy and rapid assessment tool to evaluate hospital bed control panels. To this end, a checklist was devised, and the control panel (Fig. 1.a) present in the Delta4 model (Fig. 1.b) of the beds produced by the Malvestio Spa. was evaluated. The study examined a patient's push-button panel considering a specific tool that could be potentially exploited to assess any type of bed controller.

1.1 Electrical Medical Beds

The modern history of hospital beds and related innovations has been explored in some recent reviews by Ghersi [7, 8]. In its older work, he tackles the evolution of hospital beds from the 1940s to 2000, identifying three macro stages, starting with the era of electric beds, passing through mechatronic beds up to intelligent mechatronic beds. He identified the origin of the electrical beds when the adjustable sides were invented, between 1815 and 1825 [9]. Following technology development, these supports gradually

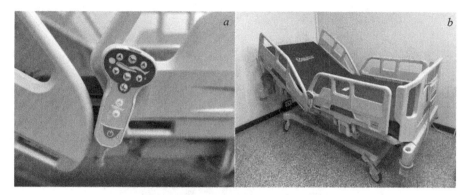

Fig. 1. a) Patient's control panel; b) Delta4 bed

acquire greater intelligence and automatisms, transforming themselves into what he defines as Intelligent Mechatronic Beds. In modern electric hospital beds, software, and hardware work together to allow the bed and its components to move in a concerted manner, thus integrating mechanics with electronics and computer science.

The most advanced versions of these tools are equipped with an electrical engine, capable of moving some of their parts (e.g., backrest) to meet people's needs in terms of personalization and comfort. The modern bed is usually divided into four different sections. This configuration, with 3 articulated parts (back, thighs or upper leg, calves or lower leg) and a central part fixed, prevents the mattress from deforming and at the same time guarantees an equal pressure distribution even if the movement of each section reaches its limit. The leg and the torso sections can also be moved thanks to electric or other actuators. Moreover, thanks to the double-section configuration of the leg section, subdivided in thighs (upper leg) and calves (lower leg), the former allows a slight elevation in its central part, at the knees level. This allows reaching a position similar to an armchair (chair position). A scheme of this structure is shown in Fig. 2.

Subsequently, another extensive work by Ghersi [8] highlighted how the hospital bed market is increasingly evolving towards their smart forms. These bed features cutting-edge technologies and are designed to have high functionality and advanced user interfaces. Nowadays, therefore, in the hospital environment, product efficiency is fundamental and has become one of the discriminating factors that will lead to its success [10]. Control panels represent the physical interfaces that allow patients and professional caregivers to control the beds' movements. Therefore, it would be desirable that the design and development of the control interfaces will consider usability aspects, such as efficacy and efficiency.

1.2 Human Factors on Medical Beds

Despite the increasingly urgent and well-recognised need to study human factors related to hospital beds. The research in this field has mainly focused on technical aspects, such as algorithms for patient monitoring systems to reduce false alarms [11], pressure-sensing mat to optimize repositioning of the patients [12] and pressure sensors to predict falling accidents and bedsores [13].

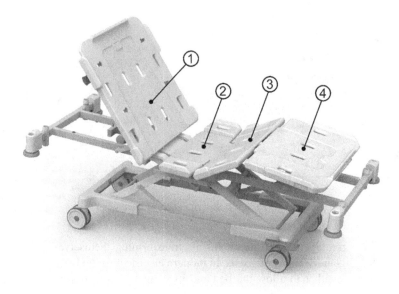

Fig. 2. Scheme of the structure of the bed. 1 – backrest; 2 – central fixed section; 3 – thighs or upper leg; 4 – calves or lower leg.

Studies investigating usability in healthcare environment are less frequent, even though there are a few exceptions. For example, a recent study [14] used semi-structured interviews and a usability questionnaire to define design guidelines for instruments in operating room. A recent review [15] sought to summarize and organize the studies carried out so far in the general field of medical devices, demonstrating the interest of human factors in hospital technologies.

However, pertaining to hospital beds, some investigations concerning their usability are present in the literature. First of all, it is interesting to know that the electric hospital bed has been tested to verify its effectiveness as a technological advance compared to previous versions, such as the hydraulic one. A video analysis study [16] has demonstrated their superiority by analyzing tasks carried out by couples of nurses who had to deal with problems relating to bed hygiene and the transfer of a patient from it to a wheelchair. In this study, the outcomes of a survey administered to 63 caregivers highlighted a high level of usability for the electric bed.

Regarding the design of the bed, an extensive study by Wiggerman [17] has shown how manufacturers are increasingly interested in the human-centric approach, in which users are involved in the development process. This work presents many usability tests (over 20 studies with more than 130 caregivers) that were carried out to identify the interfaces' potential usability problems. Again, this design approach is then concretized, in the final stages, with tests in a real environment. Regarding this last point, an example of a test is the one carried out by Cai and colleagues [18]. In their study, a smart bed, and the associated functions and technologies, was tested for 12 months in a hospital. The nurses involved were then interviewed to define any technical and usability problems.

Going more specifically to particular parts of the bed, one of the issues most encountered by hospital staff concerned the effort required to move a bed, with a patient on it, from one place to another in the hospital. In this sense, the innovations sought by the manufacturers, such as the 5th motorized wheel and alternative brake positions, have been studied to understand which solution could be the least tiring to use [19]. Thanks to quantitative and qualitative measures, these studies have shown how the 5th wheel drastically reduces perceived fatigue and the need to have the brake pedals particularly accessible to the operators, both for the patient's safety and any operators' back pain.

As for the bed controls, the attention to the usability associated with them is more recent, although, even in this field, they are often addressed to new emerging technologies, such as gestures. In a study of 2017 [20], some interviews showed how this control method (i.e., gestures) was recognized by caregivers as potentially suitable, given the possibility of hands-free control and reduced infection ability due to the reduced use of physical interfaces. Despite the advent of these innovations, the physical interface currently remains the golden standard for beds worldwide. In Lin and colleagues [21], they tested the usability of 6 different types of controllers with 20 nurses. Finally, even in one of the aforementioned studies [18], an electronic push-button panel was also tested, defined by the users interviewed as very useful and often used.

1.3 Usability Checklist

Usability checklist is a well-established methodology in Human-Computer Interaction that allow to evaluate the usability of a user interface in a rapid and cost-effective manner. Generally speaking, a usability checklist consists of a set of rules or guidelines that the user interface is expected to meet, and that a number of participants is asked to evaluate [22]. One of the main advantages of usability checklists is that they provide reliable results even with very small samples of evaluators, namely five, thereby being extremely convenient [22]. Initially, usability checklists were developed around the usability heuristics proposed by Nielsen [23]. While still being a seminal reference, such guidelines need to be adapted to the very specific case of study.

Over the years, usability checklists have been deployed to evaluate a variety of different interfaces, including websites [24], Augmented Reality applications [25], virtual environments [26], just to mention a few.

Several studies employed checklists to investigate the usability of mobile apps addressing patient monitoring of specific health issues [27] or to evaluate software for doctors' appointment management [28]. However, the user interfaces with which healthcare professionals directly interact on a daily basis have rarely been assessed using such method.

The aim of the present work is to apply a purposefully devised usability checklist for the evaluation of the control panel of an electric hospital bed.

2   Materials and Methods

2.1   Checklist Development

The checklist's creation was divided into three phases: the selection of the usability guidelines, the distribution of the same within the ten Nielsen heuristics, a first pilot to test their effectiveness, and the removal of the unsuitable ones.

- **Usability Guidelines Selection.** During the creation of usability questionnaires or checklists, one of the main limitations is forgetting some critical elements to analyze. To overcome this problem, it was decided to start from the guidelines to ensure the greatest number of controlled features. The Checklist items were elaborated based on the usability guidelines for design technology hospital settings [29]. Each guideline consistent with the purpose of the experiment was rephrased to be suitable as a checklist item and translated into Italian.
- **Items Distribution.** The ten Nielsen heuristics [30] were used to firstly define the dimensions and general usability principles of the Checklist. Subsequently, they were slightly modified and adapted, when necessary, to the context and to the evaluation of a physical interface to permit the insertion of items generated from the guidelines. The dimensions used were:

1. *Visibility of system status.* The system should provide clear and rapid feedbacks to inform the user about its current status.
2. *Match between system and the real world.* The system should use a familiar language to the user, following conventions and logical order. Possible user actions should match the real-world effects.
3. *Give the user control with comfort.* The user should be free to use the interface without impediments that facilitate errors or make the interaction less pleasant.
4. *Consistency and standard.* The user should not worry about finding conflicting elements within the system, which should follow platform conventions.
5. *Error prevention.* The system should be designed to prevent errors. In case of errors or dangerous situations, it must provide quick and punctual help for its resolution.
6. *Recognition rather than recall.* It is important to minimize the memory load elicited by the system by making the information easily accessible and intuitive.
7. *Flexibility, accessibility, and efficiency of use.* Experienced users should be able to use shortcuts to reduce system usage time. This should also be flexible and accessible enough to allow use by all types of users.
8. *Aesthetic and minimalist design.* The system should not present information that is irrelevant or infrequently used. The aesthetics should also be nice.
9. *Help users recognize, diagnose, and recover from errors.* The error messages should be clear and precise, indicating their resolutions.
10. *Help and documentation.* The system should be usable without the instructions. When a system could not achieve this objective, the information should be easy to find and centered on the user's needed actions, with step-by-step guides. The documentation should not be too long.

- **Pilot Study.** After inserting the items based on the guidelines into the most suitable usability principles categories, a first pilot experiment was carried out with some usability experts (N = 4). The purposes were to test the experimental procedure, refine the items statements eventually, remove the unsuitable items, and potentially add missing ones, according to the expert's comments. The final checklist (fundable in the Appendix section) integrated items adapted from specific guidelines and from the usability experts' comments. The total number of items created is 34.

2.2 Scoring and Measures

Participants' responses to the checklist items could be positive, negative, or not applicable (Yes; No; N.A.). Since the items were formulated to be in accordance with the guidelines, the single items score was obtained by calculating the percentage of positive responses, and as regards the dimensions, the average was then extracted. The only exception was the item 34 ("The documentation material is necessary for the use of the bed control panel"), in which the item was negatively formulated, and it was reversed. In addition, users' notes were collected in the checklist, together with any behaviour or comments that participants made during the experience. Moreover, the time spent to complete the checklist was considered. After the first analysis of the checklist, the participants fill a questionnaire to assess the level of severity of the problem detected. This Severity Questionnaire follows the scoring scale stated by Nielsen [31] that assign to every problem a score from 0 to 4: 0 = I don't agree that this is a usability problem at all; 1 = Cosmetic problem only: need not be fixed unless extra time is available on project; 2 = Minor usability problem: fixing this should be given low priority; 3 = Major usability problem: important to fix, so should be given high priority; 4 = Usability catastrophe: imperative to fix this before product can be released. Finally, the frequency in which they were reported on the Checklist or identified by users during the procedure was calculated for each problem.

2.3 Experimental Procedure

The experiment involved 5 usability experts (F = 3, Mean age = 31, SD = 5.8) and took place in a laboratory setting where a hospital bed featuring a cabled control-panel was placed. The bed presents two push-button control panels, one for patients and one for operators. The latter can lock the patient's one, to deprive people at risk of bed control. Before the participant's arrival, the experimenter blocked the control-panel to activate the LED associate with this state and permits its visualization to participants who did not have previous experience with the bed. In fact, they did not receive specific instructions on the control panel to test the intuitiveness of the system. They were asked to perform a series of actions to explore all the bed functions: turning on/off the key panel, reaching the minimum/maximum of the backrest, leg section, and bed height, finally setting the chair and safe exit positions. They could freely explore these features in the preferred order as many times as they deem necessary and in every preferred positions. Due to the starting blocked state, participants initially tried to use the panel, but it was blocked, as the experimenter explained. He unlocked the control panel only after they asked for it. After participants decided that they have completed their free exploration of the bed functions, they were administered with the Checklist. Finally, the researcher provided the control panel user manual to enable participants to fill the items of the heuristics Help and Documentation. Following the regulations for the limitations of the COVID-19 spreading, the bed was then sanitized after each use.

3   Results

This procedure has allowed the collection of different types of data, starting from the results of the items. The average percentage of positive responses showed the strengths of the control panel, while the percentage of negative responses showed the weaknesses. The results of these data analyses follow within the dimensions of the checklist. The results are shown below according to the order of dimensions and are summarized in Fig. 3.

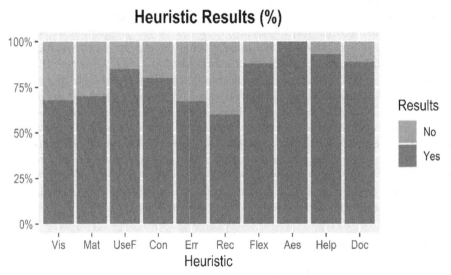

Fig. 3. The graph shows the mean percentage obtained for each heuristic. Vis = Visibility of system status; Mat = Match between system and the real world; UseF = User control and freedom; Con = Consistency and standards; Err = Error prevention; Rec = Recognition rather than recall; Flex = Flexibility and efficiency of use; Aes = Aesthetic and minimalist design; Help = Help users recognize, diagnose, and recover from errors; Doc = Help and documentation

- **Visibility of System Status.** The control panel was found to comply with the usability guidelines in 70% of the cases. In particular, the participants highlighted that there should be more feedback types and a faster bed's response to clarify the activation of the button. The lack of different types of feedback, other than the movements of the bed, was also highlighted by the experts' comments. For example: "Lack of visual feedback that indicates to continue pressing the button."; "Differences in the delay of the response to the key by the movement of the bed"; "At the beginning, it is natural to press shortly the buttons and this does not affect the bed"; "The answer is not always immediate". However, it has been noted that the materials used for the creation of the keys could create an adequate tactile sensation ("holding the button down, it became concave and gave a feeling of feedback"). The notes were also consistent, highlighting the lack of feedback, especially of a visual type ("the number of LEDs should be increased"). The participants highlight an issue regarding the backrest lifting function, which stops in correspondence of 30° without giving any indication to the user ("apart for the backrest that stops halfway").

– **Match Between System and the Real World.** 60% of responses complying with guidelines. Most of the participants noticed the same problem about the cardiologic chair button (Fig. 4), which appears to be the same both for the upper and for the lower position ("the cardiac chair should be clearer").

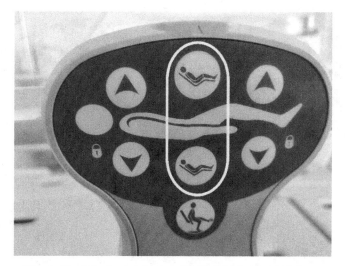

Fig. 4. Cardiologic chair buttons highlighted by the oval shape.

– **User Control and Freedom.** 80% of responses complying with guidelines. The experts highlighted issues regarding the cable that connects the control panel to the bed (e.g., "if the cable were longer it would be more comfortable"), also confirmed by the experimental notes ("too short cable"). Despite this, the checklist highlighted this problem in the comments but met all participants' approval. Moreover, the control buttons panel cannot be used with only one hand most of the times ("It would be difficult to reach all the buttons without moving the hand holding the remote control"; "Especially for the higher keys it was more comfortable to hold it with one hand and press them with the other"). The questions also highlighted that it is not clear which one is a safe position button ("It is not so intuitive what the safety positions are").

– **Consistency and Standards.** Despite the majority of responses comply with the guidelines (80%), question 11 once again highlighted the problems concerning the chair's cardiology button which, unlike the sour buttons, do not have up and down arrows ("Chair buttons do not have up or down").

- **Error Prevention.** The responses were generally positive and in according with the guidelines (71.5%). The buttons for the lowest height (Fig. 5.a) also lack a textual part to clarify its function and the only one present, the word "low" (Fig. 5.b), is in English ("English label"). It is not very clear to the participants why the backrest stop at a certain point and one of them also notice that the buttons may be pressed twice or more to reach the end of the movement due to button slippery ("No, and it is not clear that the movement has not reached the end of its travel and can continue with a further pressure of the key (30°); it is possible to lose pressure in a few moments, and the desired movement is interrupted"). The score is also significantly lowered by the absence of visibility in dark conditions.

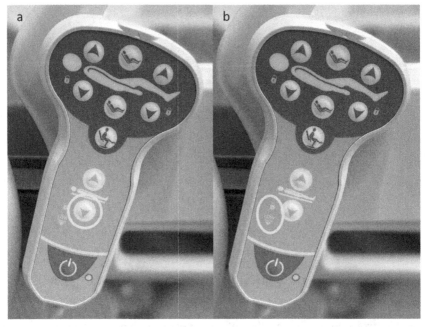

Fig. 5. (a) The left image shows the button to set the bed at the lowest height; (b) the image on the right shows the "low" label.

- **Recognition Rather than Recall.** 70% of responses complying with guidelines. The cardiologic chair button (Fig. 4) was mentioned as the major usability problem of the control panel. Three out of five participants have remarked this problem in the comments and during the procedure ("therapeutic chair not understandable"; "not all icons are understandable, the therapeutic chair is not ").
- **Flexibility and Efficiency of Use.** Despite a good average of responses in accordance with the guidelines (80%), the participants did not highlight major problems regarding visibility and accessibility of the control panel. Although, the score is lowered because of the problem with the English label "low".
- **Aesthetic and Minimalist Design.** No problems founded in this dimension (100%). Materials seem to be very well accepted and liked by all the usability experts.

- **Help Users Recognize, Diagnose, and Recover from Errors.** In general, this dimension achieved excellent compliance with the guidelines (100%).
- **Help and Documentation.** 80% of responses complying with guidelines. Two of the experts highlights that the arrows in the instruction (Fig. 6) should provide information and point to all the buttons present ("Attention to the arrows of the backrest, lower and upper legs, they should point both directions, up and down"; "they should be indicated for columns"). Also, one of the participants point out that instructions would be necessary to understand the LEDs meaning.

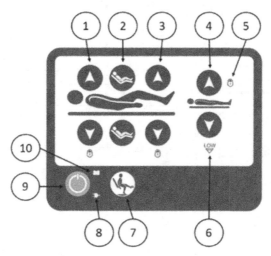

Fig. 6. Graphic part of the instructions

Concluding, the mean completion time of the Checklist was 502 s (i.e., ~9 min). The total mean percentage score of all the Checklist dimensions was 79.2% of positive answers. The analysis of the checklist results and the following administration of the Severity questionnaire are described in Table 1.

Table 1. The table shows the median of the participants' score for the severity of the usability problems found on a scale of 0 to 4. 0 = I do not agree that this is a usability problem at all; 1 = Cosmetic problem only: need not be fixed unless extra time is available on project; 2 = Minor usability problem: fixing this should be given low priority; 3 = Major usability problem: important to fix, so should be given high priority; 4 = Usability catastrophe: imperative to fix this before product can be released.

Usability Problems	Severity Score (Mdn)	Frequency (N°)
Lack of multiple feedbacks in response to a button press	2	6
Delayed response of the movement of the parts of the bed	0	6
Lack of backlight	3	6
The icons for the cardiologic chair positionare identical for both raising and lowering of these	3	10
The cable that connects the hand control and the bed appears too short	1	2
Difficulty using the hand control with one hand	2	3
It is not clear why the backrest stops at a certain height (30 °)	3	7
It is not clear what the safety positions are (minimum height and safe exit)	3	3
The push button panel is not very recognizable when hung on the side	1	1
The arrows in the information material do not point to all the drawn buttons	1	2
The label on the LED for the minimum height is in English ("low")	2	2
Sometimes it is necessary to press a button more than once to get to the end of the movement due to the loss of pressure.	2	6

4 Discussion

The objective of this study was to create a quick, easy to use and efficient tool (i.e., Usability Checklist), able to allow an in-depth analysis of the usability problems of the pushbutton panels of modern hospital beds. The motivation was to fill the absence in literature, as far as we know, of tools that evaluate hospital beds' control panel design. During the study, this instrument was then tested to assess its ability to highlight usability problems. Consistently, the Checklist devised proved to be able to highlight some critical usability issues in a reasonable time (i.e., about 9 min).

The analyses results and the subsequent categorization of the problems according to their severity have highlighted some critical issues. Firstly, the Checklist showed a lack of multiple feedback (Mdn = 2) provided to the user to assist him/her in understanding how s/he is interacting with the system. The bed itself, with the movement and noises of the actuators, is the primary feedback. Additional feedbacks, such as haptic and visual, were suggested by the experts as possible solutions. The absence of visual feedback underlined a low level of accessibility of the control panel for people in a dark environment or with visual impairment/blindness (Mdn = 3). Combined with the fact that it does not present backlights or LEDs, the checklist results suggest their implementation or the development of a surface, perhaps with elements in relief, which will enable to recognize the buttons without necessarily using the view. Therefore, this attention is necessary to allow everyone to use the control panel correctly and easily and permit an improved accessibility.

Another problem reported by the experts was the "chair position" button (Mdn = 3). To reach this position, one would need to press the button located above the man's figure while returning to the horizontal position requires to press the lower one. However, since the two icons on the buttons are the same, it was considered not very intuitive. Again, regarding the icons, users have shown how the ones indicating potentially safer positions for the patient (safe exit and minimum height) are not well highlighted (Mdn = 3).

Regarding the ease of access and use of the control panel, the checklist highlighted that the push-button panel is difficult to use with only one hand (Mdn = 2) and that it is not always sufficient to press the button once to get to the end of the movement (Mdn = 2). The latter issue could both due to the loss of grip during the pressure of the button, which is annoying when dealing with the system for a long time, and to the stop of the backrest at 30° by default without a comprehensible feedback (Mdn = 3).

Lastly, the results obtained by the observations of the "low" LED indicate the necessity to use labels in the native language (Mdn = 2).

On the other hand, the checklist was also able to highlight the strengths of the control panel. This last obtained 79.1% of positive responses in according to the guidelines, thus achieving a good degree of general usability. Furthermore, excluding the button of therapeutic chair, the icons used were clear and intuitive. The last four dimensions of the Checklist also showed how the aesthetics, the flexibility of use in terms of ease of grip and recovery from any errors, and, finally, the information materials, represent the panels' strengths.

5   Conclusions

The usability checklist and the experimental procedure showed the possibility of analyzing the usability aspects of an electric bed button panel in detail, highlighting the strengths and weaknesses of the devised tool. The ease of use and analysis of the collected data, combined with its rapidity, makes it a valid tool for improving these essential control interfaces for hospital beds quickly and at reasonable costs. A possible limitation of the present study is to use the heuristics defined by Nielsen [22], which represent rules for interfaces in general. During the development phase, the items created were then included in the usability heuristic that seemed most suitable to accommodate them. In some cases, not all the items appeared to fit perfectly with the specific heuristics definition. Future work may be necessary to redefine some of these Nielsen's heuristics, as already accessed in other areas [32, 33], to adapt them to these particular devices to improve the usability checklist. Finally, future studies could consider different versions of the checklist for assessing various types of control interfaces, such as touchscreens that start to be used in the most advanced hospital beds.

Acknowledgment. The research project was partially supported by Malvestio Spa.

Appendix

The complete list of the Checklist items is provided.

Visibility of system status

1. Pressing a key corresponds to immediate feedback from the push-button panel.
2. If present, the feedback provided is easily identifiable.
3. If present, the feedback provided takes place in multiple ways.
4. When a key is pressed, it provides tactile feedback.
5. It is easy to tell if the push of a button affects the bed.
6. Understanding when the movement has ended is easy.

Match between system and the real world

7. The movements that the bed can make are represented understandably by the buttons on the control panel.

Give the user control with comfort

8. Pushing the buttons does not require excessive physical effort.
9. It is always possible to use the push button panel while remaining in a comfortable position.
10. The push button panel can always be used with one hand.

Consistency and standard

11. The icons used are consistent with each other.

Error prevention

12. A single push of the button is enough to perform the desired movement until it ends.
13. The positioning of the push-button panel prevents accidental actions from being performed.
14. The keys for the safety positions are well identifiable.
15. The buttons are adequately spaced from each other.
16. The buttons have a surface that facilitates pressing.
17. The buttons are clearly visible even in darkness.
18. In case the wrong key is pressed, it is easy to return to the previous position.

Recognition rather than recall

19. The meaning of the icons is intuitive.
20. The icons have understandable symbols.

Flexibility, accessibility, and efficiency of use

21. The push-button panel is easily accessible.
22. The push-button panel is always visible.
23. The push-button panel can be easily grasped with both hands.
24. The travel of the buttons, i.e., the space between pressing the button and its activation, is adequate.
25. The height of the buttons is adequate.
26. The icons have both graphic and textual elements where needed.

Aesthetic and minimalist design

27. The icons used are aesthetically pleasing.
28. The icons used are large enough.
29. The materials used for the buttons are pleasant to the touch.
30. The materials used for the buttons are aesthetically pleasing.

Help users recognize, diagnose, and recover from errors

31. It is easy to understand when the hand control is locked.
32. It is easy to understand when the hand control is off.

Help and documentation

33. The documentation material is easily understandable.
34. The documentation material is necessary for the use of the bed control panel.

References

1. Büssing, A., Falkenberg, Z., Schoppe, C., et al.: Work stress associated cool down reactions among nurses and hospital physicians and their relation to burnout symptoms. BMC Health Serv. Res. **17**, 1–13 (2017). https://doi.org/10.1186/s12913-017-2445-3
2. Hämmig, O.: Explaining burnout and the intention to leave the profession among health professionals - a cross-sectional study in a hospital setting in Switzerland. BMC Health Serv. Res. **18**, 1–11 (2018). https://doi.org/10.1186/s12913-018-3556-1
3. Ma, X., Vervoort, D.: Critical care capacity during the COVID-19 pandemic: global availability of intensive care beds. J. Crit. Care **58**, 96–97 (2020). https://doi.org/10.1016/j.jcrc.2020.04.012
4. Pecoraro, F., Clemente, F., Luzi, D.: The efficiency in the ordinary hospital bed management in Italy: an in-depth analysis of intensive care unit in the areas affected by COVID-19 before the outbreak. PLoS ONE **15**, e0239249 (2020). https://doi.org/10.1371/journal.pone.0239249
5. ISO: Ergonomics of human-system interaction—Part 11: Usability: Definitions and concepts. ISO 9241-112018(E) (2018). https://www.iso.org/obp/ui/#iso:std:iso:9241:-11:ed-2:v1:en.
6. Vainiomäki, S., Aalto, A.M., Lääveri, T., et al.: Better usability and technical stability could lead to better work-related well-being among physicians. Appl. Clin. Inform. **8**, 1057–1067 (2017). https://doi.org/10.4338/ACI-2017-06-RA-0094

7. Ghersi, I., Mario, M., Miralles, M.T.: From modern push-button hospital-beds to 20th century mechatronic beds: a review. In: Journal of Physics: Conference Series, vol. 705 (2016). https://doi.org/10.1088/1742-6596/705/1/012054

8. Ghersi, I., Mariño, M., Miralles, M.T.: Smart medical beds in patient-care environments of the twenty-first century: a state-of-art survey. BMC Med. Inform. Decis. Mak. **18**, 1–12 (2018). https://doi.org/10.1186/s12911-018-0643-5

9. Who Invented Medical Beds - Medical Beds. http://www.medical-beds.co.uk/who-invented-medical-beds.html

10. de Bruin, A.M., Bekker, R., van Zanten, L., Koole, G.M.: Dimensioning hospital wards using the Erlang loss model. Ann. Oper. Res. **178**, 23–43 (2010). https://doi.org/10.1007/s10479-009-0647-8

11. Schmid, F., et al.: Reduction of clinically irrelevant alarms in patient monitoring by adaptive time delays. J. Clin. Monit. Comput. **31**(1), 213–219 (2015). https://doi.org/10.1007/s10877-015-9808-2

12. Gunningberg, L., Carli, C.: Reduced pressure for fewer pressure ulcers: can real-time feedback of interface pressure optimise repositioning in bed? Int. Wound J. **13**, 774–779 (2016). https://doi.org/10.1111/iwj.12374

13. Hong, Y.S.: Smart care beds for elderly patients with impaired mobility. Wirel. Commun. Mob. Comput. **2018** (2018). https://doi.org/10.1155/2018/1780904

14. Surma-aho, A., Hölttä-Otto, K., Nelskylä, K., Lindfors, N.C.: Usability issues in the operating room – towards contextual design guidelines for medical device design. Appl. Ergon. **90** (2021). https://doi.org/10.1016/j.apergo.2020.103221

15. Bitkina, O.V., Kim, H.K., Park, J.: Usability and user experience of medical devices: an overview of the current state, analysis methodologies, and future challenges. Int. J. Ind. Ergon. **76** (2020). https://doi.org/10.1016/j.ergon.2020.102932

16. Capodaglio, E.M.: Electric versus hydraulic hospital beds: differences in use during basic nursing tasks. Int. J. Occup. Saf. Ergon. **19**, 597–606 (2013). https://doi.org/10.1080/10803548.2013.11077010

17. Wiggermann, N., Rempel, K., Zerhusen, R.M., et al.: Human-centered design process for a hospital bed: promoting patient safety and ease of use. Ergon. Des. **27**, 4–12 (2019). https://doi.org/10.1177/1064804618805570

18. Cai, H., et al.: A qualitative study on implementation of the intelligent bed: findings from a rehabilitation ward at a large Chinese tertiary hospital. Wirel. Pers. Commun. **90**(1), 399–420 (2016). https://doi.org/10.1007/s11277-016-3375-9

19. Kim, S., Barker, L.M., Jia, B., et al.: Effects of two hospital bed design features on physical demands and usability during brake engagement and patient transportation: a repeated measures experimental study. Int. J. Nurs. Stud. **46**, 317–325 (2009). https://doi.org/10.1016/j.ijnurstu.2008.10.005

20. Fudickar, S., Flessner, J., Volkening, N., Steen, E.-E., Isken, M., Hein, A.: Gesture controlled hospital beds for home care. In: Wichert, R., Mand, B. (eds.) Ambient Assisted Living. ATSC, pp. 103–118. Springer, Cham (2017). https://doi.org/10.1007/978-3-319-52322-4_7

21. Lin, X., Zhang, Z.: Designing remote control of medical bed based on human factors. In: 2020 IEEE 7th International Conference on Industrial Engineering and Applications, ICIEA 2020, pp. 838–841 (2020). https://doi.org/10.1109/ICIEA49774.2020.9101944

22. Nielsen, J., Molich, R.: Heuristic evaluation of user interfaces. In: Conference on Human Factors in Computing Systems - Proceedings, pp. 249–256. Association for Computing Machinery (1990). https://doi.org/10.1145/97243.97281

23. Nielsen, J.: Usability inspection methods. In: Conference on Human Factors in Computing Systems - Proceedings, pp. 413–414. Association for Computing Machinery (1994). https://doi.org/10.1145/259963.260531

24. Keevil, B.: Measuring the usability index of your Web site. In: Proceedings of the 16th Annual International Conference on Computer Documentation, SIGDOC 1998, pp. 271–277. ACM Press, New York (1998). https://doi.org/10.1145/296336.296394

25. De Paiva Guimarães, M., Martins, V.F.: A checklist to evaluate augmented reality applications. In: Proceedings of 2014 16th Symposium on Virtual and Augmented Reality, SVR 2014, pp. 45–52 (2014). https://doi.org/10.1109/SVR.2014.17

26. Munoz, R., Barcelos, T., Chalegre, V.: Defining and validating virtual worlds usability heuristics. In: Proceeding of the International Conference of the Chilean Computer Science Society, SCCC, pp. 171–178 (2012). https://doi.org/10.1109/SCCC.2011.23

27. Anderson, K., Burford, O., Emmerton, L.: App chronic disease checklist: protocol to evaluate mobile apps for chronic disease self-management. JMIR Res. Protoc. **5**, e204 (2016). https://doi.org/10.2196/resprot.6194

28. Inal, Y.: Heuristic-based user interface evaluation of the mobile centralized doctor appointment system: a case study. Electron. Libr. **37**, 81–94 (2019). https://doi.org/10.1108/EL-06-2018-0114

29. Weinger, M., Wiklund, M., Gardner-Bonneau, D.: Handbook of Human Factors in Medical Device Design (2010). https://doi.org/10.1201/b10439

30. Nielsen, J.: Heuristic Evaluation Ten Usability Heuristics (2005). https://www.nngroup.com/articles/ten-usability-heuristics/

31. Nielsen, J.: Severity Ratings for Usability Problems. Nielsen Norman Group (1995). http://www.nngroup.com/articles/how-to-rate-the-severity-of-usability-problems/

32. Inostroza, R., Rusu, C., Roncagliolo, S., Rusu, V.: Usability heuristics for touchscreen-based mobile devices: update. In: Proceedings of the 2013 Chilean Conference on Human-Computer Interaction, pp. 24–29 (2013). https://doi.org/10.1145/2535597.2535602

33. Quiñones, D., Rusu, C.: How to develop usability heuristics: a systematic literature review. Comput Stand. Interfaces **53**, 89–122 (2017). https://doi.org/10.1016/j.csi.2017.03.009

Kits for Patients with Transtibial Amputation in the Pre- and Post-prosthetic Phases

Isabel Carvalho[✉], Victor Nassar[✉], and Milton Vieira[✉]

Universidade Federal de Santa Catarina, Florianópolis, Brazil
milton.vieira@ufsc.br

Abstract. This work aimed at proposing the development of novel products that provide a better transition for patients who suffered lower limb amputation. The aim is to provide more support during the transition between pre- and post-prosthetic phases in patients with lower limb (transtibial) amputations. A proposal was made for special care multifunctional kits aimed at improving the quality of life of the transtibial prosthesis user.

Keywords: Transtibial amputation · Prosthetization · Product design · Brazilian culture

1 Introduction

Patients who undergo the process of a limb's amputation, which is typically then followed by a prostheses fitting, need a certain informational support regarding the correct use of this type of assistive technology. Although they may have a prosthesis suitable for their specific need, there are cases in which patients do not have the correct support when adapting to the new equipment or in preparation for the first fitting. (Baraúna et al. 2006).

This lack of support in monitoring can cause difficulties in the use of the prosthesis, stemming, among other reasons, from lack of information and access to the most appropriate means of preparation and adaptation to the new physical situation. In addition to this initial post-amputation scenario, there is also the rehabilitation stage of using the prosthesis for the first time, where there has also been reported a lack of support that would otherwise avoid a physically uncomfortable experience, which in turn may make the use of the prosthesis temporarily or permanently unfeasible.

Benedetto et al. (2002) and Vidal et al. (2004) found that, although the use of prostheses is considered to have a good prognosis, the amputee may present important difficulties in mobility, transfer and postural changes. In addition, there may be the presence of stump pain or phantom pain, low self-esteem, fear and depression, as well as difficulties in maintaining static balance, which can lead to falls and, in more severe cases, fractures (Baraúna et al. 2006).

Within the rehabilitation team, Pullin (2009) highlights a specific role for the designer, capable of creating solutions for improving daily tasks and overall usability of prostheses more effectively than that approached by doctors, physiotherapists,

© Springer Nature Switzerland AG 2021
V. G. Duffy (Ed.): HCII 2021, LNCS 12778, pp. 20–27, 2021.
https://doi.org/10.1007/978-3-030-77820-0_2

psychologists and technicians responsible for the production of said prostheses, among others, that normally work with low interprofessional interaction.

According to Skrabe (2010), the complexity of the healthcare sector opens opportunities for multidisciplinary incorporation, in which design can propose solutions in various applications, producing effective results. Thus arises the relevance of associating the subject of prostheses with certain design concepts, which includes methodologies developed to solve problems of the most varied origins related to product use contexts. Thus, the designer is an active participant in the continuous search for the improvement of the currently available solutions, making it possible for the daily problems faced by people who have had lower limb amputations to be solved in an innovative and practical way.

In this study, the focus is on patients who have suffered lower limb amputation (transtibial) and have difficulty adhering to the use of the prosthesis in the context of the Unified Health System (SUS) in Brazil. In this context, the objective of this work is to present a proposal for special care kits aimed at improving the quality of life of users of transtibial prostheses by increasing adherence to the use of the prosthesis by the amputee.

2 Special Care of the Lower Limb Amputee in the Pre- and Post-prosthetic Phases

An amputation causes sudden changes in amputees' daily lives, directly affecting their behavior and the way they act (Botelho et al. 2003). The great challenge is the psychological adaptation to the loss of the amputated limb and the resulting condition of physical disability, which can be potentially disabling and affect health and well-being (Ephraim et al. 2003).

According to Crenshaw (1996), there are several clinical complications that can arise after an amputation, regardless of the cause, such as the formation of bruises due to the surgical procedure, which can delay wound healing and cause bacterial infection. To prevent this situation, the hematoma must be cleaned, and then solid compression is applied to the stump, or residual limb. Such compression also prevents and treats edema, benefits blood circulation and can be done with elastic bands (Boccolini 2001).

According to Carvalho et al. (2005), the infectious process must be removed, and appropriate antibiotics must be administered. Serious infections can cause complete disorganization of the wound, eventually requiring a new amputation at a more proximal level. Necrosis is another complication and, when it is of low intensity at the edges of the skin, it can be treated conservatively, but it can delay healing. The most severe cases of necrosis, however, indicate insufficient circulation at the amputation level, requiring immediate wedge resection or reamputation at a more proximal level.

Carvalho et al. (2005) also state that contractures are common in amputees and, in order for this not to happen, it is necessary to correctly position the patient on the bed immediately after the surgery, preventing the amputated limb from being in a position where the muscles are shortened. Mild contractures can be treated with positioning exercises, stretching, strengthening and mobilization, while severe ones are treated with plaster castings or the surgical release of shortened structures.

After twenty-four hours of the amputation surgery, the work of moving the stump and other parts of the body should be started to improve circulation and venous return. Thus, the patient must be referred to rehabilitation and advised on the care of the stump, so that it has good healing, avoiding infections and having correct hygienic procedures, in order to prevent further amputation. Physiotherapy is important in the postoperative period to treat edema, to benefit the circulatory system, to work on hypertrophy, to prevent adhesions and to accustom the region in contact with the prosthesis to the pressure that it will be put under. When patients start physical therapy treatment to prepare the stump for prosthesis, they must be evaluated individually, as the characteristics of the stump influence the duration and effectiveness of the treatment (Carvalho 2003).

In this context, prostheses are devices designed to complement the absence of a limb (upper or lower) or part of it. Complementation aims to replace function, composition and body support, both in gait, depending on the level of amputation, the components used and the alignment of the prosthesis during confection and training, and the gait can be completely normal (Lianza 1995).

The use of a prosthesis assists the individual in carrying out certain activities (Carmeli and Imam 2014) and in supporting functional limitations, working in the correction, rehabilitation or modification of the structure or function of the human body (WHO 2011), in addition to contributing with the development of greater confidence, improving their quality of life. Even with the prosthesis, the amputee can present important difficulties in mobility, transfer and postural changes, and still get a feeling of pain in the stump, low self-esteem, fear and depression (Benedetto et al. 2002; Vidal et al. 2004).

Thus, amputation should not be seen as the end of a therapeutic procedure, but as a new stage to be understood, assimilated and overcome. It is necessary to incorporate a series of medical, social, educational, psychological and economic measures so that patients are reincorporated into society using their own residual resources so that they may have quality of life (Carvalho 2003).

3 Quality of Life of Amputees

According to Minayo (2000), the relationship between health and quality of live exists since the birth of social medicine, in the 18th and 19th centuries, when systematic investigations began to subsidize public policies and social movements. The expression health-related quality of life means the value attributed to life, pondered through the lens of functional deterioration, perception, and social conditions induced by sickness, aggravation, and treatments, as well as the political and economic organization of the healthcare system. It can also indicate if the measured or estimated health condition is relatively desirable. In other cases, the fundamental concepts of quality of life would likewise be the perception of health, social, psychological, and physical functions, as well as the problems related to them (Minayo 2000).

Quality of life assessment has been used as a tool in the area of healthcare to measure people's health condition. Thus, different healthcare practitioners determine their patients' quality of life through the study of the results of medical interventions, as well as the perceptions of patients themselves regarding their health condition and related quality of life (Demet et al. 2002).

The quality of life assessments used for amputees were limited to the measurement of their functional status; however, this approach may be deemed insufficient, since function must not be assessed in isolation from general quality of life aspects (Demet et al. 2002). The quality of life of people who undergo lower limb amputations is characterized be abrupt changes in their routine. Thus, these people may present considerable changes; the conditions of the stump (or residual limb) or alterations in the patient's general health status can worsen the condition of their quality of life.

Patients who have undergone amputations can present psychological complications, such as conflicts, anxiety, and greater difficulties in integrating to their new condition and facing the changes in body image after the amputation (Carvalho 2003). Studies reveal that the prosthesis is fundamental to the health of the amputee, and that the better the adaptation in the use of the prosthesis, the greater the freedom and confidence to conduct activities of daily living at home and to participate in social events (Carvalho 2003).

After the amputation the use of a prosthesis enables a normal body image, helping individuals develop greater confidence and physical skills, as well as improving their quality of life (Bilodeau 2000). According to studies conducted with amputees, some authors discuss factors that influence quality of life in some way, counting among those the age of individuals, the time span from the amputation until the placement of the prosthesis, and the level of amputation (Demet et al. 2002; Carvalho et al. 2005).

Therefore, the quality of life and health of lower limb amputees includes the humanization of patient care. In the current practices of several healthcare institutions, it is a matter of a better interaction with amputated patients so as to identify what satisfies them and their rights as consumers of healthcare services, bringing to the fore their opinions as to the care received from a multidisciplinary team of healthcare professionals and those from other areas of knowledge, such as designers, with concepts of a professional action that is systemic and focused on the patient's quality of life.

In this context, the object of this study is integration between the concept of a product and the promotion of given aspects that involve quality of life. In this case, the development of a multifunctional kit with the purpose of caring for patients with transtibial amputations, to be used in the pre- and post-prosthetic phases.

4 Materials and Methods

This paper intentds to propose a practical solution, with the development of multifunctional kits that can train amputated patients on the necessary general care, before and after being fitted with a prosthesis.

According to Pazmino (2015), design methods are sets of procedures aiming to achieve a project objective; the design process model is the plan containing the sequences of operations or chains of phases and stages in a project. Therefore, the aim of the process model is to guide the designer, with a series of predefined stages and guides to aid development, in order to maximize results and minimize the chances of failure and interference in the process.

For this project, it was first sought to establish concise project requirements for innovation. Thus were defined the elements that would guide the design of the kits for this project. Afterwards, prototypes were constructed so as to understand how design solutions may work, as well as test to perceive the experiences of users. Like any process model, it serves as support and guide, and must never be seen as a process that hampers development.

Two kit proposals were created to satisfy demands detected in two different and crucial phases of the rehabilitation process for amputee patients: 1) Pre-prosthetic phase and 2) Post-prosthetic phase.

After the analysis, some shape requirements were defined among them for the pre-prosthetic kit: Removable lid; material with a durable and non-toxic finish; low profile and internal dividers that accommodate the contents; tissue paper wrapping for the contents. As for the post-prosthetic kits, the requirements established were: waterproof material; easy cleaning; shape that enables easy access to the contents.

5   Results

5.1   Pre-prosthetic Kit

The first kit was idealized to be delivered to patients at the time of their investigation for orthoses and prostheses. The kit will then serve as a complementary element to the maintenance of patients' good health for the prosthesis, because it will contain the basic and indispensable items for the postoperative period, with guidance on the patients' correct daily conduct for the preparation of the stump and useful information so that they feel more supported and better prepared to understand the new situation in which they find themselves.

The intention is that amputees begin to think of themselves less as victims of what befell them, and that they begin to feel like they are owners of their own bodies again.

The pre-prosthetic kit (Fig. 1) is a container in the shape of a rectangular box containing a lining made of plastic material so as to better accommodate the products inside, wrapped in tissue paper whose tips are positioned on top of the products, so that, to reach them, one must raise the tips, with the intention of creating a feeling of opening a gift or something important. This kit contains: elastic bandage for compression; hypoallergenic moisturizer; oil-based lotion for the prevention and treatment of pressure ulcers, lesions, and dermatitis; gel for hand sanitizing; hypoallergenic adhesive tape for bandages; soap; cotton; and an illustrated booklet.

Furthermore, the aesthetic care with the kit aims to elicit a pleasurable sensation and propose a positive relation in a life situation filled with uncertainty and a future with many opportunities, such as the opportunity to be able to walk on one's own again. The kits should be durable for future use with different purposes, after the patients' full adaptation to their new reality and to their prosthesis, with the intention that they also develop positive feelings for the kit, due to it having provided a sense of security and having been useful in the difficult moments during rehabilitation.

Fig. 1. Pre-prosthetic kit prototype.

5.2 Post-prosthetic Kit

The purpose of post-prosthetic kits (Fig. 2) is supporting and reinforcing the guidance received by patients in their first fitting. These kits contain: microfiber sports towel; 2 white socks; empty containers of various shapes for pills; moisturizing lotion; talcum powder; and an illustrated booklet.

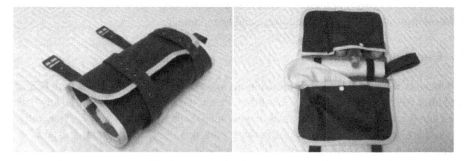

Fig. 2. Post-prosthetic kit prototype.

Given that the patients will be in a moment of transition, which is important for the rehabilitation process and that requires a certain adaptation period, maybe lasting for months, during which the patients must be persistent and confident to successfully adapt to the use of the prosthesis and not abandon it, these kits can serve as an incentive to patients, so that they continue to follow the correct guidance for their full rehabilitation.

So as to fulfill this need, the kits include an information manual, with the guidelines for a good use of the prosthesis, guidance supplied by professionals in the area, as well as a way for easy handling and transport, because, in this stage, patients are beginning to walk on their own again more independently.

6 Discussion

Amputee patients undergo variable recovery periods, because rehabilitation depends on a series of factors, such as age, cause of amputation, and the patient's physical and clinical status. In the absence of various complications, a prosthesis can be fitted in the period between eight to ten weeks, which can be longer depending on the patient's case or the city's specialized network for prosthetics.

The solution proposed to minimize this problem was the creation of kits containing the necessary items for care and a guidance manual on the preparation of the patient's stump for the prosthesis and the general information on the adaptation phases. The recommendations for the moment before the first fitting are the use of elastic bandages and the guidance for positioning, such as: not allowing the stump to hang or folding it, and not placing pillows under one's back or as a support for the stump. In the case of transtibial amputations, the patient must bandage the stump, conduct desensitization, follow the postural guidance, not sit for too long, move with the stump.

The appropriate guidance presented in the special care manual, as well as the effective use of the multifunctional kits, can stimulate patients' proactive adhesion and thus prevent injury to the residual limb and complications stemming from the inadequate use of the prosthesis, as well as enabling better adhesion to the correct use of the prosthesis, preventing its abandonment and thus enabling an improvement in the quality of life of lower limb amputee patients.

Patients with prostheses may also carry something of their own and personal daily, which can be simple towel or a variety of items. Therefore, these kits can provide a practical way of carrying these personal items, stimulating patients to be more careful with their prostheses, preventing misuse and abandonment.

7 Conclusion

All patients who have undergone amputations must adapt to a new lifestyle, both before and after their first fitting. One of the difficulties in the process of adapting to any new situation is learning all of the new rules of what should and should not be done. Generally, when there is no easy access to instructions, one runs the risk of making mistakes or giving up out of frustration.

From that point, a solution was presented to assist in the transition process, based on two multifunctional kits containing basic materials necessary for the daily care before the prosthesis, as well as in the period of adaptation to the use of the prosthesis, in addition to a printed manual containing the basic special care guidance, to be delivered to patients in their first appointment before the fitting.

One hopes that this study can be useful both for amputee patients and for the professionals in charge of their rehabilitation, and that the use of multifunctional kits stimulates patients' proactive adhesion to the use of the prosthesis, improving quality of life for those patients. One also hopes that the final result of the comprehensive care for amputees is the maintenance of their physical and mental health, as well as the development of their autonomy and social inclusion, and that, ultimately, it materializes into a full life.

References

Baraúna, M.A., et al. (eds.): Avaliação do equilíbrio estático em indivíduos amputados de membros inferiores através da biofotogrametria computadorizada. Brasilian J. Phys. Ther. **10**(1), 83–90 (2006)

Benedetto, K.M., Forgione, M.C.R., Alves, V.L.R.: Reintegração corporal em pacientes amputados e a dor fantasma. Acta Fisiátrica **9**(2), 85–89 (2002)

Bilodeau, S.: Lower Limb prosthesis utilization by elderly amputees. Prosthet. Orthot. Int. **24**(2), 126–132 (2000)

Boccolini, F.: Reabilitação: amputados, amputações e próteses. Robe Livraria e Editora, São Paulo (2001)

Botelho, N.L.P., Volpini, M., Moura, E.M.: Aspectos psicológicos em usuários de prótese ocular. Arq. Bras. Oftalmol. **66**, 637–646 (2003)

Carmeli, E., Imam, B.: Health promotion and disease prevention strategies in older adults with intellectual and developmental disabilities. Front. Public Health **2**(31), 1–7 (2014)

Carvalho, F.S., Kunz, V.C., Depieri, T.Z., Cervelini, R.: Prevalência de amputação em membros inferiores de causa vascular: análise de prontuários. Arq. Ciênc. Saúde Unipar, Umuarama **9**(1), 23–30 (2005)

Carvalho, J.A.: Amputações de membros inferiores: em busca de plena reabilitação. 2ª edn. Manole, São Paulo (2003)

Crenshaw, A.: Cirurgia ortopédica de Campbell. 8th edn. Manole, São Paulo (1996)

Demet, K., Guilherme, F., Martinet, N., André, J.: Nottingham health profile: reliability in a sample of 542 subjetcs with major amputation of one or limbs. Prosthet. Orthot. Int. **26**, 120–123 (2002)

Ephraim, P.L., Dillingham, T.R., Sector, M., Pezzin, L.E., Mackenzie, E.J.: Epidemiology of limb loss and congenital limb deficiency: a review of the literature. Arch. Physical Med. Rehabil. **84**, 747–761 (2003)

Lianza, S.: Medicina de Reabilitação 2ª Ed. Rio de Janeiro: Guanabara Koogan (1995)

Minayo, M.C.: Qualidade de vida e saúde: um debate necessário. Cien. Saude Colet. **5**(1), 7–18 (2000)

Pazimino, A.V.: Como se cria: 40 métodos para o design de produtos. Ed. Blucher, São Paulo (2015)

Pullin, G.: Design Meets Disability. MIT Press, Cambridge (2009)

Skrabe, C.: Chegou a hora e a vez do design. In: Anuário Hospital Best. Eximia Comunicação: São Paulo (2010)

Vidal, A.L.A., Santos, C.C., Nishimaru, S., Chamlian, T.R., Masiero, D.: Avaliação da qualidade de vida em pacientes amputados de membros inferiores. Med. Reabil. **23**(1), 12–17 (2004)

World Health Organization (WHO). Health technology assessment of medical devices. (Online), Medical Device Technical Series, Geneva (2011)

Research on Social Innovation Design of SCD Pre-hospital Emergency Equipment Based on IoT Technology

Kun Fang and Wei Yu[✉]

School of Art Design and Media, East China University of Science and Technology,
Shanghai 200237, China
weiyu@ecust.edu.cn

Abstract. This paper analyzes and summarizes the products in the current emergency market, and in view of the fact that there are few emergency products for sudden cardiac death in the market, and the mainstream emergency products have different degrees of disadvantages, such as poor timeliness, inconvenient transportation, difficult to use, high limitations, etc. Taking emergency equipment such as AED and automatic compression devices as examples, discuss the feasibility, necessity and specific methods of applying IoT technology to pre-hospital emergency equipment. Through the product design case, this paper puts forward the solution of the application of IoT technology in the pre-hospital emergency equipment for patients with sudden cardiac death. At present, medical emergency is an important social problem, the traditional first aid process and specific operation obviously can't deal with emergencies very well. However, it takes a long time to improve public awareness, skills training and operation process innovation, and the effect is very little. In contrast, it will be more effective and faster to make breakthroughs in the technical innovation, function improvement and social innovation design of emergency equipment. This study adheres to the concept of innovating the industry and designing to serve the society. It aims to compare the application of the existing pre-hospital emergency equipment, form a modern WITMED emergency mode through the combination of IoT and medical treatment, create perfect user experience, provide auxiliary equipment for pre-hospital emergency care, improve the survival rate of patients and improve the status of pre hospital first aid.

Keywords: Internet of Things · SCD · First aid equipment

1 Preface

The novel coronavirus epidemic situation in 2020 makes the medical and health industry get the global attention, coupled with the increase of sudden death news in recent years, how to deal with sudden illness has become a hot topic. It is an important aspect of improving medical level to ensure the sound medical emergency equipment in public places and improve the success rate of pre-hospital first aid [1].

© Springer Nature Switzerland AG 2021
V. G. Duffy (Ed.): HCII 2021, LNCS 12778, pp. 28–39, 2021.
https://doi.org/10.1007/978-3-030-77820-0_3

The death caused by cardiac arrest is sudden cardiac death (SCD). There is a saying of "golden four minutes" in emergency treatment. The first 4 min after critical illness is the most valuable and effective golden treatment time for rescuing their lives. If the first aid is implemented within 4 min of golden rescue, the success rate of first aid can reach 40%. The probability of successful rescue can be reduced by 20% for every extended 1 min, and the survival rate of more than 6 min is only 4%. The probability of successful rescue for patients with more than 10 min is almost zero [2]. For the rescue of patients with sudden cardiac arrest, it greatly depends on rapid cardiopulmonary resuscitation and defibrillation [3].

Modern people are under great pressure of work and life, and the frequency of sudden death is increasing year by year. However, the success rate of CPR in public places in developed countries is 38%, while that in most developing countries such as China is less than 1%. The first reason for this phenomenon is that the public's knowledge of cardiopulmonary resuscitation is insufficient. In many developed countries, the public's first aid training rate reaches 60%–92%, while in most developing countries it is less than 1%. The second reason is that the first-aid equipment in public places is insufficient, and there are few existing products on the market. For example, the popularity rate of AED, the recognized equipment for sudden cardiac death, is far from enough. Third, the time interval between different links in the life chain is too long. Take the ambulance call as an example. The average time from call to ambulance arrival is more than 10 min, which is even slower in crowded cities. The golden rescue time of 10 min has already been missed, and the survival rate is basically 0 [4].

In the era of digital economy, Wise Information Technology of Med (WITMED) has become a trend, and the medical industry also needs to be combined with the Internet. The core of WITMED is "patient-centered", giving patients a comprehensive, professional and personalized medical experience. First aid should no longer rely on human operation. With the most advanced Internet of things (IoT) technology, we can realize the interaction among patients, medical staff, medical institutions and medical equipment, so as to gradually achieve informatization. In the post-pandemic era, WITMED is an important way to solve the public's lack of emergency awareness and skills, and also a reliable method to improve the success rate of first aid. Medical information online connection, medical equipment linkage and real-time human-computer interaction can help the medical industry to move towards a scientific and intelligent future [5].

2 Background

The COVID-19 epidemic in 2020 is a systematic general examination. In terms of medical level, on the one hand, it tests the basic medical system and medical conditions; on the other hand, it tests the ability, style and responsibility of medical systems in various countries; in terms of the global situation, the epidemic situation tests everyone's feelings, theories and laws; in terms of the country, it also tests the governance ability and image of a big country. Calm thinking can also find some problems and room for improvement from the epidemic prevention and control [6].

Frankly speaking, the epidemic prevention and control is effective in the short term, relying on more human factors. It seems that there is still a lot of room for improvement to use scientific, intelligent and information-based means to help the epidemic prevention and control. In order to improve the precision construction of smart city, we should pay full attention to the problems and needs of epidemic situation inspection, effectively use information means in block renewal and community governance, rely on the big data function, improve the regional "people, places, things, organizations" information database, realize the accurate statistics, analysis and judgment of all kinds of data, and provide efficient support for dealing with public emergencies Convenient and scientific decision support. For example, the daily monitoring and early warning of the disabled elderly group, and the normalized non sensitive monitoring in sensitive key areas. We should infiltrate high-tech and information technology into all aspects of social governance, build an intelligent, diversified and three-dimensional social governance system, and effectively improve the efficiency of social governance [7].

In recent years, the incidence rate of sudden death has increased year by year. Taking China as an example, the number of sudden deaths more than 10 years ago is about 545 thousand, and by 2018, this figure has increased to about 1 million. At the same time, the population of sudden death is becoming younger and younger. In the past, sudden death mostly concentrated in the group of 45–50 years old, but now, more and more young people become the high-risk group of sudden death [8].

In emergency medicine, the process of emergency treatment for patients with sudden death can be divided into three stages: prehospital emergency stage, emergency treatment stage and ICU observation stage. Prehospital first aid is the first step in the emergency medical service system, which can also be said to be the key to save the lives of patients with sudden death.

When the heart of a sudden death patient stops beating, the blood flow to the brain is suddenly interrupted, and the patient will lose consciousness. Dizziness occurs when the patient's heart stops beating for 3 s. Stop beating 20 s, there will be syncope; stop beating 40 s, there will be convulsions. When the patient's heart stops beating for more than 6 min, the brain tissue will be irreversibly damaged. Studies have found that if the sudden death of patients with cardiac arrest time more than 6 min, and did not get timely and effective emergency treatment, the success rate of emergency treatment is only 4%. Therefore, within 5 min after cardiac arrest is the golden time for prehospital emergency treatment of patients with sudden death. Relevant data show that there are about 400000 patients with cardiac arrest in the United States every year, the success rate of rescue is about 10%, and the success rate of individual big cities can reach 30%. Since 1961, cardiopulmonary resuscitation (CPR) and some on-site first aid training have been included in the compulsory courses of schools in Norway. According to statistics, the public CPR rate of out of hospital cardiac arrest in Norway is as high as 70.7%. But at the same time, in most developing countries, such as China, the figure is less than 1%.

For the rescue of patients with sudden cardiac arrest, it greatly depends on rapid cardiopulmonary resuscitation and defibrillation, and puts forward requirements for emergency knowledge and professional equipment. Prehospital first aid highlights the importance of medical resource allocation, but in many developing countries, the lack of first aid equipment in public places, or although equipped with equipment, no one can use it at the critical moment, no one dares to use it, lack of basic first aid knowledge, and incorrect implementation of first aid are common problems for the public [9].

3   Current Situation of First Aid Equipment

3.1   Medical Stretcher

In general, if the public does not have sufficient first-aid knowledge, the identification of sudden death is poor, and there is no targeted first-aid equipment, medical stretcher plays an important role in pre hospital first aid. However, as an emergency equipment, it does not fully consider the practicability and pertinence, and there are some problems in rescuing patients with cardiac arrest: in order to save storage space, most stretchers on the market use folding storage structure which is too complex to be used in the first time in emergency; the load-bearing fabric is easy to be affected by patients in the process of transfer or emergency Most of them only have the function of transferring patients, and are configured in hospitals, and lack of relevant configuration in social public places (Fig. 1).

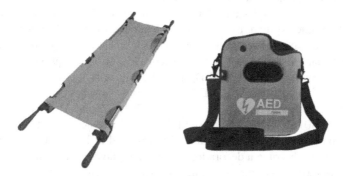

Fig. 1. Medical stretcher and AED.

3.2   AED

Electric defibrillation is the most effective first aid method to stop the heart of patients with sudden death and ventricular fibrillation (manifested as loss of consciousness, convulsion, pulse disappearance, etc.). According to relevant research reports, 70%–80% of respiratory cardiac arrest occurs in the family, public places and on the road. Before the arrival of professional rescue personnel, timely chest compressions and artificial respiration can temporarily maintain the heart and brain function of patients and buy time for the treatment of electric defibrillation. This part of the work often needs non professional witnesses to complete, and the auxiliary first aid equipment will play a key role [10].

In March 2015, the photo of Dr. Tang Ziren, deputy director of emergency department of Chaoyang Hospital, rescuing American tourists in Ocean Park of San Diego became popular on the Internet, and netizens reprinted and praised him as "a good Chinese tourist" and "a good Chinese doctor". Dr. Tang recalled that the reason why he was able to save the old man's life in the end was because of the AED, or automatic external defibrillator, which was placed everywhere in American parks. AED came out in 1979. It is easy to operate and can be used skillfully with a little training. It provides a "new weapon" for medical staff and even non-medical staff to carry out early defibrillation for patients with cardiac arrest. The success rate can be greatly improved if the rescue is carried out within 3 min in the place where AED is configured [11].

In foreign countries, the configuration rate of AED in public places is also high. In the 1990s, the United States passed relevant laws and implemented the "publicly available defibrillators" program. At present, there are 50000 AEDs in the United States according to the preliminary statistics. To install AED in public places in the United States, it is required that the automatic external defibrillator can be obtained within 10 min. Through training for non professionals such as ordinary people, the on-site defibrillation can be carried out as soon as possible in case of cardiac arrest. Japan started to promote and install them in 2004, with an average of 234.8 units per 100000 people [12].

In most other countries, the picture is less optimistic. In China, the development of AED is unbalanced, inadequate and non-standard. Except for a few big cities, such as Hangzhou, Shenzhen, Shanghai and Haikou, which focus on improving the construction of medical emergency system, issuing relevant emergency medical service regulations, and publishing the specific layout and map of AED, most cities are still in the initial stage. In 2006, capital airport installed 11 sets of AED first aid equipment in terminal 2, which is the first time to install AED first aid equipment in public places in China. However, these limited life-saving AEDs are not only not recognized by the public, but also ignored for many years. On August 16, 2015, Zhang Yonggang, director of spine surgery of 301 Hospital of Chinese PLA, died of cardiac arrest at Beijing Capital Airport. Although the life-saving artifact AED installed at Beijing Capital Airport is close at hand, it has become a decoration and has not played its due role. In a first tier city like Beijing, we can imagine the situation in other underdeveloped areas.

However, even mature emergency equipment like AED still has some problems. First of all, there are many taboos in the use of AED. For example, you can't touch the patient in the process of use, and the energy released by AED is great. You should stay away from the patient, and you can't move the patient. You can't use it when the patient has water, such as beach and swimming pool, including many SCD patients who have sweat on their body because of strenuous exercise, and the chest hair ratio More patients will also affect the rescue effect. Secondly, AED can only be used alone, can not be used in the process of patient transport and more professional rescue. Because the movement of vehicles may cause noise, it will interfere with the correct rhythm analysis. The problem of long time interval in different links of the survival chain has not been solved [13].

4 User Research

In developed countries, emergency rescue knowledge is very popular. In western developed countries, the normal rate is about 50% to 60%. In some European countries, the SOS level of citizens is 60–70%, and some have reached 92%. In Sweden, 45% of the public have participated in CPR skills training. In France, the popularization rate of emergency rescue is 40%, and in Germany, 80%. The problems such as which groups of people must receive first aid training, what proportion of enterprise employees must receive first aid training, and what rights should be protected for first-aid personnel are still fixed in the form of law. In the United States, the law stipulates that before the age of 18, any citizen must master all the basic knowledge of first aid, and receive first aid courses from kindergarten.

As early as the 1960s, the American Heart Association began to promote the popularization of primary first aid skills of cardiopulmonary resuscitation among the public. In the 1970s, it began to pay attention to the important role of "first witness" in first aid, and set up on-site first aid knowledge learning courses for the public, such as police, firefighters, drivers and other professionals. A study on the training and use of cardiopulmonary resuscitation in the United States shows that the training rate and use rate of cardiopulmonary resuscitation increased significantly from 2007 to 2009 compared with 1980 to 1982.

But at the same time, most countries in the world have no perfect first aid training system for the public. Although there is a large demand for public first aid technology training, training institutions and training resources are limited, and the public access to first aid knowledge is generally lack of standardization, systematization, scientization and normalization. In 2013, the relevant research results of police and college freshmen (high school graduates) in Shaanxi Province showed that 93.18% of high school graduates and 84.51% of police had strong willingness to first aid on the spot, but 49.4% of police and 51.4% of high school graduates were unable to help because of lack of first aid skills.

When Beijing hosted the 2008 Olympic Games, BOCOG promised the IOC that it would increase the primary ambulance training by one percentage point to 1% in 2008. In other words, before that, the level of emergency rescue training for Chinese citizens was less than 1%. Today, although the figure has increased to 3%, it is far from the level of 50% to 60% in developed countries.

5 Design Examples

5.1 Design Direction

At present, there are few emergency products for cardiac arrest in the market, and the mainstream emergency products still have some disadvantages, such as poor timeliness, inconvenient transportation, not easy to use and high limitations. After in-depth study and conception of this social phenomenon, the author hopes to design a portable, easy-to-use, professional emergency equipment for cardiac arrest, which can popularize cardiopulmonary resuscitation knowledge to the public at the same time. The portable cardiopulmonary resuscitation stretcher is designed for the three pain points: the frequency of artificial cardiopulmonary resuscitation is unstable and easy to fatigue; the operation of emergency first aid products should be simple and clear, not too complex; the time interval of different links in the survival chain should be shortened as far as possible; the patients should be transported at the same time of rescue, and the rescue time should be strived for.

5.2 Design Description

This stretcher is positioned as an emergency first aid equipment in public places, which is used to deal with sudden cardiac death in public places. It is placed in a prominent place in public places, and is equipped with strong contrast color matching, which is convenient for the public to find, and the clear operation steps are printed on the cabinet and stretcher. When a patient has cardiac arrest, open the stretcher, lift the patient to the stretcher, adjust the height and position of the air cushion on the patient's sternum, turn on the switch, the motor will drive the air cushion, and press the patient's chest. The pressing frequency is 120 times / min by default, and the frequency can be adjusted by turning the knob of the power key. At the same time, the motor will send out a sound reminder every 30 times of pressing, and use the pager The inspiratory valve can assist the patient to breathe twice, cooperate with the first aid, and at the same time, the witness can immediately transfer the patient. On the stretcher board and the cabinet where the stretcher is placed, there are simple and easy to understand steps for use, as well as two-dimensional code links for watching the use video (Figs. 2 and 3).

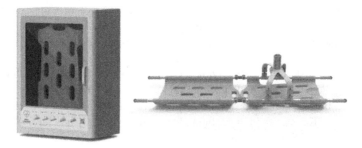

Fig. 2. Portable cardiopulmonary resuscitation stretcher.

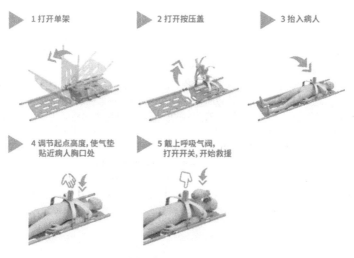

1 打开单架   2 打开按压盖   3 抬入病人

4 调节起点高度, 使气垫   5 戴上呼吸气阀,
贴近病人胸口处   打开开关, 开始救援

Fig. 3. Instructions.

5.3 Detail Design

In the process of use, when the stretcher is folded, the two stretcher plates will form two handles, which are convenient to carry. The handles of the stretcher will become supporting feet, and are equipped with wheels for convenient transportation. The back board of stretcher is designed according to the size of professional CPR board, with an angle of about 8° with the horizontal plane. And the head position has depression, which will make the patient's spine stand up, head down, so that the chest and respiratory tract open, conducive to rescue. The side uses hinge structure to retract and store. When in use, press the middle button to start pressing, and rotate the Yellow knob to adjust the pressing frequency (Fig. 4).

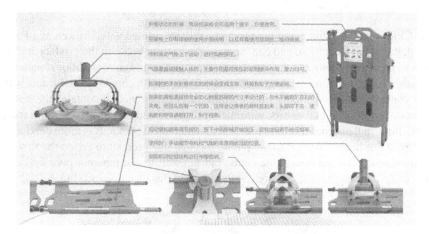

Fig. 4. Details display.

This CPR stretcher is suitable for most public places, including railway stations, subway stations, parks, etc. At the same time, we will combine with app to scan the code or directly view the exact location of the nearby CPR stretcher in the map, and click the rescue button to automatically navigate.This CPR stretcher is suitable for most public places, including railway stations, subway stations, parks, etc. At the same time, we will combine with app to scan the code or directly view the exact location of the nearby CPR stretcher in the map, and click the rescue button to automatically navigate (Fig. 5).

Fig. 5. Use environment.

5.4 Humanistic Design

In the CPR stretcher cabinet and the product itself are printed with Huiwen and Fangsheng patterns, as decoration, and can increase the friction between the product and the patient to prevent slipping. At the same time, through the design of traditional patterns, the aesthetic feeling of art is integrated into science and technology, and humanistic care is conveyed to give patients a high affinity user experience. It contains the design elements of exorcising evil spirits, eliminating diseases and protecting health in traditional culture, and also has a certain regional and humanistic color. It is more conducive to the spread of health concept to the public through this product to create the first aid equipment with Oriental design elements, bid farewell to the inherent poor and cold design of first aid equipment and convey the sense of distance to users (Fig. 6).

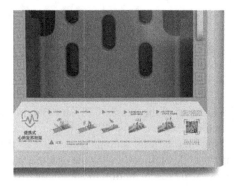

Fig. 6. Pattern design.

5.5 Technical Support

CPR cardiopulmonary resuscitation stretcher adopts high impact cardiopulmonary resuscitation device, which promotes the chest movement and blood circulation of patients to form resonance effect under the drive of external force, ensures the cardiopulmonary blood flow of patients at the most active level, and helps to restore the cardiopulmonary function of patients. Compared with the pneumatic electronic control cardiac compression resuscitator, this electric control chest compression resuscitator has the advantages of simple structure, easy to use and economic and practical.

5.6 Business Model

The portable CPR stretcher makes it clear that the customer is the management department of public places at the g-end, and the services provided are mainly divided into three dimensions: first, Internet of things + medical care: using Internet of things technology to realize the interaction among patients, equipment, medical institutions and medical staff. When SCD occurs, the nearest first aid equipment is known by positioning. At the same time, the hospital gets the information in real time and sends an ambulance to prepare for receiving patients. Realize intelligent medical treatment and strive for rescue time to the greatest extent. Second, the popularization of emergency knowledge: popularizing first aid knowledge, raising awareness of public emergency and playing soft advertising role through public poster, APP publicity and opening of network cloud classroom on official account. Third, through a comprehensive social innovation design to track the user's entire use process, analyze the user's service contacts, create a perfect user experience.

5.7 Innovation Advantage

Portability: the hinge structure is used for expansion and folding, which can be held by one hand, and is equipped with wheels, so the transportation is very convenient. Compared with similar rescue products, it doesn't need too complex adjustment steps, and can quickly start the first aid.

Professionalism: compared with artificial cardiopulmonary resuscitation, it is more scientific and reasonable. At the same time, it can avoid professional errors, too fast or too slow frequency, and fatigue.

Timeliness: cardiopulmonary resuscitation can be carried out while transporting patients, and the golden time of rescue can be achieved by saving the time interval of different links in the survival chain.

Sociality: the introduction of CPR stretcher can increase the allocation of emergency equipment in public places. At the same time, the product strengthens the concept of service design and social innovation design, and systematically and comprehensively designs the user experience of patients of all ages, witnesses and rescuers.

6 Epilogue

Under the background of digital economy, the advantage of portable CPR stretcher is that it is more professional than manual CPR, and changes the role of the public from the former rescuer to the rescue helper. Through the combination of Internet of things and medical care, it forms a new mode of modern intelligent medical emergency, tracks the user's use process, finds service contacts, and provides a perfect user service experience. At the same time, through the public welfare, it can provide a wide range of services First aid knowledge and skills should be popularized to the public by means of interaction with app. In politics, we should actively respond to the modernization reform of public health governance, form a tripartite collaborative pattern of government market society, reform health publicity and health education, improve public awareness, and reflect social care. In the social sense, after the popularization of products, it will provide auxiliary equipment for pre hospital first aid, improve the first aid conditions, significantly improve the survival rate of patients, relieve the first aid pressure of professional medical team caused by traffic congestion in big cities, improve the status quo of pre hospital first aid, comply with the trend of medical modernization with the help of innovative service design, and achieve the goal of people's life safety The ultimate medical purpose.

In a sense, CPR cardiopulmonary resuscitation stretcher is not only a kind of first aid equipment, but also a new concept of first aid. In the process of promoting the use and improving the success rate of rescue of patients with sudden death, the whole society needs to make joint efforts to popularize the knowledge of first aid, improve the awareness of first aid, and help each other in the first time. What the public on-site first aid lacks is not only the equipment, but also the concept, consciousness and first aid skills. "Design foresight" said: "human nature of the design and innovation of scientific control and correction will face unprecedented crisis and challenge." With the rapid development of emergency critical medicine, the socialization of emergency has become an inevitable trend of emergency medicine. We must fully understand the role and significance of public on-site emergency in the emergency network, and straighten out the relationship between public on-site emergency and pre hospital emergency. In the old concept, prehospital first aid is regarded as the starting point of the first aid chain, emphasizing the professional first aid activities of professional first-aid personnel. However, under the existing pre hospital emergency mode, it has become a serious shortcoming that the first aid can not be carried out within "platinum 10 min". The public on the scene can rescue the injured within the first five minutes, so the starting end of the first aid chain should be the public on-site first aid rather than pre hospital first aid. Making improvements in both hardware and software to make the public become an effective force in on-site first aid is bound to reduce more tragedies of sudden death.

References

1. Wang, P.: Epidemic prevention and control is a general examination. Beijing Daily (010), 13 April 2020
2. Wan, W.: Don't let "life saving artifact" become a decoration. Health News (002), 10 October 2017
3. Zhou, J., Mao, K.: Effect of prehospital emergency treatment for open abdominal injury. Chin. Rural Med. **23**(03), 45–46 (2016)
4. Li, C., et al.: Practice and exploration of popular science training for public self and mutual rescue in the new media era. Chin. J. Health Emerg. **3**(01), 62–64 (2017)
5. Quinlivan, M.: Providing first aid and care in the school setting. Br. J. Sch. Nurs. **13**(3), 117–120 (2018). https://doi.org/10.12968/bjsn.2018.13.3.117
6. Liu, Z.: First aid, is it necessary to "let professionals do professional work". Anhui Daily (005), 19 July 2016
7. Xu, J., et al.: Influencing factors of on-site first aid knowledge level of college students in Henan Province. Occup. Health **34**(24), 3421–3423 (2018)

8. Wang, J., Chen, C., Tie, D.: Clinical application of dynamic graphics technology. Chin. PLA J. Hosp. Manag. **27**(02), 175–176 (2020)
9. Xu, Y., Liang, A., Wang, L., Wang, J.: Development and countermeasures of cardiopulmonary resuscitation training mode for middle school students. Sch. Health China **38**(06), 803–805 (2017)
10. Alessandro, P., Francesca, F.A., Lorenzo, L., et al.: Industrial first aid equipment: a historical analysis (1840–1914). **106**(1), 48–64 (2015)
11. Yu, W.: Forward Design: Ecology Dissimilation, from Evolution and Design Progression, 1st edn. East China University of Science and Technology Press, Shanghai (2009)
12. Jiang, S., Wei, Z., Ma, D.: Investigation and research on awareness, attitude and demand of first aid knowledge among college students. J. High. Educ. (12), 194–196 (2019)
13. Chen, J., et al.: Discussion on the construction of public cardiopulmonary resuscitation training platform based on PDCA. Chin. Med. Emerg. **28**(01), 159–161 (2019)

Towards a Practical Approach for Assessing Pressure Relief Activities for Manual Wheelchair Users in Their Daily Lives

Jicheng Fu[1]([✉]), Seth Howell[1], Shuai Zhang[1], Gang Qian[1], Daniel Yan Zhao[2], and Hongwu Wang[2]

[1] University of Central Oklahoma, Edmond, OK 73034, USA
{jfu,showell112,szhang10,gqian}@uco.edu
[2] University of Oklahoma Health Sciences Center, Oklahoma City, OK 73104, USA
daniel-zhao@oushc.edu, Hongwu-Wang@ouhsc.edu

Abstract. Wheelchair users are at great risk of pressure ulcers, which are costly to treat and can seriously affect an individual's quality of life. To reduce the risk of pressure ulcers, Clinical Practice Guidelines (CPGs) recommend that manual wheelchair users perform repositioning activities, i.e., vertical pushups, lateral and forward leans, every 15 to 30 min. Despite the effectiveness of such pressure relief activities, the incidences of pressure ulcers among manual wheelchair users do not decline. Researchers hypothesize that poor compliance with CPGs could be the reason. However, no widely adopted applications are available to quantitatively evaluate whether a manual wheelchair user follows CPGs in their daily life. To fill in the gap, we have developed an iOS app that can communicate with an Apple Watch to collect the activity data of a manual wheelchair user. Based on the characteristics of sensor data specific to the iOS platform, we have developed a threshold-based algorithm to facilitate training data preparation and a neural-network-based approach to classify sensor data. Experimental results showed that our approach achieved a high classification accuracy. The outcome of this preliminary study lays a foundation for a nonintrusive and easy-to-use tool to assess a manual wheelchair user's daily pressure relief activity.

Keywords: Accelerometer · Apple watch · Firebase · Manual wheelchair · Pressure relief · Pressure ulcer

1 Introduction

There are over 1.5 million manual wheelchair users in the United States [1]. Meanwhile, the number of manual wheelchair users continues to increase substantially every year owing to the fast growth of the aging population [2, 3]. Due to their sensory or mobility impairments, wheelchair users are vulnerable to pressure ulcers [2]. Pressure ulcers can lead to pain, infection, and account for about 60,000 deaths every year in the U.S. [2, 4]. The treatments for pressure ulcers can also be costly, ranging from $20,000 to $150,000 for a single wound depending on its severity [2].

© Springer Nature Switzerland AG 2021
V. G. Duffy (Ed.): HCII 2021, LNCS 12778, pp. 40–49, 2021.
https://doi.org/10.1007/978-3-030-77820-0_4

Research has shown that pressure ulcers are mostly preventable [5]. Particularly, periodic pressure relief through repositioning is a commonly used strategy for pressure ulcer prevention. Clinical Practice Guidelines (CPGs) recommend that manual wheelchair users perform repositioning activities, i.e., vertical pushups, lateral and forward leans, every 15 to 30 min [6, 7]. Such pressure relief activities incur no costs and are easy to perform in daily life. Several studies have demonstrated the effectiveness of pressure relief activities, which can reduce seating pressure and increase blood flow to tissues around the ischial tuberosity and sacral regions [5, 8].

Despite the effectiveness of pressure relief activities, existing research found that the majority of manual wheelchair users did not adhere to CPGs [5, 9]. One study showed that on average manual wheelchair users sat in an uninterrupted position for 97 min [5], which significantly exceeded the defined periods in CPGs. Another study illustrated that the uninterrupted sitting periods could be even longer if a pressure redistributing cushion was used [10]. Researchers hypothesize that low compliance with CPGs may contribute to the high occurrence of pressure ulcers among the population of wheelchair users. The rationale is that prolonged unrelieved seating pressure has been recognized as a major causative factor of pressure ulcers [11], and the tissue breakdown may happen within an hour or even less [2].

Unfortunately, few studies are available to provide evidence to support this hypothesis. Some studies relied on qualitative approaches, e.g., questionnaires or phone calls [12]. Self-reports, however, tend to be inaccurate and biased. For example, manual wheelchair users may have false positive perceptions of their pressure relief activities. One study indicated that although wheelchair users claimed "regularly" repositioning themselves, the truth was that they might still sit for prolonged and uninterrupted time periods [8]. Hence, it is desirable to make manual wheelchair users aware of their accurate pressure relief activity rhythm and performance. To quantitatively evaluate pressure relief activities, existing research typically uses pressure sensing systems, e.g., placing sensors under cushions [8, 13], to monitor a manual wheelchair user's pressure relief activities. Besides their high cost, these systems are mostly used in controlled environments with limited lengths of use [14]. Although approaches such as SENSIMAT [15] attempt to monitor pressure reliefs in everyday life, the extra efforts required to install and maintain the data loggers for quantitative data assessments have become a barrier that prevents such systems from being widely adopted in manual wheelchair users' daily life.

To address the aforementioned challenges, we are developing a mobile-cloud system to collect a manual wheelchair user's daily activity data, which allows us to quantitatively assess the individual's repositioning activities for pressure relief. Specifically, we have developed an iOS app that can communicate with an Apple Watch to non-intrusively collect the data of forearm movements, which can be strong indicators of pressure relief activities. The app transmits the collected data to a cloud database, Firebase [16]. By analyzing the patterns intrinsic to pressure relief activities on the iOS platform, we have developed a threshold-based approach for training data preparation and a neural network-based approach for pressure relief activity identification. We have conducted experiments to evaluate the proposed approach. Experimental results showed that it is promising to use the proposed mobile-cloud approach to achieve a timely and accurate assessment of pressure relief activities.

2   Method

We propose to employ the mobile-cloud computing technique to achieve a quantitative assessment of pressure relief activities in manual wheelchair users' daily life. On the mobile side, we have developed an iOS app for Apple Watch to collect the fine-grained forearm movement data. The goal was to use the forearm movement data to recognize pressure relief activities, i.e., lateral (i.e., left and right) and forward leans and vertical pushups. The forward lean relieves pressure on the back and upper buttocks. The vertical pushup relieves all pressure from the buttocks. And the left/right leans remove pressure from the right/left half of the buttocks, respectively.

2.1   Mobile-End Specification

One of the challenges in our study was that the forearm movements associated with purposeful repositioning activities were slight, which made them difficult to detect. We observed that there was a pattern associated with repositioning activities, which consisted of a similar series of motions, i.e., people (1) adjusting their body position by leaning forward or to one side, or pushing up using the armrests to lift the buttocks off the seat; (2) holding that position for a certain duration (e.g., 30 s); and (3) moving back to their original position.

In addition, we have observed a unique pattern in the data collected by the accelerometer in the Apple Watch. An accelerometer can measure accelerations along three axes in space, namely, X, Y, and Z, as shown in Fig. 1. The total acceleration in each axis is the sum of the gravity and user accelerations imposed on the device. In this study, we only recorded the user accelerations, which was provided by the iOS SDK with the gravity being filtered out.

Fig. 1. Three Axes of an Apple Watch[1]

---

[1] Image source: https://www.21c-learning.com/my-apple-watch-dopamine-and-me-2.

Figure 2 shows an example of the patterns demonstrated by user accelerations when a left and a right lean were performed. When a repositioning activity stabilizes to a position, i.e., the user holds that position for 30 s, the accelerations along the three axes also remain unchanged.

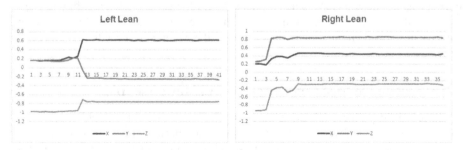

Fig. 2. Patterns demonstrated in the left and right leans

2.2   A Threshold-Based Approach to Facilitate Data Collection

These strong patterns demonstrated in accelerometer data suggest that a machine-learning approach should be suitable to accurately detect a pressure relief activity and identify its type. However, it is very time consuming to prepare and label training data to establish an intelligent model. Hence, we have developed a threshold-based algorithm to analyze and label accelerometer data. The thresholds were determined empirically through a series of experiments, which recorded user accelerations associated with pressure relief activities, i.e., forward, left, and right leans as well as vertical pushups. Along every dimension, we had identified thresholds and segments for each of the pressure relief activities. The combination of the thresholds and segments supports accurate extraction and labeling of the training data. To help other researchers explore along this direction, we have presented the thresholds for pressure relief activities in Table 1. As shown in the table, accelerations along Z need not to be considered except for pushups.

Table 1. Thresholds for pressure relief activates

Type	X	Y	Z
Left lean	[0.5, 0.7]	[−0.33, 0]	−
Right lean	[0.37, 0.7]	[0.6, 0.98]	−
Forward lean	[0.92, 1.06]	[0.25, 0.6]	−
Vertical pushup	[0.9, 0.99]	[0.07, 0.2]	[−0.5, −.0.2]

The threshold-based algorithm largely improved the efficiency for training data preparation. Whenever a piece of sensor data falls into a range defined in Table 1, the algorithm will label the data item accordingly. As a result, when an experiment finishes, the training data set is also extracted and ready to be used.

Although it is possible to use the threshold-based algorithm to classify new sensor data, it may not generalize well as people may wear the Apple Watch in different ways, e.g., on a different hand or with the face of the watch oriented differently, etc. Rather, we have developed an intelligent model to learn the patterns intrinsic to pressure relief activities.

2.3   Using Convolutional Neural Network to Classify Sensor Data

We have developed a convolutional neural network to classify the accelerometer data. The reasons for which we chose a convolution neural network rather than a traditional fully connected network are two-folds. First, the sensor data is multi-dimensional. The data items collected at each time interval consist of 3 elements, i.e., accelerations along X, Y, and Z. Hence, the input to the convolutional neural network is a $N \times 3$ matrix, representing N data items collected within a predefined time window (e.g., 5 s). Second, the convolutional neutral network is a mature technique that has achieved state-of-the-art performance in deep learning research and medical data processing [17, 18].

The label of each training example is encoded as a one-hot vector of size 5. A one-hot vector is a sequence of 0's and 1's, in which there is only one "1" value. The specification of the one-hot vectors is shown in Table 2. For example, an output of 01000 represents a left lean according to the definition.

Table 2. Output specification of the convolution neural network

	1	2	3	4	5
Position	Forward	Left	Right	Pushup	Other

Besides the input layer, our convolutional neural network consists of 4 additional layers, namely, two convolutional layers, one flatten layer, which converts the data from the previous layer into a single dimension, and one softmax layer, which calculates the probability distribution over the five position types as specified in Table 2.

2.4   Data Storage

In this study, we stored the collected accelerometer data into a Firebase [16], which is a cloud-based platform for unified app development. Firebase is featured to support mobile and web applications and real-time data storage. Therefore, our iOS app can directly store the collected accelerometer data into the Firebase system in real-time, thus offloading the storage burden of the smartphone. In this pilot study, the Firebase mainly serves a role for data storage. The data analysis and classification were conducted offline. In the next step, we will move data processing and the convolutional neural network to the cloud to automate the assessment of pressure relief activities for manual wheelchair users.

2.5 Experiments

In this pilot study, the subject was a researcher, who performed the activities of all the experiments. The subject wore the Apple Watch on the wrist of his left hand. The devices we used were iPhone 11 with iOS version 14.3 and iWatch series 5, 40mm with WatchOS 7.2. The programming environment was the Xcode 12.3 IDE running on a MacBook Pro with macOS Catalina 10.15.7.

As the sensor data demonstrates strong patterns, we were able to set the frequency of data collection at once per second. The low frequency was chosen for less battery power consumption since an Apple Watch typically has a much shorter battery life than a smartphone. We chose a time window of 5 s to determine the amount of data as input to the convolution neural network. As a result, the dimension of each data point is 5 × 3 as discussed in Sect. 2.3.

Following the instructions of CPGs, four major activities were studied: pushup, forward lean, left lean, and right lean. For the pushup experiments, the subject sat in the wheelchair with his back against the backrest. Then, the subject put both hands on the armrest and pushed his body up. For forward lean, the subject slowly reached for his toes in order to relieve pressure on the back and upper buttocks. For left lean, the subject used his right arm to push against the armrest. This forced his body weight to shift to the left. For the right lean, the opposite process was performed, i.e., used the left hand to push against the left armrest to release all the pressure from the left half of the buttocks. Any other movements performed in between two pressure relief activities were counted as "others".

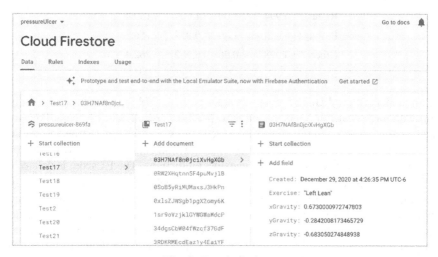

Fig. 3. Data in firebase

Each exercise had a counter that was incremented when the exercise had been successfully executed (i.e., the subject stretched enough to fall into the threshold ranges defined in Table 1). The counter was used to count how many times a specific exercise was successful. After the counter was incremented, the X, Y, and Z values were displayed on the screen of the watch so that the user could see. Afterwards, the values were stored in the Firebase. As shown in Fig. 3, each data item collected at a specific time was stored in the cloud, including the accelerations along X, Y, Z, the timestamp, and the label.

3   Results

With the threshold-based algorithm, the preparation of training data became much effective. We have collected 4522 data items (5 × 3 each), among which 819 were for left leans, 808 were for right leans, 837 were for forward leans, 771 were for pushups, and the rest was for others. We randomly selected 60% of the data as the training data, 20% as the dev data, and the remaining 20% as the testing data. The dev data was used to avoid overfitting, which happens when an intelligent model can only classify existing data well, but fails to classify new unseen data. During training, when the classification accuracy on the dev set starts to decline, training will stop.

We used the TensorFlow [19] platform to develop the convolutional neural network. We repeated the experiment five times. At each time, the data set was randomly shuffled.

Table 3. Classification report

	Precision	Recall	F1-score	Support
Forward	0.986	1.00	0.992	163.6
Left	0.988	0.994	0.994	161.8
Right	0.994	1.00	1.00	159.4
Pushup	0.980	1.00	0.988	156.8
Others	0.998	0.968	0.982	262.4

Our model achieved a high average accuracy of 99%. Table 3 shows the classification report with three evaluation metrics, namely, precision, recall, and F1-score. Precision is defined as the fraction of the true positive predictions over the sum of true positive and false positive predictions. Recall is defined as the fraction of the true positive predictions over the sum of true positive and false negative predictions. The F1 score is defined as $2 \times \frac{precision \times recall}{precision+recall}$, where precision and recall are evenly weighted. A high precision means that among the predictions for a specific class, a high fraction of them is correct. A high recall indicates that among all the data items in a specific class, a high fraction of the predictions is correct. A high F1 score means a good balance between precision and recall. The highest possible value for all three metrics is 1. As shown in Table 3, the three metrics values from the experiments are 1 or close to 1. The last column "Support" shows the average number of data instances included in each specific class in the test set.

4 Discussion

The accelerometer data demonstrates very strong and distinct patterns for different pressure relief activities, as shown in Fig. 2. Part of the reasons may attribute to the iOS SDK, which allowed our application to read only user accelerations without gravity. Had the gravity been involved, it would have been decomposed along the three dimensions of an Apple Watch, interwoven with user accelerations, thus making data analysis more challenging. The observed patterns also enabled us to develop a threshold-based algorithm to facilitate training data extraction and labeling. Actually, our algorithm can label the collected data in real-time while displaying feedback to the user.

With the prepared training data, the classifier built upon the convolutional neural network was able to effectively capture the patterns intrinsic to the repositioning activities. The experimental study showed that it achieved an average accuracy of 99%.

Through an analysis of the confusion matrices for all the experiments, we found that the majority of misclassifications occurred in the class of "Others". Among these misclassifications, the majority (on average 84%) were wrongly classified as "Pushup". A possible reason is that the forearm movements might be slight during a pushup that makes pushup classification more difficult. We will investigate this issue in the next step of our research.

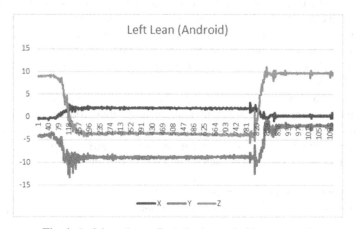

Fig. 4. Left lean data collected using android smart watch

Another observation in our experiments was that the patterns of sensor data could vary largely from iOS to Android devices. iOS and Android are the two mainstream mobile operating systems accounting for over 98% of the mobile-device market [20]. Figure 4 shows a data curve corresponding to a left lean that was collected using an Android app in a separate study. This Android app communicated with a Fossil sport smartwatch powered by Google's Wear OS. Comparing the data curves between Fig. 2 and Fig. 4, we can see very different patterns. As a result, a classifier constructed based on Apple Watch may not be directly applicable to classifying data collected from Android devices, and vice versa.

4.1 Study Limitation

The goal of this paper is to demonstrate the feasibility of using mobile-cloud computing techniques to assess manual wheelchair users' pressure relief activities. There are some limitations in this pilot study, e.g., the app only supports the iOS platform; the activity data was collected in a controlled environment; and the data source lacked diversity. These limitations will be addressed in the next step of our research.

5 Conclusion and Future Research Directions

In this paper, we have presented a preliminary study that aims to achieve a quantitative assessment of pressure relief activities in a manual wheelchair user's daily life. We have developed an iOS App that can control an Apple Watch to collect the activity data of a manual wheelchair user. We have also developed a threshold-based algorithm to facilitate training data preparation by labeling and segmenting the collected sensor data in real-time. With the training data, we were able to construct a convolutional neural network to classify repositioning activities with a high average accuracy. Hence, the preliminary study shows that our proposed approach can not only differentiate different types of pressure relief activities, but also count the number of such activities performed through a day in response to the requirements under CPGs. Furthermore, a cloud-based database backend was used to store the collected accelerometer data to offload the burden of data storage from the smartphone. The mobile- and cloud-computing setting makes our approach particularly amenable to the "new normal" caused by COVID-19 in that healthcare providers will be able to remotely monitor whether a manual wheelchair user follows the CPGs.

In the next step of our research, we will extend our research scope to Android devices. Unlike Apple's products, there are many manufacturers that produce Android devices. We will investigate whether it is possible to build a classifier that will work well with various smartwatches that use Google's Wear OS. We will also recruit manual wheelchair users to validate our proposed approach in their daily environments.

Acknowledgment. This study was supported by the Beresford Endowment Fund and the CURE-STEM Scholar Fund at the University of Central Oklahoma.

References

1. Torkia, C., Reid, D., Korner-Bitensky, N., Kairy, D., Rushton, P.W., Demers, L., et al.: Power wheelchair driving challenges in the community: a users' perspective. Disabil. Rehabil. Assist. Technol. **10**, 211–215 (2015)
2. Gefen, A.: The future of pressure ulcer prevention is here: detecting and targeting inflammation early. EWMA J **19**, 7–13 (2018)
3. Reznik, R.: Wheelchair Facts, Numbers and Figures [Infographic] (2015). http://kdsmartch air.com/blogs/news/18706123-wheelchair-facts-numbers-and-figures-infographic
4. Byrne, D.W., Salzberg, C.A.: Major risk factors for pressure ulcers in the spinal cord disabled: a literature review. Spinal Cord **34**, 255–263 (1996)

5. Schofield, R., Porter-Armstrong, A., Stinson, M.: Reviewing the literature on the effectiveness of pressure relieving movements. Nurs. Res. Pract. **2013**, 1–13 (2013). https://doi.org/10.1155/2013/124095

6. Consortium for Spinal Cord Medicine Clinical Practice Guidelines: Pressure ulcer prevention and treatment following spinal cord injury: a clinical practice guideline for health-care professionals. J. Spinal Cord Med. **24**, S40 (2001)

7. Makhsous, M., Rowles, D.M., Rymer, W.Z., Bankard, J., Nam, E.K., Chen, D., et al.: Periodically relieving ischial sitting load to decrease the risk of pressure ulcers. Arch. Phys. Med. Rehabil. **88**, 862–870 (2007)

8. Sonenblum, S., Sprigle, S., Martin, J.: Everyday sitting behavior of full-time wheelchair users. J. Rehabil. Res. Dev. **53**(5), 585–598 (2016)

9. Demarré, L., Van Lancker, A., Van Hecke, A., Verhaeghe, S., Grypdonck, M., Lemey, J., et al.: The cost of prevention and treatment of pressure ulcers: a systematic review. Int. J. Nurs. Stud. **52**, 1754–1774 (2015)

10. Uenishi, K., Tanaka, M., Yoshida, H., Tsutsumi, S., Miyamoto, N.: Driver's fatigue evaluation during long term driving for automotive seat development. SAE Technical Paper 0148-7191 (2002)

11. Nixon, J., Cranny, G., Bond, S.: Pathology, diagnosis, and classification of pressure ulcers: comparing clinical and imaging techniques. Wound Repair Regener. **13**(4), 365–372 (2005)

12. Groah, S.L., Schladen, M., Pineda, C.G., Hsieh, C.-H.J.: Prevention of pressure ulcers among people with spinal cord injury: a systematic review. Pm&r **7**, 613–636 (2015)

13. Gabison, S., Mathur, S., Nussbaum, E.L., Popovic, M.R., Verrier, M.C.: Trunk Function and ischial pressure offloading in individuals with spinal cord injury. J. Spinal Cord Med. **40**, 723–732 (2017)

14. Stockton, L., Flynn, M.: Sitting and pressure ulcers. 1: risk factors, self-repositioning and other interventions. Nurs. Times **105**, 12–14 (2009)

15. SENSIMAT Systems. https://sensimat.wordpress.com/

16. Firebase: Firebase Realtime Database. https://firebase.google.com/docs/database

17. Li, D., Zhang, J., Zhang, Q., Wei, X.: Classification of ECG signals based on 1D convolution neural network. In: 2017 IEEE 19th International Conference on e-Health Networking, Applications and Services (Healthcom), pp. 1–6 (2017)

18. Silver, D., Schrittwieser, J., Simonyan, K., Antonoglou, I., Huang, A., Guez, A., et al.: Mastering the game of go without human knowledge. Nature **550**, 354 (2017)

19. TensorFlow: (2/17). TensorFlow. https://www.tensorflow.org/

20. Mobile operating systems' market share worldwide from January 2012 to October 2020. https://www.statista.com/statistics/272698/global-market-share-held-by-mobile-operating-systems-since-2009/

Principles for Designing an mHealth App for Participatory Research and Management of Chronic Pain

Eileen Mary Holowka[1], Sandra Woods[2], Amber Pahayahay[3], Mathieu Roy[4], and Najmeh Khalili-Mahani[1,5(✉)]

[1] Technoculture, Arts and Games, Milieux Institute for Art, Culture and Technology, Concordia University, Montreal, QC, Canada
{eileen.holowka,najmeh.khalili-mahani}@concordia.ca
[2] Montréal, Canada
[3] University of Waterloo, Waterloo, ON, Canada
acpahayahay@uwaterloo.ca
[4] Department of Psychology, McGill University, Montréal, QC, Canada
mathieu.roy3@mcgill.ca
[5] PERFORM Centre, Concordia University, Montreal, QC, Canada

Abstract. Collecting data from the lived experiences of those with chronic health conditions is a delicate and challenging matter that must account for the individual differences of coping with a personally-embodied condition in psychosocial contexts. In this paper, we describe our research process for designing a mobile application that will serve as a portal for participatory research into non-pharmacological interventions which could improve the daily experiences of chronic pain patients. The process is informed by our empirical framework "affective game planning for health applications" (AGPHA), which postulates that for digital health interventions to be effective, they must minimize a user's stress by maximizing their sense of control and agency in self-expression and self-care. We have evaluated our hypotheses through literature review, focus groups, anonymous online surveying, and participatory research with stakeholders (patients, caregivers, researchers). From this, we have designed and implemented a prototype application, *PlaythePain,* which includes five main features: *Talk, Track, Play, Share* and *Report*. The app incorporates elements of choice, playfulness, and social engagement, by 1) allowing users to select and introduce their own complementary and alternative forms of self-care for their pain, and 2) adding a humorous and empathetic chatbot that guides patient-partners to conduct self-research (qualitative and quantitative). Further sharing of data with designated doctors or personal stories with other community members is also available at the discretion of the user. We believe that this approach will facilitate it for users to increase awareness about the psychosocial and environmental contexts of their conditions.

Keywords: mHealth · Participatory research · Patient-centered design · Chatbot · Health tracking apps · Stress · Chronic pain · User experience

---

S. Woods—Patient Partner.

© Springer Nature Switzerland AG 2021
V. G. Duffy (Ed.): HCII 2021, LNCS 12778, pp. 50–67, 2021.
https://doi.org/10.1007/978-3-030-77820-0_5

1   Introduction

Caring for chronic pain (CP) is not only a medical challenge, but also a cultural and psychosocial one. The primary concern for many pain patients is how to communicate their pain and the first challenge of communication is quantification. When pain is not associated with a medically explained injury, the burden of pain quantification is left to patients' subjective assessment of the pain scales often used to measure pain severity. The second challenge of communication is qualification. In the absence of objective biomarkers, many chronic pain patients face isolation, dismissal, stigma, and difficulty qualifying for care programs [1–3].

Today, there is consensus that patient-partnerships are the key to advancing pain research and personalizing CP management [4]. The participatory action research model (PAR) puts patients at the heart of research and dissemination of knowledge gained through self-experimentation and self-observation [5, 6]. Digital pain management tools show promise for improving the challenges of communication, and are often considered the preferred tool for patients to record and report the contextual variations in their daily experiences of pain [7, 8].

With the increasing popularity of digital technologies, additional methods of representing and communicating chronic pain have become available. Beyond tracking, mHealth (mobile health) tools also offer opportunities for patients to learn pain self-management techniques outside of a clinical setting where there may be time and resource constraints [9]. As Stephen A. Rains writes in his 2018 book, *Coping with Illness Digitally*, the primary reasons for which individuals turn to digital tools in the face of chronic illnesses are to make and reinforce connections; to solicit and provide social support; to share experiences and seek information; and/or to change patient-provider relationships [10].

There are a number of digital tools already on the market for people living with CP, however few are dedicated to creating patient-partnership in research. Most mHealth apps provide patients with coping strategies and tools to assist them with the self-management of their CP [9, 11, 12]. However, sustained engagement with such software seems to be a recurring challenge in studies of their efficacy [13].

Because pain is a personal experience, which varies under different contexts and over time, limiting user's and patient's participation to one type of app risks making the participation inaccessible or ineffective for many of them. This limitation is not exclusive to behavioral interventions using mHealth apps, but a reality that has forced clinical researchers to seek new methodologies that leverage current advances in data science which involve participant observation and the continued adjustment of process based on those observations [14].

Creating flexible tools and processes is essential for maximizing participants' engagement. We aimed to address this need by creating a digital platform that functions as a self-laboratory for investigating the efficacy of non-pharmacological methods, especially those delivered through mHealth apps, in coping with chronic pain. The self-laboratory design allows participants to engage in ways that most suit their needs, schedule and interests.

In this paper, we describe our iterative design process from a scientific hypothesis through its evolution, integration of patient partners, investigation of the issue of user-engagement via market review, literature review, user survey, and prototyping.

2   Conceptual Framework and Scientific Basis

Melzack's neuromatrix theory of pain emphasizes that personal and social factors significantly influence resilience to pain. One must account for these myriad of psychosocial factors in order to effectively design a patient-oriented digital environment for chronic pain [15].

Chronic health conditions are inherently stressful, thus we have suggested an empirical framework, Affective Game Planning for Health Applications (AGPHA), in order to minimize user stress while engaging with a digital health application [16]. AGPHA builds on Lazarus' Transactional Theory of Stress and Adaptation and advocates for iterative quantification of physiological stress responses in relation to variation in how players evaluate a challenge with regards to their own cognitive and emotional resources, and coping strategies [17]. According to AGPHA, the primary appraisal of an interaction (e.g. with an app or game) plays a critical role in its adoption. In many cases, primary appraisal (e.g. about usefulness or meaningfulness of an experience) may be negative, but iterative engagements that enhance fun, meaningfulness, and effectiveness can alter the user's experience over time. In fact, we have obtained preliminary evidence indicating that enjoyment and relatedness while playing a mobile app game increase analgesia in an experimental setting [18].

In order to assess the variations in primary appraisal of digital pain research, we engaged in an iterative process that is summarized in Fig. 1. Based on AGPHA, we were interested in answering four questions which evolved during this process:

1. What factors are important to consider in creating patient-partnership in research?
2. Do playful, creative and social activities matter in a digital citizen laboratory?
3. What motivates CP patients to engage with a digital citizen laboratory?
4. What functionalities address the needs identified in 1, 2, and 3?

3   Research Process and Findings

3.1   Literature Review of Considerations for Creating a Digital Laboratory for Studying Chronic Pain

Communicating About Chronic Pain. Chronic pain is a debilitating condition that affects one in every five people in Canada and the United States. Those living with CP may suffer long-term disability, depression, and even suicidal ideation [19]. Cultural and psychosocial challenges, such as shame and stigmatization or mistreatment (due to prejudice and implicit biases or cultural and linguistic misunderstandings) are reported often [1, 20, 21].

Even the act of communicating pain in a clinical setting can be difficult. Patients are often asked to use a numerical "Pain Scale" to describe their pain even though this system has been critiqued extensively for its subjectivity and unreliability [22, 23]. In medicine, fiction, and theoretical discourses pain is often framed as something unrepresentable, despite the wealth of art and poetry that still tries to represent it [24]. Although pain resists representation in so many ways, the imagination, exploration, and empowerment of communicating pain remain necessary and critical practices for those living with CP.

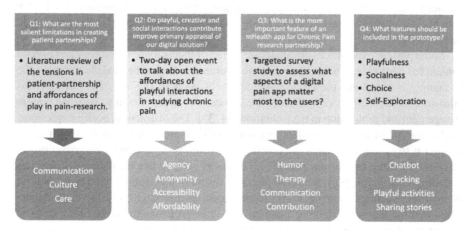

Fig. 1. Research steps to improve the primary appraisal of the digital laboratory

Choice and Self-determination. Clinical researchers are increasingly aware that putting patients at the centre of their care and giving them agency in their treatment creates the best outcomes [25, 26]. Centring patients in their own care can help them improve self-esteem, mastery, self-empowerment, understanding, or acceptance of their illness. Further, those who take an active role in their treatment tend to be more resilient and live and function better with their illness(es) [27]. Self-determination and psychological well-being have also proven beneficial in improving the overall quality of life of individuals living with CP conditions specifically [28]. Digital health apps offer more accessible ways to practice patient-centred care in a world with limited health resources. They also offload many of the more time-consuming and frustrating aspects of self-monitoring (such as recording dates or compiling/visualizing information) to the smartphone [29]. Having flexibility over features, such as controlling whether the app reminds the user to engage, can also be important for both improving self-knowledge and empowerment, as well as providing patients control and agency [29].

A necessary feature of implementing patient-centered care into digital health apps involves ensuring that users have full control over their health data, both in terms of what data they are willing to share, as well as how they wish their data to be used [29]. One of the predominant concerns when it comes to digital health tools is the risk of further compromising the rights, agency, and data security of already vulnerable individuals or groups [30]. Apps (and wearable health technologies) have the power to "normalize (and sometimes antagonize) human bodies" [31], for example using gamification to mask their collection of data from players without compensating them. In contrast, implementing patient-centred care into design puts control over data back into the hands of the patients who can choose to use it as they wish, whether for research into CP or for their own use (ie: to share with their friends and loved ones, patients, peers, or healthcare professionals).

Playfulness. When playfulness is incorporated into digital health it increases the opportunities for more light-hearted and interactive pain management, coping, and care for CP patients. There are several playful elements to consider for design of a digital research framework.

Some playful experiences are analgesic in and of themselves. Humorous and playful content has been proven to improve the pain tolerance in both acute and chronic pain due to changes in mood and the physiologic effects of laughter [32, 33]. The effectiveness of distraction and immersion afforded by games or VR are shown to increase patient engagement and motivation in rehabilitation [34, 35]. The distraction, positive emotions, and/or placebo analgesia provided by games, music therapy, meditation, mindfulness, or other distraction techniques can be effective methods of reducing pain sensations in cases of both acute and chronic pain [36, 37]. Studies suggest that interactive distractions, including video game play, are more effective for pain management than more passive alternatives, such as listening to music or watching television [18, 38]. Researchers found that the more entertaining a patient finds a given game, the more likely they are to continue their rehabilitation and to benefit from it [39].

Other playful experiences are about sense-making and meaning-making, both of which are key components of living with and communicating chronic pain [24]. Self-expression and meaning-making are central to the practices of art therapy, which can also be digitized [40, 41]. Play is not solely a motivational distraction, it is also a mode of communication that provides a space for cultural and metaphorical approaches to studying and making sense of body-mind relations [42]. If self-expression can be integrated into play, and digitized, then we will have a framework for both experimentation with and production of experience and knowledge [43]. Digital play creates a structured system to experiment with experiential learning; it provides an opportunity for creating and revising new modes of expression and communication; and because it is 'play', it makes it possible to explore paradoxical--even conflictual--ideas across cultures and realities. Therefore, beyond distraction, playfulness can also offer a space in which CP patients can simulate control over hypothetical situations and improve mastery, self-esteem, and resilience.

Social Interactivity. A high proportion of people living with chronic illnesses turn to digital communities in search of social support, shared illness experiences, and even therapeutic advice. Although social eHealth interventions (such as online support groups) have a number of downsides in terms of spreading misinformation, increasing potential exposure to difficult content, or inducing anxiety, they constitute an important resource for many of those living with chronic conditions [10, 44].

Although imperfect, digital spaces such as CP Facebook groups or websites can provide spaces in which individuals can express their experiences of persistent pain on their own terms and represent themselves as they wish to be seen, without the restriction of a clinical checklist or pain scale [10, 45]. Our previous work has shown that social networks provide an important outlet for those who are burdened by emotional stress [46, 47]. Digital spaces of social interactivity can offer CP patients opportunities to explore their understanding of pain and meaning-making, both on their own and in collaboration with others. This meaning-making (both individual and social), as we have discussed, is an important tool for self-empowerment and exercising mastery.

3.2 Public Consultation: Can We Play the Pain Digitally?

From the literature review above, we concluded that digital platforms afford the opportunity to communicate, exercise choice and mastery, distract and express oneself in various creative manners, individually or socially. Our next step was to evaluate these assumptions in consultation with the public. ·

We organized a public two-day event ay Concordia's 4TH Space, an exhibition centre which is located in a visible high-traffic space in downtown Montréal, easily accessible and open to the public (information about the event can be found here: https://www.concordia.ca/cuevents/offices/provost/fourth-space/2019/10/01/play-the-pain-in-4th-space.html). Information about the event were shared through various social media by patient partners and event moderators who worked with CP patients. The event was structured around the theme of healing through creativity, and was integrated into the backdrop of an ongoing research exhibit by our lab (Media Spa) where different types of games were made available to visitors to explore and discuss. The main questions for participants were: "Do you see any advantage in digitizing art-therapy?" and "Do you see an advantage in creating an app that enables you to research the analgesic effect of different non pharmacological therapies?".

In order to create a natural conversational space, we did not perform any formal data collection (to avoid the artificiality and the 'stress' of being recorded) or studies. Observational notes indicated that following themes, in terms of the promises or challenges of our proposal, were salient:

- **Accessibility** of digital platforms was seen as a double-edge sword. On the one hand, almost all participants with whom we spoke concurred that the "digital" can break the geographical barriers and become particularly useful to those who could not be physically participating due to illness or disability. On the other hand, concerns were expressed about the cost of access (cell phones, price of WiFi) and the fact that such digital interventions would not be necessarily accessible to those who might need them most.
- **Anonymity** was an important feature, especially to those who did not wish to publicly share their personal stories, but who acknowledged the importance of sharing them in a more protective setting.
- **Ownership** of data, and agency in decision-making about how to express, evaluate, and contribute knowledge about pain was important to those who self-identified as suffering from chronic pain.
- **Respect for individual narratives** and recognition of personal needs and philosophical dispositions was also considered an important factor in designing pain applications. Participants were not interested in apps that forced users to fit their complex experiences of pain into reductionist numerical and categorical representations.

- **Social playfulness** was appreciated, although we observed an initial trepidation in joining some group activities such as dancing, playing music, and creative writing, but no one hesitated to join Yoga, play VR, or discuss pain symbolism (Fig. 2).

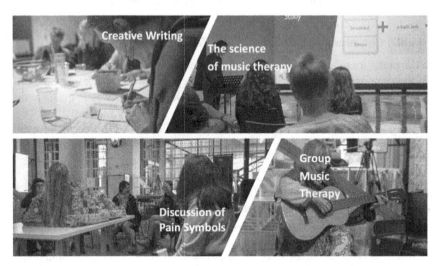

Fig. 2. A few sample activities that took place during the 2-day Play the Pain event.

3.3 Affordances of Digital Platforms for CP Research and Management

Surveying Existing Apps for Coping with Chronic Pain. First, we surveyed existing apps specifically designed for coping with chronic pain. Between October 2019 and May 2020, we searched for all applications that were advertised specifically for coping with chronic pain. In total, we found 137 applications. We excluded any that were not implemented on a mobile device and categorized the remaining 114 apps based on their primary advertised feature. As can be seen in Fig. 2, the majority of existing products were dedicated to tracking (n = 38, with 6/38 incorporating a social networking option as well). The subsequent most frequent applications were games (n = 19), followed by various therapeutic applications (12 forms of physical therapy; 8 meditations, 5 cognitive behavioral therapies (CBT), 4 audio- and 3 forms of art-therapy (drawing, coloring and image-guided). There were also 12 apps for providing pain management information (Fig. 3).

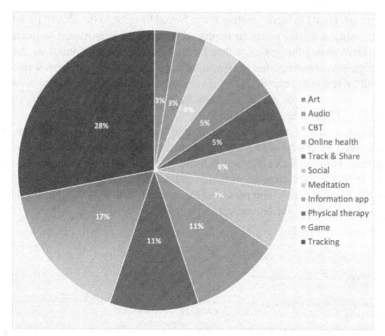

Fig. 3. Distribution of the surveyed mobile applications advertised or developed with the primary objective of serving chronic pain patients.

Survey Study: Are CP Patients Interested in Becoming Research-Partners?

Second, we launched an online anonymous survey through the social media of patient and clinical partners as well as PERFORM Centre's mailing list, calling for CP patients or their caregivers to help us design the app.

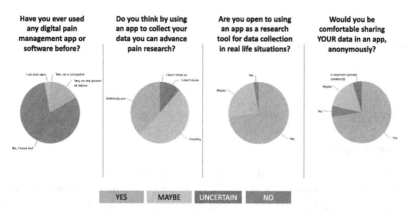

Fig. 4. Frequency of survey respondents' answers to the questions of familiarity with similar apps (more than 80% were unfamiliar), believing in potential benefits for advancing research (more than 40% strongly agreed) and willingness to share data (more than 70% agreed).

We were interested to learn whether users would be open to the idea of participating in research using a digital platform deployed on an app. Results are summarized in Fig. 4, and show that, although more than 80% of the respondents (out of 98) had never used any digital pain management software or apps, the majority of them were open to sharing data for research purposes. Only a very small percentage felt that such strategies would not be useful. About half of the participants considered it a possibility that such approaches would advance pain research.

In addition, we asked participants to answer questions about how best to collect data about their pain. As can be seen from Fig. 5, tracking of psychosocial factors was the most important factor in data collection (absolutely true for 42% and somewhat true for 43%). The majority of the respondents believed that they could accurately describe their pain experience numerically, and preferred scientific terminology. That said, more than 78% of participants thought humor was a preferred method for describing one's pain experience.

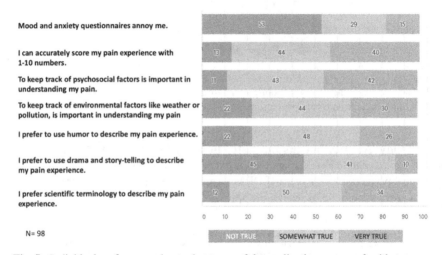

Fig. 5. Individual preferences about what types of data collection were preferable to users.

4   Prototype

4.1   Design Elements

Based on the research described above, we concluded the following:

First, that potential users are on board with providing anonymous data about their pain experience to advance science; second, that tracking psychological and environmental factors is important; and third, that scientific terminology and humor were both important for communicating pain.

Based on these principles, we designed *Play the Pain* (Fig. 6) as an mHealth research partnership hub incorporating three elements into a typical digital pain diary:

1. **Patient-oriented**: It allows patients to choose what type of intervention they prefer and what type of data they wish to gather [**Track**, **Talk** and view pain/play **Report**];
2. **Playful**: It adds playfulness through the use of a chatbot agent, which draws the users' attention to a range of creative activities for self-expression and exploration [**Talk & Play**]; and
3. **Social**: It allows users to share their stories within a community of other CP users or with their 'doctors' (clinicians or researchers) [**Share**].

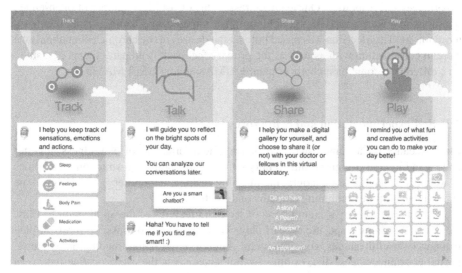

Fig. 6. An overview of the main features of the *PlaythePain* app prototype.

4.2 Data Collection

Data collection respects both an individual's privacy and agency, making it possible for them to become research-partners with a 'doctor', who will have access to the user's data if the user chooses to share it with them. This is done through a secure backend data-management system that will be described elsewhere.

The app collects two types of data, quantitative (**Track**) and qualitative (**Talk**).

Track. Quantitative data is collected using standard instruments which can be accessed through the Track feature. Users can quantify their pain (type of pain, location of pain, sensation, and intensity of each), sleep (standard sleep questionnaires are implemented in a chatbot), and emotions (type of emotions experienced during the day are presented on a dial with a scale to help users assign a rating to them), and provide information about their medications and activities. They can later reflect on their data in an individual report which will be explained later in this section.

Talk. Qualitative data is collected by providing the patient-partner the option to share additional stories about their daily experiences. These conversations are guided by a chatbot.

Chatbots have proven to be useful for mHealth tools in a variety of situations (from mental health diagnostics and adolescent coaching, to interventions in COVID-19 screening), but they require careful design that considers the varying needs of app users, the possible severity of their symptoms, and acts in a way that is beneficial while not off-putting or controlling [48–50]. A chatbot can be pre-scripted, as in the case of *Play the Pain*. With pre-scripted dialogue, the challenge is to accommodate a wide array of experiences and responses. Our team addressed this by asking a number of open-ended questions into which app users could input their thoughts and feelings using their own terminology. This decision was based both on the desires of the chronic pain patients we were in conversation with as well as the primary feedback from participants of a study on a different chronic pain chatbot "painSELfMAnagment" (SELMA) [51].

4.3   Self-experimentation and Self Expression

Play. Because we are interested in exploring the affordances of playfulness in better understanding and designing interventions for CP (for both its distraction capabilities as well as its potential for encouraging meaning-making and mastery), we designed the app with an attitude combining empathy and lightness.

We achieved this by assigning one of the main features of the application to **Play**. Instead of assigning a specific type of play, we provide a list of possible forms of play that can be useful (games, cognitive brain training, art-creation, meditation, exercise, music, watching videos, diet, or other) which encourages the user to define their own category of playful intervention, assign applications to it, and **Share** the ways in which it is helpful to them, if they so choose.

Share. Digital communities are an important source of information and perspective from shared illness and therapeutic experiences, and offer the possibility for increasing a sense of empowerment through self-expression [10]. We implemented the **Share** option which is accessible the main menu and also prompted from other app features (different **Talk** and **Track** branches) to encourage patient-partners to contribute to knowledge creation.

Access to this open-ended narrative data gathering portal is controlled by the user who chooses whether to share their stories with a 'doctor', with the public (a community of anonymous users of the app), or keep private. The stories told by the user on this portal can be accessed, deleted, or edited by the user, and are retained in their personal pain diary for later review. If their stories are shared publicly, users can search and interact with others' stories by keyword. Aware of the potential of social networks for propagation of misinformation and toxic or disrespectful interactions, the interactions on others' posts is limited to two emoticons, "heart" and "broken heart" to express empathy.

Talk. Under our patient-centred approach, the focus in the current implementation of our chatbot is on providing patients with choices and agency, while also pointing them towards relevant activities that may be helpful, e.g. meditation, tracking, or social inter-activity. In addition to being a tool for qualitative data collection, **Talk** (chatbot) is designed to draw the user's attention to possible positive aspects (*making lemonade out of a lemon*), and encourage them to self-express using the **Share** option (Fig 7 presents an example).

An important design consideration in chatbot implementation has been to make it playful while also being empathic and casual. We address this, for example, by using emojis and affirming the user's experiences while reminding them that they are talking to 'just a bot' so that *they themselves* can later reflect on their experiences.

We are interested in adapting the wording of some of the standard psychometric questionnaires into an organic, empathetic, and playful interaction to help users self-express and encourage them to experiment with how new modalities (diet, activities, perspectives) which might help them cope better with CP.

An example of semi-structured interview in Talk, and the report where the data collected in the interview is saved and made available to the user.

Fig. 7. An example of the flow of semi-structured conversations in **Talk** (chatbot). (1) The user selects **Talk** from main menu and is presented with a list of topics. (2) Each topic is divided into subtopics from which the user can select one at a time. In this case the user has chosen "I have a story". (3) Each story can have different subcategories, a selection scheme that avoids producing incomprehensible or unempathetic responses to the user. (4) The chatbot asks some general questions to encourage the user to dig deeper into their story and reminds them that they are interacting with a chatbot, encouraging them to **Share** their story with actual humans. (5) The user is directed to the **Share** menu and talk about their story about a relationship. They opt to share the with the Doctor. (6) When the user consults the report, they would see a list of quantitative data that they have recorded. (7) When they select the *Gallery* button in the 'day' report, they are directed to their personal gallery and can see that they shared a story on that date. The story has an icon to show its privacy setting (only me, doctord, public). The user can also edit and delete the stories in the gallery. In this case the access was granted only to the 'doctor' and received one 'broken-heart' reaction. (8) When the user selects the *Chats* button, they see the topics that they have chatted about on this date. (9) When they select the topic ("I have a story") they can view a log of their conversations with the chatbot.

We have chosen not to use AI technology; instead, a writer and one of our chronic pain patient partner/researchers designed the chatbot. Although AI is becoming more useful in medical diagnosis [48, 52], its capabilities in providing empathy (a critical factor for CP patients) are still very limited [53] and subject to implicit bias.

4.4 Personal Reports and Galleries

Fig 8 shows a more comprehensive view of **Report** features. Users have full access to every data-point, accessible by date, or averaged over months, and year. The graphs quantify the number of times that the user has reported pain, and the number of interactions (playing, talking). The app does not include any hidden data collection capabilities, and users have the option of selecting whether they share their data with a designated 'doctor'. At any given time, the user can revoke the doctor's access to their data. The following data categories are retained in a secure remote database: pain, feelings, sleep, activities, and medication (from the **Track** menu) as well interactions with the chatbot (from the **Talk** menu) and stories (gallery of pictures, stories, and videos from **the Report**).

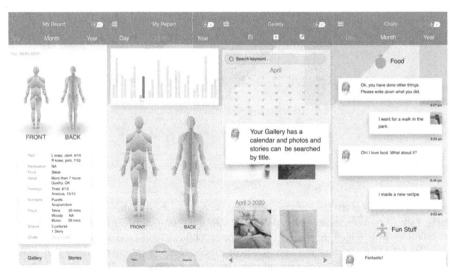

Fig. 8. An example of a report accessible to a user. If they choose to share this information with a doctor, the same data will become visible and downloadable to them. Simple statistical graphs of the volume of self-tracking and playing are shown by month and year in diagrams. All report elements are searchable by date or keyword.

5 Conclusion

5.1 Summary

Caring for chronic pain requires attention to the cultural and psychosocial contexts in which pain is evaluated and communicated. Our work is inspired by the recognition of the necessity of patient-partnerships in advancing health research and personalizing care through community and creative communications [4, 54]. In line with the objectives of the participatory action-research model (PAR), we aimed to design a patient-centric application that would put people with CP at the heart of both research and the dissemination of knowledge gained through self-experimentation and self-observation. We hope that this app can be used by patients and research-partners to further explore options to improve the quality of life and CP care.

Starting from a theoretical framework (Neuromatrix of Pain and Transactional Theory of Stress Appraisal and Coping), we aimed to investigate the most important elements to consider in the design of a digital citizen laboratory for CP patients. We set out to answer four questions to inform our design:

1. What are the most important factors to consider in creating patient-partnership in research?
2. What are the affordances of playful, creative and social activities in a digital citizen laboratory?
3. For chronic pain patients, what is the greatest motivation for engaging with a digital citizen laboratory?
4. What are the app features that can address the above needs?

We reviewed the literature, performed a CP public consultation, and conducted a general survey study addressed to CP patients and their caregivers. We also reviewed more than 137 digital mHealth tools for those living with CP, which pointed to the following design requirements:

I.   **A patient-oriented approach** is the most important feature for potential users. Any digital app for PAR must respect individual differences in focus, interests, modes of self-evaluation and self-expression, and self-care, allowing users to select which data to share and how they choose to engage.
II.   **Incorporating playful activities into the app** is important. It is also critical to strike a balance between collecting accurate data and providing enough freedom to acknowledge and express empathy for the lived experiences of CP patients.
III. **Sharing data with designated researchers and clinicians** offers an opportunity to contribute to research while incorporating an element of social purpose to the engagement.
IV.   **Creating knowledge** from the lived experiences of patients from a searchable archival gallery is an empowering tool for CP patients.

This prototype has been launched in both English and French and includes 5 principal features:

- **Talk**: An empathic chatbot that promotes self-reflective and semi-structured qualitative data collection about various aspects of daily experiences.
- **Track**: A digital pain diary that also gathers information about sleep, activities, feelings, and medication.

- **Share**: A restricted social network that allows users to create a gallery of their stories, artwork, and videos about various activities or experiences that they deem to be worth sharing.
- **Play**: A library of different mHealth-mediated interventions that can be added by the user.
- **Report**: A comprehensive report of all data collected within the app, transparently available to the user which can be shared only if they grant access to a designated research-partner.

5.2　Future Work

Our app design has not yet undergone extensive user testing and validation.

We have been consulting and refining the UI/UX iteratively and in partnership with potential stakeholders (patients, caregivers, and researchers). We are in the process of planning a focus group study with the participation of additional CP patients and pain clinicians to validate our approach.

The future work will involve releasing the app on the App Store and Google Play to monitor its uptake as well as refining its backend data management in order to maximize data-security.

Further, we plan to implement additional computational algorithms to allow users to analyze and interpret their own data.

Our ultimate hope is to increase the involvement of CP patients as partners in research. This app aims to be a tool to incorporate ecological and qualitative data into clinical research, where psychosocial and environmental monitoring of the context of an individual's experience and the behavioral adaptation are currently lacking.

References

1. Kleinman, A.: The Illness Narratives: Suffering, Healing, and the Human Condition. The University of Michigan Press, Ann Arbor (1988)
2. Werner, A., Malterud, K.: It is hard work behaving as a credible patient: encounters between women with chronic pain and their doctors. Soc. Sci. Med. **57**(8), 1409–1419 (2003)
3. Thernstrom, M.: The Pain Chronicles: Cures, Myths, Mysteries, Prayers, Diaries, Brain Scans, Healing, and the Science of Suffering. Farrar Straus and Giroux, New York (2010)
4. Mintzberg, H.: Managing the Myths of Health Care: Bridging the Separations Between Care, Cure, Control, and Community. 1st ed, vol. Viii, 262 p. Berrett-Koehler Publishers, Inc., Oakland (2017)
5. Fals-Borda, O., Rahman, M.A.: Action and Knowledge: Breaking the Monopoly With Participatory Action Research, vol. viii, 182 p. Apex Press. Intermediate Technology Publications, New York (1991)
6. Warriner, D.S., Bigelow, M.: Critical Reflections on Research Methods: Power and Equity in Complex Multilingual Contexts, vol. xi, 200 p. Researching Multilingually, Blue Ridge Summit: Multilingual Matters, Bristol (2019)
7. Jibb, L., et al.: Electronic data capture versus conventional data collection methods in clinical pain studies: systematic review and meta-analysis. J. Med. Internet Res. **22**(6), e16480 (2020)
8. Lazaridou, A., Elbaridi, N., Edwards, R.R.: Chapter 5: Pain Assessment. In: Essentials of Pain Medicine. Elsevier, St. Louis (2018)

9. Vilardaga, R., et al.: Theoretical grounds of Pain tracker self manager: an acceptance and commitment therapy digital intervention for patients with chronic pain. J. Contextual Behav. Sci. **15**, 172–180 (2020)
10. Rains, S.A.: Coping with Illness Digitally. MIT Press, Cambridge (2018)
11. Hamine, S., et al.: Impact of mHealth chronic disease management on treatment adherence and patient outcomes: a systematic review. J. Med. Internet Res. **17**(2), e52 (2015)
12. Birnie, K.A., et al.: iCanCope PostOp: user-centered design of a smartphone-based app for self-management of postoperative pain in children and adolescents. JMIR Form. Res. **3**(2), e12028 (2019)
13. Ross, E., et al.: Clinical integration of a smartphone app for patients with chronic pain: retrospective analysis of predictors of benefits and patient engagement between clinic visits. J. Med. Internet Res. **22**(4), e16939 (2020)
14. Bothwell, L., et al.: Adaptive design clinical trials: a review of the literature and ClinicalTrials.gov. BMJ Open **8**(2), e018320 (2018)
15. Melzack, R.: Pain and the neuromatrix in the brain. J. Dent. Educ. **65**(12), 1378–1382 (2001)
16. Khalili-Mahani, N., Schutter, B.D.: Affective game planning for health applications: quantitative extension of gerontoludic design based on the appraisal theory of stress and coping. JMIR Serious Games **7**(2), e13303 (2019)
17. Lazarus, R.S., Folkman, S.: Transactional theory and research on emotions and coping. Eur. J. Pers. **1**(3), 141–169 (2020)
18. Goodman-Vincent, E., Roy, M., Khalili-Mahani, N.: Affective game planning for playing the pain. In: Extended Abstracts of the 2020 Annual Symposium on Computer-Human Interaction in Play, pp. 122–128 (2020)
19. Choinière, M., et al.: The Canadian STOP-PAIN project – Part 1: who are the patients on the waitlists of multidisciplinary pain treatment facilities? Can. J. Anesth./J. canadien d'anesthésie **57**(6), 539–548 (2010)
20. Dusenbery, M., Doing Harm: The Truth About How Bad Medicine and Lazy Science Leave Women Dismissed, Misdiagnosed, and Sick. First ed, 390 p. HarperOne, New York (2017)
21. Meints, S.M., et al.: Racial and ethnic differences in the experience and treatment of noncancer pain. Pain Manag. **9**(3), 317–334 (2019)
22. Krebs, E., Carey, T., Weinberger, M.: Accuracy of the pain numeric rating scale as a screening test in primary care. J. Gener. Intern. Med. **22**(10), 1453–1458 (2007). https://doi.org/10.1007/s11606-007-0321-2
23. Melzack, R.: The McGill pain questionnaire: from description to measurement. Anesthesiology **103**(1), 199–202 (2005)
24. Scarry, E.: The Body in Pain: The Making and Unmaking of the World. Oxford UP, New York (1987)
25. Haverfield, M.C., Giannitrapani, K., Timko, C., Lorenz, K.: Patient-centered pain management communication from the patient perspective. J. Gen. Intern. Med. **33**(8), 1374–1380 (2018). https://doi.org/10.1007/s11606-018-4490-y
26. Gagliardi, A.R., et al.: How is patient-centred care conceptualized in women's health: a scoping review. BMC Womens Health **19**(1), 156 (2019)
27. Barbis, J.: Chapter 7: a physiotherapeutic, biopsychosocial approach to the management of patients with peripheral neuropathic pain and complex regional pain syndrome. In: Challenging Neuropathic Pain Syndromes: Evaluation and Evidence-Based Treatment. Elsevier, St. Louis (2018)
28. Brooks, J., et al.: Towards an integration of the health promotion models of self-determination theory and theory of planned behavior among people with chronic pain. Rehabil. Psychol. **63**, 553–562 (2018)

29. He, B.J., et al.: Abstracts of Presentations at the International Conference on Basic and Clinical Multimodal Imaging (BaCI), a Joint Conference of the International Society for Neuroimaging in Psychiatry (ISNIP), the International Society for Functional Source Imaging (ISFSI), the International Society for Bioelectromagnetism (ISBEM), the International Society for Brain Electromagnetic Topography (ISBET), and the EEG and Clinical Neuroscience Society (ECNS), in Geneva, Switzerland, 5–8 September2013. Clin. EEG Neurosci. (2013)
30. Boyd, D., Crawford, K.: Critical questions for big data. Inf. Commun. Soc. **15**(5), 662–679 (2012)
31. Crawford, K., Lingel, J., Karppi, T.: Our metrics, ourselves: a hundred years of self-tracking from the weight scale to the wrist wearable device. Eur. J. Cult. Stud. **18**(4–5), 479–496 (2015)
32. Lapierre, S.S., Baker, B.D., Tanaka, H.: Effects of mirthful laughter on pain tolerance: a randomized controlled investigation. J. Bodyw. Mov. Ther. **23**(4), 733–738 (2019)
33. Dunbar, R.I.M., et al.: Social laughter is correlated with an elevated pain threshold. Proc. R. Soc. B: Biol. Sci. **279**(1731), 1161–1167 (2011)
34. Tabak, M., et al.: Dinner is ready. In: Extended Abstracts Publication of the Annual Symposium on Computer-Human Interaction in Play, pp. 283–289 (2017)
35. Gromala, D., et al.: The virtual meditative walk. In: Proceedings of the 33rd Annual ACM Conference on Human Factors in Computing Systems, pp. 521–524 (2015)
36. Garza-Villarreal, E.A., et al.: Music reduces pain and increases resting state fMRI BOLD signal amplitude in the left angular gyrus in fibromyalgia patients. Front. Psychol. **6** (2015)
37. Garland, E., et al.: Therapeutic mechanisms of a mindfulness-based treatment for IBS: effects on visceral sensitivity, catastrophizing, and affective processing of pain sensations. J. Behav. Med. **35**(6), 591–602 (2011). https://doi.org/10.1007/s10865-011-9391-z
38. Nilsson, S., et al.: Active and passive distraction in children undergoing wound dressings. J. Pediatr. Nurs. **28**(2), 158–166 (2013)
39. Ushaw, G., et al.: Adopting best practices from the games industry in development of serious games for health. In: Proceedings of the 5th International Conference on Digital Health, pp. 1–8 (2015)
40. Garner, R.L.: Digital Art Therapy: Material, Methods and Applications, p. 1. Jessica Kingsley Publishers, London (2016)
41. Malchiodi, C.A.: The handbook of art therapy and digital technology, p. 1. Jessica Kingsley Publishers, London (2018)
42. Bateson, G.: Steps to an Ecology of Mind. University of Chicago Press ed, vol. xxxii, 533 p. University of Chicago Press. Chicago (2000)
43. Sicart, M.: Play Matters. MIT Press, Cambridge (2014)
44. Shoebotham, A., Coulson, N.S.: Therapeutic affordances of online support group use in women with endometriosis. J. Med. Internet Res. **18**(5), e109 (2016)
45. Suls, J., et al.: Hystersisters online: social support and social comparison among hysterectomy patients on the internet. Ann. Behav. Med. **31**(3), 271–278 (2006). https://doi.org/10.1207/s15324796abm3103_9
46. Khalili-Mahani, N., Smyrnova, A., Kakinami, L.: To each stress its own screen: a cross-sectional survey of the patterns of stress and various screen uses in relation to self-admitted screen addiction. J. Med. Internet Res. **21**(4), e11485 (2019)
47. Pahayahay, A., Khalili-Mahani, N.: What media helps, what media hurts: a mixed methods survey study of coping with COVID-19 using the media repertoire framework and the appraisal theory of stress. J. Med. Internet Res. **22**(8), e20186 (2020)
48. Philip, P., et al.: Virtual human as a new diagnostic tool, a proof of concept study in the field of major depressive disorders. Sci. Rep. **7**(1), 1–7 (2017)
49. Gabrielli, S., et al.: A chatbot-based coaching intervention for adolescents to promote life skills: pilot study. JMIR Human Factors **7**(1), 1–7 (2020)

50. Zhang, J., et al.: Artificial intelligence chatbot behavior change model for designing artificial intelligence chatbots to promote physical activity and a healthy diet: viewpoint. J. Med. Internet Res. **22**(9), e22845 (2020)

51. Hauser-Ulrich, S., et al.: A smartphone-based health care chatbot to promote self-management of chronic pain (SELMA): pilot randomized controlled trial. JMIR mHealth uHealth **8**(4), e15806 (2020)

52. Shen, J., et al.: Artificial intelligence versus clinicians in disease diagnosis: systematic review. JMIR Med. Inform. **7**(3), e10010 (2019)

53. Ellis, D., Tucker, I.: Emotion in the digital age: technologies, data and psychosocial life. In: Routledge Studies in Science, Technology and Society, p. 1. Routledge, London (2020)

54. Mintz, S.: On a scale from 1 to 10: life writing and lyrical pain. J. Lit. Cult. Disabil. Stud. **5**(3), 243–259 (2011)

Automated Escalation and Incident Management in Healthcare During Mass Casualties and Pandemic Events

Md. Yousuf Hossain[1], Umar Azhar[2], Yvonne To[2], Joseph Choi[2], and Loutfouz Zaman[1(✉)]

[1] Ontario Tech University, Oshawa, 2000 Simcoe St N, Oshawa, ON L1G 0C5, Canada
`loutfouz.zaman@ontariotechu.ca`
[2] Hypercare, 313 Queen St W Summit Room, Toronto, ON M5V 25, Canada

Abstract. We present Hypercare – a system for automated escalation and incident management in healthcare, which allows clinicians to create escalation logic in the hospitals. We present eight common escalation use cases and the results of a heuristic evaluation of the front-end of the system. We have completed designing the front-end and creating backend API endpoints of this application. The API endpoints have been collaboratively documented and tested using Postman. Examples for creating an escalation ladder and fetching active escalations are provided.

Keywords: Incident management · Escalation · Agent-based interaction · Communication in healthcare

1 Introduction

Incident escalation, a process that users are informed sequentially (i.e., trying to reach different people in a pre-defined order until a response is received), is a critical component of communication in healthcare. Despite its importance, outdated pagers are still the primary way using which incidents are escalated in healthcare, leading to potential patient harm [21]. This is especially true during the COVID-19 pandemic, where patients may deteriorate rapidly.

We developed an interactive logic tool to allow clinicians to create escalation logic. The tool shows a visual representation of the state diagram that is backing the rule engine (the state machine governing the escalation policies). Once the policy is set, whenever a page is triggered through Hypercare, it is cross-checked with the rule engine to determine the appropriate recipient.

One of the main advantages of using this escalation system is that the user/admin does not need to manually contact and keep track of every person in the hospital. In a clinical setting, a health worker can just start this escalation and leave the rest to Hypercare application. This could be helpful in a complex clinical environment where different patients need to be taken care of by different clinicians. Moreover, the admins can keep track all the information in a hospital and this may result in more responsible behavior from the clinicians.

© Springer Nature Switzerland AG 2021
V. G. Duffy (Ed.): HCII 2021, LNCS 12778, pp. 68–85, 2021.
https://doi.org/10.1007/978-3-030-77820-0_6

In this paper we present our solution and describe eight use cases how the system can be potentially used. We also describe the limitations of the solution. Preliminary evaluation of the system has been conducted using Nielsen's heuristics [20], the results of which are also provided.

2 Background

An agent is a software entity that applies AI techniques to choose the best set of actions to perform in order to reach a goal specified by the user [17]. For decades they have been used to solve many different kinds of problems in healthcare [17]. Relevant earlier examples of use include decision support systems [17] to diagnose the state of the patient (e.g., [2]), support co-operative medical decision making (e.g., [9, 11]), and for internal hospital tasks [17], such as supporting transaction workflow between healthcare workers (e.g., [6]), application of protocols (e.g.,[1]), and management of patients in critical conditions (e.g., [14, 23]). Agent-based interaction in healthcare practice is popular for conversations and unconstrainted natural language input. Systematic reviews of those have been recently conducted [10, 16]. The works reviewed there are concerned with psychotherapy, social skills practice, education, personal assistance, clinical interview, data collection. None appear to be directed at communication and collaboration among the healthcare workers or at escalation.

A mixed-method study has been recently conducted by Tang et al. [27] to evaluate the impact of an electronic interprofessional communication and collaboration platform on teamwork, communication and adverse events in a clinical setting. The results suggest that the impact of the use of such tools is mixed but can be positive in some settings. A system literature review in 2018 has been conducted by Pourmand et al. [21] on smartphone application-based text messaging in emergency department and revealed that 40% of works were concerned with facilitation of communication. The notable works mentioned are as follows: A study by Przybylo et al. [25] demonstrated that HCGMs (Compliant Group Messaging) were rated as significantly more effective in facilitating clear and efficient communication during rounds and patient discharge than traditional paging systems, a study by Mehrzad et al. [15] demonstrated that paging among healthcare workers create a financial time loss of $2,370-$17,250, and a study by Ellanti et al. [5] found that 93% of messages on WhatsApp were related to patient care and that 100% participants found WhatsApp to be more efficient than pagers. Furthermore, a study showed that 14% of pages were sent to the wrong physician, with 47% of those pages requiring immediate or urgent attention [29]. Hypercare addresses this shortcoming in clinical communication by allowing users to create and manage personnel work schedules. As hospitals have a daily turnover in on-call roles and responsibility, this on-call schedule is important for coordinating team-based patient care. Traditionally, this required a switchboard operator as an intermediary. A provider would call the switchboard operator, who then sends a page to the intended receiver. This process wastes time on the sender, as they have to sit by the phone and wait for a call back. Since the page is a one-way communication modality, the sender has no confirmation that the page was even successfully sent and received. This process is also disruptive for the receiver, as they often get a page with little to no context – only a call back number. This does not convey the urgency of the message, and the receiver has to make a decision whether to stop what they are doing to return the page, or let it wait. This can be potentially disastrous in time sensitive scenarios with critically ill patients. Hypercare solves this problem by digesting work schedules and creates a concise list of currently on-call providers for various roles and specialties in the hospital. With this system, it bypasses the need for a switchboard operator, and the platform provides closed-loop communication to confirm that the message was successfully sent.

Prochaska et al. [22] conducted a survey on medicine residents and found that the majority of respondents preferred SMS text messaging for efficiency and ease of use, but traditional paging systems for security purposes, although 71% of respondents admit to having received patient identifiers via SMS text message. Hypercare is a mobile-first digital healthcare communication and collaboration platform. The platform is encrypted and meets all the healthcare privacy and security regulations pertaining to electronic communications and transmission of personal health information. The foundation is a secure text messaging and file sharing platform that is designed to be familiar and easy to use. Extra healthcare features, such as priority messages and templated messages (e.g., consultation requests) are added to further help clinicians sort messages and help them plan their workflow. Previous studies replacing pagers with mobile communication solutions in clinical settings have found improvement in both speed and quality of information, with 94% of clinicians favoring wireless modes of communication [7].

Even though escalation tools are present (very few in healthcare) there is little to no research available in regards to its effectiveness. To the best of our knowledge, there is no tool available that can handle the complex situations faced in a healthcare setting. The best example available is PagerDuty [30] that allows users to acknowledge escalations through phone/app. The best example available is PagerDuty [30] that allows users to acknowledge escalations through phone/app. The best example available is PagerDuty [30] that allows users to acknowledge escalations through phone/app. However, they still lack the ability to provide proper context or trigger manual escalation when needed. Hypercare's advantage of being a messaging and scheduling platform allows a more comprehensive solution. Hypercare allow users to escalate issues themselves rather than being completely automated and provide more context. The interactive visualization tool has the flexibility to allow admins/schedulers to customize and build custom logic for escalation rules.

Hypercare has created automated alerts that have integrated with electronic health records to automatically send messages to select providers. A current example is that for patients with COVID-19, when their oxygen requirements reach a certain threshold (which indicates deterioration and need for critical care). A message is sent to the most responsible physician informing them of this and to advise consultation with an intensivist. Various automated alert systems have been shown to improve clinical workflows. A 6-month study conducted in Johns Hopkins Hospital utilizing an alarm notification to escalate critical cardiac monitor signals to nurses found improvement in perceptive alarm response time and decreased alarm fatigue for nurses [4]. Another 2-year study utilized a voice-activated communication badge to escalate between nurses. Successful closure of communication loops were recorded in 100% of events, compared to 26% when pagers were utilized [3].

Compared to the above protocols, Hypercare can further improve escalations in more complex and dynamic scenarios. The sender can send a single message and rely on the Hypercare platform to keep trying in a structured and hierarchical way to ensure that the intended recipient(s) receive the message. Providers would be able to customize scenarios that would trigger an escalation. Furthermore, users can label messages with different levels of priority, which result in different escalation protocols.

Through our literature review, we found a lack of automated systems that could implement rule-based escalation policies taking into context of priority and urgency through a modern communication text-based platform. The closest in vision was a patent implemented by General Electric [26] which leveraged various platforms including pagers. The escalations were limited unfortunately by the technology system such as email and pagers, which limits the capability of having a closed loop feedback system to ensure escalations are prompted when necessary. Given the newer technology stack that is under analyzation there is belief our automation engine will be much more precise when escalating.

3 Hypercare Escalation

Here we present the Hypercare automated escalation and incident management solution, which accommodates various clinical settings (e.g., escalation to certain providers, organization-wide 'code' alerts, critical results), and facilitates prompt provider responses and action. Hypercare's escalation feature will enable clinicians to trigger the organization's escalation policy and automatically communicate clinical concerns to the next appropriate provider if the appropriate response is not received. By streamlining and automating portions of the escalation process, Hypercare will facilitate a quicker provider response time, thereby optimizing the use of clinical resources and maximizing patient health outcomes. Based on the organization's policy, the escalation feature will also provide clinical decision support by prompting clinicians to escalate when appropriate.

3.1 Creating Escalation Logic

In the Hypercare solution, the user creates an *escalation ladder* through a drag-and-drop interface as shown in Fig. 1–4. We use the term escalation ladder to represent *escalation logic*. The landing page for building escalation logic is shown in Fig. 1. An escalation ladder can be defined as the hierarchies of communication for a particular department, e.g., weekday or weekend escalation. This is configured by the admins on the *admin portal*. To create an escalation ladder, the user clicks on the "Create new escalation" button.

Fig. 1. Escalations landing page.

3.2 Creating Escalation Level

After clicking on the "Create new escalation" button a new window (Fig. 2) appears where the user/admin can drag specific roles or a person from the left window and drop them into the square in the middle. Each role can consist of multiple staff in a hospital, e.g., senior consultant, resident, intern, etc. Here, the user has dragged the role titled "Cardiology Resident On-Call" in the 1st level of escalation ladder. This means when an admin starts this escalation, the person assigned to the "Cardiology Resident On-Call" will be the first to be contacted. The escalation will only move to the next level if no one in the first level responded within a given response time limit.

Fig. 2. Creating an escalation ladder in the 1st level.

3.3   Creating Escalation Policy

Escalation policies are configured on an organization level and can be applied to individual departments. Admins can edit organizational policies to be applied to a department on an ad-hoc basis. An example of a policy which will "Try every communication channel every 10 min for 3 attempts" is shown in Fig. 3.

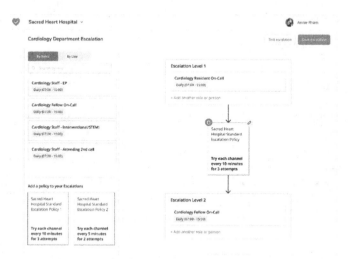

Fig. 3. Adding escalation rule/policy and 2nd level.

The admins can also edit the escalation policy by hovering the mouse above the policy. When the admin is satisfied with the escalation ladder, they can save it. This will save the escalation in the backend server. See Fig. 4.

3.4   Testing Escalation Ladder

The admin can test the escalation by checking on the schedule test escalation button as shown in Fig. 4 and save the escalation. After that another window is going to appear as shown in Fig. 5 which will give a prompt to the admin to confirm it. After confirming the escalation testing, every individual in the escalation ladder will receive a notification and will they need to confirm it.

3.5   Activating Escalation

The Hypercare solution supports two modes of escalations: departmental and individual.

Departmental Escalation.   There are two ways to activate the departmental escalation. One way is from the inbox of a user. This whole approach is shown in Fig. 6. To start this escalation, the admin/user needs to long presses a message (Fig. 6-a). An option menu appears where the user should choose "Escalate" (Fig. 6-b). After that a new

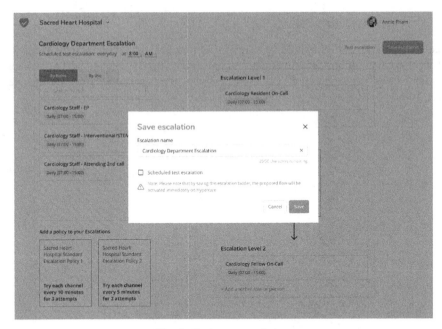

Fig. 4. Saving an escalation.

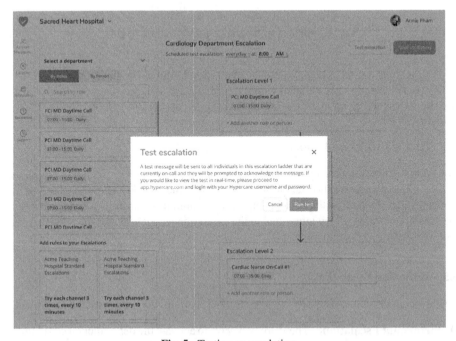

Fig. 5. Testing an escalation.

window appears where the user needs to choose between department and individual escalation (Fig. 6-c). Suppose the user chooses departmental escalation. After that, a window appears if the user is part of multiple escalations. Here the user is only part of one escalation. Therefore, no window appears for selecting which escalation to start. After that, a review escalation window (Fig. 6-d) will appear where the user can see a detailed information about the escalation, e.g., who is the responder in each level, escalation policy between two escalation levels, and the staring level. By de-fault, the escalation will start from level one. Although the user can change the starting level from the first to any other levels by clicking on the level. Lastly, the user needs to click on the send button to start this escalation. After the escalation is created a new chat window is going to be created where all the escalated persons will be automatically added.

Another way to activate the department escalation is to start from the locating window. This whole approach is shown in shown in Fig. 7. The admin/user needs to go to the locating window and select the department they want to start the escalation for (Fig. 7-a, b). Then the user needs to select the escalation that they want to start from the next window (Fig. 7-c). Here the user has chosen "Cardiology" as the department and "Weekday escalation" as the escalation. Then another window will appear where the user can add important information or message regarding this escalation. After adding the information, the user needs to click on "Review". Then, Fig. 6-d will appear where the user can see the detailed information of the escalation. Lastly, the user needs to click on the send button to start this escalation.

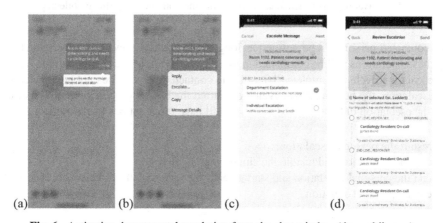

(a) (b) (c) (d)

Fig. 6. Activating departmental escalation from the chat window (the mobile app).

Personal Escalation. To activate the personal escalation, the user/admin needs to open the inbox of the person that they want to send the escalation to. After opening the chat window, the user needs to long press a message and choose personal escalation from the menu just like departmental escalation (Fig. 6- a, b). For personal escalation, there is no escalation ladder because only one person is connected. The contacted person needs to respond to the message or else they will continuously get notified after a certain period.

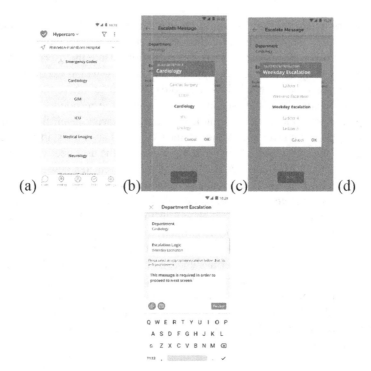

(a)   (b)   (c)   (d)

Fig. 7. Activating departmental escalation from the home window (the mobile app).

The contacted person will be notified as long as the escalation cycle is not completed. All these operations will be completed in the backend without user participation. When the escalation cycle is completed but still the contacted person does not acknowledge the escalation, the person who activated or started the escalation will get a notification that the escalation did not succeed and they will have three options to choose from:

a) restart the personal escalation,
b) end the escalation and handle the situation manually,
c) end the personal escalation and start a departmental escalation so that someone else can help in that situation.

In an emergency scenario, the user who activates the escalation can end the personal escalation at any time and start another departmental escalation (Fig. 8).

Fig. 8. (a-c) Activating personal escalation, d) Ending personal escalation.

Acknowledging Escalation. For both personal and departmental escalations, the user needs to acknowledge the escalation. For the departmental escalation only one user needs to acknowledge to stop the cycle. If no one from the first level responds, only then the user from the second level is contacted. To acknowledge the escalation message, the user needs to open the app. As shown in Fig. 9-a, there is a tooltip on the app that says "You have 2 escalations in progress", if an escalation is waiting for acknowledgment. Now, if the user clicks on the tooltip another window will show all the active escalation details. To acknowledge the escalation, the user needs to click on view option that will open the chat for that escalation. After opening the chat box, the user needs to tap on the pink button that says "Tap to acknowledge and end escalation" (Fig. 9-c). Now, the escalation is completed (Fig. 9-d).

Fig. 9. Acknowledging the escalation.

3.6 Escalation Status

The user who activated the escalation can see the details info of the escalation at any time. They can review the previously activated levels, currently active escalation level, next levels to be activated and their details, such as member's details, number of attempts, next attempt's time, etc (Fig. 10).

Fig. 10. Escalation status.

3.7 Escalation Endpoints

The escalation features in the Hypercare app are not ready to use yet. GraphQL is a query language for API, which is used to load the data from a server to a client [31]. We have created all the API endpoints and tested them through Postman [32], which is a popular API client that helps the developers to create, share, test and document APIs. We have used Postman to collaboratively test and document the API endpoints. We have mainly used Node.js [33] to develop the backend APIs, which is an open-source, cross-platform, back-end JavaScript runtime environment that runs on the Chrome V8 engine and executes JavaScript code [33].

Here, we have added some of the snapshots of the API endpoints. Figure 11 shows which parameters need to be passed from the front-end of the application to be able to create an escalation ladder. The process of creating an escalation ladder is shown in Fig. 1–4.

Figure 12 shows another API endpoint to fetch all active escalations for a user. This API endpoint takes *escalationTemplateId* as the only parameter and it returns all the related information for that active escalation, such as active escalation id, type, chat,

Fig. 11. Creating escalation ladder GraphQL API endpoint.

message, all the active levels and their members or roles, escalation policy/rule for each level, etc. The API will only return the information that the front-end application would ask for. This endpoint can be used in Fig. 9 when the user would open the inbox for acknowledging the escalation.

Fig. 12. Fetching an active escalation for a user GraphQL API endpoint.

3.8 Limitations

There are limitations to the Hypercare's solution. Receivers may not receive or read messages for a multitude of reasons. They may be scrubbed in an operation, and they cannot physically look at their phone. They may be having an end-of-life discussion with a dying patient, and do not want to interrupt the conversation. Or simply, their phone may be unknowingly out of battery. In these scenarios where the intended recipient does not receive or respond to the message, there is often an escalation policy, where different providers are contacted in a systematic way when the first provider does not respond. This is still a time-consuming process that adds one more issue that the sender must think about, which is not ideal in the scenario where they are actively managing a critically ill patient. Furthermore, this process often requires familiarity with the processes that may be specific to a certain use case, department, or even organization which could result in issues for newer staff members or locums (temporary staff).

4   Escalation Use Cases

Below we present eight common use cases for the Hypercare solution.

4.1   Getting Ahead of Patient Deterioration

Actor. Registered Nurse.

Description.   In the event that the physician on call is not responding to an urgent clinical message due to unforeseen circumstances, Hypercare can be used to prompt the registered nurse to escalate concerns to the next responsible physician as per organizational policy. This will facilitate interdisciplinary communication to ensure a quicker response time and optimal patient health outcomes.

Trigger. Patient deterioration.

4.2   Quality Improvement Audits/Post-mortem Assessments

Actor. Administrative Staff.

Description.   In the event that an urgent concern is escalated with undesirable, adverse, or unexpected results, the administrative staff of the organization can review Hypercare's Audit Trail to assist clinical leads in identifying accomplishments and areas for further improvement. This will facilitate quality improvement initiatives within the organization and help.

Trigger. Escalation Activation.

4.3 Attempting to Get in Contact with a Hypercare User

Actor. Chief of Department.

Description. When a staff physician fails to show up to his assigned day shift on the Orthopedic Surgery unit, the Chief of Department must contact the assigned staff member before finding an appropriate substitute within a timely manner. Individual escalations will be beneficial in automating the process of searching for/contacting the staff physician.

Trigger. Triggering Individual Escalations.

4.4 Escalations to Individual Members/Roles Within a Group Message

Actor. Physician.

Description. In the case of a code activation (e.g., Code STEMI), each member of the team is sent a priority message with escalation. Administrators can define an escalation policy for each role/member of the team (e.g., there may be an escalation ladder for the cath lab nurse, the interventional cardiologist, the cath lab administrator, etc.). If a role/member fails to acknowledge the message, the person next in line in the escalation policy is added to the group chat, and the escalation process continues until either someone responds, or the escalation ladder is exhausted.

Trigger. Code Team Activation.

4.5 Critical Results Notifications

Actor. Electronic Health Record Administrator.

Description. There would be a steering committee (e.g., the medical advisory committee) that would determine which critical results (e.g., labs, other alarms) are flagged to be sent via Hypercare to members of the care team. The relevant provider(s) should be identified in the EHR. This result is then sent as a priority message to the provider and may be escalated in the case of non-response, as determined by the steering committee.

Trigger. Clinical EMR Alerts.

4.6 Contacting Proxies in the Escalation Ladder (Sender)

Actor. Clinician.

Description. When triggering an escalation where a user has a designated proxy, the proxy will be added into the group chat alongside the original recipient.

Trigger. Designated Proxy User Assigned.

4.7 Acknowledging Escalations on Another User's Behalf

Actor. Manager/Provider.

Description. In the event that a code team member is already responding to the code, a designated member of that team (Manager, Code Team Leader, Front Desk Admin) can "acknowledge" the alert on behalf of that member. This will prevent further escalations to that member and users can then review this information in the audit trail. E.g., Victoria Chen (Manager) acknowledged on behalf of Michelle Williams (Physician) at x time on y date.

Trigger. Code Activation.

4.8 Code Orange (Disaster/Mass Casualty)

Actor. Manager/Provider.

Description. In the event that there is a code orange (a medical incident that overwhelms capacity of the hospital), there are active calls out to available providers to come into the hospital to help.

The current process involves activating a fan-out list. Currently, this is most often done by telephone manually. For example, when a code orange is called, a person in the hospital would call five people, and those five people would call five people, and so on, until a certain response is achieved and confirmed. The nuances of the process are different but the overall concept is that successively larger groups of contacts are called until you get a certain number of people confirming that they can respond to the incident within a certain amount of time. Ideally this group is to grow exponentially as quickly as possible (i.e., the maximum number of calls made per unit time), but at the same time not lose track of what is happening and who is being triggered.

In the Hypercare context, successive groups should be contacted until a certain threshold of people confirm that they can reach the hospital in a certain time period. There are many ways one can define these groups, and often it is distance based (i.e., those who live the closest are called first since they will get there the fastest). How that is determined is outside the scope of Hypercare, and these groups will be defined by the organization.

Trigger. Code Activation.

5 Heuristic Evaluation

To perform an initial evolution, we have employed a revised version [18] of the traditional heuristic evaluation by Nielsen and Molich [20]. Salgado and Freire [12] performed a systematic mapping of the literature on the use of heuristics for mobile usability evaluation and found that the traditional set of heuristics [20] is the most used for usability evaluations of mobile devices. In the follow up work, Salgado et al. [13] suggested that the traditional heuristics [20] are sufficiently generic to be used for identifying usability issues effectively in mobile interaction, among other contexts. Although, it was revealed that heuristic evaluation is not normally associated with mobile applications [8].To perform an initial evolution, we have employed a revised version [18] of the traditional heuristic evaluation by Nielsen and Molich [20]. Salgado and Freire [12] performed a systematic mapping of the literature on the use of heuristics for mobile usability evaluation and found that the traditional set of heuristics [20] is the most used for usability evaluations of mobile devices. In the follow up work, Salgado et al. [13] suggested that the traditional heuristics [20] are sufficiently generic to be used for identifying usability issues effectively in mobile interaction, among other contexts. Although, it was revealed that heuristic evaluation is not normally associated with mobile applications [8].

We have broken down the evaluation into three main stages: briefing, evaluation, and debriefing, as has been previously suggested [19, 24]. Two passes have been taken by each of the two researchers who co-authored this work. The researchers who participated in the evaluation were not involved in the development of the front-end of the system. However, one researcher was fully involved in its back-end development. The two researchers agreed that the system conformed to 9 out of 10 heuristics. *Help and documentation* was the heuristic the system did not pass, as the feature has not been implemented at the time.

6   Discussion and Future Work

We have presented Hypercare – a system for automated escalation and incident manage- ment in healthcare, which allows clinicians to create escalation policies. We presented eight common escalation use cases and results of a heuristic evaluation of the front-end of the system.

Our main focus was to develop a system that would facilitate clinicians' workflow by allowing them to focus on their patients and leaving the rest to our application. There could be many more escalation uses other than the eight that we presented in this work. Since the Hypercare application is not fully ready for deployment yet, we had to focus on evaluating the UI. The revised Neilson's heuristic evaluation [18] was used to formally evaluate the system. The Hypercare app passed all the heuristics except for *help and documentation* at the time of evaluation.

In the future further evaluations will be conducted. Testing will be performed by simulating various different user profiles in different environments (Web, Android and iOS). The algorithm for escalation will be tested through both manual and automated test process. For the manual testing, the tester will act as an actual user of the final application and iterate over all the functionality of the system manually. For the automated testing process, the tester will write a unit testing script to see if all the functions are working as they are supposed to. Each iteration contains numerous users with varying traits including but not limited to creating escalations, activating escalations, acknowledging escalation, not acknowledging escalations. Within each iteration, at least 50 escalations will be sent. The average response time will be calculated for each iteration for each environment and compared to determine effectiveness of automated escalation. In the final evaluation stage, the system will be evaluated with healthcare workers and actors using a cognitive walk-through [28], where the tasks will be based on the use cases described above.

Acknowledgements. This research has been funded by Mitacs Accelerate.

References

1. Alsinet, T., Ansótegui, C., Béjar, R., Fernández, C., Manyà, F.: Automated monitoring of medical protocols: a secure and distributed architecture. Artif. Intell. Med. **27**, 367–392 (2003). https://doi.org/10.1016/s0933-3657(03)00010-1
2. Barro, S., et al.: Intelligent telemonitoring of critical-care patients. IEEE Eng. Med. Biol. Mag. **18**, 80–88 (1999). https://doi.org/10.1109/51.775492
3. Bonzheim, K.A., et al.: Communication strategies and timeliness of response to life critical telemetry alarms. Telemed. J. E Health **17**, 241–246 (2011). https://doi.org/10.1089/tmj.2010.0139
4. Cvach, M.M., Frank, R.J., Doyle, P., Stevens, Z.K.: Use of pagers with an alarm escalation system to reduce cardiac monitor alarm signals. J. Nurs. Care Qual. **29**, 9–18 (2014). https://doi.org/10.1097/NCQ.0b013e3182a61887
5. Ellanti, P., Moriarty, A., Coughlan, F., McCarthy, T.:The Use of WhatsApp Smartphone Messaging Improves Communication Efficiency within an Orthopaedic Surgery Team. Cureus **9**(2) (2017) https://doi.org/10.7759/cureus.1040
6. Huhns, M.N., Singh, M.P.: Managing heterogeneous transaction workflows with co-operating agents. In: Jennings, N.R., Wooldridge, M.J. (eds.) Agent Technology: Foundations, Applications, and Markets, pp. 219–239. Springer, Berlin, Heidelberg (1998)
7. Joseph, B., et al.: Improving communication in level 1 trauma centers: replacing pagers with smartphones. Telemed. e-Health **19**, 150–154 (2013). https://doi.org/10.1089/tmj.2012.0114
8. Joyce, G., Lilley, M., Barker, T., Jefferies, A.: Heuristic evaluation for mobile applications: extending a map of the literature. In: Ahram, T.Z., Falcão, C. (eds.) AHFE 2018. AISC, vol. 794, pp. 15–26. Springer, Cham (2019). https://doi.org/10.1007/978-3-319-94947-5_2
9. Lanzola, G., Gatti, L., Falasconi, S., Stefanelli, M.: A framework for building cooperative software agents in medical applications. Artif. Intell. Med. **16**, 223–249 (1999). https://doi.org/10.1016/s0933-3657(99)00008-1
10. Laranjo, L., et al.: Conversational agents in healthcare: a systematic review. J. Am. Med. Inform. Assoc. **25**, 1248–1258 (2018). https://doi.org/10.1093/jamia/ocy072
11. Larssan, J.E., Hayes-Roth, B.: Guardian: intelligent autonomous agent for medical monitoring and diagnosis. IEEE Intell. Syst. Appl. **13**, 58–64 (1998). https://doi.org/10.1109/5254.653225
12. de Lima Salgado, A., Freire, A.P.: Heuristic Evaluation of Mobile Usability: A Mapping Study. In: Kurosu, M. (ed.) HCI 2014. LNCS, vol. 8512, pp. 178–188. Springer, Cham (2014). https://doi.org/10.1007/978-3-319-07227-2_18
13. de Lima Salgado, A., Rodrigues, S.S., Fortes, R.P.M.: Evolving Heuristic Evaluation for multiple contexts and audiences: Perspectives from a mapping study. In: Proceedings of the 34th ACM International Conference on the Design of Communication. Association for Computing Machinery, New York, NY, USA, pp. 1–8 (2016)
14. Marchetti, D., Lanzola, G., Stefanelli, M.: An ai-based approach to support communication in health care organizations. In: Quaglini, S., Barahona, P., Andreassen, S. (eds.) AIME 2001. LNCS (LNAI), vol. 2101, pp. 384–394. Springer, Heidelberg (2001). https://doi.org/10.1007/3-540-48229-6_52
15. Mehrzad, R., Barza, M.: Are physician pagers an outmoded technology? Technol Health Care **23**, 233–241 (2015). https://doi.org/10.3233/THC-140865
16. Montenegro, J.L.Z., da Costa, C.A., da Rosa, R.R.: Survey of conversational agents in health. Expert Syst. Appl. **129**, 56–67 (2019). https://doi.org/10.1016/j.eswa.2019.03.054

17. Nealon, J., Moreno, A.: Agent-based applications in health care. In: Moreno A, Nealon JL (eds) Applications of Software Agent Technology in the Health Care Domain. Birkhäuser, Basel, pp. 3–18 (2003)

18. Nielsen, J.: Enhancing the explanatory power of usability heuristics. In: Proceedings of the SIGCHI Conference on Human Factors in Computing Systems. Association for Computing Machinery, New York, NY, USA, pp. 152–158 (1994)

19. Nielsen, J., Mack, R.L.: Usability Inspection Methods. Wiley, Hoboken (1994)

20. Nielsen, J., Molich, R.: Heuristic evaluation of user interfaces. In: Proceedings of the SIGCHI Conference on Human Factors in Computing Systems. Association for Computing Machinery, New York, NY, USA, pp. 249–256 (1990)

21. Pourmand, A., Roberson, J., Gallugi, A., Sabha, Y., O'Connell, F.: Secure smartphone application-based text messaging in emergency department, a system implementation and review of literature. Am. J. Emerg. Med. **36**, 1680–1685 (2018). https://doi.org/10.1016/j.ajem.2018.06.067

22. Prochaska, M.T., Bird, A.-N., Chadaga, A., Arora, V.M.: Resident use of text messaging for patient care: ease of use or breach of privacy? JMIR Med. Inform. **3**, e4797 (2015). https://doi.org/10.2196/medinform.4797

23. Quaglini, S., Stefanelli, M., Cavallini, A., Micieli, G., Fassino, C., Mossa, C.: Guideline-based careflow systems. Artif. Intell. Med. **20**, 5–22 (2000). https://doi.org/10.1016/S0933-3657(00)00050-6

24. Sharp, H., Preece, J., Rogers, Y.: Interaction Design: Beyond Human-Computer Interaction. Wiley, Hoboken (2019)

25. Shieh, L., et al.: Smarter hospital communication: secure smartphone text messaging improves provider satisfaction and perception of efficacy, workflow. J. Hosp. Med. **9**(9), 573–578 (2014). https://doi.org/10.1002/jhm.2228

26. Susai J, Randazzo, M.: System and method for alert escalation processing in healthcare information systems

27. Tang, T., et al.: Using an electronic tool to improve teamwork and interprofessional communication to meet the needs of complex hospitalized patients: A mixed methods study. Int. J. Med. Inform. **127**, 35–42 (2019). https://doi.org/10.1016/j.ijmedinf.2019.04.010

28. Wharton, C., Rieman, J., Lewis, C., Polson, P.: The Cognitive Walkthrough Method: a Practitioner's Guide. In: Usability inspection methods, pp. 105–140. John Wiley, USA (1994)

29. Wong, B.M., et al.: Frequency and clinical importance of pages sent to the wrong physician. Arch. Intern. Med. **169**, 1072–1073 (2009). https://doi.org/10.1001/archinternmed.2009.117

30. PagerDuty | Real-Time Operations | Incident Response | On-Call. In: PagerDuty. https://www.pagerduty.com/. Accessed 12 Feb 2021

31. GraphQL | A query language for your API. https://graphql.org/. Accessed 13 Feb 2021

32. Postman | The Collaboration Platform for API Development. In: Postman. https://www.postman.com/. Accessed 13 Feb 2021

33. Node.js. https://nodejs.org/en/. Accessed 13 Feb 2021

Different Patterns of Medication Administration Between Inside and Outside the Patient Room Using Electronic Medical Record Log Data

Alireza Kasaie[1]([✉]), Jung Hyup Kim[1], Wenbin Guo[1], Roland Nazareth[1], Thomas Shotton[1], and Laurel Despins[2]

[1] Industrial and Manufacturing Systems Engineering Department, University of Missouri, Columbia, MO, USA
{skdx2,wgk95,rnbh6,tmsv22}@umsystem.edu, kijung@missouri.edu
[2] Sinclair School of Nursing, University of Missouri, Columbia, MO, USA
DespinsL@health.missouri.edu

Abstract. The primary object of this study is to analyze the different patterns of medication administration in a medical intensive care unit (MICU) using an electronic medical record (EMR) log data and how these patterns can be different inside and outside the patient room in terms of average process time. To analyze ICU nurses' workflow related to the EMR documentation, the real-time measurement system (RTMS) data was used, and multiple hierarchical task analysis (HTA) charts were developed. The results revealed that there was no significant different pattern between the medication administration inside and outside the patient room. However, we found a significant difference in medication administration's average process time between inside and outside the patient room. The findings of this study highlight the behavioral differences in performing medication administration in an ICU.

Keywords: Electronic medical record · Medication administration · Health information technology

1 Introduction

An intensive care unit is one of the most complex and dynamic areas in a hospital [1]. According to the study done by Ross, et al. [2], medication errors may cause or lead to inappropriate medication usage. As a result, those errors will affect patient outcomes, increasing patient morbidity, mortality, and costs [3, 4]. The significant errors related to the medication orders in ICUs are prescribing, transcribing, dispensing, and administration [5]. More than 50% of medical errors occur at the prescribing stage and 34% at the administration stage [6]. According to Vazin and Delfani [7] medication errors account for 78% of serious medical errors in an ICU. They state that the most common causes of errors are rule violations, slip and memory lapses, and lack of knowledge. According to a study done by Freedman, et al. [8], the occurrence and scope of medication errors are described by an American Heart Association Scientific Statement. Based on this

© Springer Nature Switzerland AG 2021
V. G. Duffy (Ed.): HCII 2021, LNCS 12778, pp. 86–95, 2021.
https://doi.org/10.1007/978-3-030-77820-0_7

report, improved methods, like automated information systems, are needed to identify and reduce medication errors.

Various strategies could improve the quality of care and operational efficiency. One strategy is improving health information technology, which helps ICU nurses quickly access patient information and support clinical decision-making [9]. Electronic medical record (EMR) is a type of IT system introduced to help physicians and nurses carry out their tasks more efficiently while improving the quality of care, safety, and patient outcome [10]. Despite the advantages of EMR systems, they still have several shortcomings. First, EMR systems generate and process a large amount of digital information regarding a patient's treatment and conditions. EMR systems will increase the spending time on documentation due to the massive amount of the patient conditions and treatment information delivered to nurses, limiting the ability of ICU nurses to provide timely and appropriate healthcare services [11–13].

Although the electronic health record systems should make the medication administration process safer, error rates may increase due to order complexity [14]. According to a study done by Warrick, et al. [15], the rate of new errors, like incorrect selections of multiple dosage options for some drugs, raised after deploying the EMR system in a pediatric ICU.

To advance our understanding of ICU nurses' EMR documentation process, a time-motion study was conducted in a medical ICU at the University of Missouri Hospital. By combining data obtained from the time-motion study and real-time measurement system (RTMS), multiple hierarchical task analysis (HTA) charts were developed to understand ICU nurses' workflow. HTA charts can be used as a tool to show the nurse's workflow [16]. According to the previous study done by Guo, et al. [17], four primary categories, including 1) update assessment results, 2) review documents, 3) medication administration, 4) check lab specimen orders were identified which must be conducted to complete the EMR documentation. In this study, we investigated the patterns of medication administration and how these patterns in EMRs can be different in terms of average process time inside and outside the patient room.

2 Literature Review

One of the most essential and vital parts of nurses' work since the time of Florence Nightingale is nursing documentation [18]. The objectives of documentation in a healthcare system are to ensure continuity of care, provide legal evidence of the process of care, and support evaluation of patient care quality [19]. Further, EMR documentation should help the healthcare team deliver a higher quality of care and evaluate nurses' progress and patients' health outcomes [20]. However, achieving these objectives might be challenging when nurses spend more time documenting due to the large amount of information regarding patients' complex conditions and treatments. While healthcare information technology (HIT) is reducing error inside the ICU, the current EMR system increases the incidence of certain types of mistakes that produce hazard risk related to patient safety and even mortality [21–23]. According to a study done by Bates, et al. [24], incorrect selection of medications similarly spelled appearing nearby the computer screen and physicians writing orders in the wrong electronic record are some of these errors. Also, healthcare information technology can cause new kinds of errors, specific to the inherent cognitive complexity of human-computer interaction [24]. According to a study done by Vicente [25], inconsistencies in the system, like buttons, menus, and entry fields, may prolong medication order completion time or increase user errors by concealing or misrepresenting stored information. Also, disruption, incompleteness, and inappropriate charting are three major issues of EMR documentation [19]. The quality of nursing care crucially depends on accessing high-quality information related to patient's conditions [26].

In this research, we look deeper into the nurses' workflow related to EMR documentation to discover how medication administration patterns in EMRs can differ in terms of average process time and frequency inside and outside the patient room.

3   Methodology

The time-motion study was conducted in the medical ICU (MICU) at the University Hospital, University of Missouri-Columbia. Nine ICU nurses participated in this study, and one to three nurses were observed on each observation day from 7:00 a.m. to 7:30 p.m. for 15 days from 2/17/2020 to 3/11/2020. All participants were registered nurses with a range of 1 to 26 years of ICU work experience. All participating nurses were informed about the time-motion study, and all collected information related to the nurses and patients was kept confidential. To minimize the Hawthorne effect, observers maintained a considerable distance from the participants and did not initiate any conversation with them. Besides, to maintain patient privacy, observers were not allowed to enter a patient room.

The studied MICU had two pods and a reception area in the center of the unit. There were nine single-patient rooms in each pod and a nurse station equipped with computers, monitors, tables, telephones, and a medicine cabinet.

All information related to the nursing documentation in the EMR system were recorded in the Real-Time Measurement System (RTMS) database. In this study, the RTMS log data was used to analyze nursing work patterns related to the EMR charting. All procedures done in this study were approved by the University of Missouri IRB.

Three graduate industrial and manufacturing systems engineering students and one senior undergraduate engineering student collected time and activity data during this study. The observers recorded the start and end time of each task done by ICU nurses and took notes about any special events in an observation form. Figure 1 shows the manual observation form used in this study for a time-motion study.

All nursing activities are categorized into five main groups: verbal report, primary care, peer support, out-of-room activities, and non-nursing activities [27]. RTMS data shows the time and EMR windows related to nurses' documentation. Nurse log ID, login time, number of clicks, pages accessed, every keystroke, and computer name for charting were provided in the RTMS.

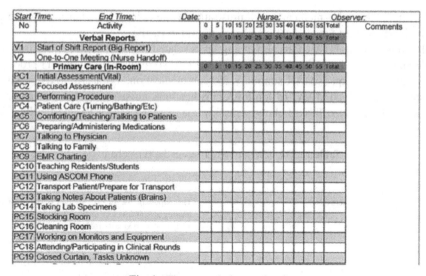

No	Activity	0	5	10	15	20	25	30	35	40	45	50	55	Total	Comments
	Verbal Reports	0	5	10	15	20	25	30	35	40	45	50	55	Total	
V1	Start of Shift Report (Big Report)														
V2	One-to-One Meeting (Nurse Handoff)														
	Primary Care (In-Room)	0	5	10	15	20	25	30	35	40	45	50	55	Total	
PC1	Initial Assessment(Vital)														
PC2	Focused Assessment														
PC3	Performing Procedure														
PC4	Patient Care (Turning/Bathing/Etc)														
PC5	Comforting/Teaching/Talking to Patients														
PC6	Preparing/Administering Medications														
PC7	Talking to Physician														
PC8	Talking to Family														
PC9	EMR Charting														
PC10	Teaching Residents/Students														
PC11	Using ASCOM Phone														
PC12	Transport Patient/Prepare for Transport														
PC13	Taking Notes About Patients (Brains)														
PC14	Taking Lab Specimens														
PC15	Stocking Room														
PC16	Cleaning Room														
PC17	Working on Monitors and Equipment														
PC18	Attending/Participating in Clinical Rounds														
PC19	Closed Curtain, Tasks Unknown														

Fig. 1. The manual observation form

4 Data Analysis

In this study, we combined data obtained from the time-motion study and RTMS to develop a hierarchical task analysis (HTA) chart for having a detailed view of the nurses' documentation workflow.

4.1 Hierarchical Task Analysis (HTA) Chart

By combining the data gained from the time-motion study and RTMS system, multiple HTA charts related to EMR documentation were created both inside and outside the patient room. The advantage of HTA chart is to break down a nurses' task into sub-tasks and provide a model for task execution, which helps us better understand ICU nurses'

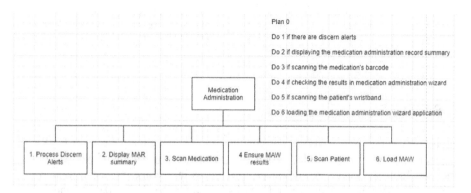

Fig. 2. The HTA chart for medication administration in EMRs

work patterns related to medication administration while doing EMR charting. Figure 2 shows the HTA chart for medication administration in EMRs.

To construct the HTA chart, all nursing tasks related to medication administration inside and outside the patient room categorized into six groups, including 1) process discern alerts, 2) display MAR summery, 3) scan medication, 4) ensure MAW results, 5) scan patient, 6) load MAW. To administer medications, nurses must complete all or a part of the above tasks. Table 1 shows a description of each of the HTA chart tasks.

Table 1. The description of tasks in the HTA chart

Task number	Task name	Description
1	Process discern alerts	The purpose of discern alerts window is to warn of missing patient data such as height/weight or allergies that provide decision support for an order. Also, this window will show nurses any discern alerts regarding the conflictions of a new medication order with the current one. There are several types of discern alerts depending on the nature of the nurses' activity
2	Display Medication Administration Record (MAR) summary	The Medication Administration Record (MAR) Summary is a view-only section that allows nurses to view all active, scheduled, unscheduled, PRN, and continuous medications for a specific patient. The MAR displays the medication orders, tasks, and documented administrations for the specific time frame
3	Scan medication	Scanning a medication's barcode to verify that the nurse is administrating the right medication, at the right dose, at the right time, to the right patient
4	Ensure Medication Administration Wizard (MAW) results	Reviewing and confirming all information related to the medication orders and sign them to store the results in the database
5	Scan patient	Scanning a patient's wristband can automatically show the patient's medications due, medical history, and verify the patient's identity. It also shows all the medications and dosages required or procedure about to be performed based on the records
6	Load Medication Administration Wizard (MAW)	Launching the Medication Administration Wizard (CareAdmin) application by clicking the Medication Administration icon on the organizer toolbar

5   Results

In this study, a one-way ANOVA was conducted to compare the patterns of EMRs for medication administration inside and outside the patient room in terms of average process time (see Table 2). There are significant differences in average process time between inside and outside the patient's room for tasks 1 ($P = 0.010$), 3 ($P = 0.009$), and 6 ($P = 0.038$) (see Table 3). These results will be further discussed in the next section.

Table 2. ANOVA results for the average process time of medication administration in EMRs

Location	Avg process time	StDev	F	P
In-Room	2.789	4.540	24.80	**0.00**
Out-of-Room	3.529	5.280		

Table 3. ANOVA results for the average process time of HTA chart tasks

Task number	Location	Average process time	StDev	F	P
1	In-Room	2.516	4.410	6.72	**0.010**
	Out-of-Room	3.613	5.573		
2	In-Room	1.811	3.163	1.95	0.163
	Out-of-Room	2.155	3.740		
3	In-Room	3.230	4.409	6.82	**0.009**
	Out-of-Room	4.453	6.404		
4	In-Room	3.920	5.673	3.32	0.069
	Out-of-Room	4.791	6.205		
5	In-Room	3.890	6.485	2.13	0.145
	Out-of-Room	4.689	6.195		
6	In-Room	2.283	3.506	4.32	**0.038**
	Out-of-Room	2.856	3.790		

6 Discussion and Limitations

The primary goal of this study was to analyze the different patterns of medication administration using EMR log data in a medical ICU and how these patterns can be different inside and outside the patient room in terms of average process time.

When nurses open the medication orders window by clicking the orders icon on the navigation ribbon at the left side of the EMR, they will see all of the patient's active orders, including medication orders. There are several types of alerts that nurses might see during the medication administration process including:

- An alert may appear when medication is hazardous to handle and requires appropriate personal protective equipment or should not be handled by pregnant or breastfeeding nurses.
- An alert may appear regarding the timing of giving the medication to the patient (too early or overdue).
- An alert may appear in case of the potential drug interaction between the administered medication and other medications that the patient has already taken. In this case, a drop-down box will be shown up with options for resolving the alert.

- An alert may appear regarding parameters under which medication should not be given (see Fig. 3).

Fig. 3. A screenshot of a discern alerts regarding the medication issue

Table 3 shows a significant process time difference in task 1 (process the discern alerts) between inside and outside the patient room. ICU nurses usually spend more time processing discern alerts while working outside the patient room. One possible explanation might be related to the behavioral preferences of ICU nurses. Typically, ICU nurses prefer to check the potential conflicts between the new and current medication orders while working outside the patient room, because checking and reviewing the patient documentation for processing the discern alerts is a time-consuming process.

Fig. 4. A screenshot of scanning medication process in medication administration wizard

For task 3 (Scan Medication), ICU nurses need to scan a barcode on the box or a bottle of the medication when they administer and check expiration dates. A successful scan indicates that a medication order matches the results represented on the medication administration wizard (MAW) via a checkmark (see Fig. 4).

If the required dose is more than what has been shown in the system, the nurse needs to scan the medication's barcode multiple times to meet a required dose. Table 3 shows a significant difference in scanning medication between outside and inside the patient room. ICU nurses usually spend more time to scan a medication's barcode while working outside the patient room. One possible explanation could be an additional process time for checking the expiration date of the medicines outside the patient room. Nurses will get medication from medicine cabinets and prefer to check expiration dates outside a patient room while preparing and giving them to patients inside the room. Checking the expiration date of medication will take longer since nurses need to open the medication boxes or look for the medication bottle expiration date.

For task 6, the medication administration wizard (MAW) shows ICU nurses which medication is currently due to be given and scheduled in the future up to 75 min, overdue medication, PRN medication, and any continuous infusions. Also, MAW provides detailed information about each patient's medications (see Fig. 5). According to the results, ICU nurses spend a longer time using the MAW outside the patient room compared to the in-room. One of the ICU nurses' top priorities is preparing and giving the patient medication while doing focused assessments in a patient room. Thus, ICU nurses usually use the MAW to see what medicine is currently due to be given while working inside the patient room. However, they will spend more time using the MAW to check

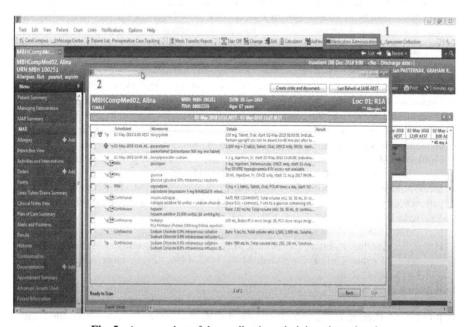

Fig. 5. A screenshot of the medication administration wizard

the medication orders for the future and complete additional medication orders while working outside the patient room. ICU nurses must process more information while reviewing and updating medication orders.

Although the findings of this study revealed some of the patterns related to medication administration inside and outside the patient room, there are several limitations. First, nurses' interruption was not considered when we developed the HTA chart. Even Though ICU nurses experience multiple interruptions during EMR documentation, those interruptions were not included in the data analysis. Also, we only collected data from day-shift nurses. Thus, we recommend including night-shift nurses to compare how their patterns are different than our findings. Another limitation of this study is the small sample size. We only collected the data from nine nurses. It would be better to have more participants for supporting our results in a future study. Lastly, we did not consider the effect of urgent situations, such as surgeries, patient coding. These situations might affect ICU nurses' workflow and process time in the ICU.

References

1. Beckmann, U., Baldwin, I., Hart, G., Runciman, W., Intensive Care Units Participating in the AIMS-ICU Project: The Australian incident monitoring study in intensive care: AIMS-ICU. An analysis of the first year of reporting. Anaesth. Intensive Care **24**(3), 320–329 (1996)
2. Ross, L., Wallace, J., Paton, J.: Medication errors in a paediatric teaching hospital in the UK: five years operational experience. Arch. Dis. Child. **83**(6), 492–497 (2000)
3. Allan, E.A., Barker, K.N.: Fundamentals of medication error research. Am. J. Hosp. Pharm. **47**(3), 555–571 (1990)
4. Koska, M.: Drug errors: dangerous, costly, and avoidable. Hospitals **63**(11), 24 (1989)
5. American Society of Health-System Pharmacists: Best Practices for Hospital and Health System Pharmacy. American Society of Health-System Pharmacists (2007)
6. Bates, D.W., et al.: Incidence of adverse drug events and potential adverse drug events: implications for prevention. JAMA **274**(1), 29–34 (1995)
7. Vazin, A., Delfani, S.: Medication errors in an internal intensive care unit of a large teaching hospital: a direct observation study. Acta Medica Iranica **50**, 425–432 (2012)
8. Freedman, J.E., et al.: Medication errors in acute cardiac care: an American heart association scientific statement from the council on clinical cardiology subcommittee on acute cardiac care, council on cardiopulmonary and critical care, council on cardiovascular nursing, and council on stroke. Circulation **106**(20), 2623–2629 (2002)
9. Furukawa, M.F.: Electronic medical records and the efficiency of hospital emergency departments. Med. Care Res. Rev. **68**(1), 75–95 (2011)
10. Sreeramakavacham, S., Kim, J.H., Despins, L., Sommerfeldt, M., Bessette, N.: Effect of patient acuity of illness and nurse experience on EMR works in intensive care unit. In: Duffy, V.G. (ed.) DHM 2018. LNCS, vol. 10917, pp. 547–557. Springer, Cham (2018). https://doi.org/10.1007/978-3-319-91397-1_44
11. Hefter, Y., Madahar, P., Eisen, L.A., Gong, M.N.: A time-motion study of ICU workflow and the impact of strain. Critical Care Med. **44**(8), 1482–1489, (2016). https://doi.org/10.1007/978-3-319-21602-7_8
12. Hendrich, A., Chow, M.P., Skierczynski, B.A., Lu, Z.: A 36-hospital time and motion study: how do medical-surgical nurses spend their time? Permanente J. **12**(3), 25 (2008)
13. Poissant, L., Pereira, J., Tamblyn, R., Kawasumi, Y.: The impact of electronic health records on time efficiency of physicians and nurses: a systematic review. J. Am. Med. Inform. Assoc. **12**(5), 505–516 (2005)

14. Cho, I., Park, H., Choi, Y.J., Hwang, M.H., Bates, D.W.: Understanding the nature of medication errors in an ICU with a computerized physician order entry system. PLoS ONE **9**(12), e114243 (2014)
15. Warrick, C., Naik, H., Avis, S., Fletcher, P., Franklin, B.D., Inwald, D.: A clinical information system reduces medication errors in paediatric intensive care. Intensive Care Med. **37**(4), 691–694 (2011)
16. Parameshwara, N., Kim, J.H., Guo, W., Pasupathy, K.S.: NGOMSL simulation model in an emergency department. In: 2016 Winter Simulation Conference (WSC), pp. 1938–1949. IEEE (2016)
17. Guo, W., Kim, J.H., Smith, B., Despins, L.: How nurse experience influences the patterns of electronic medical record documentation in an intensive care unit. In: Proceedings of the Human Factors and Ergonomics Society Annual Meeting, vol. 63, no. 1, pp. 708–712. SAGE Publications Sage CA, Los Angeles (2019)
18. Iyer, P.W., Camp, N.H.: Nursing Documentation: a Nursing Process Approach. Mosby Inc. (1999)
19. Cheevakasemsook, A., Chapman, Y., Francis, K., Davies, C.: The study of nursing documentation complexities. Int. J. Nurs. Pract. **12**(6), 366–374 (2006)
20. Jefferies, D., Johnson, M., Griffiths, R.: A meta-study of the essentials of quality nursing documentation. Int. J. Nurs. Pract. **16**(2), 112–124 (2010)
21. Harrington, L., Kennerly, D., Johnson, C.: Safety issues related to the electronic medical record (EMR): synthesis of the literature from the last decade, 2000–2009. J. Healthc. Manage. **56**(1), 31–44 (2011)
22. Horsky, J., Kuperman, G.J., Patel, V.L.: Comprehensive analysis of a medication dosing error related to CPOE. J. Am. Med. Inform. Assoc. **12**(4), 377–382 (2005)
23. Koppel, R., et al.: Role of computerized physician order entry systems in facilitating medication errors. JAMA **293**(10), 1197–1203 (2005)
24. Bates, D.W., Cohen, M., Leape, L.L., Overhage, J.M., Shabot, M.M., Sheridan, T.: Reducing the frequency of errors in medicine using information technology. J. Am. Med. Inform. Assoc. **8**(4), 299–308 (2001)
25. Vicente, K.J.: Ecological interface design: Progress and challenges. Hum. Factors **44**(1), 62–78 (2002)
26. Saranto, K., Kinnunen, U.M.: Evaluating nursing documentation–research designs and methods: systematic review. J. Adv. Nurs. **65**(3), 464–476 (2009)
27. Song, X., Kim, J.H., Despins, L.: A time-motion study in an intensive care unit using the near field electromagnetic ranging system. In: IIE Annual Conference. Proceedings, 2017: Institute of Industrial and Systems Engineers (IISE), pp. 470–475 (2017)

Systematic Review of the Importance of Human Factors in Incorporating Healthcare Automation

Jessica Kurniawan[✉] and Vincent G. Duffy

Purdue University, West Lafayette, IN 47906, USA
jkurniaw@purdue.edu

Abstract. Automations are meant to help reduce human workload and/or to reduce the need of humans to operate production processes and giving services. One of the most prominent users of automation is the people that are working in the healthcare sector. There are a lot of benefits from healthcare automation applications. One of them is by reducing error rates as illustrated by Felder (2003), virus infected patients 29 times (approx.) for every million transfusions, healthcare automation can mitigate this. Alongside the exponential growth of automation, some adjustments are required, thus, the role of human factors is very important to adjust changes and get the most value of the human-automation system. This paper demonstrates a systematic literature review of scientific papers on human factors in healthcare automation usage. To further understand this relationship several analyses were done by using the keywords "healthcare", "automation", and "human factors" and extracting those keywords from articles to see trends. The analyses were conducted using VOSViewer, Harzing's Publish or Perish, AuthorMapper, and MAXQDA to obtain emerging keywords (co-occurrence), co-author analysis, and co-citation analysis. Not only that, but several articles were also extracted from different databases named; Google Scholar, Springer-Link, Scopus, and WebofScience to understand the relationship between human factors and healthcare automation in detail. One takeaway from this review is that the trend of using automation to streamline healthcare institution processes is increasing and it has been proven that human factors theories are needed to incorporate the new technology properly.

Keywords: Healthcare · Automation · Human factors

1 Introduction and Background

The emerging discoveries of Artificial Intelligence have increased the usage of automation in different occupation fields nowadays and the healthcare industry is not an exception. Automation is a state where machines or processes in a system (or even the system itself) operates automatically to aid the human operator such as reducing their workload (Dias 2014). Hence, healthcare automation is the processes and services that operate automatically in a healthcare institution.

According to Sriram and Lide (2009), healthcare institutions rely heavily on automation in two different aspects; (1) Healthcare informatics; and (2) Medical Devices.

© Springer Nature Switzerland AG 2021
V. G. Duffy (Ed.): HCII 2021, LNCS 12778, pp. 96–110, 2021.
https://doi.org/10.1007/978-3-030-77820-0_8

Healthcare informatics deals with various data processes and information coming from different sides of the healthcare institution(s) or even the government. With the help of automation, different types of software are provided to streamline the supply chain processes, simulations, algorithm modeling, information and data management for clinical practice and research, and many more. As for the latter, it deals more with the "hardware" aspects of healthcare such as designing, testing, and manufacturing surgical instruments and devices.

Due to the rapidly increasing demand for healthcare services, automation has become a necessity. However, automation often fails due to eliminated feedbacks that should have been received by the operators and which can lead people to be less prepared when facing and detecting automation failure (Lee and Bobbie 2006). Some adjustments are required because of the implementation of automated instruments (software, medical devices, etc.), this is where human factors application comes into the scene. Human factors examine the relationship between operators and the system that they interact with. Multiple challenges will likely emerge including; cognitive aspects of automation bias and human performance, information trade between clinicians and AI systems, situation awareness, and the impact on the interaction with patients (Sujan et al. 2019). Human factors practitioners play a crucial role in finding ways to incorporate AI or automation into healthcare clinical processes and services (Fig. 1).

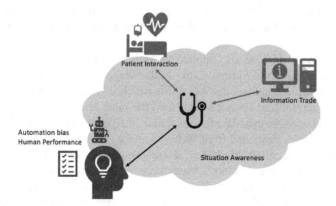

Fig. 1. Challenges in healthcare-related human-automation interaction (adapted from Sujan et al. 2019).

2 Purpose of the Study

The purpose of this study is to perform a systematic literature review on scientific papers about healthcare automation and human factors. The study primarily focuses on disclosing the importance of human factors theories to incorporate automation in healthcare institutions. For instance, workflows that integrate informatics tools will be able to coordinate and track patients' demands with more ease (Saleem et al. 2011). With the right procedures, AI can augment human capabilities, and health institutions will benefit from this relationship and reduce the possibilities of human errors.

3 Methodologies

The research was started with data collection by searching 3 keywords in several different databases; SpringerLink, Google Scholar, Scopus, and Web of Science. I used "Human Factors", "Healthcare", and "Automation" to look for articles that talk about topics that are related to my keywords. To extract articles from Google Scholar database, I used a software called "Harzing's Publish or Perish". Harzing can search for articles and extract the bibliometric data from different databases such as Crossref, Google Scholar, Google Scholar Profile, Pubmed, and several other databases, however, an external subscription is required to access the other databases and is only limited to 1000 articles from a search. The second search was conducted on Web of Science database through the Purdue Library website. The same keywords were typed into the search bar to look up the articles and obtain the metadata that is necessary to conduct the systematic literature review. The metadata from Web of Science includes the article title, author, abstract, keywords, and citations which Harzing's metadata did not have.

The next step was conducted using the VOSviewer software, which is a tool that can generate cluster diagrams of co-citations, co-author, and keywords. By using the metadata from WoS, a cluster diagram of keywords and co-citations was formulated. On top of that, keywords and co-author analysis were conducted by exporting the bibliometric data from Google Scholar to VOSviewer. One note when reading the cluster diagrams is that the size of the bubbles for each author represents the number of his or her publication and the line between authors or citation represents the co-authorship or the co-citation links.

The same keywords were also applied to AuthorMapper, which is an online tool used to extract articles from SpringerLink. AuthorMapper was able to obtain not only articles but also leading authors and keywords which will help to analyze the content of the articles later on. Last but not least, I used the same keywords to look for articles from Scopus and used the metadata for co-citation analysis on VOSviewer in case there are not a lot of articles generated from Web of Science.

Using the software called "Mendeley", I was able to retrieve 4 articles of my interest that are relevant to "human factors", "healthcare", and "automation" and generate a Chicago-style citation. An extended lexical search was performed using MAXQDA by exporting the selected articles (4 articles that I chose, articles that were derived from the co-citation analysis, and two chapters from the "*Handbook of Human Factors and Ergonomics*"). Not only that, but a word cloud was also generated to analyze the most used terms within those selected articles. Trend analysis was conducted as the last step of this systematic review to see the trend of published articles throughout the year.

4 Results

The research started with data collection by searching 3 keywords in 4 different databases; SpringerLink, Google Scholar, Scopus, and Web of Science. Table 1 below illustrates the database and the corresponding number of articles that were obtained from the inputted keywords.

Table 1. Table of different databases, number of articles generated, and inputted keywords

Database	Number of articles	Keywords
Google Scholar (via Harzing)	980	Healthcare and automation and human factors
SpringerLink (via AuthorMapper)	2766	Healthcare and automation and human factors
Web of science	5	Human factor and healthcare and automation
Scopus	23	Human factor and healthcare and automation

4.1 Co-authorship Analysis

The Co-Authorship cluster diagrams were generated using extracted bibliometric data from Google Scholar with the help of Harzing's Publish or Perish software. Co-Authorship networks are powerful tools that could be utilized to "assess collaboration trends and to identify leading scientists and organizations" (Fonseca et al. 2016). The bibliometric data from Harzing was exported to VOSviewer to help visualize the bibliometric networks by generating a cluster diagram of co-authorship analysis. I set the minimum number of documents of an author as 5 and out of 1896 authors, 19 met the threshold.

Fig. 2. Co-Authorship cluster diagram that was generated using VOSviewer by exporting the extracted bibliometric data from Harzing and consisted of 19 authors out of the 980 articles that were discovered.

The author who has the strongest link strength of 6 is Robert L. Wears with 7 documents and 281 citations, however, the author who has the most document numbers and citations is Pascale Carayon with 22 documents and 3088 citations. It is shown in Fig. 2. That Pascale Carayon has the biggest bubble which represents the total number of publications or documents that he has while Robert L. Wears has the most links attached to his bubble towards other authors.

4.2 Co-citation Analysis

The co-citation analysis was conducted using metadata that was downloaded from the Web of Science and includes the article title, author, abstract, keywords, and citations. The co-citation analysis was conducted to identify cross-disciplinary ideas (Trujillo and Long 2018) and to determine the frequency of two documents that are cited together by other articles. The more co-citations two documents receive, the higher their co-citation strength which also means that it is more likely that they are semantically related. I uploaded the metadata from the 5 articles that were displayed in Web of Science with the keywords "healthcare" AND "automation" AND "human factors" to VOSviewer. Based on the statement that was presented in the earlier paragraph, 2 was chosen as the minimum number of citations of a cited reference. 4 cited references met the threshold and have the greatest total link strength out of the 232 cited references.

Fig. 3. Co-Citation cluster diagram was visualized using VOSviewer by exporting metadata from Web of Science based on 5 articles.

All citations have the same number of citations which is 2 and the same amount of total link strength which is 4. However, as shown in Fig. 3, 3 of the 4 cited references are Jason J. Saleem's articles and most of the cited references are from the International Journal of Medical Informatics.

Due to the lack of articles generated by Web of Science, I decided to export the metadata from 20 newest articles from Scopus (2010–2020) to VOSviewer to generate another co-citation analysis. The parameters that were used were; 1 as the minimum number of citations of a cited reference, and out of the 387 cited references, all of them were selected because they had great link strength.

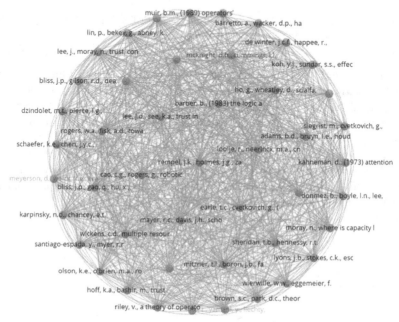

Fig. 4. Co-Citation cluster diagram was visualized using VOSviewer by exporting metadata from Scopus based on the 20 newest articles from 2010 to 2020 (Scopus, n.d.)

4.3 Co-occurrence Keywords Analysis

The Co-occurrence analysis operates by searching for words that are commonly used in the selected articles (Krishan 2017). A co-occurrence map would help us capture the relationships between words that "co-occur" together in articles. The bibliometric data from 980 articles that were generated via Harzing's Publish or Perish which consisted only of key terms from the list of keywords in the article and also from the titles was exported to VOSviewer to generate a visualized bibliometric network or a cluster diagram to obtain the most frequently used words. The counting method that was used to generate the desired diagram was "binary counting". The keywords were extracted from the title and abstract fields. 10 was selected as the minimum number of occurrences of a term and out of the 6438 terms detected, 169 meet the threshold. Hence, 101 keywords were selected as the 60% most relevant items (Fig. 4).

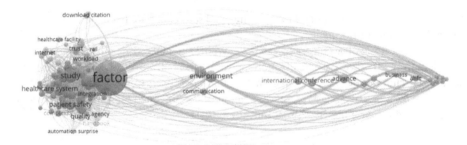

Fig. 5. Co-Occurrence map based on text data from Harzing's Publish or Perish that consists of 101 number of terms selected that meets the threshold.

As illustrated in Fig. 5, the word "Factor" occurs the most out of the other words followed by study, environment, proceeding, research, patient safety, and healthcare system which all have a similar number of occurrences. Some interesting keywords that were also included in the diagram were workload, healthcare facility, and automation surprise.

Another Co-Occurrence analysis was conducted using the metadata from the Web of Science. The same procedure as before was implemented (extracting keywords from the title and abstract fields by using the binary counting method). However, the parameters were set to 3 as the minimum number of occurrences of a term, and out of the 312 terms discovered, only 4 met the circumstances (Fig. 6).

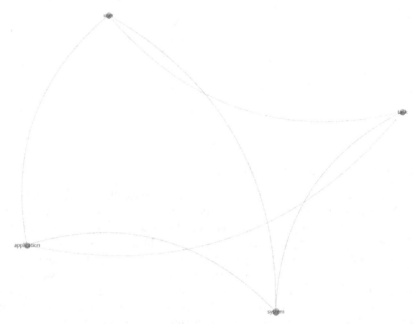

Fig. 6. The Co-Occurrence map consists of 4 key terms out of the 312 terms discovered from the generated 5 articles in Web of Science (Web of Science, n.d.).

The term "system" has the highest number of occurrences which is 4 and a relevance point of 1.31.

4.4   Leading Tables from AuthorMapper

AuthorMapper was utilized to create leading tables that could summarize leading articles and its component from Springer's database. The keywords "Healthcare", "Automation", and "Human factors" were inputted into the search bar to generate articles and authors that are relevant to the key-terms. A total of 2766 articles were discovered alongside several 8049 authors from the year 1986 to 2021. Table 2 below is a table of 5 leading authors out of 8049 followed by their publication years, keywords, and count.

Table 2. Table of Leading authors listed in AuthorMapper from SpringerLink database alongside their years of publication and keywords.

Author	Years	Keywords	Count
Ziefle, Martina	2010–2011, 2013–2015, 2017–2021	Technology acceptance, demographic change, life-logging, privacy, smart textiles, ubiquitous computing, human factors	19
Serpa-Andrade, Luis	2018, 2020	Intraocular pressure, Prosthesis, actuators, ADC, anthropometry, biomechanics, design, artificial neural networks	12
Caporusso, Nicholas	2018–2021	Classification, cybersecurity, Machine learning, Support vector machine, Artificial Intelligence	8
Fuller, Helen J. A	2018–2020	Human factors, patient safety, usability, heuristic evaluation, change management, conceptual models, health care	8
Nozaki, Manami	2017, 2019, 2020	Cultural competence, intercultural competence, nursing, cross-cultural communication, Healthcare education	8

It can be concluded that more articles related to "Healthcare" AND "Automation" AND "Human Factors" were published by the leading authors around the year 2017 to 2020. However, Martina Ziefle still has the highest count compared to the other authors. Similar keywords were also used between the leading authors (although each of them has different ranks for different authors) such as Human Factors, Artificial Intelligence, and Healthcare.

Another table was generated based on the leading countries that have significant relevance with the keyword "healthcare", "automation", and "human factors". There was a total of 93 countries contributed to the topic of healthcare automation and human factors with the biggest contribution went to The United States. The following table demonstrates the leading countries with the years of related publications were published, top keywords, and count.

As shown in Table 3, multiple countries have been publishing articles related to "healthcare", "human factors", and "automation" since the early 2000s. Multiple keywords that are similar or the same were also used in articles between the leading

Table 3. Table of Leading countries listed in AuthorMapper from SpringerLink database alongside their years of publication and keywords.

Country	Years	Keywords	Count
United States	2006–2021	Human factors, patient safety, usability, artificial intelligence, healthcare, safety, machine learning	586
United Kingdom	2000–2021	Healthcare, trust, artificial intelligence, human factors, smart homes, technology, assistive technology	266
Germany	2006–2021	Technology acceptance, Human factors, technology, human-robot interaction, older adults, smart home	230
Italy	2005–2021	Human factors, human-robot interaction, healthcare, internet of things, machine learning, safety	182
Canada	2007–2021	Artificial Intelligence, aging, machine learning, medical error, assistive technology, deep learning, human factors	119

countries such as; Human factors, Healthcare, Trust, Safety, Technology, and Artificial Intelligence.

Overall, the leading keywords for the theme "healthcare" AND "automation" AND "human factors" are displayed in the following Table 4.

Table 4. Leading keywords based on the search "healthcare" AND "automation" AND "human factors"

Rank	Keywords
1	Human factors
2	Healthcare
3	Artificial intelligence
4	Usability
5	Patient safety

4.5 Content Analysis from MAXQDA

Word Cloud. 8 Articles and two chapters from the *Handbook of Human Factors and Ergonomics* were selected to generate a word cloud. 4 articles of interest were selected from multiple sources by typing "healthcare" AND" automation" AND "human factors" on Mendeley's search bar. Chapter 57 "Human Factors and Ergonomics in Health care" and chapter 59 "Human Factors and Ergonomics in Automation Design" from *Handbook of Human Factors and Ergonomics* were also utilized. The last 4 articles were obtained from the co-citation analysis using the Web of Science metadata. A stop list was created to acquire meaningful words by disposing of all prepositions, numbers, symbols, and other words that are irrelevant to the topic of Healthcare Automation and Human Factors (Fig. 7).

Extended Lexical Search. Through co-occurrences analysis, leading tables, and the generated word cloud, multiple key-terms were selected for an extended lexical search in MAXQDA of the 8 selected articles and 2 chapters from *The Handbook of Human Factors and Ergonomics*. The following are the list of the selected keywords;

Fig. 7. Word cloud generated based on 8 articles and 2 chapters from The Handbook of Human Factors and Ergonomics (#3-5, 9, 12, 15-17, 20, 21 in the reference list) using MAXQDA software.

Human Factor: The term Human Factor appears several times in the reference section of Chapter 57 Human Factors and Ergonomics in Healthcare by Pascale Carayon (Carayon et al. 2012) from *The Handbook of Human Factors and Ergonomics.* The word also resurfaces multiple times in other articles by Sujan et al. (2019), Carayon and Wood (2010), Saleem et al. (2009). The article titled "Human-Supervisory Distributed Robotic System Architecture for Healthcare Operation Automation" emphasized that human factors theorems were used in the automation workflow "to provide a flexible and robust human-knowledge-based supervision and control for safe, reliable, and automated process for the healthcare industry." (Tan et al. 2015). It was also pointed out that the discipline of human factors and ergonomics could be utilized to enhance the performance, quality, and safety of the health care system (Carayon et al. 2012).

Healthcare System: According to Carayon and Wood (2010) six sectors were proposed to be improved in the healthcare system; safe, effective, patient-centered, timely, efficient, and equitable. The goal of implementing human factors and ergonomics in the healthcare system is to produce high-quality safe patient care. The keyword "healthcare system" was also mentioned in other papers by Berg (1999) that talks about a sociotechnical approach to patient care information systems by developing and evaluating IT applications in the healthcare system, Saleem et al. (2005), Tan et al. (2015) with their Robotic system architecture to be applied on healthcare processes, Carayon et al. (2012) in his chapter from *The Handbook of Human Factors and Ergonomics.*

Artificial Intelligence: Artificial Intelligence was mentioned several times and has become the leading keywords for several authors based on the search in AuthorMapper such as; Nicholas Caporruso and also was included in the leading keywords in several countries named; The United States, United Kingdom, and Canada. The article by Gambino et al. (2019) titled "Digital Doctors and Robot Receptionists: User Attributes that Predict Acceptance of Automation in Healthcare Facilities" emphasized that artificial intelligence could offer refined accessibility, precision, and personalized care in healthcare settings. However, the growth of automation in the healthcare industry is sometimes hard to be accepted or implemented correctly, thus the human factors practitioners play their role in this aspect.

Patient Safety: The word "patient safety" appears the most in *The Handbook of Human Factors and Ergonomics* Chapter 57 by Carayon et al. (2012). It was stated that the discipline of Human Factors and Ergonomics has much to provide in terms of understanding, reduction, and prevention of medical errors that could lead to a significant improvement in patient safety. The chapter also defined the critical role of HFE's contribution to mitigating medical errors to enhance patient safety.

Usability: As mentioned by Carayon et al. (2012), "Human factors input typically consists of the identification of human factors criteria to the list of system requirements"; such as the usability requirements. When discussing human factors, most of the time it will be associated with usability. The article by Carayon and Wood (2010) brought up the importance of knowing the usability of medical equipment before the procurement and whether they are ergonomically designed to decrease the stress and workload of the clinicians. The statement itself expressed the association between human factors and usability in healthcare industries. Chapter 59 from *The Handbook of Human Factors and Ergonomics* also referenced a couple of articles about usability.

4.6 Trend Analysis

Multiple trends were generated through AuthorMapper which used SpringerLink as the database and with Scopus to see whether there is more article published throughout the years and discuss whether this issue became increasingly significant. Figure 8 below illustrates the number of articles published based on each year from 1986 to 2021 generated by AuthorMapper.

As shown above, there was a significant increase in the number of published articles from 2019 (515 articles) to 2020 (813 articles) due to COVID-19 and the hopes of human factor practitioners to decrease the workload and mental stress of healthcare workers.

The same conclusion is shown in Fig. 9 which displayed the trend for the number of articles or documents published throughout the year based on the Scopus database. From one document published in 2019 to 7 documents in 2020.

An analysis was obtained using Vicinitas by searching the keyword "healthcare" and "automation" and "human factors". The engagement surrounding the topic is also increasing throughout the year based on the tweets that Vicinitas inspected from Twitter. This proves that the subject of human factors in healthcare automation is getting more important and starts to engage more people (Fig. 10).

Fig. 8. The bar graph illustrates a significant increase in the number of articles published from the year 1986 to 2021.

5   Discussion and Future Work

The systematic review shows numerous numbers of the conducted research and written scientific papers that contribute to illustrate the importance of human factor roles in healthcare automation. Not only that HFE can mitigate medical error that will lead to an improvement in patient safety, but also it will play a significant role in decreasing the workload and stress for the clinicians in healthcare facilities. On top of that, with the right procedure established by the human factor practitioner, the implementation of

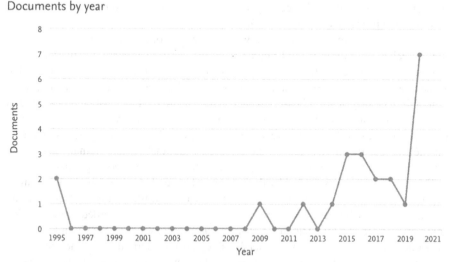

Fig. 9. The line graph illustrates an increase of published articles especially the sharp increase from the year 2019 to 2020 based on the Scopus database.

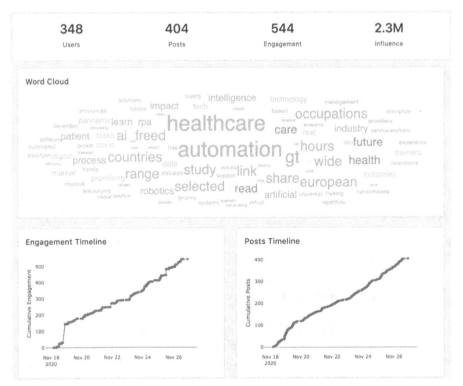

Fig. 10. Engagement trend line configured by Vicinitas based on the tweets on Twitter by searching the keywords "healthcare" and "automation" and "human factors" (Twitter, n.d.).

automation can provide a chance to give clinicians more time to do their other tasks because some processes will be automated.

The co-citation and co-author analyses that were conducted proved that a lot of authors realize the importance of human factors' role in healthcare automation, especially in a pandemic era. The co-occurrence analysis, the generated word cloud, and the extended lexical search displayed that human factor theories contribute to the improvement of the usability of artificial intelligence in healthcare facilities, which is classified as healthcare automation, and could lead to augmented patient safety and ensured the processes/procedures in the healthcare system. Moreover, the trend analysis also showed that the number of publications about healthcare automation and human factors are increasing as the year goes by, which contributes to the highlighted importance.

Recent work that was funded by the National Science Foundation in the USA highlighted the importance of teamwork between human and artificial intelligence with the implementation of human factors even more. The title of the awarded work is "The Future of Work in Health Analytics and Automation: Investigating the Communication that Builds Human-Technology Partnerships" by Joshua Barbour from the University of Texas at Austin. The project will investigate how automation would benefit workers instead of discouraging them in healthcare work. The proposal also emphasizes that automation in healthcare prevents medical errors, lower the costs of caregiving, and augment or create new forms of job opportunity (Barbour 2020) instead of eliminating them. The author reminded us that the improvement in automation would also mean inevitable changes in the technologies and organization of work, hence some adjustments must be implemented. The project will also focus on how to communicate these benefits to students at community colleges and universities in the hopes to help them prepare for the upcoming challenges in automation. For further details, the project can be found at NSF.gov by searching them with the keywords "healthcare automation" and "human factors".

References

AuthorMapper. https://www.authormapper.com/. Accessed 30 Nov 2020

Barbour, J.B.: Paperwork. Health Commun. (2020). Country unknown/Code not available. https://doi.org/10.1080/10410236.2019.1613481, https://par.nsf.gov/biblio/10110618

Berg, M.: Patient care information systems and health care work: a sociotechnical approach. Int. J. Med. Inform. **55**(2), 87–101 (1999)

Carayon, P., Alyousef, B., Xie, A.: Human factors and ergonomics in health care. Handbook Hum. Factors Ergon. **4**, 1574–1595 (2012)

Carayon, P., Wood, K.E.: Patient safety: the role of human factors and systems engineering. In: Studies in Health Technology and Informatics, vol. 153, pp. 23–46. IOS Press (2010). https://doi.org/10.3233/978-1-60750-533-4-23

Dias, J.: 6 Big Benefits of Applying Automation to Healthcare, 30 November 2020, 15 December 2014. https://hitcon-sultant.net/2014/07/21/6-big-benefits-of-applying-automation-to-healthcare/

E Fonseca, B.D.P.F., Sampaio, R.B., de Araújo Fonseca, M.V., Zicker, F.: Co-authorship network analysis in health research: method and potential use. Health Res. Pol. Syst (2016).https://doi.org/10.1186/s12961-016-0104-5, BioMed Central Ltd.

Felder, R.: Medical automation - a technologically enhanced work environment to reduce the burden of care on nursing staff and a solution to the health care cost crisis. In: Nursing Outlook, vol. 51. Mosby Inc. (2003). https://doi.org/10.1016/S0029-6554(03)00102-7

Gambino, A., Kim, J., Sundar, S.S.: Digital doctors and robot receptionists: user attributes that predict acceptance of automation in healthcare facilities. In: Extended Abstracts of the 2019 CHI Conference on Human Factors in Computing Systems, pp. 1–6 (2019)

Google Scholar. https://scholar.google.com/. Accessed 30 Nov 2020

Harzing's Publish or Perish. https://harzing.com/resources/publish-or-perish/. Accessed 30 Nov 2020

Lee, J.D., Bobbie, D.S.: Human factors and ergonomics in automation design. In: Handbook of Human Factors and Ergonomics, vol. 3 (2006)

MAXQDA. https://www.maxqda.com/. Accessed 30 Nov 2020

Mendeley. https://www.mendeley.com/?interaction_required=true. Accessed 30 Nov 2020

Saleem, J.J., Patterson, E.S., Militello, L., Render, M.L., Orshansky, G., Asch, S.M.: Exploring barriers and facilitators to the use of computerized clinical reminders. J. Am. Med. Inform. Assoc. **12**(4), 438–447 (2005)

Saleem, J.J., et al.: Exploring the persistence of paper with the electronic health record. Int. J. Med. Inform. **78**(9), 618–628 (2009)

Saleem, J.J., Russ, A.L., Neddo, A., Blades, P.T., Doebbeling, B.N., Foresman, B.H.: Paper persistence, workarounds, and communication breakdowns in computerized consultation management. Int. J. Med. Inform. **80**(7), 466–479 (2011)

Scopus.   https://www-scopus-com.ezproxy.lib.purdue.edu/search/form.uri?display=basic. Accessed 30 Nov 2020

Sriram, R.D., Lide, B.: The role of standards in healthcare automation. In: 2009 IEEE International Conference on Automation Science and Engineering, CASE 2009, pp. 79–82 (2009) https://doi.org/10.1109/COASE.2009.5234111

Sujan, M., et al.: Human factors challenges for the safe use of artificial intelligence in patient care. BMJ Health Care Inform. **26** (1) (2019). https://doi.org/10.1136/bmjhci-2019-100081, BMJ Publishing Group

Tan, H., Holovashchenko, V., Mao, Y., Kannan, B., DeRose, L.: Human-supervisory distributed robotic system architecture for healthcare operation automation. In: 2015 IEEE International Conference on Systems, Man, and Cybernetics, pp. 133–138. IEEE (2015)

Trujillo, C.M., Long, T.M.: Document co-citation analysis to enhance transdisciplinary research. Sci. Adv. **4**(1) (2018). https://doi.org/10.1126/sciadv.1701130, American Association for the Advancement of Science

Krishan: How to Use Words Co-Occurrence Statistics to Map Words to Vectors, 30 November 2020, 18 December 2017.https://iksinc.online/2015/06/23/how-to-use-words-co-occurrence-statistics-to-map-words-to-vectors/

VOSviewer. https://www.vosviewer.com/. Accessed 30 Nov 2020

Web of Science. https://apps.webofknowledge.com. Accessed 30 Nov 2020

Scenario Planning in Healthcare Development in the VUCA World

Hiroyuki Nishimoto[(✉)]

Kochi University, Nankoku, Japan
hiroyuki.nishimoto@kochi-u.ac.jp

Abstract. VUCA is an acronym that stands for Volatility, Uncertainty, Complexity and Ambiguity. This VUCA classification encourages creating new strategize ac-cording to unknown situations, rather than copying traditional patterns from good practices. Firstly, in order to respond to rapid changes, it is necessary for everyone to make quick decisions. To do that, a vision is required in terms of environmental volatility. Secondly, since success means continuing until achieved, which means being sustainable. Therefore, to stay successful, choose affordable losses within tolerance, rather than maximizing profits. Modeling simplifies complex phenomena. It is possible to understand complicated phenomena as they are. Lastly, if the object is not visible, it is possible that an obstacle is blocking your view. Switching perspectives, looking for the object from a different view-point may works. After analyzing the situation, design thinking is effective at the stage of creating a concrete solution. And in the current complex societies, causal loop diagram is a particularly effective method to explore a vision for sustainable business ecosystems.

Keywords: VUCA · Healthcare data science · Future design

1 In the World of VUCA

1.1 What is VUCA

The world is undergoing rapid structural changes as it faces various challenges from the COVID-19 pandemic declared by WHO on March 11, 2020. Structural change is often sparked by technological innovation, new economic developments, global shifts in the pools of capital and labor, changes in resource availability, changes in supply and demand of resources, and changes in the political landscape. Unfortunately, however, many structural changes are being caused by unknown viruses this time.

The battle between humans and viruses has been repeated over the years. Since the virus is carried by humans, the development of transportation is accelerating the spread of the virus. It can be said that structural changes have occurred in the tactics against viruses. Fighting unknown enemies requires a new method of situational judgment. One of the methods is VUCA [1], which is an acronym that stands for Volatility, Uncertainty, Complexity and Ambiguity as shown in Fig. 1. In this context, volatility refers to the volatility of the environment.

© Springer Nature Switzerland AG 2021
V. G. Duffy (Ed.): HCII 2021, LNCS 12778, pp. 111–125, 2021.
https://doi.org/10.1007/978-3-030-77820-0_9

1.2   How to Get Through the VUCA

General Approach to Volatility. In order to respond to rapid changes, it is necessary for everyone to make quick decisions. To do that, a vision is required to choose the adequate action for changes in environment [1]. By presenting the vision to all members, each of them will be able to clarify their own objectives and act autonomously. Without enough time to communicate, visioning is more flexible and agile than creating rules. To achieve this, source credibility, discussion transparency, information sharing, and a short message of vision are important.

General Approach to Uncertain. Causal models focus on maximizing returns by selecting optimal strategies. In general, the higher the expectations, the higher the risk. However, the risk should not be a fatal loss to stop all actions because success means continuing until achieved, which means being sustainable. Unfortunately, if you encounter a fatal failure, the path to success is cut off. Therefore, unsustainable failures should be avoided anyway. Given some options, you need to determine if the loss is acceptable, rather than expecting a profit. To stay successful, first choose affordable losses within tolerance, rather than maximizing profits [2]. Further development of this perspective will lead to an ecosystem for sustainability. This is the royal road to success and avoiding uncertain.

General Approach to Complexity. Modeling simplifies complex phenomena. In addition to modelling, modularization is to make a model divided into units that can be driven independently with minimal association with others. Modularization narrows down factors to consider and makes problem solving easier. By utilizing the modularization, it would be possible to understand complicated phenomena as they are.

General Approach to Ambiguity. If an object is not visible, it is possible that an obstacle is blocking your view. In order to solve this problem, one way to solve this problem is to switch perspectives and look at them from different perspectives. Factor analysis is a method of analyzing emotional value using different perspectives. In the analysis, the emotional value is measured as the length of the shadow projected on the axis of a certain interest. Since vector cosine is defined as the cosine of the angle between the vector and the axis, the length of the shadow on the axis is also defined as the cosine of the value vector. Therefore, the cosine of the new angle vector can be defined as a new viewpoint in factor analysis. The image of factor loading plot in Fig. 2 shows a factor loading plot in terms of power generation efficiency. The vertical axis shows the value of power generation efficiency. The horizontal axis shows the value of eco-friendly.

Figure 2 shows four vectors, which are Nuclear power generation before and after the accident, thermal-power generation, wind-power generation. Each vector component shows the characteristics in the power generation methods. Wind power is eco-friendly, but the efficiency is poor. Thermal power generation is more efficient than wind power generation, but it is not eco-friendly. On the other hand, in the nuclear power generation, the efficiency before and after the accident is the same, however it seems that there looks a significant change from eco-friendly to not eco-friendly. In this way, each axis component defined as the cosine of the value vector is compared to understand the characteristics of each vector.

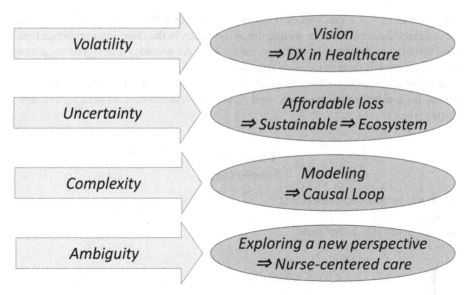

Fig. 1. How to get through the VUCA

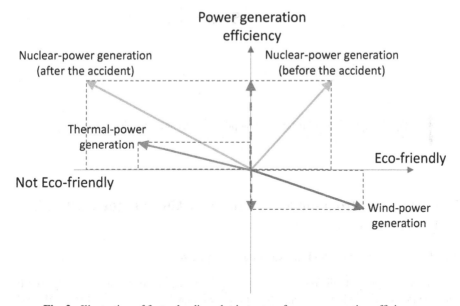

Fig. 2. Illustration of factor loading plot in terms of power generation efficiency

As shown in, Fig. 3 economic parameters are closely related to economic profit, so they are along the axis of economic profit. For this reason, factor analysis uses this phenomenon to explore the axis that maximizes the component variance. In exact terms, this variance is called the covariance. The larger the variance, the larger the difference, which means the axis that makes it easier to distinguish the data. It is the axis that characterizes the data. In other words, the axis extends in the direction to represent the characteristics of the data. In this way, factor analysis provides a new axis as a new perspective, even if there is no suitable existing perspective.

In order to solve the ambiguous situation, one way is to switch perspectives and look at them from different perspectives. And factor analysis can be also used to find new perspectives.

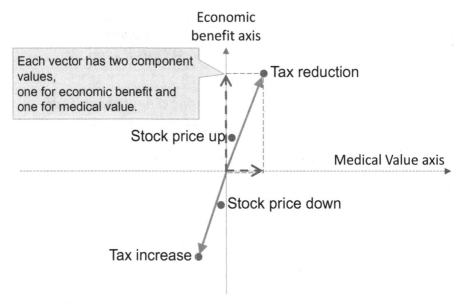

Fig. 3. Illustration of factor loading plot in terms of economic parameters

2 Backcasting from the Future 10 years Ahead in the Healthcare Development

2.1 Game Changer in the Healthcare Development

Our future is unpredictable, but signs of change can be detected. We will identify significant changes and envision the scenarios. The scenario analysis is not for future prediction, but it is for discussing how to deal with various structural changes. Since one of the ideal solutions is to create an autonomous virtuous cycle, we use a causal loop diagram to explore the ideal business ecosystem.

Standing 10 years in the future, backcasting [3] the current turmoil as follows:

Figure 4 shows the causal loop of healthcare development with an ecosystem. As shown in the diagram, rapid aging was a fundamental problem in Japan. In addition, the COVID-19 pandemic caused a lot of confusion. There was a growing need for telemedicine to resolve them. Nurse-centered care was important for the realization of telemedicine. With the promotion of home medical care, the development of home medical devices has progressed. The development of home medical devices is ahead of drug development due to lower development costs and reduced health risks. And more home medical devices were used for lifelong data and disease analysis.

Many personal health records (PHRs) are stored on the device and merged with electronic medical records (EMRs) into big data. This data is used in precision medicine and contributes to extending the healthy life expectancy of people. Finally, the promotion of National Health Insurance has continuously reduced medical costs.

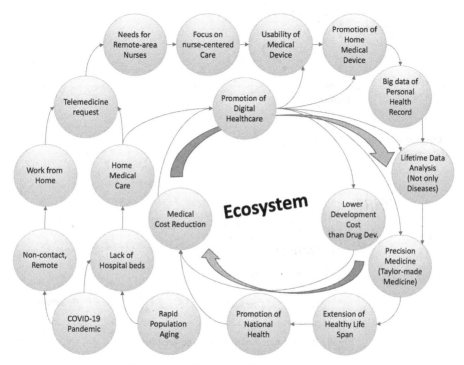

Fig. 4. Causal loop of healthcare development

2.2 Nurse-Centered Care

Figure 5 shows the case of telemedicine without a remote-area nurse to support home medical care on the patient side. In this case, there was concern that the medical treatment will not go smoothly, including administrative issues, such as online connection. One of the best solutions was to assign remote-area nurses to the patient side, as shown in Fig. 6. The nurses were able to provide a variety of care, including ECG, vital signs, intravenous injections, and blood collection. The mobile medical devices for nurses have been replaced by personal home medical devices for daily measurements.

This success has promoted nurse-centered care. Improvements in the hospital were made from the nurses' perspective, on behalf of patients who could not speak well of their demands. The nurses' working environment was improved, work efficiency increased, and patient satisfaction increased. As shown in Fig. 7, by focusing on the new perspective of nurse-centered care, issues that had not been noticed before were clarified. The importance of the third perspective, following the physician's and patient's perspectives, was recognized. ICT-related developments, such as the application of wearable devices and robotics, were further promoted. Big data on personal health records generated through the network.

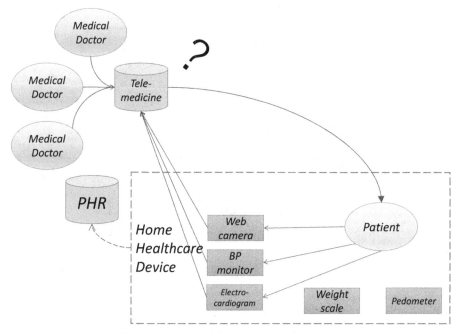

Fig. 5. Telemedicine without remote-area nurses

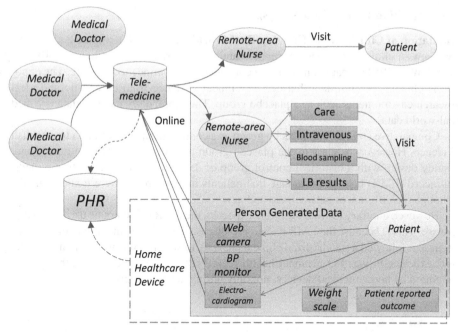

Fig. 6. Active telemedicine with remote-area nurses

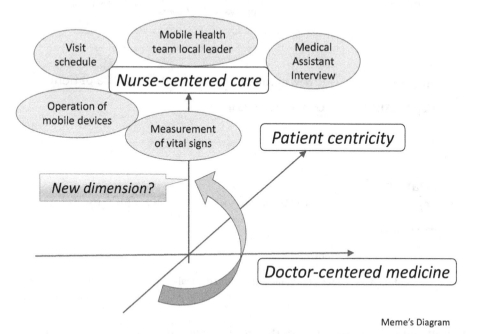

Meme's Diagram

Fig. 7. Nurse-centered care in telemedicine

2.3 Algorithm-Driven Data Analysis

Limitation of Clinical Trial Utilizing Real-World Data (RWD). Figure 8 shows the overview of clinical development process and clinical trial design utilizing real-world data (RWD). RWD is patient health data collected from routine medical care. The opposite is clinical research data that derives clinical evidence from unrealistic and ideal research environments such as a placebo group. Therefore, daily medical data is called real-world data.

Comparative studies with placebo group as a control group are common to establish evidence. However, patients in the placebo group are not treated. On the other hand, a study design with a historical control group of data extracted from electronic medical record (EMR) had the advantage that patients in both groups were treated equally, although the differences between old and new.

However, contrary to what everyone expected, the EMR could not be used to predict disease. This is because the EMR had no pre-disease data, and no individual differences because it followed a standardized clinical pathway to simplify receipt calculations. The next expectation was the personal health record (PHR). It was daily health big data measured by home medical devices, not only during hospital visits.

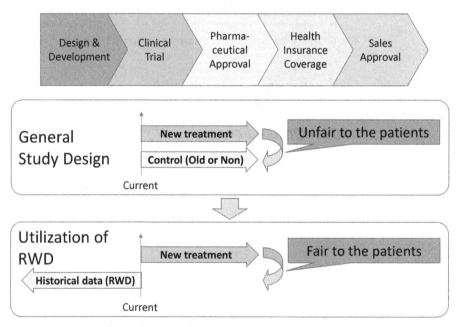

Fig. 8. Potentials for clinical trial utilizing real-world data (RWD)

Growth of PHR (Personal Health Record) into Big Data. Figure 9 shows the PHRs (Personal Health Records) positioning around 2020 in Japan and Fig. 10 shows the PHRs (Personal Health Records) positioning around 2030 in Japan. The horizontal axis indicates whether source of data is medical data or personal generated data. The vertical axis

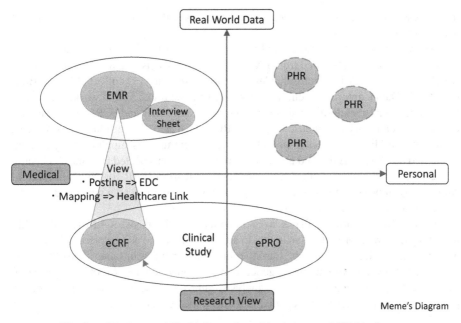

Fig. 9. PHR (Personal Health Record) positioning around 2020 in Japan

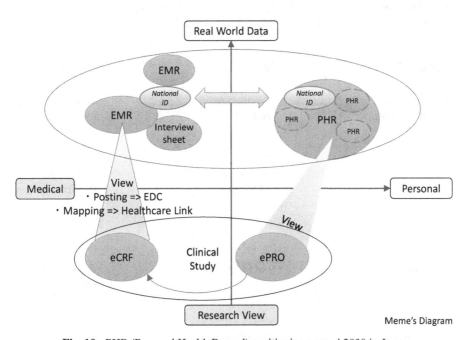

Fig. 10. PHR (Personal Health Record) positioning around 2030 in Japan

indicates whether daily observational data, defined as real-world data, or interventional data for clinical research.

PHRs around 2020 were scattered as small data and had low interoperability. For this reason, the data transcribed from EMR was mainly used as data for clinical research, which was called eCRF (electronic Case Report Form) and was collected by the EDC (Electronic Data Capture) system. In order to reduce the transcription work, the goal of development was an automatic direct mapping between EMR and eCRF called Health-care Link. For lifestyle-related diseases, ePRO (electronic Patient Outcome) records, such as patient diaries collected on tablet devices, were used as supplementary clinical research data. A view is defined as a table with information selected to make a decision. Therefore, eCRF can be defined as a view extracted from EMR for clinical research. And ePRO can be configured as a view extracted from general person generated data for clinical research, but around 2020 it was still undeveloped.

Around 2030, scattered PHRs were integrated on the basis of EMR, and highly useful big data was formed in Japan due to advances in online access, acceleration of e-government development, and the introduction of national IDs in Japan. The ePRO was developed as a view extracted from general person generated data for clinical research. The patient big data enabled lifetime analysis, improved medical treatment outcomes, promoted preventive care, and resulted in reduced medical costs.

Lifetime Analysis Utilizing Personal Health Records. Figure 11 shows the causal loop of the business ecosystem brought about by lifetime analysis utilizing personal health records. Around 2030, PHR was actively used as real-world evidence (RWE),

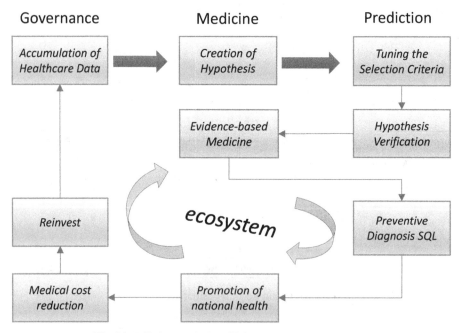

Fig. 11. Lifetime analysis utilizing personal health records

patient selection criteria were used in SQL were applied for preventive medicine, national health was promoted, and medical costs were reduced as a result.

Deep Neural Network (DNN). On the other hand, structural changes have also progressed in the method of analyzing clinical research data. The application of AI in the healthcare field has advanced. Figure 12 shows the illustration of three typical types of deep neural network. One is a CNN (Convolutional Neural Network), which is a neural network suitable for analyzing visual images. This corresponds to human visual function. Another is RNN (Recurrent Neural Network), a neural network suitable for analyzing audio time series data. This corresponds to human auditory function. The last one is a neural network used for multivariate analysis. It is classified as applied mathematics.

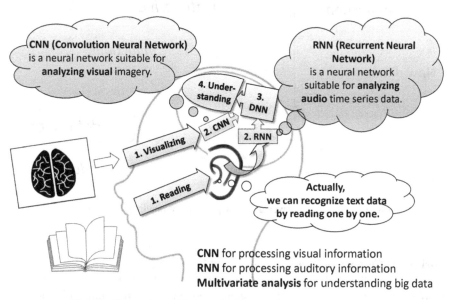

Fig. 12. Illustration of three typical types of Deep Neural Network

Lifetime Analysis Utilizing Personal Health Records. Figure 13 shows a movement of statistical methods, starting with model-driven, data-driven, and algorithm-driven approaches. In a sense, the mainstream of clinical statistics was a model-driven approach that utilizes probability distribution models such as the normal distribution. Since Statistical thinking is based on methodological discipline, wrong hypotheses are rejected and correct hypotheses are uniquely obtained. The next mainstream was data-driven methodology based on deep neural networks to find one of the better solutions in its walking domain to explore it. It was classified as applied mathematics rather than statistics, because the solution changes depending on the given data, such as Taylor series model with numerical derivatives for initial value problem.

Finally, a new perspective on clinical statistics focuses on algorithm-driven approach. In a sense, deep neural networks can be defined as big data analysis, but as an evolution, sparse analysis, which derives hypotheses from a small amount of data, is attracting attention. The algorithm-driven approach has been found to lead to different results, even if the initial values are the same, such as lasso regression and ridge regression.

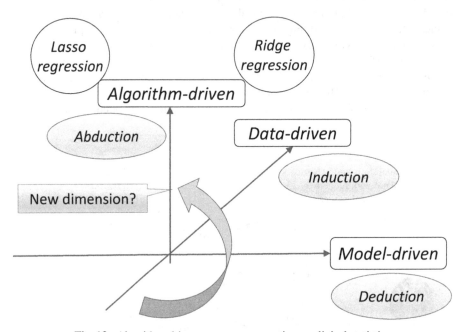

Fig. 13. Algorithm-driven as a new perspective on clinical statistics

Algorithm Difference Between L1-Norm and L2-Norm.

Figure 14 shows the method of Lagrange multiplier with L2-norm (Ridge regression). The solution obtained is indicated by the contact point between the limited distance (L2 norm), which is indicated by the Pythagorean theorem, and the log-likelihood function, which is the solution of the generalized linear model. When the probability distribution of the log-likelihood function is changed in order to find the optimal solution, the contact point moves in the same way. This means that the solution of the ridge regression is unstable, and the simulation is a time-consuming algorithm.

On the other hand, Fig. 15 shows the method of Lagrange multiplier with L1 norm (Lasso regression). The solution obtained is indicated by the contact point between the limited distance (L1 norm), which is indicated by the Manhattan distance, and the log-likelihood function, which is the solution of the generalized linear model. Even if the probability distribution of the log-likelihood function is changed in order to find the optimal solution, the contact point does not move in the contrary. This means that the solution of the lasso regression is stable, and the simulation is a time-efficient algorithm.

In this way, from the new perspective of the algorithm-driven approach, ridge regression when precision is required and lasso regression when speed is required can be used appropriately according to the clinical research design.

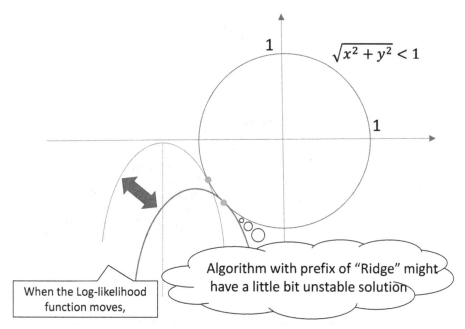

Fig. 14. The method of Lagrange multiplier with L2 norm (Ridge regression)

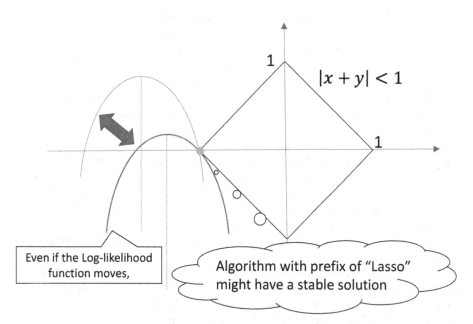

Fig. 15. The method of Lagrange multiplier with L1 norm (Lasso regression)

Design Thinking Tools in Healthcare Data Science. After the situation analysis, it is necessary create a concrete solution and introduce it appropriately. Figure 16 shows an

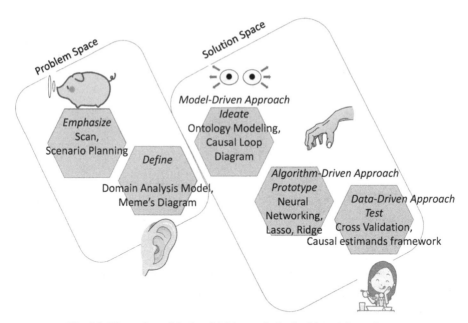

Fig. 16. Illustration of design thinking tools for healthcare data science.

illustration of design thinking [5] tools for healthcare data science. In the case of the five human senses, the five stages of design thinking could correspond to the sense of smell, hearing, sight, touch, and taste, respectively. The first stage in design thinking, "empathy", is likened to the sense of smell to detect risk. The sense of smell is the most dominant of the five senses, as it has evolved as the first function in detecting danger in the evolutionary history of animals. Therefore, to avoid ingestion of toxic substances, about 90% of our taste is determined by the sense of smell, not the tongue. This is the reason why we cannot taste food when we have a cold.

In the first stage of design thinking, leading tools for empathy include Scan [4] and scenario planning. Before starting with scenario planning in order to make a strategic long-term planning, we have to scan for signs of change. The Scan cannot accurately predict the future, but it can help us find signs of change that will follow in the future. Next, combine the signs of change and create a scenario, which is intended to discuss how to handle structural change, the title is never good or bad scenario. The purpose of scenario planning is to create enough options to discuss various structural changes for the unpredictable future.

The second stage of design thinking, "definition," is likened to hearing, listening to a problem. In the second stage of design thinking as a stage of "define", leading tools for defining problems includes domain analysis model [6] and Meme's diagram [7]. Both "empathy" and "define" stages are classified into problem space.

The solution space includes "ideate" to visualize the solution, "prototype" to create a prototype model that the sense of touch can recognize it, and "test" to finally verify like "tasting". The leading tools of "ideate" are the ontology modelling [8] and causal loop diagram mentioned above, which are classified in model-driven approach. And the leading tools of "prototype" are neural networking, lasso regression, and ridge regression mentioned above, which are classified in algorithm-driven approach. And the leading tools for deep learning "test" include cross validation and causal estimands framework [9], which are classified in data-driven approach. In particular, the causal estimands framework consider that normal health conditions create null values because no need for blood tests, and uses all observational data (FAS: complete analysis set) including null values, and efficient analysis is possible without dropout records.

3 Conclusion

As described above, the "VUCA" is highly likely to be the practical situational judgment method in clinical data science. This VUCA classification encourages creating new strategies according to unknown situations, rather than copying traditional patterns from good practices. After analyzing the situation, design thinking is effective at the stage of creating a concrete solution. In the current complex societies, causal loop diagram is a particularly effective method to explore a vision for sustainable business ecosystems.

Acknowledgement. The author would like to acknowledge the contribution of Associate Professor Keiichi Yamamoto, Manabu Mizobuchi, Ippei Akiya and other PR team members of Japan CDISC User Group.

References

1. Lawrence, K.: Developing leaders in a VUCA environment. UNC Executive Development, pp. 1–15 (2013)
2. Sarasvathy, S.D.: Effectuation: Elements of Entrepreneurial Expertise. Edward Elgar Publishing (2009)
3. Timilsina, R.R., Nakagawa, Y., Kotani, K.: Exploring the possibility of linking and incorporating future design in backcasting and scenario planning. Sustainability, **12**(23), 9907 (2020)
4. Scan: http://www.strategicbusinessinsights.com/Scan//
5. Stages in the Design Thinking Process: https://www.interaction-design.org/literature/article/5-stages-in-the-design-thinking-process
6. HL7 Version 3 Domain Analysis Model: https://www.hl7.org/implement/standards/product_brief.cfm?product_id=71/
7. Nishimoto, H., Koyanagi, T., Sarata, M., Kinoshita, A., Okuda, M.: "Memes" UX-Design methodology based on cognitive science regarding instrumental activities of daily living. In: Human Computer Interaction 2019, LNCS, vol. 11582, pp. 264-273 (2019). https://doi.org/10.1007/978-3-030-22219-2_20
8. Osterwalder, A.: The Business Model Ontology: A Proposition in a Design Science Approach (2004)
9. Little, R.J., Tchetgen, E.J.T., Troxel, A.B.: University of Pennsylvania 11th annual conference on statistical issues in clinical trials: estimands, missing data and sensitivity analysis (afternoon panel session), Clin. Trials **16**(4), 381–390 (2019)

The Digital Dilemma and the Healthy Nation

Xueying Niu[✉]

Beijing Normal University, No.19, Xinjiekouwai Street, Haidian District, Beijing 100875, People's Republic of China

Abstract. The digital dilemma is a unique social phenomenon that emerges in the digital era. It results from a mismatch between the speed of development of digital applications and the strength of educational guidance and supervision. The over-dependence of young people on the Internet, the disorientation of the elderly in digital life, and the excessive interference of big data in people's lives have created such social problems. This leads to the manifestation of Internet addiction and the digital divide. Based on a healthy nation's strategic background, the health industry has become a global hot spot. In this paper, we will analyze the digital dilemma faced by young and older people from the national situation of China, and take the game guidance combined with reinforced learning design as the entry point to study the solution of digital dilemma, advocate the establishment of media literacy, cooperate and win-win, and promote the concept of a healthy nation.

Keywords: Digital dilemma · Enhanced learning · Educational games · Healthy nation

1 The Digital Dilemma in the Age of Big Data Based on China's National Context

1.1 Digital Dilemma for the Masses

With the continuous development of science and technology, the rapid development and popularization of 5G, the Internet of Things, artificial intelligence, and other technologies have opened the fourth industrial revolution wave. The integration of 5G and artificial intelligence and other technologies has expanded a new dimension of network development, and digital applications have gradually penetrated all aspects of people's lives. The network has changed the depth and breadth of Chinese people's lives beyond imagination. Twenty years ago, the network meant a new life; 20 years later, the network has become life itself. China is now the most widely used country globally for digital applications, such as education, social networking, entertainment, e-commerce, food delivery, Etc. Digital applications are all over the world, and there is no life without the Internet. The Internet is like a catalyst for society's rapid development while also promoting changes in its composition. It has brought convenience to our lives and created a series of social problems that have inspired researchers to think about the healthy development of society. The digital dilemma, a social phenomenon unique to the digital age, has emerged. The International Telecommunication Union (ITU) defines

© Springer Nature Switzerland AG 2021
V. G. Duffy (Ed.): HCII 2021, LNCS 12778, pp. 126–134, 2021.
https://doi.org/10.1007/978-3-030-77820-0_10

the digital divide as: "The digital divide can be understood as the inequality in access to new information and communication technologies between developing countries and rich developed countries, between urban and rural areas, and between younger and older generations, due to poverty, lack of modern technology in educational facilities, and illiteracy. It can be manifested in four areas: Access, Basic skills, Content, and Desire [1]. It can be seen as a result of the mismatch between the speed of digital application development and the strength of educational guidance and supervision. The over-dependence of young people on the Internet, the disorientation of the elderly on digital life, and the excessive interference of big data in people's lives, Etc., have caused such social problems. This has led to the manifestation of Internet addiction and the digital divide.

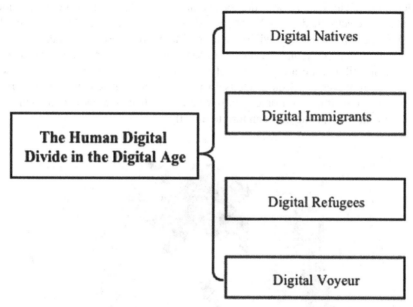

Fig. 1. A figure of the human digital divide in the digital age

As society evolves and science and technology continue to improve, the information society subtly affects every inhabitant in this era. In 2001, educational technologist Mark Prensky published the article "Digital natives, digital immigrants," and inspired by Mark Prensky, Wesley Fryer used the term digital refugees for the first time in his book "Digital refugees and bridges" in 2006 [2]. Wesley fryer divided the human digital divide in the digital age Wesley fryer divides the human digital divide in the digital age into four major categories: digital natives, digital immigrants, digital refugees, and digital voyeur (see Fig. 1). Dividing these categories with age groups, digital natives will most likely correspond to teenagers, while digital refugees will represent older age groups. It is undeniable that modern technology has brought great convenience to people's production and life, but it has also brought many dilemmas. The digital dilemma here refers more to understanding the inconvenience caused by information for different age groups and the discovery of these problems so that the diverse science and technology in the information age can give the audience a better user experience.

1.2 Health Nation

The Requirement for Aging-Friendly Services. As aging continues to increase and more and more older people live alone, the living environment of the elderly is facing significant challenges. Through the group's research on the situation of the elderly in one area of Beijing, most of the problems are focused on infrastructure, garbage classification, greening, and community feedback. We can divide the elderly into four simple categories: those who live alone and can use electronic devices, those who live alone and do not use electronic devices, those who do not live alone, and those who do not live alone and do not use electronic devices. When the elderly group encounters difficulties in life, these four types of elderly fever will often have different responses. When these seniors encounter problems, they may be unable to seek help from their nearest and dearest because their children are away or do not have children, so they can only seek help from society. However, many older adults do not choose to seek help directly in a crisis. Electronic devices' impact on older adults who do not live alone is not so significant because they have someone they can turn to directly.

Fig. 2. A figure of digital society (Source:Tencent Media Research Institute. Deloitte Digital Media Trends Survey Report (2019).https://xw.qq.com/cmsid/20190508A0JOOP/20190508A0JOOP00, 2019.)

Although modern society's technological advances have made it more convenient (see Fig. 2), the elderly, as a particular group, have difficulty acquiring specific digital skills through self-learning. When the elderly do not have access to these skills and the society does not provide them with some exceptional guidance, the elderly will undoubtedly lag behind the times and become a "disadvantaged group." In an article, Song Baozhen suggested that "with the concept of 'disadvantaged' in sociology, we can refer to these disadvantaged groups in data access and use as 'data vulnerable groups ''' [3]. This situation mostly occurs in developing or backward developing countries, and the 45th Statistical Report on the Development of the Internet in China released by the China Internet Network Information Center (CNNIC) shows that as of March 2020, there were about 60,568,000 Internet users over 60 years of age in China. This figure corresponds to a tiny fraction of the 200 million older people across China who do not use the Internet. These elderly groups, born in the 1940s-60s, used to receive information mainly through newspapers and radio, and with the widespread use of the Internet, there are still many older adults who learn about society in real-time through paper media. This contradiction, which was not apparent at first, became increasingly clear after the beginning of the 2020 epidemic. Most people in the elderly group believe more in their lifestyles and basic knowledge accumulated over the years than in the new technologies of the times, and they are influenced by multiple factors that are resistant to learning new technologies. For example, economic factors and cognitive ability make it difficult for the elderly to "re-educate" themselves. During the epidemic, the various health codes caused extreme inconvenience to these older people, many of whom did not use smartphones and only used an old phone for daily communication. So when the health code green code was issued, it added an insurmountable gap to these seniors' digital dilemma, from getting to and from the hospital to getting on and off the bus. The health code, a digital age product, has instead blocked many older people from traveling, living, and aging among the difficulties. The construction of a healthy country needs to pay attention to these "disadvantaged groups" that exist in our society, rather than ignoring and abandoning them.

A Youth Group in Need of Change. Another notable group in the healthy nation is teenagers, who are prone to many problems if they do not learn to live in harmony with this digital society when they are born in society all over the Internet. For example, many teenagers are now addicted to the Internet, and many of them are playing games with kryptonite and charging money to the game by tricking their parents into performing facial recognition. People usually have three aspects of satisfaction when they do something: a sense of accomplishment, a sense of belonging, and autonomy. When children are in leisure and entertainment, the game is just a medium and platform for them, and this medium can meet the above three needs at the same time. However, China currently lacks a game classification between good games and bad games, and the evaluation system of the whole society is single. Many such similar cases appeared in the Tencent Multiparty Governance Conference previously. The exquisite graphics and operation of video games, while satisfying people's satisfaction of constantly pursuing something better - upgrading - are irresistible to children who cannot still discriminate in their growth process. For teenagers, their self-control is a huge problem, but intergenerational parenting in Chinese society is an important social issue. When faced with these group problems that cannot be ignored in a healthy country, we cannot offer a quick, one-size-fits-all solution. Many parents do not have the time for in-depth media learning, and the "youth guardian platforms" that society has set up to address these issues are a path that cannot fully reach the ideal place for parents, and we should have rational expectations of these initiatives. Simultaneously, over-control can cause children to lose their internal drive and motivation to communicate with their parents. The advantage of games is not that they make children remember specific knowledge, but they are conveying soft skills (resource deployment, sense of history, hand-brain coordination, Etc.). On the road to building a healthy nation, it is worthwhile to explore how to promote the proper treatment of games by young people and even the use of games to refine their worldview and promote their diversity.

2 Artificial Intelligence Reinforcement Learning

2.1 Overview of Reinforcement Learning

Reinforcement learning is known to be one of the methodologies of machine learning. Reinforcement learning is the process of concluding continuous attempts without preconceptions, then adjusting the previous behavior through continuous trial and error and feedback, and finally arriving at the best result within an algorithmic calculation by adjusting again and again. This whole process is an interactive and mutual change process. When one party finds an error, it will be passed to the platform through the data, and then the so-called learning method will be changed and corrected (see Fig. 3). When we train a dog, the dogs do not understand human language, but they can judge their owner's reaction after various commands. When we want to train a dog to shake hands with a human, if the dog ignores or does not understand, it is not given a treat. If by chance it stretches out its hand to get food, then the next time it does not reach out, it can not get food, repeatedly carry out this training process, the dog will gradually recognize the "shake hands = food" command. The face recognition technology that is currently very popular in a society based on a similar principle, and before using the machine will let the user carry out a full range of facial information collection; the purpose is to identify which one is the user's photo, which one is not, to distinguish the actual user. However, there is still a fundamental difference between the two: the dog learns to shake hands entirely through its learning, while the information collection of facial recognition is based on the existence of an information source to provide a reference for it, and then the machine uses this reference to make a distinction. We are pursuing the first type

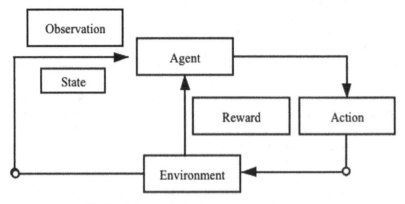

Fig. 3. A figure of reinforcement learning process

of independent animal learning, which does not require the user to teach continually, but active learning through the environment. Reinforcement learning is most currently known as Go, and artificial intelligence has been able to play one of the world's top Go masters in Go, all of which relies on the machine's own learning and exploration. So reinforcement learning is a promising technology.

2.2 Problems Facing Reinforcement Learning

Likewise, reinforcement learning has many drawbacks. The first and most important one is the high cost. This cost can be understood very clearly by a real-life example. For example, online shopping platforms use reinforcement learning to recommend products, but initially, there may be many unsuitable recommendations, which can make the user's experience very bad. Alternatively, a takeaway website, the operator wants to increase the price of food seen in the interface by the old users to increase the revenue to some extent. Although this is terrible behavior indeed many websites are increasing the effectiveness by increasing the price of the old customers, while the new users just absorbed will not be affected by the price. The way the platform identifies whether a person is a regular user is determined by an algorithm based on the frequency of that user's logins and purchases, and this way, if a regular user finds out, he or she may not continue to use the platform.

Although we do not advocate this kind of "killing" situation, both examples are good examples of how AI is not "smart" yet. When reinforcement learning is used in real-world scenarios, the cost of trial and error is extremely high. A movie from 2005 already showed a pilotless fighter jet fighting autonomously, and now this movie is being played out in reality. In recognition, we need to clarify how reinforcement learning can better serve human beings, increase science and technology investment to master better resources and perpetuate positive value.

2.3 Video Games Provide an Environmental Field for Reinforcement Learning

Initially, enhanced learning techniques applied to games, and the process of machine learning and trial and error can be seen in Go. Nevertheless, when we want to develop reinforcement learning techniques, we will first take the techniques out of the original game and put them in a realistic environment. However, when we train to enhance learning after the extraction, we may also be able to pull the game back. Aristotle's definition of play is "play is a rest and pastime after work, a behavioral activity that does not have any purpose in itself." When we are playing games, whether they are video games or other recreational activities in life, the human psyche is a purposeless rest. When people are in this state, mental relaxation is easier to accept the game's information.

As a particular virtual environmental field, the game can provide the factors needed to enhance the learning process. It can provide a complete virtual situation and treat the real game used as a trial. This approach can significantly alleviate the real-life situation of high trial and error costs and user churn.

3 Video Games Can Lead to Different Types of Reinforcement Learning

3.1 The Current Status of Game Typing

First, we need game typing. Different games have various labels, and the implantation process corresponding to reinforcement learning is also different. The above figure (see Fig. 4) shows the game's typing with a desert theme. The authors have selected some representative games and put them on the table. We can intuitively see that the game typing is roughly RPG, SLG, MMORPG, FSP, TSP, AAG, RTS, TAB, Etc. There are many other categories not shown in the figure. Then an essential basis for game typing is the gameplay. When we choose an RPG game, we construct our characters in a virtual scene of the game. Players can be hunters, witches, warriors, Etc. These role experiences that are untouchable in the real world are the focus of such games. Players can play as anyone in the game. There is a game called "Chinese parents" in China, widely acclaimed since its launch. The whole game process simulates a person's process from birth to adulthood, in which players can experience a complete set of education processes from childhood to adulthood. Many teenagers have gained a better understanding of their parents through playing this game, while middle-aged parents have gained a deeper understanding of education after playing this game. This game can bring people a wide

	Game Type	Game Name
China	Role-playing Game(RPG)	XuanYuan Sword:The Scar of the Sky
		Phantom Sword Record of the City of Ghosts(YouChengHuanJianLu)
		ZiSaiQiuFeng
		Chinese Paladin 5 Prequel
		Gujian3
	Simulation Game(SLG)	My Time At Portia/My Time at Sandrock
Other countries	Massive Multiplayer Online Role Playing Game(MMORPG)	World of Warcraft
		Final Fantasy XIV:A Realm Reborn
	First-person shooting game(FSP)	Borderlands1-3
		Fallout: New Vegas
		Rage
		Metro Exodus
	Third-person shooting game(TSP)	Lost Planet 2
		Spec Ops: The Line
	Act Adventure Game(AAG)	Raji: An Ancient Epic
		Uncharted 3: Drake's Deception
		Super Mario Odyssey
		Assassin's Creed Origins
		Prince of Persia: The Sands of Time
		Shadow of the Colossus
		Journey
		Mad Max
		Gun.Smoke
	Real-Time Strategy Game(RTS)	Homeworld: Deserts of Kharak
	Table Game(TAB)	Forbidden Desert
		Camel Up
		Mexica
		Blacksmith of the Sand Kingdom
		Through the desert

Fig. 4. A figure of game typology with desert games as an example

range of meanings. The virtual environment provides people with the opportunity to try and has the characteristics of inclusion and diversity.

However, with the development of society, players accumulate more and more games to play, and their requirements for games become higher and higher. In such a general background, game typing slowly becomes less noticeable. In the past, the typology was that different types of players played different types of games, and this distinction was even somewhat related to gender. Now it is concentrated in various scenes of a big game to change. Different typologies are gradually integrated into the same large game, and a big game may have a variety of scenes with different styles and themes so that players can experience a variety of game feelings in one game. Such a background allows us to do game psychology and data with advantages and disadvantages. The advantage is that the psychological orientation can be analyzed through a giant game's data; however, there is no way to complete players' categorization through the precise classification of game typology, so the data will appear inaccurate.

3.2   The Concept of Combining Video Games with Reinforced Learning

Reinforcement learning requires realistic scenarios that are too costly, and real e-commerce users cannot afford trial and error. When we want to add a user, it may take ten or hundreds of attempts to attract the user through various means and increase their stickiness. Nevertheless, once we give them a bad experience, there will be different reactions for different personalities. Some users are more loyal to the game or do not want to make other choices out of inertia, and reinforcement learning by trial and error once or twice will not make such users leave. However, if most users are not so patient and give them one bad experience, they may leave the game forever, and it may take hundreds or thousands of times more effort to get them back the next time. Our concept is to place this reinforcement learning process of testing user experience in a virtual environment, but this virtual environment cannot attract people to join actively, so we need to think about what kind of ways to complete the virtual environment's construction.

Games come with a projection of people's real psychology and are excellent virtual scenarios. People's demand for games lies more in the playability of the game, so if carefully and cleverly designed, the process of reinforcement learning can be embedded in the game's virtual environment. When we do this kind of implantation, there is a background that there should be enough data to support it first, and the trial and error cost will be significantly reduced. First of all, the reinforcement learning process in the virtual environment can significantly reduce the cost, followed by the game scene through extensive data analysis to get the psychology of the players so that they can design some game environment they can accept to get what we want to the purpose of reinforcement learning and can significantly reduce the cost. Data analysis uses some previous data, cooperation with game companies to obtain different types of game players, or through the same large game in various scenes of the player extensive data analysis, to get the basis of big data. For example, in a video game, data is collected from players during normal channels. After a new level is developed, when the player cannot pass, he may play a few times and give up. Suppose one million people play the game, 100,000 people play three times and give up, 300,000 people play five times and give up, and 500,000 people play seven times and give up, then the conclusion is that the level difficulty can be maintained at 6–7 (play 6–7 times to pass) so that at least half of the users can be retained. For the other half of the users, thirty percent of them (who play 4–5 times and give up) could be given some default trigger points to pass the game the next time they enter the game. Various measures can be taken to increase users' stickiness with different levels of familiarity and visits, but all of them should have a good user experience.

At the same time, users can be classified (those who have not logged in three days, those who have not logged in five days, those who have not logged in a week), and then they can be pushed, and data analysis this type of push. For the game, when there is boredom, the player will log in to the game. For example, there is a situation when a player has had a bad experience in the game, or the game is too difficult or tedious, Etc., which can cause the player to give up temporarily. However, if they do not want to play for a short period, it is hard to stop playing for the rest of their life, and they may get an enormous reward after a while. The game company's data about the players playing the game is not personal. The data is used for the overall situation statistics. The data includes how many times a player logs in, how long he/she will experience the game at a time, in what scenarios he/she will quickly give up playing the game, Etc. Through such general data analysis to complete the construction of the player's psychology. Different games have different age groups, and game companies need to develop new levels after the game is developed to increase player stickiness. We work with them to develop the game and add the factors we want to understand, and then we pay the game company a fee to incorporate the points we want to understand into the level design through preliminary research. The players' feedback in the new levels will also provide the game company with ideas for redesign.

So the core of this idea is strategic cooperation and win-win cooperation. Big data does not know enough about users' psychology, so people get a poor user experience while using it. Many platforms are also using big data to master users' preferences and tendencies, but this way tests real users. The psychology of making games and running other platforms is different. This way uses virtual users to do objective user analysis of reinforcement learning, and the ultimate goal of experimenting through games is to make different kinds of users have a good user experience.

References

1. Qingguan, G.: Communication Studies Tutorial, 2nd edn., p. 218. People's University of China Press, Beijing (2011)
2. Fryer, W.: Digital refugees and bridges (2006)
3. Baozhen, S.: The rights of the digitally disadvantaged and their protection under the rule of law. Soc. Sci. Dig. **12**, 76–78 (2020)

Development of Autonomous UVC Disinfectant Robot

Vishal Reddy Gade, Deep Seth$^{(\boxtimes)}$, Manish Kumar Agrawal, and Bhaskar Tamma

Ecole Centrale School of Engineering, Mahindra University, 1A Survey No: 62, Bahadurpally, Hyderabad 500043, Telangana, India
`Deep.Seth@mahindrauniversity.edu.in`

Abstract. Surfaces contaminated with SARS-CoV-2 or other such viruses pose a grave threat to the safety of individuals. Mobile robots mounted with ultraviolet (UV) light attachments are ideal for disinfecting hospital rooms, shopping centers and other public spaces. This paper mainly discusses the steps involved in making an autonomous UV Disinfectant robot and its functionalities. The UV Disinfectant robot initially maps the environment with the help of a user and subsequently localizes itself in the map and is able to autonomously navigate to a selected location in the map. The user must select waypoints in the generated map determining the locations where disinfection is required. After the waypoint generation of a map, the robot can autonomously navigate through the map disinfecting given locations. The robot is equipped with 6 UVC lights around a central column, which is fixed to a mobile robotic platform that has required sensors. The robot can be used as a part of the regular cleaning crew and it aids in reducing the spread of infectious diseases, viruses, bacteria, and other types of harmful microorganisms in the environment. ROS framework is used to program the robot.

Keywords: Robotics · ROS · Autonomous · Navigation · UV disinfection

1 Introduction

Due to the COVID-19 pandemic, there is a worldwide necessity to disinfect surfaces. As we slowly get back to our workplaces, sanitation plays the most important role. In the pre-pandemic era, sanitation involved electrostatic sprayers, hazing machines, and manual cleaning but now the efficiency needs to be increased.

Despite the evolution in utilization of disinfectants, there are constraints to quality work. It also exposes cleaning crew to many health concerns. An alternative, to regular dis-infection using liquids, which is safe and cost-effective is the use of UVC light. It is a non-chemical approach and requires only electricity and minimal maintenance. The light source is to be held at various positions to disinfect tables, doors, chairs, etc., and this prolonged exposure time is also detrimental to humans. Therefore, a UV disinfectant robot will make the disinfection process safe, reliable and eliminates human error.

The UVC energy required to disinfectant a surface depends on UVC intensity and exposure duration. UVC Intensity in turn depends on the intensity of light source and

© Springer Nature Switzerland AG 2021
V. G. Duffy (Ed.): HCII 2021, LNCS 12778, pp. 135–151, 2021.
https://doi.org/10.1007/978-3-030-77820-0_11

distance of surface to be disinfected. The reduction in intensity, or power, of UVC light drops very rapidly with distance as the intensity is inversely proportional to square of the distance.

$$(Ed = P/(d^2).$$

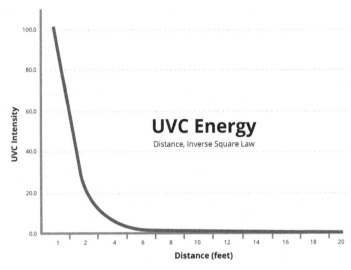

Fig. 1. UVC energy

As shown in Fig. 1, starting with a "100%" energy value, the UVC intensity at four feet is reduced to "6.3%" of the original energy. At ten feet, the energy is only 1% of the initial energy. The key point is that distance from surface to disinfectant is a significant parameter in the design of the UVC disinfectant robot [1].

UV dosage can be directed to surfaces in different ways. For example, fixed UV lights can be placed near the surfaces but since that is not an efficient way to use UV energy, a mobile unit with UVC lights has been chosen to be built.

Since the UVC energy decreases with increase in distance, the robot should cover a room's multiple positions for a certain duration of time and as direct exposure of UV light is harmful to humans, an autonomous robot is made to satisfy the needs. The autonomous UV Disinfectant robot thus made is equipped with 6 UVC lights around a central column, which is fixed on a mobile robotic platform that has all the sensors needed for obstacle avoidance and autonomous navigation.

2   Literature Survey

Studies on various bacteria have shown that the dose required for disinfection for bacteria varies between 2 to 25 mJ/cm^2 and a slightly higher values in general for viruses [2]. Different viruses in the Corona virus family, requires a dose of just under 30 mJ/cm^2

Table 1. UVC dose required for a 99.99% reduction of different micro-organisms [3]

MICROBE	Dose mJ/cm2	Type
Campylobacter jejuni	5	Bacteria
Helicobacter	7.5	Bacteria
Staphylococcus aureus	10	Bacteria
Streptococcus faecalis	11	Bacteria
Escherichi coli	13	Bacteria
Enterococcus faecalis	13	Bacteria
SARS coronavirus CoV P9	16	Virus
Murine coronavirus	26	Virus
Murine norovirus	27	Virus
Calicivirus feline	30	Virus
Clostridium pasteurianum	10	Spore
Streptomyces griseus	26	Spore
Penicillium expansum	65	Spore
Saccharomyces cerevisiae (yeast)	130	Fungi
Tetraselmis suecica	1000	Algea

on average for a reduction of 99.99% [3]. Data of UV dose required for reduction of different microbes are shown in Table 1.

Previous work done with respect to UVC Devices is discussed below to understand the current status and identify gaps.

The UVC-LEDs are semiconductors consisting of stable structure doped in precious metals. The power supply of the sources can be continuous or pulsed, so the light emitted by the sources, the lifetime, and the spectrum emission depends on the nature of source and the power supply type [4]. The advantage of UVC-LEDs is their compact size and energy saving, which is four to nine times more efficient than the UVC lamps in water treatment. However, their use is still limited as a result of their high cost.

Stibich et al. [5] have compared the conventional lamps and pulsed Xenon systems for the reduction of the healthcare-associated pathogens in hospital rooms. They have shown that pulsed Xenon and mercury lamps have the same effectiveness at relatively short exposure time, about 10 min.

Song et al. [6] have used continuous and pulsed Xenon UV to inactivate micro-organisms in ambulances. They have reported that the device does not need to use chemical agents and reduce 90% of E. coli, Staphylococcus albus, and environmental pathogens in 30 min.

Anderson et al. [7] have reported that the addition of UVC disinfection treatment to standard protocol, with chemical agents, had a direct positive effect on the Clostridium difficile and vancomycin-resistant contamination.

Haddad et al. [8] have reported that combining portable xenon–pulsed ultraviolet germicidal light device and standard manual cleaning of surfaces decreases the bacterial load by 70%.

Bentancor and Vidal [9] have presented a remotely programmed device using an Android mobile and an infrared detection security. It can be operated from a wide range of Android mobile devices.

Recent developments in technology have led to the creation of different types of UVC sources, but the UVC germicidal lamps are the most frequently used due to their relatively low cost. Devices such as humidifiers, and wall reflectors decrease disinfection time when used with UVC. Combining disinfectant chemical agents with UVC is an emergent technology but has the disadvantage of damaging the surrounding material. But due to the robot's mobility, disinfection time is reduced without using any complementary devices or chemical agents. Remote control robots require technical assistance making it hard for the cleaning staff to manage the robot. By considering all the above restrictions, an autonomous mobile robot with UV lights on the top is made. Motion detection sensors are also added for the safety of individuals which help the robot to turn off the UV lights if there is any human presence.

Autonomous mobile robot navigation plays a vital role in self-driving cars, warehouse robots, personal assistant robots, and smart wheelchairs, particularly with a lack of labor force and a steadily expanding aging populace. Various mobile robots are used in factories and warehouses to automate the production lines and inventory, sharing the staff's workload [10]. Personal robots such as PR2 [11, 12] and Care-O-bot [13] have demonstrated their ability to perform a variety of integrated tasks such as long-distance navigation and complex manipulation.

3   Objective

The main objective of the current work is to develop a mobile robot with UVC lights that can; a) move from one location to another b) avoides obstacles while disinfecting the surfaces c) control UVC light exposure for a certain duration of time and d) run without any human intervention as direct exposure of UVC light is harmful to humans.

4   Methodology

Primary groundwork is laid to visualize the dimensions of surfaces that need to be disinfected. Upon which, a design is finalized based on its functionalities and a CAD model is developed for visualization. Using this CAD model, a chassis is made in which all the components are assembled. The end product of the robot is shown in Fig. 2. The robot should mainly disinfect surfaces that are in reach of human touch like desks, chairs, cubical wall tops, and computer peripherals etc.

Fig. 2. Completely assembled UVD robot

4.1 Design

Initially, the height of the robot should be estimated in accordance with the elevation of the surfaces to be disinfected, such as desks, chairs etc. Heights of surfaces to be disinfected around a typical office cubical (Fig. 3) are measured.

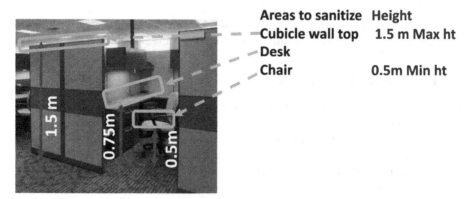

Fig. 3. A typical office cubical

The total height of the robot is chosen to be 1.7 m. For simplicity, a 2-wheel differential drive mechanism with 2 castor wheels is selected.

4.2 Structure

The chassis of the robot is made by aluminum extrusion profiles (Fig. 4) as it results in maximum design and assembly possibilities with minimal time investment. It is light weight, and has outstanding torsion and load resistance.

Dimensions of the robot: 450 X 450 X 1700 mm.

Fig. 4. Chassis with aluminum profiles

4.3 Modeling

Considering the required height and the drive mechanism, a CAD model of the robot is designed (Fig. 5). AutoCAD educational version 2020 is used for this modelling.

4.4 Electrical and Electronics Architecture

All subsystems must be connected to a main computing unit, which runs ROS (Robot Operating System). Signal Path and Power Path are planned before assembling the components. Power from the battery (Li-ion battery pack, battery capacity, voltage, current) is shared with all the components as shown in the Fig. 6. A main switch and a fuse are added directly to the battery output for safety.

All messages from sensors to actuators are communicated through ROS as shown in Fig. 7. Here, Jetson Nano is the computing unit that runs on ROS. The micro controllers, motor driver, sensors and LIDAR are connected to ROS directly and the Jetson Nano is Wi-Fi enabled to share the data or receive the commands from the user.

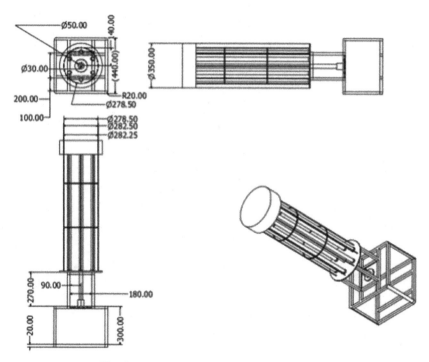

Fig. 5. CAD model for the structure of the robot

4.5 Component's Used

Two DC geared motors (12V, 200 rpm) with a torque of 13.5 kg-cm are attached to the bottom of the chassis. These motors are controlled by Roboclaw 2x7A with up to 15 Amps peak per channel. It can also read data from the encoders. Six UVC lights (30W, Philips TUV) are connected to its ballast's which are controlled by an 8-channel relay module. The technical specifications of the UV-C lights are mentioned in Table 2.

Four Ultrasonic Sensors are used to avoid obstacle collision in close proximity and 2 PIR (Full form of PIR) motion detection sensors are included to detect any human presence or motion. RPLidar A1M8 is a 360-degree 2D laser Scanner. It produces 2-D point cloud data which is used for Mapping, Localization and Environment Modelling. RPLidar and its specifications are shown in Fig. 8 and Table 3, respectively. Jetson Nano is the brain of the robot that runs Robot Operating System (ROS) architecture and connects all hardware components. Technical specifications of Jetson Nano are specified in Table 4. It has AC8265 Wireless NIC which enables Wi-Fi and Bluetooth communications.

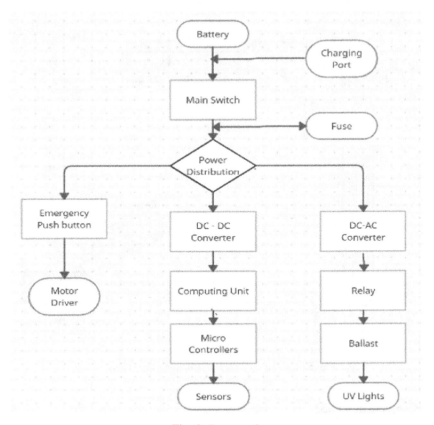

Fig. 6. Power path

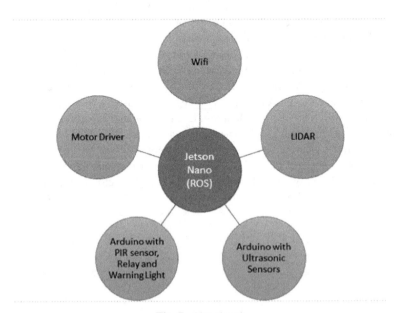

Fig. 7. Signal path

Table 2. Nominal technical specifications of UV-C lights

Power	30 W
Lamp current	0.37 A
UV-C radiation at 100 h	12 W
Voltage	102 V
Useful life	9000 h

Table 3. Specifications of RPLidar A1M8

Dimensions	98.5 mm × 70 mm × 60 mm
Weight	G.W 170 g
Distance range	0.15–6 m, white objects
Angular range	0–360°
Distance resolution	< 0.5 mm
Angular resolution	≤ 1
Sample duration	0.5 ms
Sample frequency	2000–2010 Hz
Scan rate	1–10 Hz, typical 5.5 Hz,

Fig. 8. RPLidar A1M8

4.6 Software Architecture

Roboclaw

Roboclaw has a software called BasicMicro Motion Studio that allows pre-configuration of Controller values of the closed-loop control or debugs any specific problem in general.

Table 4. Technical specifications of jetson nano

GPU	128-core maxwell
CPU	Quad-core ARM A57 @ 1.43 GHz
Memory	4 GB 64-bit LPDDR4 25.6 GB/s
Storage	64 GB micro-SD

The Roboclaw has supported drivers for Robot Operating System, Arduino, Python in RaspberryPi and LabView. It requires a sensor for closed-loop control and in the case of terrestrial robots, wheel encoders are the best choice. The Roboclaw works well with 2-Phase Rotary encoders and brings a whole new level of functionality to the motor controller, enabling it to perform accurate maneuvers. With the encoders, the Roboclaw can Autotune itself when commanded to [14]. The connections to the motor driver are shown in the Fig. 9.

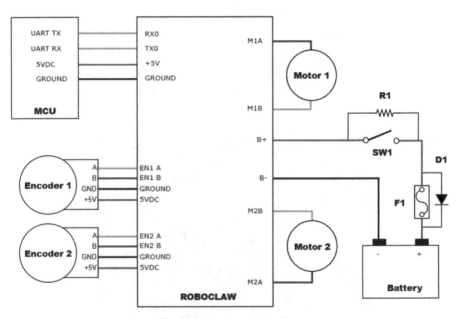

Fig. 9. Roboclaw connections

Robot Operating System (ROS)

The Robot Operating System (ROS) is an open-source framework for robotics software development with its roots at Willow Garage and Stanford University. The philosophy is to make a piece of software that could work in other robots by making minor changes in the code and refrain from reinventing the wheel. It consists of modular tools that are divided into libraries and supports various languages such as C++, Python and LISP.

The sensors and actuators that we use in robotics have also been adapted to be used with ROS.

ROS provides standard operating system facilities such as hardware abstraction, low-level device control, implementation of commonly used functionalities, message passing between processes, and package management. It is based on graph architecture with a centralized topology where processing takes place in nodes that may receive or post data in the form of standard message formats, such as multiplex sensor, control, state, planning, actuator, and so on. Many of the capabilities frequently associated with ROS are the libraries that provide a powerful set of tools to work with ROS easily. Of these, navigation library, gmapping package, rviz visualizer, simulators, and debugging tools are the most important ones [15].

Gmapping

Maps in ROS are basically a bitmap image representing an occupancy grid, where white pixels represent free space, black pixels represent obstacles, and grey pixels indicate "unknown". Therefore, the map is built using graphical program. Since the mobile platform is equipped with Lidars, we can create our own map by using Gmapping. In our case, we used SLAM gmapping as it combines the data from the lidar (for depth), and odometry into the occupancy map.

Gmapping is one of the more popular SLAM algorithms used in robotics. Pairing with the Rao-Blackwellized Particle Filter (PF), it uses the filter to sort out laser data. It then takes into account the altered movements and the recent observations of the robot. PFs utilize a system where each particle is a sample containing both its own map of the environment and a robot pose. Each individual particle in the system is associated with a weight and every time the robot moves, the particles are updated with a new map and pose corrected to the movement. This algorithm helps to reduce the chances of uncertainty in the robots pose for the prediction step of filtering. This weight is utilized by the algorithm to filter out the weakest samples and converge towards the strongest representation [16].

Adaptive Monte Carlo Localization (AMCL)

Monte Carlo Localization (MCL) is a package commonly used in robotics. AMCL is one of the ROS packages used on the turtlebot (reference). This package is particularly special as it helps the turtlebot to self-localize itself when it is navigating through different environments. This is accomplished by using the current scan of the environment and odometry data taken to pinpoint present location of robot. This then allows user to point and click on previously built map to a new location, thus allowing the robot to travel to the designated destination while avoiding obstacles.

This package is paired with SLAM gmapping. These two packages help robot know its present environment and localize itself. The robot can then go to any destination in the mapped environment [17].

Simultaneous Localization and Mapping (SLAM)

The robot relies on a relative coordinate system and dead reckoning to drive autonomously by knowing its location and destination. The Turtlebot will simultaneously and computationally construct a map of the environment, as well as its known relative position, in accordance with its location, by using Simultaneous Localization and Mapping (SLAM).

ROS enables the robot to create a map of its environment using the SLAM gmapping. package.

Once the map is available, ROS provides the AMCL package (Adaptive Monte Carlo localization) for automatically localizing the robot based on its current scan and odometry data.

Frame-Base Motion

In the present work, we have considered Frame-based motion by employing "move base" package. The "move base" package is a very sophisticated path planner and combines odometry data with both local and global cost maps when selecting a path for the robot to follow.

4.7 Final Assembly

All the components are integrated according to Signal and Power Path (from topic 4.4). Jetson Nano is the main computing unit in the robot which runs ROS. All the sub systems are connected to it. DC-motors with encoders are connected to a motor driver i.e., Roboclaw. The Roboclaw is serially connected to a Jetson Nano. Lidar is directly connected to Jetson Nano as ROS nodes. UV-C tubes are connected to the ballast, relay module and finally to the Jetson Nano. Ultrasonic Sensors are connected to an Arduino which is also connected to the Jetson Nano. The connections of the components are shown in the Fig. 10.

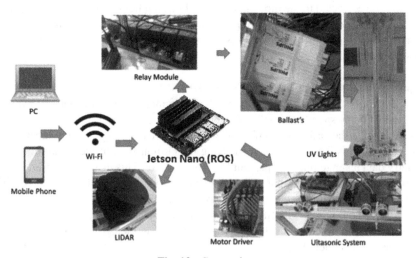

Fig. 10. Connections

5   Testing and Results

For a robot to perform autonomous navigation, initially environment mapping must be performed by the user and the map is to be saved for further purposes. At each point of time, the robot should be aware of its position and orientation with reference to the map. Hence, localization must run all the time. After mapping, when a goal is given to the robot it should plan the shortest global path to the goal and start navigating. While moving, it should continuously plan a local path to avoid obstacles along the way.

5.1   Mapping

Mapping an area to be disinfected consists of 4-step process. Initially, the user loads the GMapping demo software. The Rvizrobot's front-end live map visualization tool needs to be loaded so the user can visualize the map as they create it. Then, the user drives the robot around the desired environment until the user is satisfied with the map coverage, as seen in RViz. Finally, the user saves the map to the desired location in the computer's file system (for example refer Fig. 11). This last step creates and saves the map with the output in the form of a ". pgm" image of the map, as well as a ". yaml"(Yet Another Markup Language) configuration file.

Mapping starts as soon as the Gmapping package is launched. The robot needs to be manually moved around the region to complete the map. A 2-D Lidar is used to obtain the data from the surroundings. Once the map is created, gmapping is stopped and the map is saved. This map will be used for further navigation tasks.

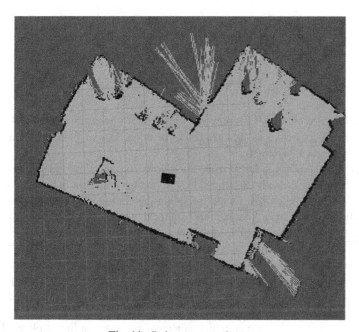

Fig. 11. Robot generated map

5.2 Localization

It is important for the robot to know its current position in the map with respect to its surroundings. This is called Localization. ROS navigation stack implements Monte-Carlo Localization. It is an algorithm that generates several guesses about where the robot's next move could be and then update itself as the robot moves through the environment, while collecting real time data. ROS navigation implements this algorithm in a node called AMCL node provided by the AMCL package.

Once the Localization package is launched, the robot in the visualizer will spawn at the given initial co-ordinates. It uses laser scan topic and odom (please check if the word is correct "odom") frame to spawn the base frame in the map.

5.3 Path Planning and Navigation

The path planning part of navigation is implemented in a package called "move_base".

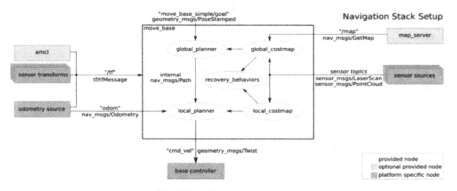

Fig. 12. ROS navigation stack

The middle box of Fig. 12 represents move_base node, the core of ROS navigation stack. It subscribes to several features, including global_planner, local_planner, global_costmap, local_costmap.

Planner calculates a path for the robot to follow from its current position to the goal position provided by the user. Within ROS, the planner relies on map called costmaps to generate a plan. The global planner relies on generating global plans based on the global_costmap and the local_planner relies on local_costmap for generating local plans.

In Fig. 13, the rectangular boxes are topics whereas ovals are nodes. We can see a move-base node that publishes and subscribes to several topics.

Path Planning involves both global planning and local planning. Apart from the laser sensor, 4 ultrasonic sensors are also installed to avoid the obstacles at close proximity. In order to observe the path planning process of the robot, rviz can be used for Map display (Cost maps) and Path display (Plans).

From Fig. 14. The global path which is shown as the green line is planned when a goal is given and the local path which is shown as the red line is short and is continuously planned based on the obstacles on the global path.

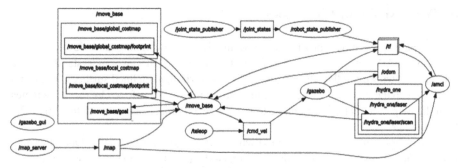

Fig. 13. ROS topics & nodes

Fig. 14. Green line indicates global path and red line indicates local path

5.4 Safety and Obstacle Avoidance

Since direct exposure of UV-C lights is harmful to humans, two motion detection sensors are used to detect human presence during the UV-C lights operation. If any motion is detected, then the UV-C lights turn-off automatically and an Emergency warning light will turn on as a warning indication.

After a path is planned and the robot starts moving, the local planner will update its local path continuously helping the robot to avoid obstacles.

5.5 Disinfection

Disinfection is done by turning-on the 6 UV-C lights at a single location for specified period. Once the waypoints for the robot to disinfect are generated by the user a patrolling algorithm is used to feed the robot with each waypoint one after the other by using a client server application socket. Specific conditions are also implemented for the robot to skip a waypoint if there is a difficulty in planning a path to the waypoint or if there is any object in that location.

6 Discussion and Conclusion

In this paper, we have shown the steps involved in designing and developing an autonomous UV Disinfectant robot. From testing and results, we understand that the robot navigates well in flat surfaces but difficulties arises on inclined surfaces. The robot cannot go up the inclined surfaces due to insufficient tractive effort. The robot navigates with the help of a 2D map but unable to recognize 3D objects as we are using only a 2D laser scanner.

This robot can create its own map when a user moves it manually. Once the map is made and the user determines the locations to be disinfected the robot autonomously moves from one location to another and starts disinfecting for a certain amount of time. While disinfecting i.e., when the UV lights are ON, if any person comes closer to the robot, it will detect the motion and turns OFF the UV lights for safety purposes. This process is more consistent than manual cleaning since the robot follows the same path with higher precision, and thanks to its autonomy, human staff will not be exposed to contagious viruses.

7 Perspective/Future Scope

Adding a camera to the robot enables more flexible process, as the evaluated image data can be used to precisely control the robotic movements. Object detection allows the robot to decide which places to disinfect instead of a user selecting the waypoints manually. 4-wheel drive can be implemented to make movement on the uneven surfaces easy. Since the robot needs to recharge, a self-docking station can be implemented where the robot can return after completing a task. A user-friendly mobile application should be developed for the cleaning staff to operate without any difficulty. A self-diagnostics system can also be implemented to find out a faulty system before the robot's daily tasks.

Acknowledgements. The authors would like to thank MU Vice-chancellor Medury Yajulu, Professor Arya K Bhattacharya and Professor Bishnu Pal for providing support and key inputs during this work. We would Also like to thanks Prof. S.K.Saha from IIT Delhi who introduces us to mobile platform Robomuse 5 from where we tool the inspiration to develop this UVC robot.

References

1. Solution Design. http://solutionsdesignedforhealthcare.com/solutions/products/uv-disinfection/physics-101-inverse-square-law. Accesses 12 Dec 2020
2. Malayeri, A., Mohseni, M., Cairns, B., Bolton, J.: Fluence (UV dose) required to achieve incremental log inactivation of bacteria, Protozoa. Viruses. Algae. IUVA News. **18**, 4–6 (2016)
3. Kowalski, W., Walsh, T., Petraitis, V.: 2020 COVID-19 Coronavirus Ultraviolet Susceptibility (2020)
4. Harris, T.R., Pagan, J.G., Batoni, P.: Optical and fluidic co-design of a UV-LED water disinfection chamber. ECS Trans., vol. **45**(17) (2012). 221st ECS Meeting, May 6 – May 10. Seattle, WA

5. Stibich, M., et al.: Evaluation of a pulsed-xenon ultraviolet room disinfection device for impact on hospital operations and microbial reduction. Infect. Control. Hosp. Epidemiol. **32**, 286–288 (2011). https://doi.org/10.1086/658329

6. Song, L., Li, W., Li, J.H.L., Li, T., Gu, D., Tang, H.: Development of a pulsed xenon ultraviolet disinfection device for real-time air disinfection in ambulances. Hind. J. Healthc. Eng. 1–5 (2020). https://doi.org/10.1155/2020/6053065

7. Anderson, D.J., et al.: The benefits of enhanced terminal room (BETR) disinfection study: a prospective, cluster randomized, multicenter, crossover study to evaluate the impact of enhanced terminal room disinfection on acquisition and infection caused by multidrug-resistant organisms. Lancet. Infect. Dis. **389**, 805–814 (2017). https://doi.org/10.1016/S0140-6736(16)31588-4

8. Haddad, L.E., et al.: Evaluation of a pulsed xenon ultraviolet disinfection system to decrease bacterial contamination in operating rooms. BMC Infect. Dis. **17**, 672–677 (2017). https://doi.org/10.1186/s12879-017-2792-z

9. Bentancor, M., Vidal, S.: Programmable and low-cost ultraviolet room disinfection device. HardwareX. **4**, 1–13 (2018). https://doi.org/10.1016/j.ohx.2018.e00046

10. D'Andrea, R.: Guest editorial: a revolution in the warehouse: a retrospective on Kiva systems and the grand challenges ahead. IEEE Trans. Autom. Sci. Eng. **9**, 638–639 (2012)

11. Marder-Eppstein, E., Berger, E., Foote, T., Gerkey, B., Konolige, K.: The office Marathon. In: ICRA (2010)

12. Hornung, A., Phillips, M., Jones, E.G., Bennewitz, M., Likhachev, M., Chitta, S.: Navigation in three-dimensional cluttered environments for mobile manipulation. In: ICRA (2012)

13. Reiser, U., Jacobs, T., Arbeiter, G., Parlitz, C., Dautenhahn, K.: Care-O-bot® 3 – vision of a robot butler. In: Trappl, R. (ed.) Your Virtual Butler, pp. 97–116. Springer Berlin Heidelberg, Berlin, Heidelberg (2013). https://doi.org/10.1007/978-3-642-37346-6_9

14. Ionmc webpage. http://downloads.ionmc.com/docs/roboclaw_user_manual.pdf. Accessed 10 Dec 2020

15. Conley, K., et al.: Ros: an open-source robot operating system. In: ICRA Workshop on Open Source Software (2009)

16. Goncalves, J., Lima, J., Costa, P.: Real-time localization of an omnidi-rectional mobile robot resorting to odometry and global vision data fusion: an ekfapproach, 1275 – 1280 (2008)

17. Liu, S., Li, S., Pang, L., Hu, J., Chen, H., Zhang, X.: Autonomous exploration and map construction of a mobile robot based onthe tghm algorithm. Sensors **20**, 490 (2020)

Requirements for a Game-Based Approach to Strengthen Leadership in Health Care

Mareike Sorge[1]([⊠]), Christina Mayer[2], Judith Schöner[3], Robert Kummer[1], and Melanie Rentzsch[1]

[1] Logistics and Factory Systems, Fraunhofer Institute for Factory Operation and Automation IFF, Magdeburg, Germany
{mareike.sorge,robert.kummer,melanie.rentzsch}@iff.fraunhofer.de
[2] Institute of Industrial Engineering and Ergonomics, RWTH Aachen University, Aachen, Germany
c.mayer@iaw.rwth-aachen.de
[3] EUMEDIAS, Magdeburg, Germany
jschoener@eumedias.de
https://www.iff.fraunhofer.de/en.html

Abstract. The growing technological progress and the concomitant complexity in professional life poses new challenges for executives. These complexities are particularly noticeable in the health care sector at the middle management level on a daily basis. The executives are in an intermediate position: Both care work and managerial functions must be matched up sophisticatedly to meet and satisfy all target groups. Many decisions (especially for questions that arise for the first time or those that are unique) are commonly made based on intuition or trial-and-error principle. Usually, the possible consequences of alternative decisions cannot be reliably determined in advance. This paper addresses these issues and describes methods for dealing with them. Therefore, initial results of a respective analysis are going to be introduced.

Keywords: Leadership · Health care · Virtual learning environment

1 Introduction

In the context of multi-layered patient and employee requirements as well as political and economic demands, leaders in the health care sector are more and more frequently acting at the complex interface of conflicting objectives such as ensuring high-quality patient care, promoting employee satisfaction and motivation as well as fulfilling efficiency needs and political regulations. In coping with the resulting challenges, managers are increasingly moving to the center of corresponding requirements for decision-making and thus influencing the degree of goal achievement in a relevant way through leadership actions within the scope of their responsibility. Although their decision-making is therefore of central importance for the success of an organization, in practice it is usually based on experience and intuition as well as personal and social competencies developed over the course of their biographies, what especially applies to issues with strong

V. G. Duffy (Ed.): HCII 2021, LNCS 12778, pp. 152–164, 2021.
https://doi.org/10.1007/978-3-030-77820-0_12

corporate cultural or organizational links. Ultimately, this means that consequences of different decision alternatives cannot be reliably determined in advance.

In comparison to that, various technology-based systems such as monitoring, simulation and support systems have increasingly established to accompany product- and process-related decision-making processes in the industrial context throughout the last decade. Large proportions of a manager's decision portfolio in the industrial sector can thus be covered by available solutions, whilst systems for addressing specific cultural and organizational issues in the context of health care remain to be developed.

Therefore, the aim of the LUTZ[1] research project is to utilize the opportunities of appropriate solutions to support decision-making in a new perspective by developing a system for accompanying culture- and organization-related events, which will support leaders in the health care sector in complex decision-making processes in the context of leadership, corporate culture and organization. For the realization of that, the project addresses the following questions:

- What specifics can be used to characterize leadership work in the health care sector?
- Which challenging decision-making situations can be identified in the context of leadership, corporate culture and organization?
- How can corporate cultural and organizational effects of different decisions and decision-making processes be represented?

Within the scope of the overall objective, the present paper pursues two goals: On the one hand, the paper intends to give a rough overview of the methodological approach used in the analysis and requirement phase of the LUTZ project. On the other hand, two methods are then emphasized to illustrate the initial results and present them for discussion.

The paper aims to present first results from a literature research regarding the topic "attributes of leadership in health care". Furthermore, the paper presents initial results of one part of the qualitative study[2]. Herein, the focus is on the presentation of first results from the evaluation phase of an interview that was conducted on the topic of "leadership", and targeted to get an overview of all relevant information of leadership tasks, challenges and areas of tension. Based on the results of the literature review and the interview, first assignments of possible learning scenarios are to be made, which could be discounted in a learning environment and therefore be made available to managers for qualification in their management activities. Overall, the paper will focus on the following questions:

- What are the characteristics of leadership in health care?
- Which characteristics are to be considered for the development of the learning environment?

[1] The project "LUTZ - Learning Environment for Transformational Leadership of the Future/02L18B534" is funded by the German Federal Ministry of Education and Research and the European Social Fund as part of the "Future of Work" program for a period of three years from May 2020.

[2] With regard to the duration of the project, the paper does not claim to present all results in the complete form. From these aspects the research questions were formed, which are central in the LUTZ project and especially for the interview evaluation.

The process of the initial analysis that is considered in the LUTZ project will be discussed below. The first results from the literature review and the interview will then be presented. The paper ends with a comprehensive discussion of the respective results with regard to the two focused questions of the paper as well as a possible design of learning scenarios.

2   Method

The main objective of the first phase of the project LUTZ is to get an overview of the health care sector in Germany as well as the management styles in middle management, while different methods are applied. On the one hand, there is a literature research of the topic of leadership behavior and styles in the German health care sector. On the other hand, a qualitative and quantitative study is carried out in order to complement and enhance the theoretical and scientific results.

The aim of the literature review is to gather the existing state of research on the central research question of "What is ideal leadership in health care?". The research aims to verify the research needs and to get to know the leadership culture as well as the particularities of organization and structure of the German health care system. In addition, the review will also serve to highlight the needs within the health care sector in terms of support for managerial qualification. Last but not least, the results of the literature review constitute an important basis for the design of the concrete learning scenarios for the learning environment which is developed in the research project LUTZ.

As part of the qualitative study, several guided interviews were carried out with health care managers. The focus was on interviews with nursing service managers of a private nursing service manager in Saxony-Anhalt. The aim of the interviews was to develop a feeling for tasks that managers in the health care sector have to deal with, how they work on these tasks as well as what requirements to consider. The previous examination with the research topic revealed that decision-making processes are always part of leadership. Decision-making is an individual complex process which is based on experiences that have already been made, on the basis of which situations are perceived, evaluated and reflected upon differently. Therefore, the study focuses on questions about managerial tasks and also includes the individual and manifold decision-making situations.

In addition, further interviews were conducted with executives from other institutions and areas of health care, such as dentistry or general medicine. This approach must be justified by the fact that the previously identified management tasks and decision-making situations as well as the findings on leadership and decision-making behavior, the framework conditions, and the challenges of one health care sector should be compared with other results and expanded accordingly. Furthermore, interviews are performed with the upper management level in order to become acquainted with and understand the organizational culture. Leadership and corporate culture are closely related [1].

All interviews are evaluated using the method of qualitative content analysis by the psychologist and sociologist Philipp Mayring. After the transcription of the interviews, the evaluation was carried out taking into account concrete research questions on the topic of leadership such as "Which management tasks characterize the health care sector?" and "Which challenges exist for the managers in the health care sector?". At the beginning of the evaluation, the interviews were divided into sections of meaning, according to the research questions. The sequences were paraphrased then, before categories were derived. These categories are discussed and tested in the evaluation team with the aim of designing a common category system.

On the one hand, this paper will outline initial results from the literature review, which refers in particular to the question of which features leadership in German health care has. On the other hand, the first findings from the qualitative study of the project will be presented. This is a first, exemplary category system, which was elaborated by means of the content analysis of an interview with a nursing service manager. In this interview, the focus was placed on the topic of leadership. The following categories will be expanded and concretized in the further course of the project until a uniform category system exists, which is considered to be saturated.

3   Results

Within a systematic literature search using the databases of PubMed, PubPsych, LIVIVO, EconBiz and SCOPUS, a variety of several hundred publications was to be found under the application of an intentionally broad defined search string representing the core elements of the matter of interest. Papers had to be published from 2016 until present, be written in English or German language and full texts available. After a content-guided inclusion-exclusion-procedure, taking into account titles as well as abstracts and full texts, a selection of 37 publications referring to leadership issues in health care in either explicit or implicit form got integrated in the following review, the intention of which is to provide an initial overview of the appearance of leadership in health care.

In a meta-reflection, it is to be stated that issues of leadership in health care are broadly discussed in international literature with special consideration in territories such as the United States, Europe and Germany, the latter of which was of special interest for the review on hand. Thereby, the publications reviewed allowed statements as well as conclusions along the following categories that were to be identified in order to describe the phenomenon of leadership in health care: understanding, importance, tasks, competence and qualification. A synthesis of selected findings of each category is presented below.

Understanding of Leadership. Within the scope of the selected contributions, management and leadership are described as two disparate concepts. While management is described to primarily focus on tasks, leadership is characterized to predominantly concentrate on people [2]. In other perspectives, integrated understandings are to be found, conceptualizing leadership as ability to initiate influence, innovation and engagement towards reasonable actions or goals in order to foster desired outcomes [3]. Thereby, leadership is also being described as not necessarily being tied to specific roles or hierarchies, but to embody competences that can be represented by various staff members who bring initiatives forward, shape change and work together [4]. The extent to which a leader does actively promote encouraging work climate, provide orientation and clarity and engage in achieving common goals is thereby described as attribute of good quality leadership [5].

Importance of Leadership. Evidence on the importance of leadership on manifold outcomes is to be found across various health care professions such as nurses and physicians as well as diverse health care settings like nursing homes and hospitals. Within this, it becomes apparent that not only does leadership influence goal achievement in aspects as patient and employee well-being as well as terms of politics and economics, but also does so in both direct and indirect ways. Additionally, the responsibility of leaders in the health care sector covers a broad spectrum of professional subjects including health care-related aspects as well as matters of work design. Thereby, amongst the most highlighted issues in the scope of leadership liabilities, patient-related objectives such as health care quality and outcome [6], employee-related aspects like promoting well-being and commitment [7] as well as work design-related matters as process management and safety building [8, 9] were to be derived. Additionally, single specifications of leadership objectives, namely optimizing treatment quality and cost efficiency [10, 11] were to be identified according to this.

Leadership Tasks. Closely associated with this, a broad range of leadership tasks was to be found within the contributions, documenting different horizons of operational and strategic integration as well as multi-faceted dimensions amongst routines of health care leaders. Attempting to cluster the according activities, the following emphases can be summarized: In terms of management along upper hierarchy levels, main duties include strategy building, budget accountability, implementation of laws and regulations applicable to the facility, personnel, patient and process as well as quality, error and incident management [11, 12]. In respects of leadership along varying hierarchy levels, central tasks imply encouraging social support [13], empowering staff in the interest of good quality care [2], fostering organizational learning [8], shaping development and change [8] as well as taking care of oneself and others [14]. Further assignments thereby finally include fostering justice [6], promoting trust [15] and building common values.

Leadership Competences. According to the variety of tasks, a corresponding rich spectrum of competence needs could be identified to comply with leadership requirements in health care. Along both, nursing and medical leaders, competence profiles encompass several dimensions including professional, personal, social, procedural, methodical as well as reflexive perspectives [11, 14, 16], the scope of which thereby vividly maps the different ranges affected by health care leaders. Namely, these can be described as representing micro-, meso- and macro-level perspectives, accordingly addressing the leader itself as well as cooperation within and in between teams, intra- and inter-professional collaboration, health care organizations, stakeholder networks and health care system.

Leadership Qualification. In contrast to that, studies across various settings have consistently reported that even though the necessity of gaining leadership competences has been recognized and the extent of leadership-associated responsibilities increases over the course of nursing and medical professionalization, a systematic consideration of sound leadership qualification within primary health care education remains an open issue to date. Subsequently, competence acquisition and role development occur spontaneously through confrontation with according events, implicitly during performance in practice and through adoption from superiors and role models without explicit reflection [11, 17, 18, 19].

Following these essential findings of the review, the results of one of the interviews with a nursing service manager are presented below. This is, as already mentioned, a first category system that must not be understood as saturated and solid yet. Despite its exemplary nature, this category system makes it possible to make first derivations for the design of learning scenarios.

The presented interview was conducted with a nursing service manager that has been working in the company for several years and holding responsibility for an own team since. The interview reveals the complexity of the daily work of nursing managers. In addition to the formation of fixed routines designed to create a structure, as specific management tasks such as routing, billing or budget planning are always repeated at fixed times, the head of care must always be able to deal with unpredictable tasks. No day is like the other, so a clear head, spontaneous solutions (not solution) and complexity management are needed. It also became clear that the nursing manager is not only a manager but still needs to be a specialist. For example, it is characterized by emergency availability, because, as a last resort, it feeds into care when there is a shortage of staff: *"I don't work in shift work anymore, except for exceptions"*. In addition, it needs a high level of expertise to act as an adviser to staff, patients and relatives. It could also be identified that the manager is in a state of conflict with different tensions between parties. This tension is attributable to its own person, the staff, patients, relatives and management. The head of the care service practices self-care and has, for example, *"learnt to say no"*, as well as to apply self-leadership and above all to ensure that the workforce is well served."

If the atmosphere in the team is perceived as good, such as when the manager constantly has *"an open ear"* while listening to problems and valuing the staff, the internal processes and the quality of work is right, which was reported to be very important. As a result, the manager is encouraged to behave and build trust in staff for care. Furthermore, in order to be able to assume responsibilities, it is necessary to know the strengths and weaknesses of the personnel, as well as the individual personalities of the staff because *"everyone needs something else to be happy."* Therefore, it is also important that the manager takes into account the satisfaction of patients, relatives and management.

The organizational structure provides that in addition to the role as care and administrative officer, a nursing service manager also has to act as adviser for the staff, the patients and the relatives. The manager has to know the care services and to discuss about these with the families concerning to their relatives to be cared for. Thus, in order to carry out its tasks, the manager must develop not only social and technical skills, but also a certain level of numerical and management skills.

The following category system was derived as a summary from the results of the content analysis of the previously presented interview. The categories were established inductively. Table 1 shows the categories, their respective definitions as well as illustrating anchor examples that are borrowed from the meaning of original quotations and exemplify the content of the categories in natural language.

The discussion of the results found follows in the next section.

Table 1. Category System

Category	Definition	Anchor example
Solicitousness	Text indicating caring (pleasant, protective) behavior	*I always try to make sure that the patients are doing well - that they feel valued and involved*
To get to know the staff	To get to know the staff with their strengths, weaknesses and characteristics	*Every employee has individual needs.* *A care manager should know these needs and understand how they affect an employee's reaction in certain situations*
Self-care	The manager takes care of himself/herself	*It is important for me to take care for myself and to listen to my own needs and limits*
Employees wellbeing	The staff members should feel good	*We always try to do a little something together every once in a while, be it having lunch together or celebrating birthdays with an afternoon of games – the main thing is that the team is doing well*
Patient welfare	The patients should feel good	*It is also important to me that our residents feel comfortable with us*
Relatives welfare	The relatives should feel good	*I try to take time to listen to the concerns of the family members of our residents and to provide them with whatever advice I can to support their care for their loved ones*
Inclusion of the staff	Passages that point out that the manager integrates their employees into processes	*When it comes to decisions regarding the way we organize our work, I always try to involve my team. If you want a decision to be supported by everyone, I think it is a necessity to do it like that*

(continued)

Table 1. (*continued*)

Category	Definition	Anchor example
Respect	Passages pointing to each other's attention	*Sometimes I am just like 'What a great team!'. The way my colleagues take care for our residents but also keep everything running in the background is remarkable and truly deserves my fullest respect*
Honesty	Passages suggesting that one treats one another sincerely and avoids lies	*Honesty is key. No matter whether it concerns praise or criticism*
Administrative office	Tasks falling within the administrative area	*Some days I spend almost entirely at my desk, answering e-mails and making phone calls*
Personnel management	Tasks related to staff and, in particular, operational planning	*Who takes care of which residents and when is something I usually coordinate together with my deputy*
Dealing with unpredictable situations	There are events during the day that arrive unplanned and surprisingly	*Some things you simply just cannot predict. Like sick notes, for example, or emergencies. You just have to deal with it*
Tracing the daily routine of the qualified nurses	The manager participates in the daily life of skilled workers	*I think it is important to keep a sense of what occupies the team in their daily work and to stay involved, whether it is through participating in shift changes or a quick little chat in the hallway*
Routines	There are fixed processes in the day-to-day work that structure it	*Some of my tasks are defined by certain specifications, as are some sequences in our daily routine*
Mediation between requests	Actions of the executive to achieve a balance of interests	*Sometimes, interests diverge quite a bit so that you have to put quite some effort into it to reconcile them*
Emergency availability	The manager jumps in as a specialist in an emergency case	*I don't normally take on nursing tasks anymore, but when it hits the fan, sure, I step in*

(*continued*)

Table 1. (*continued*)

Category	Definition	Anchor example
Advisory activity	The executive informs and makes recommendations	*I get back to the relatives of our residents whenever possible – especially when there is news from our facility or when I came upon a helpful advice*
Quality management	The manager controls the quality of the work and establishment	*I am aware of my responsibility to both set the standards for what we aim to achieve in care as well as to make my employees fit to provide according high quality work*
Quick and well-founded finding of solutions	Passages suggesting that solutions must be found spontaneously	*Our work also always holds the unexpected. You must embrace that – and remain open to spontaneity*

4 Discussion

In order to approach the answer to the research questions and thus to contribute to the further development of the overall project, the following section aims to put the presented findings into perspective as well as to derive according conclusions.

Within the scoping review, a set of five associated categories delivering information on understanding, importance, tasks, competences and qualification of leadership has been developed, referring to which a summary of the inherent key implications is going to be introduced below.

Understanding of Leadership. Regarding the understanding of leadership, different approaches of conceptualization became apparent, most notably represented in a concise distinction of management and leadership on the one hand, as well as integrated perspectives on the other hand. To what extent these understandings are determined by differing working contexts and varying processes of professional socialization remains to be examined in further research, which also applies to the question of underlying interpretations and metaphors of the nature of leadership.

Importance of Leadership. The far-reaching significance of leadership in the health care sector came up to be uncontested across varying health care services as well as health care professions. Given its both direct and indirect effects on patient- and employee-related concerns as well as economic and political issues, leadership thereby appeared to become effective on its own, e.g. in terms of social support, as well as in association with further variables, e.g. in terms of designing beneficial health care and working environments.

Leadership Tasks. Considering the manifold spectrum of leadership tasks in health care, an essential finding pertained the hybrid involvement of health care leaders in both the nursing respectively medical as well as managerial system. Additionally, it was to be revealed that the relationship of health care- and leadership-related tasks is of reciprocal nature, unfolding that just as original health care-related tasks are part of leadership roles, embodying leadership roles is part of concise health care-related duties as well.

Leadership Competences. Representing the reciprocal connection of nursing respectively medical responsibilities and leadership issues in the provision of health care, the very same relation was to be found in the description of according competence needs, thereby including professional as well as extra-professional requirements.

Following the conclusions derived from the review, the results of the interview are being discussed and interpreted in the following section. Its relevance to the research question "What are the characteristics of leadership in health care?" is the focus.

Leadership Qualification. In strong contrast to the requirements associated with performing complex health care leadership tasks, the systematic integration of their development beginning in the early stages of nursing and medical education as well as in processes of lifelong work-related learning remains an open issue to date.

Aligned with the category system, it can be pointed out that leadership in health care is characterized by the need for managers to occupy multiple tasks. Especially with regard to care, it has become clear that in addition to human resources management, the care service also carries out management and sales activities, as well as emotional and rescue activities. On the other hand, the health care is characterized by the tension of a manager, composed of different groups of stakeholders: Himself/Herself (not Yourself), the patient, relatives, staff and management. On the one hand, other features include the fact that leadership in the health care also means being ready for technical use. The reason is that it is not only about carrying out specific management tasks such as human resources management, but also about being able to take on care activities. On the other hand, quick and informed solutions must always be found.

Until now, it has been mainly assumed that the manager was in a sandwich position between the upper management level and their staff, care recipients and relatives. The analysis of the interview has shown that the manager also has to carry out self-care and faces this challenge. It is therefore required not only to take into account the welfare of employees, patients and relatives and to meet the more economic management requirements. The executive must also always pay attention and try to attain a balance between all stakeholders. The balance between yourself, staff, patients and relatives is, among other things, necessary in order to assure a level of satisfaction and thus the quality of care and the facility. The findings reveal other research questions such as "What is the role of emotion in day-to-day management?", "What is the role of self-care?", and "How will and how can the balance be established between stakeholders?" that will be taken into account later during the evaluation.

Synoptically, a broad consistency was to be found within the present findings in terms of the issues raised, allowing for the conclusion of having come upon the following particularities of leadership in health care:

Leadership in the health care sector is characterized by a specific complexity and contradictoriness that can be traced back to a multitude of patient- and employee-related requirements, economic and political boundary conditions as well as the particularities of service provision in an area of health- and safety-relevant interactive work. Within this context, health care leaders operate in multiple fields of tension, within a variety of paradoxes and role conflicts unfolds (not unfold), such as those arising from the relationship between economic rationality and professional self-conception. In the scope of this, leaders are regularly required to cope with unstructured challenges in non-routine situations and hardly predictable outcomes and thereby to solve problems of a system they themselves are a part of which. Consequently, leaders in health care need skills that enable them to remain capable of acting in situations like these and to successfully deal with uncertainty.

Finally, these characteristics are to be highlighted as particularities of leadership in health care and thus to be considered in the development of a reasonable learning environment that intents to provide an effective approach to build sound competences for leading in health care.

To that effect, established requirements regarding the conception and design of stimulating learning environments need to be taken into account. Above all, these refer to providing learning scenarios that meet relevant demands in terms of content and context, striving for simulation-based approaches reflecting realistic situations and specific behaviors as well as addressing skills being interconnected in practice accordingly together.

In order to meet these requirements, a digital learning environment combining aspects of simulation, gaming and reflection is going to be developed and thereby striving for the overall goal to enable health care executives to put different decisional options to the test, experience their respective effects and hence strengthen their abilities to design successful decision-making processes in practice. Within a protected environment, they are going to be confronted with relevant learning scenarios allowing for transferable learning experiences.

For the design of the learning scenarios, it is necessary to depict the identified area of conflict. Not only staff members or patients must be satisfied with a decision of the manager. The managers themselves must also be taken into account with their personality and attitudes, meaning that their welfare should also be in the focus. In addition, the learning scenarios should take into account the diversity of responsibilities of the manager and thus allow the training of different leadership behaviors as part of a high work complexity. For example, it is not sufficient to depict human resources management tasks alone. Contrarily, it is necessary to include possible unforeseeable events in the scenarios that have the potential to disrupt routines, and require an immediate and profound troubleshooting. Consequently, just as important, when designing the learning scenarios, one must take into account, which tasks or problems the managers consider to be particularly challenging, which situations they can already deal with appropriately and where they are more likely to need awareness and training.

This paper did not put emphasis on decision-makings though. During the project progression, however, this subject is going to be considered equally intensively. This also includes the separation of existing models for determining effective leadership styles (e.g. Blanchard & Hersey 1969) and dealing with the topic of leadership and decision-making processes (e.g. Vroom & Yetton 1973), which will be based on the learning scenarios.

5 Conclusion

The applied combination of a systematic literature research and a qualitative interview study enables a very detailed insight into the day-to-day management of leaders in the health care sector. While the review gives an overview of existing findings on the topic of leadership and creates an understanding of its complexity and variety, the personal and direct exchange with care providers offers deep insights into the multi-faceted and ambitious practice of leadership in health care. Given its meaning for multiple direct and indirect effects on patients, employees and health care organizations, its importance in balancing a variety of opposing interests of patients, employees, economics and politics as well as its inherence in diverse professional roles, an incontestable need to system-atically support a comprehensive development of profound leadership competences in health care professionals became apparent and will thus be addressed by the project LUTZ.

References

1. Rowold, J., Heinitz, K.: Führungsstile als Stressbarrieren. Zeitschrift für Personalpsychologie **7**(3), 129–140 (2008)
2. Tewes, R., Fischer, T.: Too busy to lead? Current challenges for German nurse leaders. J. Nurs. Manag. **25**(1), 1–3 (2017)
3. Kurtzman, J., Goldsmith, M.: Common Purpose: How Great Leaders Get Organizations to Achieve the Extraordinary. Wiley, San Francisco, CA (2010). as cited in: Bowles, J.R., Adams, J.M., Batcheller, J., Zimmermann, D., Pappas, S.: The Role of the Nurse Leader in Advancing the Quadruple Aim. Nurse Lead. **16**(4), 244–248 (2018)
4. Bass, B.M., Bass, R.: The bass Handbook of Leadership: theory, research, and managerial applications. FreePress, NewYork (2008). as cited in: Blanck-Köster, K., Roes, M., Gaidys, U.: Clinical-Leadership-Kompetenzen auf der Grundlage einer erweiterten und vertieften Pflegepraxis (Advanced Nursing Practice). Med Klin Intensivmed Notfmed 115, 466–476 (2020) https://doi.org/10.1007/s00063-020-00716-w
5. Northouse, P.G.: Leadership: Theory and Practice. Sage, London (1997). as cited In: Van Der Heijden, B.I.J.M., Mulder, R.H., König, C., Anselmann, V.: Toward a mediation model for nurses' well-being and psychological distress effects of quality of leadership and social support at work. Medicine (United States) **96**(15), e6505 (2017)
6. Stuber, F., et al.: The effectiveness of health-oriented leadership interventions for the improve-ment of mental health of employees in the health care sector: a systematic review. Int. Arch. Occup. Environ. Health **94**(2), 203–220 (2020). https://doi.org/10.1007/s00420-020-01583-w
7. Horstmann, D., Remdisch, S.: Health-oriented leadership in the geriatric care sector. the role of social job demands and resources for employees' health and commitment. Zeitschrift für Arbeits- und Organisationspsychologie **60**(4), 199–211 (2016)
8. Wagner, A., et al.: and on behalf of the WorkSafeMed Consortium: Healthcare professionals' perspectives on working conditions, leadership, and safety climate: A cross-sectional study. BMC Health Serv. Res. **19**(1), 53 (2019)

9. Jungbauer, K.-L., Loewenbrück, K., Reichmann, H., Wendsche, J., Wegge, J.: How does leadership influence incident reporting intention in healthcare? A dual process model of leader–member exchange. German J. Hum. Resour. Manag. **32**(1), 27–51 (2018)
10. Genrich, M., Worringer, B., Angerer, P., Müller, A.: Hospital Medical and Nursing Managers' Perspectives on Health-Related Work Design Interventions. A Qual. Study Front. Psychol. **11**, 869 (2020). https://doi.org/10.3389/fpsyg.2020.00869
11. Schmidt, T., Büchler, M.W.: Managementaufgaben in der Chirurgie: Herausforderungen und Chancen. Chirurg **92**,. 219–226 (2021) https://doi.org/10.1007/s00104-020-01349-7
12. Thume, J., Klahold, P.: Anforderungen an die moderne einrichtungsleitung in NRW. Komplexität rechtfertigt akademische Ausbildung. Pflegezeitschrift **69**(3), 172–175 (2016)
13. Van Der Heijden, B.I.J.M., Mulder, R.H., König, C., Anselmann, V.: Toward a mediation model for nurses' well-being and psychological distress effects of quality of leadership and social support at work. Medicine (United States) **96**(15), e6505 (2017)
14. Sylke, M.: Jung und Alt im Team - Chancen und Risiken: Altersheterogenität als Führungsaufgabe am Beispiel von Pflegeteams auf Station im Krankenhaus; Einblicke in aktuelle Diskurse und Forschungsstände sowie arbeits- und organisationspsychologische Einordnung. artec-paper, 208 (2016). https://nbn-resolving.org/urn:nbn:de:0168-ssoar-58735-1
15. Pfaff, H., Braithwaite, J.: A parsonian approach to patient safety: transformational leadership and social capital as preconditions for clinical risk management—the GI factor. Int. J. Environ. Res. Public Health **17**(11), 3989 (2020)
16. Hellmann, W., Meyer, F.: Management competence in leading positions in clinical surgery - what does a surgeon need to know? Zentralbl. Chir. **141**(6), 682–687 (2016)
17. Rothdiener, M., et al.: Surgeons' participation in the development of collaboration and management competencies in undergraduate medical education. PLoS ONE **15**(6), e0233400 (2020) https://doi.org/10.1371/journal.pone.0233400
18. Bowles, J.R., Adams, J.M., Batcheller, J., Zimmermann, D., Pappas, S.: The role of the nurse leader in advancing the quadruple aim. Nurse Lead. **16**(4), 244–248 (2018)
19. Bowles, J.R., Batcheller, J., Adams, J.M., Zimmermann, D., Pappas, S.: Nursing's leadership role in advancing professional practice/work environments as part of the quadruple aim. Nurs. Adm. Q. **43**(2), 157–163 (2019)

Towards an Effective Web-Based Virtual Health Intervention: The Impact of Media Platform, Visual Framing, and Race on Social Presence and Transportation Ratings

Fatemeh Tavassoli[1]([✉]) [iD], Mohan Zalake[1] [iD], Alexandre Gomes de Siqueira[1] [iD], François Modave[2] [iD], Janice Krieger[3] [iD], Benjamin Lok[1] [iD], and Juan Gilbert[1] [iD]

[1] Department of Computer and Information Science and Engineering, University of Florida, Gainesville, FL 32611, USA
{ftavassoli,mohanzalake,agomesdesiqueira,lok,juan}@ufl.edu
[2] Department of Health Outcomes and Biomedical Informatics in the College of Medicine, University of Florida, Gainesville, FL 32611, USA
modavefp@ufl.edu
[3] College of Journalism and Communications, University of Florida, Gainesville, FL 32611, USA
janicekrieger@ufl.edu

Abstract. Effectively delivering health-promoting messages can persuade users to adopt healthy life-saving behaviors. Research in health-promoting media messages shows that higher social presence and transportation ratings can positively impact users' trust and intentions to adopt healthy behaviors. Hence, social presence and transportation are essential measures for the quality of virtual health communication. This study aims to identify the factors that can increase social presence and transportation in the context of virtual human interventions for promoting colorectal cancer screening. To promote colorectal cancer screening and increase awareness, we developed a virtual healthcare assistant named ALEX (*A*gent *L*everaging *E*mpathy for e*X*ams). ALEX is a web-based intervention that incorporates high-fidelity 3D models with human voices and gestures to inform patients about colorectal cancer risks and screening information. In this paper, we study the effect of three independent variables on users' self-reported ratings of the social presence and transportation scales: 1) media platforms (smartphones vs. computers), 2) visual framing conditions (near vs. far), and 3) ALEX-user race relationship (concordance vs. dis-concordance). We conducted a between-subjects user study with 755 users (genders: male, female; races: Black, White; and age range: 50–73) using Qualtrics. All users completed the web-based virtual appointment with a gender-concordant ALEX on their preferred media platform and then completed the post-survey. The results show that the main effect of media platform was significant ($F_{1,747} = 5.18, p = 0.02$), but there were no significant differences between visual framing conditions and the Alex-user race rela-

© Springer Nature Switzerland AG 2021
V. G. Duffy (Ed.): HCII 2021, LNCS 12778, pp. 165–181, 2021.
https://doi.org/10.1007/978-3-030-77820-0_13

tionship ($p > 0.05$). Our analysis indicates that smartphones can induce higher social presence and transportation than computers.

Keywords: Virtual human · Virtual health intervention · Colorectal cancer

1   Introduction

Virtual human health interventions are shown to be useful for delivering health messages and changing users' health-related behaviors [28]. Virtual humans can effectively promote healthy behaviors and address health disparities by providing accessible information and decreasing the barriers for initiating care [37,39]. Virtual humans are computer-generated characters with an anthropomorphic embodiment which can engage human users in a credible conversation using speech, facial expression, and body language [11]. Virtual humans can play the role of Virtual Healthcare Assistant (VHA).

Fig. 1. All four versions of ALEX (Black Female, Black Male, White Female, and White Male) with the two visual framing conditions (left: near and right: far) is demonstrated on the two media platforms (smartphones and computers).

We built a VHA named ALEX (*A*gent *L*everaging *E*mpathy for e*X*ams), in collaboration with a multidisciplinary research team [17]. ALEX was designed and developed through a user-centered design by performing iterative user studies with potential users [45]. ALEX is a web-based virtual health intervention which features high-fidelity 3D models that can talk and behave like humans to inform patients about Colorectal Cancer (CRC) risks and screening information. ALEX aims to encourage CRC screening among older adults (above 50) who, according to health guidelines, are at a higher risk of getting CRC.

CRC is the third leading cause of cancer-related deaths in the United States among both men and women. The best way of reducing CRC risk is to get screened regularly starting at the age of 50, which can decrease CRC mortality rates by approximately 50% [1]. There are several barriers to CRC screening, such as lack of information and doctor recommendations [26].

Telehealth and virtual health interventions can facilitate educating patients on the CRC risk factors and screening options. Social presence and transportation can significantly affect the quality of virtual health communication by increasing users' trust and intentions to adopt healthy behaviors [13,41]. Social presence is defined as the communicators' salience and their interpersonal relationship during the mediated conversation [40]. Social presence is characterized as *"the sense of being there"* [29] or *"being together with another"* [22]. Transportation is defined as absorption in a story that contains attention, imagery, and emotional affect [15]. Users' beliefs and attitudes might change after returning to the real world from being transported to the virtual world, and they may experience strong emotions and motivations [15]. This study aims to identify the factors that can increase social presence and transportation in the context of virtual human interventions for promoting colorectal cancer screening.

Three influential factors of social presence and transportation ratings are: 1) inherent features of communication medium, 2) proxemics, and 3) VHA demographic. Inherent features of communication medium such as screen size can affect the social presence and transportation ratings [2,8,40]. We investigate the impact of two media platforms: 1) smartphones, 2) computers. Proxemics, which is defined as the interpersonal distance between communicators, can influence the perception of users' attribution, affect, and judgment of the virtual human [25], which in turn can impact the social presence and transportation ratings. We explore ALEX's two different visual framing conditions: 1) near, 2) far. ALEX's race and gender can be customized for the patient's demographic to improve patients' satisfaction and adherence to the provided health guidelines [27,37]. We developed four versions of ALEX representing different demographic groups, including: 1) Black Female, 2) Black Male, 3) White Female, and 4) White Male. Research suggests that race concordance between the user and virtual human is more influential than gender concordance and results in a more socially present, enjoyable, and useful interaction [38]. Hence, we decided to use the gender concordant ALEX and only examine the ALEX-user race relationship's role: 1) concordance, 2) dis-concordance.

We performed a between-subjects user study with 755 users (genders: male, female; races: Black, White; and age range: 50–73) from Qualtrics (Table 1). First, users completed the web-based virtual appointment with a gender-concordant ALEX on their preferred media platform (Fig. 1). Then, users filled a post-survey and answered 5-point Likert scale questionnaires related to social presence and transportation.

In this paper, we address the following research questions:

RQ1: Do different media platforms (smartphones, computers) impact social presence and transportation ratings?

RQ2: Do different visual framing conditions (near, far) impact social presence and transportation ratings?

RQ3: Does ALEX-user race relationship (concordance, dis-concordance) impact social presence and transportation ratings?

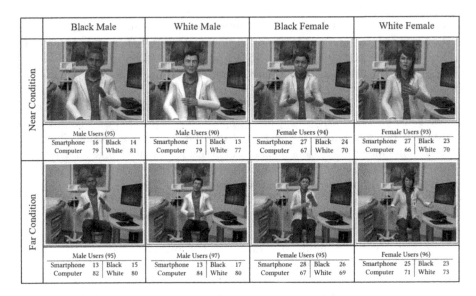

Fig. 2. All variations of ALEX and two visual framing conditions (First row: near condition, Second row: far condition). The information provided for each variation of ALEX indicates: 1) gender of users, 2) total number of users, 3) number of users in each media platform condition (Smartphone vs. Computers), 4) number of users in each race condition (Black vs. White)

2   Background

2.1   Virtual Healthcare Assistants

Virtual humans are considered a type of computer-generated Embodied Conversational Agents with an anthropomorphic embodiment that can be engaged in a conversation using human communication means such as speech, facial expression, and body language [11]. Virtual humans have been used in different health care domains such as mental health [3], pain management [43], and physician-patient interaction [32]. Virtual humans can play the role of a Virtual Healthcare Assistant (VHA). VHAs are non-judgemental and offer a sense of anonymity [35]. Hence, patients may be more willing to trust them and disclose sensitive health-related information [31]. Another advantage is that the race and gender of VHAs can be customized for the patient's demographic to improve patients' satisfaction and adherence to the provided health guidelines [27,37]. The contents and the recommended health guidelines that are delivered by VHAs can be tailored for patients to meet their needs better [21]. In addition, VHAs can better convey the health message to patients with low-reading and low-health literacy or not tech-savvy individuals [6]. VHAs are shown to be useful for lung cancer risk awareness [37] and increasing patient satisfactions [32]. This study explores the results of a user study with a VHA named ALEX that aims to inform patients about CRC risks and screening information in an accessible virtual appointment.

2.2   Social Presence

Social psychologists first defined the concept of social presence as the salience of the communicators and their interpersonal relationship during the mediated conversation [40]. Social presence is an important measure for the quality of virtual communication and is associated with positive communication outcomes. For example, authors in [14] found that social presence is associated with persuasion and attraction. The study in [20] found that social presence led to a higher purchase intention, while being positively associated with trust, enjoyment, and perceived usefulness of an online shopping website. Social presence can help build trust between individuals that assists with in-person or online interactions [30]. These factors have led researchers in both academia and industry to seek ways to increase social presence. Social presence has two main elements: 1) intimacy: a feeling of closeness that communicators feel during an interaction, and 2) immediacy: a psychological distance between the communicators. Many verbal and nonverbal communication factors can affect intimacy and immediacy, such as voice features, facial expressions, gestures, and physical appearance [18]. Prior research suggests that a communication medium's inherent and technological qualities can lead to different levels of social presence [40]. Thus, there has been significant interest from researchers in exploring the impact of modality on social presence, and the most common themes are: 1) Computer-mediated communication compared with face-to-face communication, 2) text-based Computer-mediated communication compared with other audio-visual modalities, and 3) comparison of immersive and non-immersive virtual environments [36]. The majority of the prior research has focused on the immersive qualities of the media. However, social presence is a subjective experience, and contextual and individual factors can impact it. Thus, the main predictors for social presence are: 1) immersive qualities, 2) contextual properties, and 3) individual traits [36].

Social Presence and Display Size: Some studies have looked at the impact of variations in display parameters on social presence. These parameters typically consist of image definition and display size. These studies have not led to definitive results, leaving room for further research. Some studies have found a higher definition larger display promotes higher social presence (e.g., [2,8]), while others did not find the display parameters to have a significant impact on the social presence (e.g., [24,42]). This disparity among prior research results is a significant motivation for us to consider two form factors with different display sizes in our analysis, namely smartphones and computers. This is the basis of our first research question *RQ1*: measuring the impact of smartphones vs. computers on social presence, transportation, and usability.

2.3   Transportation

Transportation is defined as absorption in a story that contains imagery, emotional affect, and attention [15]. As a result of transportation, a user may become less aware of the real-world events in favor of being immersed in the narrative that is happening in the virtual world. Loss of awareness towards real-world events can occur both on a physical level; for example, a user may not notice if someone enters the room, and on a psychological level, for example, a user may feel a subjective distancing from reality. Prior studies suggest that users' beliefs and attitudes might change after returning to the real world from being transported to the narrative virtual world, and they may experience strong emotions and motivations [15].

Transportation and social presence are close in nature; a general tendency towards transportation and being absorbed in a narrative can increase the feeling of social presence in the mediated communication [16]. Thus, transportation has some similar predictors to social presence such as: 1) media effect: visual media requires less mental effort than print media to imagine, therefore easing transportation [16], 2) individual traits: Tendency towards absorption into a story is also a subjective experience [12]. However, some individual differences remain stable across stories and contexts.

Authors in [13] looked into the experience of transportation to health-promoting media messages in the context of health communication. Their findings included two examples of health-related messages on smoking and skin protection. When presented with anti-smoking messages, smokers with a higher degree of transportation revealed an increased sense of persuasion to make an effort to quit smoking. They also found associations between experiential responses to skin protection messages and intentions of self-protection.

In order to improve the rate of CRC screening, patients need to be persuaded by ALEX to get screened. Therefore, we investigated the effects of transportation, which is shown to have a substantial impact on persuasion.

3   System Design

This section briefly describes the collective effort of a team of researchers from computer science, communication, and clinical medicine backgrounds. We designed and developed an internet-based health intervention featuring four VHAs called ALEX (*A*gent *L*everaging *E*mpathy for e*X*ams). ALEX has been developed through a user-centered design, which involves going through iterative user studies with potential users and aims to design a final product that can meet their individual needs along four areas: 1) credibility, 2) usability, 3) effectiveness, and 4) accessibility. Complete details of the system can be found in our design process paper [17]. The rest of this section is organized as follows: 1) Script, 2) ALEX development, 3) Visual Framing, 4) Responsive Interface development.

3.1   Script

ALEX aims to communicate accurate medical information regarding CRC's risk factors and the importance of getting CRC screening to reduce the barriers associated with CRC screening [17]. The conversational script of ALEX was iteratively improved through a user-centered design process and included empirically-based constructs respecting CRC communication best practices. ALEX script consists of 12 tailoring components including: 1) susceptibility, 2) severity, 3) benefits, 4) barriers, 5) self-efficacy, 6) response efficacy, 7) comparative risk feedback, 8) risk probability, 9) message source, 10) narrative persuasion, 11) demographic matching, and 12) message framing.

3.2   ALEX Development

Research shows that demographic discordance with a healthcare provider can reduce patient satisfaction and lead to lower adherence to the recommended health guidelines [27]. Taking into account the US population demography information, we developed four versions of ALEX representing different demographic groups, including: 1) Black Female, 2) Black Male, 3) White Female, and 4) White Male. All four versions of ALEX deliver an identical health message regarding the colon cancer risk factor and a screening recommendation. ALEX 3D models were first designed using Adobe Fuse, and then the quality was further improved by a professional 3D artist. To enable the creation of high-quality and realistic animations, we recruited a male and a female actor. Vicon Shogun Motion Capture System was used to record gestures and body movements. For each version of ALEX, the scenario was recorded by a race and gender concordant professional voice actor. Lip-sync and facial expressions were created based on audio files using FaceFX Store. For background, an actual image of a local clinical room was used to increase the realism. During the virtual appointment, ALEX was posed seated on a clinical stool and used gestures while having conversations with patients. In a prior study, we detailed the emerged design-guidelines of ALEX development [45].

3.3   Visual Framing

Research in cinematography literature, suggest that the camera shot of a character in a scene can affect source credibility and interpersonal-attraction [33,34], which could influence a user's perception of the character. We developed two visual framings by placing a virtual camera in a near and a far distance from the ALEX to create medium and full shots, respectively. The near condition, which is captured using a medium shot, shows ALEX from the waist up and reveals detailed information about the character. Medium shots are usually used in dialog scenes where facial expressions and body language play an important role [23]. The far condition, which is captured using a full shot, shows the whole body of ALEX and the character is smaller in relation to the background and more detail of the background are in the view. Full shots are used to show the overall look of the characters, how they are dressed and whether they move awkwardly or confidently. Full shots are considered emotionally neutral and more informative [23].

Table 1. Number of users in different demographic groups and study conditions.

Total number of users	Media platform		Visual framing conditions		Race		Gender		Age		
	Smartphone	Computer	Near	Far	Black	White	Female	Male	Range	M	SD
755	160	595	372	383	155	600	378	377	50–73	59.25	6.05

3.4 Responsive Interface Development

The user interface is designed to be simplistic to better serve the target users' needs who are older population (50 and older) and might not be tech-savvy. ALEX is the main part of the interface and located at the center of the view. To enhance accessibility, ALEX supports common browsers and operating systems. The interface was developed using Bootstrap, which is an open-source framework for mobile-first responsive front-end web development. Hence, ALEX can be easily accessed from devices with different aspect ratios, such as smartphones or computers. In addition, captions with recommended font and text-size were provided to assist people with visual or hearing aids [9]. Users can interact with the system through buttons containing relevant and appropriate text. Buttons are used 1) To collect users' responses to the questions 2) Play and pause ALEX, 3) close the intervention.

4 Experiment

This research is part of a more extensive and multidisciplinary research project funded by the National Institutes of Health (NIH). In this paper, we focus on data collected through an initial pilot study to ensure the soundness of different components and make improvements before deploying the intervention into patients' health portals.

We plan to examine the effect of media platforms, visual framing conditions, and user-ALEX race-concordance on social presence and transportation ratings using the pilot study data.

4.1 Participants

We recruited 755 users aged between 50–73 (M = 59.25, SD = 6.05), to follow the age recommendation for CRC screening and be consistent with the demographic of the patients that are our target audience. For this pilot test, all users were recruited from a Qualtrics online pool of participants. Users were nearly equally balanced between the two gender groups (378 males, and 377 females) and the two visual framing conditions (372 near, 383 far). To roughly follow the race distribution of White and Black population in the United States, we recruited different numbers of users from the two race groups (155 Black, and

Table 2. The modified items of the social presence and transportation scales. The items marked with * are reverse coded.

Social Presence Items (1 = Strongly disagree - 5 = Strongly agree)	Transportation Items (1 = Strongly disagree - 5 = Strongly agree)
1. I felt that Alex was aware of my presence	1. During the virtual appointment, I could easily picture myself in the exam room.
*2. I often thought about Alex not being a real person	*2. After finishing the virtual appointment, I found it easy to put it out of my mind.
*3. I perceived Alex as being only a computerized image, not as a real person	3. The virtual appointment affected me emotionally.
	*4. I found my mind wandering during the virtual appointment.
	5. The events in the virtual appointment are relevant to my everyday life

600 White). Besides, to replicate a real-world scenario with our target patients, users had a choice to open the intervention link on their own preferred devices. Based on our analysis of devices, the number of users in the computer medium platform was higher (160 smartphones and 595 computers). Table 1 summarizes the demographic information of the users.

4.2   Study Design and Procedure

ALEX links were distributed to the eligible participants through Qualtrics. All users were gender concordant with the version of ALEX that they received, but users could be race concordant or dis-concordant with ALEX. For example, a Black male user could receive a link for Black male or White male ALEX in the near or far condition. We attempted to balance the number users in each of the following four groups: 1) race concordant near condition, 2) race concordant far condition, 3) race dis-concordant near condition, and 4) race dis-concordant far condition. Figure. 2 summarizes the number of users in each race and gender of ALEX as well as near and far conditions.

After receiving the link, users opened the ALEX intervention using their preferred device. To compute the number of users for each media platform, we parsed the User-Agent string for each individual user, which was recorded in our data-base during the interaction with ALEX. A parsed User-Agent string identifies the characteristics of the end-user devise, such as operating system, and device model. Figure 2 shows the number of users for each media platform (phone vs. users) for each version of ALEX and visual framing conditions. After finishing the ALEX intervention, users filled out a post-survey questionnaire which includes the social presence and transportation scales.

4.3   Measures

In this section, we describe the social presence and transportation scales used in this study. To reduce the total number questions in the post-survey, we had to be selective with the number of items per scale and used the ones that are most relevant to our study's context.

Social Presence. We modified the original social presence scale to better fit our study. We adopted the most relevant subset of social presence questionnaire from [4] with some modifications to better fit our study's context. We also used the typical 5-point Likert-type scale (from 1 = "Strongly disagree" to 5 = "Strongly agree"). See Table 2 for the list of items included. Note that items 2 and 3 are reverse coded.

Transportation. We selected the five most relevant items from the transportation scale introduced in [15] that measure imagery, emotional affect and attention. We slightly modified the five selected items to become suitable for our context. All five items were presented in a 5-point Likert-scale type (from 1 = "Strongly disagree" to 5 = "Strongly agree"). Table 2 lists the selected items. Items 2 and 4 are reverse coded because they are negatively worded.

5   Results

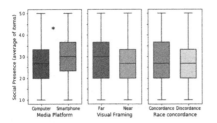 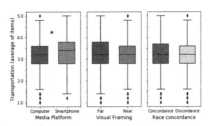

Fig. 3. Box-plot presentation of the average of items for Left: social presence, Right: transportation. X-axis: 3 independent variables and their respective groups. Y-axis: 5-point Likert scale 1: strongly disagree, 5: strongly agree.

The parametric assumptions for the three-way MANOVA were not met. So, we used the non-parametric Aligned Ranked Transform (ART) test to analyze the data [44]. The independent variables are media platforms (smartphone vs. computer), visual framing conditions (near vs. far), and user-ALEX race (concordance, dis-concordance). The outcome variables are the average of items for social presence scale and the average of items for transportation scale.

5.1   Social Presence

For social presence ratings, we averaged the three responses to the questionnaire to provide an overall social presence score. To explore the effects of the media platform, visual framing, and race-concordance on *social presence*, we performed ART analysis. We found that the main effect of media platform was significant $(F_{1,747} = 5.18, p = 0.02)$. There were no significant differences in visual framing and race concordance $(p > 0.05)$. The interaction effect between these independent variables was also not significant $(p > 0.05)$. The post-hoc analysis suggested that social presence was significantly higher in smartphones than computers $(t_{747} = -2.28, p = 0.02)$. This means that smartphone users reported a higher subjective feeling that they were in the presence of a "real" person while interacting with ALEX. Figure 3 shows the distribution of the overall social presence score for each independent variable.

5.2   Transportation

Similarly, we averaged the five responses to the transportation questionnaire to provide an overall transportation score. We examined the effects of the media platform, visual framing, and race-concordance on *transportation* by performing ART analysis. The main effect of media platform was significant $(F_{1,747} = 9.35, p = 0.002)$. There were no significant differences for visual framing and race concordance $(p > 0.05)$. The interaction effect between these independent variables was also not significant $(p > 0.05)$. The post-hoc test indicated that transportation was significantly higher in smartphones as compared to computers $(t_{747} = -3.06, p = 0.002)$. This suggests that users with smartphones were more absorbed into the story, had more affect, and attention towards the health intervention by ALEX. Figure 3 shows the distribution of the overall social transportation score for the independent variables.

The two different visual framing conditions were expected to have an effect on transportation ratings. Therefore, we did additional analysis for the first item "During the virtual appointment, I could easily picture myself in the exam room". (TR1) since it might be impacted by the far condition which shows a wider view of the exam-room background and could enhance users' imagination. We found that the main effect of media platform was significant $(F_{1,747} = 9.56, p = 0.002)$ and also observed a clear trend for visual framing $(F_{1,747} = 3.19, p = 0.07)$. There is an interaction effect between media platform and visual framing $(F_{1,747} = 7.13, p = 0.007)$.

The post-hoc analysis on media platform indicated that users in the smartphone group had a significantly higher rating on TR1 item than users in the computer group $(t_{747} = -3.09, p = 0.002)$. The post-hoc analysis on visual framing also showed that users in the far condition had a clear trend towards higher TR1 rating than users in the near condition $(t_{747} = -1.79, p = 0.07)$. In addition, the post-hoc analysis suggested that the difference in the TR1 rating in near and far conditions was significantly different in phone and computer $(t_{747} = 7.13, p = 0.007)$.

6 Discussion

In this paper, we set out to understand how the media platform and visual framing conditions affect users' self-reported social presence and transportation ratings. We now discuss the implications of our findings in the following.

6.1 Smartphone Users Reported Higher Social Presence and Transportation

We addressed the RQ1, which was concerned with the impact of media platforms (smartphones and computers) on users' self-reported social presence and transportation ratings. Our findings suggest that there is a significant difference between the two media platforms in users' self-reported responses to social presence and transportation scales. These results show that users in the smartphone group reported higher ratings for social presence and transportation scale.

Social Presence. Surprisingly, our results did not follow the same trend as prior works. Several studies showed that larger screen sizes positively impacted the social presence ratings [2,8], and some did not find any significant results [24,42]. However, our result showed that smartphone users reported higher social presence ratings than computer users despite the smaller screen sizes of smartphones. Other specific technological affordances of the smartphone medium platform may explain these results. Two potential reasons are discussed next. First, research has shown that people are more intimate with their smartphones than other devices. Authors in [10] established the concept of a digital companionship and showed that people feel less distance with their smartphones compared to computers, colleagues, or even neighbors. This points to intimacy as an inherent quality of the smartphone medium. Intimacy is also a main component of social presence [40]. Second, social presence involves the psychological processes which induce the feeling of being together, even through a screen. Users have grown accustomed to video-calling with other people that appear on their smartphones in a similar size to ALEX, as an alternative to face-to-face communication, a gold standard for social presence [7]. These two affordances of smartphones might affect users' self-reported ratings of the social presence towards the contents delivered through the smartphone medium.

Transportation. First, transportation and social presence are closely related and share the same common core of feeling immersed in a narrative world [16], and the digital companionship and users' feeling of being closer to smartphones may induce immersion into the ALEX narrative. Second, another study has shown that users tend to experience higher cognitive absorption towards the smartphone medium platform [5], a main factor for transportation [15]. Cognitive absorption and transportation share some components, such as immersion. Therefore, higher cognitive absorption in smartphones might explain higher transportation ratings. Our discussion offers insight into how other inherent technological features of the smartphone medium (e.g., digital companionship, a popular communication medium, and cognitive absorption) might influence higher social presence and transportation. As smartphones have become increasingly pervasive and indispensable to the general public, VHA interventions could leverage this medium to effectively deliver health messages to affect users' intentions to pick up healthier habits. This requires further research on the social presence associated with smartphones, which seems to be lacking [36]. To our knowledge, this is the first study to compare the social presence and transportation of VHAs between smartphone and computer media platforms.

6.2 Effect of Visual Framing Conditions on Social Presence and Transportation Ratings

Regarding the (RQ2), we first hypothesized that visual framing could influence the ratings for social presence and transportation. However, there were no significant differences between the visual framing conditions and the overall average scores for the social presence and transportation scales, except for (TR1) which seemed to be the most relevant item to visual framing conditions. Next, we discuss the potential reasons for these findings.

Social Presence. The near condition makes virtual humans appear larger on screen, showing more details of ALEX's facial expressions and body language than the far condition. Based on prior research [36], we expected to see more social presence in the near condition due to the users' ability to perceive higher visual realism [19]. However, the closer shot could also expose minor flaws with lip-syncing or animations that were not as salient in the far condition, leading to negatively impacted sense of behavioral realism and lowered social presence.

Transportation. The far condition's wider view of the background was expected to help participants feel higher immersion in the virtual world than the near condition. However, overall transportation score did not show any significant difference between the two conditions, except on TR1. We think a reason could be the lack of notable differences in the background of the near and far conditions, and users in both conditions could see enough visual cues to infer that they are in an exam room which needs further research.

6.3 Limitations

One limitation of our study is that our results came from users with a specific age range (50 and older) and further research is needed to generalize the findings for other demographics especially the younger population. Additionally, both social presence and transportation are subjective experiences and can be impacted by individual and psychological factors which we did not consider in this study.

7   Conclusion and Future Work

In this study, we investigated the impact of three independent factors, namely 1) media platform (smartphones vs. computers), 2) visual framing conditions (near vs. far), and user-ALEX race concordance on the overall average of self-reported ratings for social presence and transportation. Social presence and transportation scales are essential for influencing users' trust and intentions, which may affect an increased rate of early CRC screening and significantly improved outcomes. A user study was conducted with 755 users (aged 50–73) who completed an intervention with ALEX. ALEX is an internet-based virtual healthcare assistant designed for promoting colorectal cancer awareness for at-risk patients.

The results showed that the effect of media platforms on users' self-reported ratings of the social presence and transportation scale was significant. Surprisingly, despite the smaller smartphone screens, the smartphone group users reported a higher social presence and transportation ratings than users in a computer group. These findings strengthen the importance of smartphone-based delivery of virtual healthcare assistant interventions. We hope this study motivates researchers further to explore the factors affecting live-saving interventions through smartphone-based virtual healthcare assistants.

7.1   Future Work

The findings from this study motivate us to explore the technological affordances of the smartphone further. We plan to conduct an additional study with younger individuals, who possibly have a more intimate relationship with their smartphones, to confirm our findings are not age-specific as well as investigating other outcome variables such as persuasion and behavior change. A higher immersion and cognitive absorption towards the content delivered through the smartphone can lead to more attentional focus, suggesting a potential for improved learning. We are interested in studying the effectiveness of the virtual human training delivered through smartphones compared to other platforms such as computers.

References

1. Centers for disease control and prevention - colorectal awareness, February 2020. https://www.cdc.gov/cancer/dcpc/resources/features/colorectalawareness/
2. Ahn, D., et al.: The effects of actual human size display and stereoscopic presentation on users' sense of being together with and of psychological immersion in a virtual character. Cyberpsychol. Behav. Soc. Netw. **17**(7), 483–487 (2014)
3. Albright, G., Bryan, C., Adam, C., McMillan, J., Shockley, K.: Using virtual patient simulations to prepare primary health care professionals to conduct substance use and mental health screening and brief intervention. J. Am. Psychiatric Nurses Assoc. **24**, 247–259 (2018)
4. Bailenson, J.N., Blascovich, J., Beall, A.C., Loomis, J.M.: Interpersonal distance in immersive virtual environments. Pers. Soc. Psychol. Bull. **29**(7), 819–833 (2003)

5. Barnes, S.J., Pressey, A.D., Scornavacca, E.: Mobile ubiquity: understanding the relationship between cognitive absorption, smartphone addiction and social network services. Comput. Hum. Behav. **90**, 246–258 (2019)

6. Bickmore, T.W., Pfeifer, L.M., Jack, B.W.: Taking the time to care: empowering low health literacy hospital patients with virtual nurse agents. In: Proceedings of the SIGCHI Conference, pp. 1265–1274 (2009)

7. Biocca, F., Burgoon, J., Harms, C., Stoner, M.: Criteria and scope conditions for a theory and measure of social presence. Presence: Teleoper. Virtual Environ. (2001)

8. Bracken, C.C.: Presence and image quality: the case of high-definition television. Media Psychol. **7**(2), 191–205 (2005)

9. Caldwell, B., et al.: Web content accessibility guidelines (WCAG) 2.0. WWW Consortium (W3C) (2008)

10. Carolus, A., Binder, J.F., Muench, R., Schmidt, C., Schneider, F., Buglass, S.L.: Smartphones as digital companions: characterizing the relationship between users and their phones. New Media Soc. **21**(4), 914–938 (2019)

11. Cassell, J., Sullivan, J., Churchill, E., Prevost, S.: Embodied Conversational Agents. MIT Press, Cambridge (2000)

12. Dal Cin, S., Zanna, M.P., Fong, G.T.: Narrative persuasion and overcoming resistance. Resist. Persuas. **2**, 175–191 (2004)

13. Dunlop, S.M., Wakefield, M., Kashima, Y.: Pathways to persuasion: cognitive and experiential responses to health-promoting mass media messages. Commun. Res. **37**(1), 133–164 (2010)

14. Fogg, B.J., Tseng, H.: The elements of computer credibility. In: Proceedings of the SIGCHI Conference on Human Factors in Computing Systems, pp. 80–87 (1999)

15. Green, M.C., Brock, T.C.: The role of transportation in the persuasiveness of public narratives. J. Pers. Soc. Psychol. **79**(5), 701 (2000)

16. Green, M.C., Kass, S., Carrey, J., Herzig, B., Feeney, R., Sabini, J.: Transportation across media: repeated exposure to print and film. Media Psychol. **11**(4), 512–539 (2008)

17. Griffin, L., et al.: Creating an mHealth app for colorectal cancer screening: user-centered design approach. JMIR Hum. Factors **6**(2), e12700 (2019)

18. Gunawardena, C.N., Zittle, F.J.: Social presence as a predictor of satisfaction within a computer-mediated conferencing environment. Am. J. Dist. Educ. **11**(3), 8–26 (1997)

19. Harris, H., Bailenson, J.N., Nielsen, A., Yee, N.: The evolution of social behavior over time in second life. Presence: Teleoper. Virtual Environ. **18**(6), 434–448 (2009)

20. Hassanein, K., Head, M.: Manipulating perceived social presence through the web interface and its impact on attitude towards online shopping. Int. J. Hum. Comput. Stud. **65**(8), 689–708 (2007)

21. Hawkins, R.P., Kreuter, M., Resnicow, K., Fishbein, M., Dijkstra, A.: Understanding tailoring in communicating about health. Health Educ. Res. **23**(3), 454–466 (2008)

22. Heeter, C.: Being there: the subjective experience of presence. Presence: Teleoper. Virtual Environ. **1**(2), 262–271 (1992)

23. Heiderich, T.: Cinematography techniques: the different types of shots in film. Ontario Mining Assosiation (2012). https://www.oma.on.ca/en/contestpages/resources/free-report-cinematography.pdf

24. James, C.A., Haustein, K., Bednarz, T.P., Alem, L., Caris, C., Castleden, A.: Remote operation of mining equipment using panoramic display systems: exploring the sense of presence. Ergon. Open J. **4**(1) (2011)

25. Jeong, D.C., Feng, D., Krämer, N.C., Miller, L.C., Marsella, S.: Negative feedback in your face: examining the effects of proxemics and gender on learning. In: Beskow, J., Peters, C., Castellano, G., O'Sullivan, C., Leite, I., Kopp, S. (eds.) IVA 2017. LNCS (LNAI), vol. 10498, pp. 170–183. Springer, Cham (2017). https://doi.org/10.1007/978-3-319-67401-8_19

26. Jones, R.M., Devers, K.J., Kuzel, A.J., Woolf, S.H.: Patient-reported barriers to colorectal cancer screening: a mixed-methods analysis. Am. J. Prev. Med. **38**(5), 508–516 (2010)

27. LaVeist, T.A., Nuru-Jeter, A.: Is doctor-patient race concordance associated with greater satisfaction with care? J. Health Soc. Behav. 296–306 (2002)

28. Lisetti, C., Amini, R., Yasavur, U., Rishe, N.: I can help you change! An empathic virtual agent delivers behavior change health interventions. ACM TMIS **4**, 1–28 (2013)

29. Lombard, M., Ditton, T.: At the heart of it all: the concept of presence. J. Comput.-Mediat. Commun. **3**(2), JCMC321 (1997)

30. Lu, B., Fan, W., Zhou, M.: Social presence, trust, and social commerce purchase intention: an empirical research. Comput. Hum. Behav. **56**, 225–237 (2016)

31. Lucas, G.M., Gratch, J., King, A., Morency, L.P.: It's only a computer: virtual humans increase willingness to disclose. Comput. Hum. Behav. **37**, 94–100 (2014)

32. Mast, M.S., Hall, J.A., Roter, D.L.: Disentangling physician sex and physician communication style: their effects on patient satisfaction in a virtual medical visit. Patient Educ. Counsel. **68**, 16–22 (2007)

33. McCain, T.A., Divers, L.: The effect of body type and camera shot on interpersonal attraction and source credibility (1973)

34. McCain, T.A., Repensky, G.R.: The effect of camera shot on interpersonal attraction for comedy performers (1972)

35. Meeker, D., Cerully, J.L., Johnson, M., Iyer, N., Kurz, J., Scharf, D.M.: Simcoach evaluation: a virtual human intervention to encourage service-member help-seeking for posttraumatic stress disorder and depression. Rand Health Q. **5**(3) (2016)

36. Oh, C.S., Bailenson, J.N., Welch, G.F.: A systematic review of social presence: definition, antecedents, and implications. Front. Robot. AI **5**, 114 (2018)

37. Persky, S., Kaphingst, K.A., Allen, V.C., Jr., Senay, I.: Effects of patient-provider race concordance and smoking status on lung cancer risk perception accuracy among African-Americans. Ann. Behav. Med. **45**(3), 308–317 (2013)

38. Qiu, L., Benbasat, I.: A study of demographic embodiments of product recommendation agents in electronic commerce. Int. J. Hum. Comput. Stud. **68**(10), 669–688 (2010)

39. Rizzo, A.A., et al.: An intelligent virtual human system for providing healthcare information and support. Technical report, Madigan Army Medical Center, Tacoma WA (2011)

40. Short, J., Williams, E., Christie, B.: The Social Psychology of Telecommunications. Wiley, Hoboken (1976)

41. Skalski, P., Tamborini, R.: The role of social presence in interactive agent-based persuasion. Media Psychol. **10**(3), 385–413 (2007)

42. Skalski, P., Whitbred, R.: Image versus sound: a comparison of formal feature effects on presence and video game enjoyment. PsychNol. J. **8**(1) (2010)

43. Wandner, L.D., et al.: The impact of patients' gender, race, and age on health care professionals' pain management decisions: an online survey using virtual human technology. Int. J. Nurs. Stud. **51**(5), 726–733 (2014)

44. Wobbrock, J.O., Findlater, L., Gergle, D., Higgins, J.J.: The aligned rank transform for nonparametric factorial analyses using only ANOVA procedures. In: Proceedings of the SIGCHI Conference, pp. 143–146 (2011)
45. Zalake, M., Tavassoli, F., Griffin, L., Krieger, J., Lok, B.: Internet-based tailored virtual human health intervention to promote colorectal cancer screening: design guidelines from two user studies. In: Proceedings of the 19th ACM International Conference on Intelligent Virtual Agents, pp. 73–80 (2019)

The Design of Outpatient Services in Children's Hospitals Based on the Double Diamond Model

ZhiWei Zhou, Xi Han, and Tao Xi[✉]

Shanghai Jiao Tong University, Minhang District, Shanghai, China
torchx@sjtu.edu.cn

Abstract. With the opening of the two-child policy, the user base of children's hospitals continues to expand. However, in the service environment of children's hospitals, the service targets are not single; their direct users are children, but parents also play a key role. Therefore, this paper redesigns the children's hospital outpatient service system based on the service design process under the double diamond model in four stages: discover, define, develop and deliver. In this paper, we optimize both the service system and the service touchpoints. At the service system level, the design of the consultation app simplifies part of the consultation process and improves the consultation efficiency, thus saving parents' time and relieving children's anxiety; at the service touch point level, the use of a guide robot instead of a manual contact saves labor costs and optimizes the interaction form of the robot to improve children's consultation experience.

Keywords: Double diamond model · Service design · Children's hospital · Guide robot

1 Introduction

With the opening of the two-child policy, the children's medical industry is being paid more and more attention. As early as in the 2019 China New Pediatric Clinic Development Report, it has been suggested that 2020–2030 will be the "golden decade" with the largest number of potential customers and the largest market for the children's medical economy. The children's medical economy is not the same as traditional pediatric clinics, but refers to independent medical institutions with children as the main target group [1]. However, children are a special group with unique physiological and psychological characteristics, and their emotional perception of hospitals is different from that of adults. The long waiting time and fear of the unknown can cause children's experience of consultation to decrease. As far as children's medical institutions in China are concerned, most children's hospitals are still a subdivision of hospitals, providing "impersonal" mass-produced services [2]. A small number of private children's hospitals can realize the importance of children's consultation experience, and improve children's consultation experience through color and space layout changes from a visual perspective. However, few children's medical institutions will improve the user experience by optimizing the service system from the service design perspective.

V. G. Duffy (Ed.): HCII 2021, LNCS 12778, pp. 182–193, 2021.
https://doi.org/10.1007/978-3-030-77820-0_14

In order to improve the experience of children's medical care, this paper proposes a design solution for outpatient services in children's hospitals from two aspects: service systems and service touchpoints through the Double Diamond model theory combined with the service design approach.

2 Theoretical Research

2.1 Service Design Concept

With the advent of experience economy, more and more scholars are shifting their attention from product-based industry to service-based industry. As an emerging discipline, service design takes a broader approach to design research, requiring an understanding of service operators and social practices in addition to user context, and applying these insights to the development of evidence and interaction of service systems [3]. Shostach first introduced the design concept of combining tangible products with intangible services in 1984, i.e., service design emphasizes the creation of a better user experience by providing a quality service system from a system and process perspective through both intangible and tangible media [4]. Professor He Renke has pointed out that service design follows the development of the economic model, which focuses not only on the design of individual products but also on the design of integrated service systems [5].

2.2 Double Diamond Model Concept

In 2005, the British Design Council proposed a double dispersion-focused double diamond design model, called "The 'Double Diamond' Design Process Model". The Double Diamond Model is a process that allows for continuous exploration, testing, and iteration. The process is divided into two phases: discovering the right problem and discovering the right solution, with four steps of discover, define, develop, and deliver, as shown in Fig. 3. The entire model framework visualizes the transformation of design thinking into Divergent and Convergent during the design process, which confirms the idea that design is not a purely linear process [6, 7] (Fig. 1).

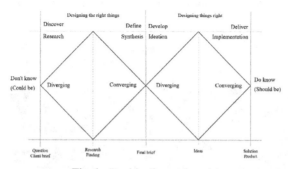

Fig. 1. Double diamond model

2.3 Service Design Process Under the Double Diamond Model

On the one hand, the reason is that service design is the design of a service system and the process is more complex, so thinking with this model helps to find the bridge between the problem and the solution [8]. On the other hand, the model can be used to get a comprehensive understanding of the needs of multiple users and get a reasonable solution [9].

For the research objectives in different stages of the double diamond design process, it is necessary to select the appropriate design methods to accomplish the expected results. For the content studied in this paper, the corresponding design methods and tools are organized based on the research phases of the double diamond model, as Table 1.

Table 1. The service design method based on double diamond model

Discover	Define	Develop	Deliver
User interviews	Persona	Brainstorming	Service system map
User tracking	Journey map	Business canvas	Business canvas
	Design outline		

3 Status Research

3.1 Discover

Children's Hospital Research. Stickdorn et al. put forward the basic principles about service design in the book "This is Service Design Thinking", clearly stating that most of the methods of service design are based on users' psychological activities and behavioral patterns, and that all designs should be built from the user's perspective and centered on user experience. In order to get a realistic picture of the current state of medical care in children's hospitals and to provide a reference base for subsequent service system improvements, a scenario study through field research and user research is a necessary

Fig. 2. Field research situation

prerequisite for service design research. This process is also the "discover" phase of the Double Diamond model.

The study investigated four children's medical institutions (pediatric clinics) in Wuhan, Hubei Province, China, all of which had a high volume of people and a noisy environment in common (as shown in Fig. 2).

Combined with the relevant literature, different questionnaires were designed for child patients and accompanying parents, and the research was conducted on the consultation environment, consultation process, consultation length, and consultation experience in turn. The following results (Fig. 3 and Fig. 4) were obtained by compiling data on the length of consultation and the feeling of consultation.

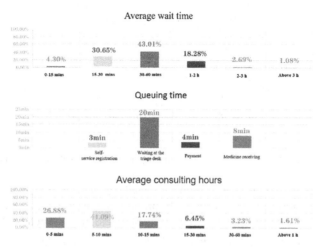

Fig. 3. Results of the pediatric patient visit length study

In the research data of waiting time and consultation length, it can be found that most patients' waiting time in the hospital (about 1 h) far exceeds the consultation time (5–10 min), and the waiting time at the triage desk accounts for the largest proportion of all waiting time. Research on the perception of the visit also reveals that more than 90% of both child patients and accompanying parents have negative feelings about the hospital. For instance, the children's ability to regulate their own emotions is weak, and they are extremely vulnerable to anxiety. For the accompanying parents, the complicated consultation process, the long waiting time and the child's anxiety make the accompanying parents also have a bad emotional experience.

Service System Status Research. *Stakeholders.* The stakeholders involved in this service system are divided into two parties: the service recipient (patient) and the service provider (hospital), whose responsibilities are shown in Fig. 5. The system serves both the child patient and the accompanying parent, both of whom go through the same service process and play similar roles in the broader context, but with some differences. Because of the special nature of children and their low cognitive ability, steps such as registration, payment, and finding a department are done by parents, so these links in

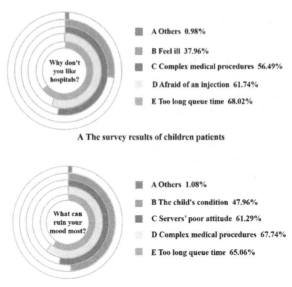

A Others 0.98%

B Feel ill 37.96%

C Complex medical procedures 56.49%

D Afraid of an injection 61.74%

E Too long queue time 68.02%

A The survey results of children patients

A Others 1.08%

B The child's condition 47.96%

C Servers' poor attitude 61.29%

D Complex medical procedures 67.74%

E Too long queue time 65.06%

B The survey results of parents escort

Fig. 4. Results of consultation experience

this service chain are accompanying parents in direct contact with the various service touchpoints.

Stakeholders on the provider side include medical staff, all guidance staff, online customer service staff, etc. The doctor, as the primary service provider, provides consultation services to the patient and offers treatment plans based on the condition. Customer service staff and guidance staff mainly provide operational guidance work to patients for different aspects of online and offline to help patients to have a smooth visit.

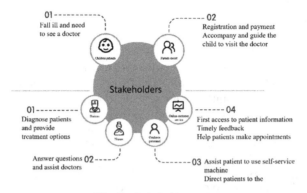

Fig. 5. Stakeholder map

Service Process. In the field research, we used the tracking research method to track the whole process of a patient's consultation, and combined with the user interviews, the paper summarized the complete outpatient consultation process, including inquiry, reservation, going to the hospital, queuing, registration, going to the department, waiting for consultation at the triage, consultation and other stages, and sorted out the corresponding location of each stage and the service demand when the location is switched (Fig. 6).

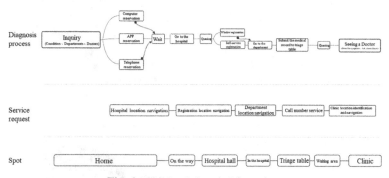

Fig. 6. Children's hospital flow chart

Service Touchpoint. There are three major categories of touchpoints in service design: physical touchpoints, digital touchpoints, and human touchpoints. Each of them plays a vital role in the service process and is an important indicator of the service experience. The service touch points of the system can be summarized from the above summarized visit service flow, as shown in the Table 2.

Table 2. Service touchpoints in hospital service system

Physical touchpoints	Digital touchpoints	Human touchpoints
Signs, cases, screens, call-in announcements, printed materials (receipts, flyers, etc.)	(Patient) cell phone or computer, autonomous service terminal, (hospital) computer	Online customer service, billing staff, guidance staff, doctors, nurses, patients (as a service vehicle to provide information to medical staff)

3.2 Define

The second phase of the double diamond model is to define the problem to be explored. Real data from the hospital and patient side have been obtained through the discover phase above, and through the generalization and organization of these data, further analysis is carried out to identify the problems in the design.

Persona

Through user research feedback, set up virtual persona, using the persona method, comprehensive target user characteristics and attributes, as shown in the Fig. 7.

Fig. 7. Personas

According to the personas, it can be found that the basic need of users in the children's hospital outpatient environment is medical consultation, and there are many links in the completion of this service, which can be divided into two parts: online and offline. The degree of connection between these two parts determines the user's experience of the consultation demand.

Journey Map

Using the journey map can more clearly discover the user's emotional changes throughout the service process, which helps us identify pain points.

As can be seen in Fig. 8, the emotional changes of the child patients and the accompanying parents during the consultation session are different. Therefore, the emotional needs of both are different. For example, the emotional turmoil of child patients during the consultation process lies in the fear of the treatment process and the anxiety of waiting for the consultation process, but they do not have too much need for the whole process to be connected and progressed. For parents, they are more sensitive to the emotional expression of "waiting" and "queuing". Therefore, they are more concerned about the progress of each step of the process, and their anxiety is reflected in three areas: the emotional changes of the child, the long waiting time, and the unknown steps of the consultation.

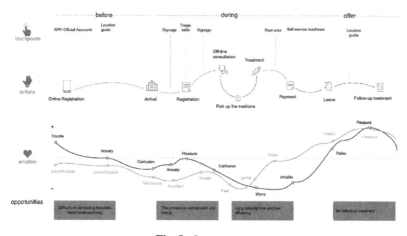

Fig. 8. Journey map

Through the discover phase and the above design approach, the following pain points can be summarized:

1. Waiting time is not proportional to consultation time.
2. Negative emotions in children increase time of consultation.
3. Different direct users at variable steps of the consultation process.

4 Design Results

4.1 Develop

Based on the above pain points, this paper proposes three areas of optimization for the outpatient service system of children's hospitals: (1) Improve the efficiency of consultation by streamlining the service process. (2) Optimize the degree of articulation of the consultation process so that there is no disconnection between the online and offline consultation steps. (3) Through the means of emotional design, optimize the interaction form of service touchpoints and users to improve user experience.

4.2 Deliver

Service System
In the service system design of the children's hospital, O2O's service model is used to realize online APP appointment registration, electronic medical record, condition monitoring and offline 1v1 consultation experience through the information transmission of the Internet. The entire service system composition is shown in Fig. 9.

APP Design
In order to improve efficiency and reduce unnecessary queuing time during consultation, the service system includes an App that matches doctors in advance for an initial

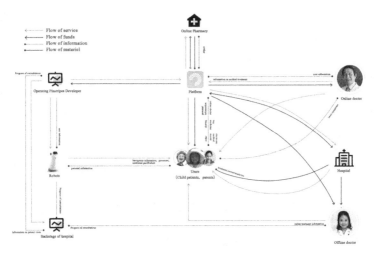

Fig. 9. Service system

diagnosis; automatic scheduling to estimate waiting times and reminders for departure as well as online one-click billing.

Considering the direct users of the app are parents of children, the design of the app's interface is simple and clear, filtering out unnecessary information so that parents can quickly access important information (Fig. 10).

Fig. 10. Interface design

Guided Robot Design

In this design solution, a service robot (Fig. 11) is used to replace part of the manual touchpoints, which saves human resources and at the same time allows the robot to soothe the children's negative emotions by emotional interaction, so that the children can have a better emotional experience during the consultation process.

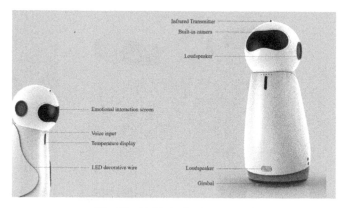

Fig. 11. Guided robot's structure

Function Introduction

1. Consultation guidance. The robot can replace lobby attendants, operation instructors, and triage desk guides for location navigation, voice reminders, and face recognition to read medical records. It can save excess labor resources, make the consultation process easier and faster, and facilitate user access.
2. Infrared temperature measurement. Using infrared technology to measure the forehead temperature, the basic temperature measurement can be completed before entering the consultation room, saving the consultation time and improving the efficiency of the doctor's consultation.

Emotional Interaction Design

Typically, robots interact with users in both visual and auditory terms. However, during childhood, the most direct way people receive information from the outside world is through their own perception, which is generated through each sense [10]. Therefore, the

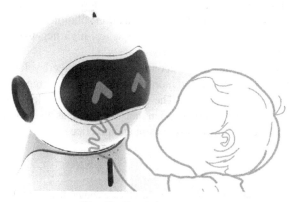

Fig. 12. Touch interaction

Fig. 13. Morphological changes

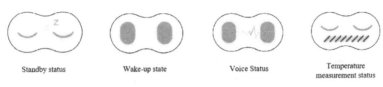

Standby status   Wake-up state   Voice Status   Temperature measurement status

Fig. 14. Emotional interaction

guide robot designed in this paper can interact with the users through interactive behaviors in terms of voice interaction (auditory), touch-based interaction (haptic, Fig. 12), morphological changes (visual, Fig. 13), and expression changes (visual, Fig. 14), so that children can interact with the robot during the consultation process to soothe their emotions and enhance their experience.

5   Conclusion

In this paper, we use the research methodology of the Double Diamond Model to optimize the design of outpatient services for children's hospitals from the perspective of service design. Through four phases of discover, define, develop and deliver, existing problems in children's hospitals are identified and optimization solutions are derived. This paper proposes a solution to the problems of long queues, high negative emotions among children, and differences in service targets.

In the future, children's healthcare economy will be further developed and intelligent public services will become more and more popular. Service design as a design tool can better improve the user's experience. The combination of double diamond model and service design also helps designers broaden their design ideas and better tap into design pain points, which is worth further discussion and practice.

References

1. Cn-healthcare Homepage. https://www.cn-healthcare.com/articlewm/20191014/content-107 2571.html. Accessed 14 Oct 2019

2. Yang, L.: Research on the optimal design of medical appointment registration system based on service design theory. Southeast University (2018)
3. Evenson, S.: A designer's view of SSME. In: Hefley, B., Murphy, W. (eds.) Service Science, Management and Engineering Education for the 21st Century, pp. 25–30. Springer, Boston (2008). https://doi.org/10.1007/978-0-387-76578-5_4
4. Shostack, G.L.: Designing services that deliver. Harv. Bus. Rev. **62**(1), 133–139 (1984)
5. He, R., Hu, Y.: Research on the design patterns and strategies of service design concept derivation stage. Design **01**, 40–49 (2015)
6. Design Council. Eleven lessons: managing design in eleven global companies, desk research report. Engineering **44**, 18 (2007)
7. Chen, G.D., Pan, R., Chen, S.Y., Wang, J.: Product design of Liangzhu ancient culture based on improved double diamond design model. Packag. Eng. **40**(12), 242–248 (2019)
8. Dubberly, H., Evenson, S., Robinson, R.: The analysis-synthesis bridge model. Interactions **15**(2), 57–61 (2008)
9. Patrício, L., Fisk, R.P., Cunha, J.F.E., et al.: Multilevel service design: from customer value constellation to service experience blueprinting. J. Serv. Res. **14**(2), 180–200 (2011)
10. Fang, Y.: Exploration of contemporary children's hospital design based on perceptual care. China Hospit. Archit. Equip. **21**(07), 59–61 (2020)

Artificial Intelligence Applications and Ethical Issues

Brown Hands Aren't Terrorists: Challenges in Image Classification of Violent Extremist Content

Margeret Hall[(✉)] and Christian Haas

University of Nebraska at Omaha, Omaha 68182, USA
{mahall,christianhaas}@unomaha.edu

Abstract. The Internet eases the broadcasting of data, information, and propaganda. The availability of myriad social media has turned the spotlight on violent extremism and expanded the scope and impact of ideology-oriented acts of violence. Automated image classification for this content is a highly sought-after goal, yet raises the question of potential bias and discrimination in case of incorrect classification. A requirement for addressing, and potentially counter-acting, bias, is the existence of a reliable training dataset. To demonstrate how such a dataset can be developed for highly sensitive topics, this article operationalizes the process of human-coding images posted on the open social web by violent religious extremists into four master categories and four subcategories. We concentrate on the group ISIS due to their prolific digital content creation. The developed training dataset is used to train a convolutional neural network to automatically detect extremist visual content on social media and determine its category. Using inter-coder reliability, we show that the training data can be reliably coded despite highly nuanced data and the existence of various categories and subcategories.

Keywords: Social media · Mixed methods · Algorithmic bias · Image processing · Violent extremist organizations

1 Introduction

Visual digital propaganda is voluminous and growing. The volume is well beyond the ability of humans to manually treat and make tracible decisions upon at a per-content item level. Due to the closed nature of the various social platforms, the specific attributes of images and content which are removed due to Terms of Service violations is currently unknown.[1] This is problematic on several points. The lack of visibility creates knowledge gaps in the evolution of propaganda-related research. The research community is also unable to evaluate the degree to which the algorithmic treatment of propaganda suffers from bias in its modelling of data and classifications. Bias, for example, can arise if

---

[1] Generalized descriptions of removable/censor-provoking content is available in the Terms of Service sections of the platforms, see for example Facebook's Community Standards Enforcement page: https://govtrequests.facebook.com/community-standards-enforcement.

© Springer Nature Switzerland AG 2021
V. G. Duffy (Ed.): HCII 2021, LNCS 12778, pp. 197–207, 2021.
https://doi.org/10.1007/978-3-030-77820-0_15

misclassification rates are higher for certain 'sensitive' characteristics such as ethnicity, skin color, or gender.

This manuscript details the process of qualitatively coding visual terror propaganda for use in computer vision scenarios where potential bias can be particularly harmful. Two trends have converged forming the research imperative. One is the increasing use of the internet to broadcast and recruit to fringe ideologies [1]. Particular to the case of terror groups, the often violent and sometimes illegal content is generally outside of the bounds of terms and conditions of various platforms which can be used to post and host [2]. The other trend is increasing realization worldwide of the dangers associated with non-tracible biased algorithms [3, 4].

1.1 Challenges Associated with Coding Violent Extremist Content

From both the perspectives of content generation and research, the next frontier of social media is in visual media [5]. Image processing has been employed recently to combat human trafficking [6] and child pornography [7] but has yet to be trained and tested on radical, violent extremist organization (VEO) content. The attributes of (and intentions behind) gang or human trafficking content and VEO content on online social media (OSM) are vastly different. A particularly acute need for computational image analysis exists as in spite of the voluminous (and growing) quantity of visual data available, the impact of such propaganda remains poorly understood [8]. Due to the particularly disturbing context of violent extremism, an automated image tagging algorithm is a broadly desirable goal [9, 10]. At a time of increasing awareness of the causes of algorithmic bias, research teams must be exceedingly careful in curating training data [11]. While it is desirable to (automatedly) tag images of the Islamic State (ISIS) actively engaging in propaganda as potentially sensitive content, it is not desirable to tag any image of a Muslim going about their daily life in the same way (see i.e., Fig. 1). Likewise, even as ISIS co-opts imagery and symbolism from Islam, an outcome where any and all Islamic images are classified as potentially sensitive content is inappropriate. Tightly linked to the challenge is the normative commentary that one person's terrorist is another person's freedom fighter. In scenarios where humans do not agree, computers are hardly expected to classify content well.

The widespread application of Machine Learning (ML) techniques for automated decision making also incurs an increased risk of potential negative effects on people affected by such decisions. Various studies in criminal justice [12], image classification and computer vision [13], automated hiring recommendations [14], healthcare budgets [15], and natural language processing [16] show that predictions from algorithms can lead to significant discrimination against certain groups. In the previous examples, the predictions created by algorithms exhibited biases based on Race, Gender, or a combination of both.

While the sources of biases can be manifold and not restricted to the data itself, making sure that training data is reliable and not inherently biased itself is the goal of a subset of approaches in Algorithmic Fairness [17]. Due to the potentially serious ramifications of being tagged a potential terrorist in automated image classification, a methodology that creates reliable, unbiased training data as a ground truth that the algorithms can use is of utmost importance. Furthermore, potential bias in algorithmic decision making is often measured through various fairness metrics that are themselves calculated based on the training data, reinforcing the need for reliable data.

A required first step and the challenge this work addresses is mitigation via qualitatively defining the attributes of VEO propaganda. The specific research challenge addressed in here is reliably and validly coding VEO images such that an image processing algorithm would have good performance (reliability), without replicating bias against Muslims and Islamic imagery. The HCI contribution follows Oulasvirta and Hornbæk's taxonomy of constructive problem-solving [18]; the companion article evaluating computational performance is: [10].

2 Approach

Our proprietary database houses 1.5 million images swept from ISIS-linked OSM accounts and web pages since August 2015 (see [2, 10]). We create the training data by manually classifying a subset of these images (n = 95,242). The manual classification is performed by an interdisciplinary team of two undergraduate students with expertise in computer science and international law and one postdoctoral researcher, overseen by one faculty advisor, each with 20–40 h of manual coding training [19]. The team was comprised of 50% Muslims and one Arabic speaker in case disambiguation between image and text was required. The project team concentrated on the depiction of the image and nor corresponding text. While the nuance level is higher and thus more difficult to find agreement on, the aim and scope of the project was to concentrate on visual propaganda.

Our work concentrates on VEO propaganda: "a systematic form of purposeful persuasion that attempts to influence the emotions, attitudes, opinions, and actions of specified target audiences for ideological, political or commercial purposes through the controlled transmission of one-sided messages (which may or may not be factual) via mass and direct media channels [20]". When coding images, two main questions are asked: what is the intent and focus of the image, and does the image contain attributable markings to ISIS or other VEOs.

We model the method of establishing coder agreement upon Bolognesi and colleagues [21] due to the similarity in coding images and other semantically rich data. The training data is used to train the algorithm to automatically detect VEO propaganda on Web and OSM and classify it by category.

The overall goal of the project is to improve social media content monitoring and to create an artificial intelligence that could surveil social media without infringing on the rights of Muslim individuals. This would provide researchers valuable data on posts with VEO propaganda, give valuable military insights, and provide (counter)narrative context inside ISIS-controlled regions. Moreover, as deep learning and artificial neural network technology become more advanced, the creation and training of such programs becomes easier. The initial manual classification of these of images supports the trained algorithm to automatically categorize images more quickly and efficiently, as well as helping reduce potential bias if the classification in the training data is reliable. A greater and more accurate understanding of attributable propaganda will also hopefully reduce inappropriate automated censorship on social media platforms. The subsequent steps include deploying convolutional neural networks (CNNs), which are appropriate for computer vision tasks and which have become a common benchmark algorithm. The model of choice is AlexNet, a specific architecture of CNN consisting of 5 convolutional layers and 3 fully connected layers [10, 22].

Fig. 1. Sharing religious materials with fighters in the Kurdish-held Kirkuk region. The black caption bar and black square logo with the territory name at the bottom right typify images which are released by ISIS's official media services. Images depicting arms but no faces or other identifying markers are commonly used to display daily activities as a form of normalization of ISIS rule. Are these the hands of terrorists?

3   Categorizing Violent Extremist Propaganda

The project team worked over a calendar year to code the data. Students processed between 4,000–5,000 images per week. The variance has a strong correlation to the number of violent images in the set; images depicting violence are often immediately obvious and can be sorted within seconds, without need for close inspection. Due to the sometime graphic nature of the data and its weighty subject matter, then entire team had access to free mental health services via the university's counseling office and were given mandated vacation time periodically throughout the year to enforce disengagement with the content.

Hard, Soft, Symbolic, and None were the initial categories used, but throughout the process it became evident that many images were important but conceptually different than the four initial groups. These are included as Training Materials, Landscapes, Official Communications, and non-ISIS groups. Table 1 lists the final categories used, any subcategories, and the number of images in each.

Hard. This category intends to show the coercive strength of the group through violence and weapon capabilities. More than just images of weapons, this category includes the aftermath of attacks, punishments such as people being tied to posts with signs around their necks, whipping or stoning, as well as extreme blood and limb loss are categorized here. Examples of hard content include: dead bodies, severed body parts, or blood; weapons; modified vehicles; people being punished; rocket/missile being prepared and launching; destruction clearly caused by warfare (bombs, guns, etc.); men wearing all black standing over figures in orange jumpsuits; executions; masked men giving speeches; militants training. We do not include sample images of hard propaganda due to its potentially disturbing nature.

Fig. 2. An unattributed soft propaganda image of a militant holding a kitten. Fighters typically wear confiscated fatigues or drabs whereas officials dress in all black.

Soft. This category is intended to show the social perks and culture of the group, as well as how people enjoy their involvement within the group. Agriculture and civilians receiving regular medical care are classified here. Martyrdom images are also considered to be soft propaganda, despite occasional present of battlefield aspects in the image as weapons are not the focus of the image. Interactions such as traffic stops are considered soft even when weapons are present if the weapons are in a passive position. Other typical examples of soft propaganda published by ISIS include young children happy and smiling (but not child soldiers); goods being sold; pamphlets being shared among people; civilians at a mosque; martyrs; an Imam giving khutbah (sermon) to his congregation; a muezzin calling people to prayer, or groups of people praying; distribution of zakat (Fig. 2).

Fig. 3. A sample symbolic image of a presumed ISIS fighter holding up the One Finger and an ISIS flag. Symbolic Non-ISIS includes images that are clearly symbolic but are not attributable to ISIS.

Symbolic. This category shows easily identifiable symbols and imagery related to the group are often intend to idealize the group and mission as well as recruiting new members. We make distinct the acts of communally praying (soft) and co-opted iconography of Islam (symbolic). The One finger is a symbol from the Islamic community as a whole but has been co-opted by ISIS as a victory signifier, thus is classified as symbolic when present. Common symbolic content includes the One Finger (Fig. 3); lions; the Quran; children or militants studying the Quran; militants praying.

None. This category is broad as it contains any content that does not fall into the previously mentioned criteria. Although there may be elements that are hard or symbolic, images where the focus of the image may be on large amounts of text or represent many contrasting categories are classified here. In Hashemi and Hall [10] None is separated into two categories, None ISIS and None Irrelevant to separate images that are attributable and those that are not. Typical images may include a dusty road with no people or cars on it; a picture of a small, far off helicopter with no identifying markings; graffiti on a wall; half chopped down trees; professional, regular military forces; logos.

None is distinct from *Useless* as a category. Useless refers to banner ads which are included in the data, or other items which were encoded as images and scraped but are not actually part of the content (page icons, assets).

General Training Materials. This category includes images that are intended as jihadist training material or instructions for contacting recruiters, as shown in Fig. 4. It may include instructions on proxies and VPNs, manuals for lone wolf attacks, and instructions for secure communication (Fig. 4). The category was subsumed into Official Communications in the second round of coding.

Landscapes. This category includes images that depict landscapes as well as flowers and fauna that can be attributed to ISIS. Landscapes can be urban or natural and are presumably intended to inspire warm feelings about the quality of life under the Caliphate. Figure 4 also partially depicts an idealized landscape. It was added as a subcategory in the second round of coding.

Fig. 4. Example of a training image where the user is taught to register for secured communications (left) overlaid with an idealized landscape (right).

Official Communications. This category includes official ISIS communications. Two types of communications are included: ISIS magazine covers, and communiques which follow a specific format and design and include the logo of the group. Communiques from other groups are not included here (Fig. 5).

Fig. 5. Example of a communique; text and image purposefully blurred. The red banner on blue background with a logo watermark is typical of the official media arm of ISIS. (Color figure online)

Non-ISIS Groups. When images are able to be attributed to other violent extremist organizations, they are categorized in their own categories regardless of the above categories. The main representation of other groups in the data are:

- Al Kataib (Al-Shabaab) is an Al-Qaeda affiliated rebel group in Somalia.
- Al-Qaeda is a well known organization with many affiliates in other countries. Their Iraq affiliate would later become ISIS.
- Ansar al-Sharia is an ISIS affiliated group in Libya and Yemen.
- Islamic Front (Syria) consists of different groups that merged and have one common media logo attached to individual groups' logos.

4 Evaluation of Approach

Following [21] we employ Cohen's κ to evaluate the agreement between coders. Table 1 contains each of the eight categories (4 main, 4 subcategories) and the cross tabulation of each category. Cohen's κ = 0.857 for two raters over 95,242 images (z = 486, p = 0.000). This is considered in the range of 'very good' or 'almost perfect agreement' [23].

Due to differences driven by the inclusion or exclusion of the two categories "Flags of ISIS" and "Training Materials" Fleiss' κ is also evaluated, as Fleiss' calculation is considered robust to raters coding different items (Table 2). Also allows for a by-class statistical evaluation (Table 3). The test statistics between the two calculations are nearly identical, which is to be expected as Fleiss κ is widely considered an extension of Cohen's κ.

The high agreement level between raters is largely driven by agreement in Hard Propaganda. This is likely due to the unambiguous nature of the violent and warlike imagery. Categories which are more ambiguous, i.e., Soft and Symbolic propaganda, have lower (though still meritorious) inter-rate agreement. We take note of the low inter-rater agreement of Non-ISIS groups. The low agreement is likely driven by the fact that the dataset precedes the development of ISIS as a stand-alone group. While the group was developing and professionalizing its own brand parts of other groups insignia remained present in the content.

Table 1. Image classes and cross tabulations displaying agreement/disagreement between coders. Agreed classified images are **bolded**. A disagreement between Coding rounds 1 and 2 exists in the categories "Flags" and "Training Materials" shows that these two are to be considered unreliable in their context.

Second round classification

First round classification		Training materials	Hard	Non ISIS	None	Communications	Soft	Symbolic	Useless	
	Flags of Isis	**0**	0	0	36	0	0	0	0	36
	Hard propaganda	0	**35511**	268	723	13	96	40	0	36651
	Non ISIS groups	0	17	**1291**	31	0	4	6	2	1351
	None	452	520	586	**18522**	946	242	102	76	21446
	Official communications	0	0	1	23	**4411**	0	0	0	4435
	Soft propaganda	0	123	739	4392	1	**4163**	40	0	9458
	Symbolic propaganda	0	193	10	134	4	249	**933**	0	1523
	Useless	0	6	4	18	0	6	1	**20307**	20342
Total		452	36370	2899	23879	5375	4760	1122	20385	95242

Table 2. Evaluation metrics of Fleiss κ

	Kappa	Asymptotic			Asymptotic 95% confidence interval	
		Standard error	z	Sig.	Lower bound	Upper bound
Overall agreement	0.857	0.002	483.591	0.000	0.854	0.860

Of the main categories, only Soft Propaganda has an agreement level below 'Substantial.' While overall pleased with our results, we identify the weakness of the Soft Propaganda inter-rater agreement as an area of future work and a major limitation. The weakness of this category leads to the real-life change of misclassification if such a schema were to be employed in a real-life scenario [10]. Soft Propaganda is large class of every day, and highly stylized, 'influencer'-style content; we suspect that category refinement would improve the results.

Table 3. Evaluation of rater agreement on individual categories

Rating category	Conditional probability	Kappa	Asymptotic			Asymptotic 95% confidence interval	
			Standard error	z	Sig.	Lower bound	Upper bound
Flags of Isis	0.000	0.000	0.003	−0.058	0.953	−0.007	0.006
General training materials	0.000	−0.002	0.003	−0.734	0.463	−0.009	0.004
Hard propaganda	0.973	0.956	0.003	294.913	0.000	0.949	0.962
Non ISIS groups	0.608	0.599	0.003	184.727	0.000	0.592	0.605
None	0.817	0.760	0.003	234.623	0.000	0.754	0.767
Official communications	0.899	0.894	0.003	275.844	0.000	0.887	0.900
Soft propaganda	0.586	0.552	0.003	170.407	0.000	0.546	0.559
Symbolic propaganda	0.705	0.701	0.003	216.441	0.000	0.695	0.708
Useless	0.997	0.996	0.003	307.524	0.000	0.990	1.003

a. Sample data contains 95242 effective subjects and 2 raters.

5 Summary and Future Work

The extreme nature and volume of visual digital propaganda makes its treatment a foremost task for researchers and practitioners. Reliably coding VEO images is a necessary first step in larger-scale applications of automated image classification. This article introduces and serves as a methods companion for works attempting to inject qualitative methods and meaning into applied computer vision and machine learning tasks (i.e., [2, 10]). The research team first defined four overarching themes present in digital VEO propaganda, recursively adding four additional themes during the course of the coding efforts. In the definition phases of the project care was taken to create thematic schema that would not replicate bias against Muslims and Islam when deployed in live systems. The identified themes and their allocated images have generally high inter-coder reliability, which gives a strong basis for future computational pattern analyses and prediction tasks.

While the easiest of the coding tasks are quickly resolved both by human and machines (i.e., hard propaganda and impertinent items like page assets), the disagreement level on the most nuanced (thus difficult and important) items is still too high. A broader conversation around a better and more unified understanding of visual terror propaganda is necessary to achieve the explainability level required for wide-scale deployment of machine-forward regimes like automated classification and removal of content. Additionally, further bias mitigation steps in the general image classification pipeline should be considered due to the high negative impact of misclassifications in this scenario.

This article reports on the process of qualitatively understanding and coding visual terror propaganda. The four main categories may apply to other use cases, but are likely to require tailoring if applied to other VEO groups such as far left or far right groups. Given the centrality of public digital social platforms in the current rise of far-right groups as well as the fluency in which these groups communication in imagery, future work should concentrate on fine-tuning the categories for this use case.

References

1. Ligon, G.S., Hall, M., Braun, C.: Digital participation roles of the global jihad: social media's role in bringing together vulnerable individuals and VEO content. In: Nah, F.F.-H., Xiao, B.S. (eds.) HCIBGO 2018. LNCS, vol. 10923, pp. 485–495. Springer, Cham (2018). https://doi.org/10.1007/978-3-319-91716-0_39

2. Hall, M., Logan, M., Ligon, G.S., Derrick, D.C.: Do machines replicate humans? Toward a unified understanding of radicalizing content on the open social web. Policy Internet 12(1) (2020). https://doi.org/10.1002/poi3.223

3. Bradshaw, S.: Disinformation optimised: gaming search engine algorithms to amplify junk news. Internet Policy Rev. 8(4), 1–24 (2019). https://doi.org/10.14763/2019.4.1442

4. De-Arteaga, M., Fogliato, R., Chouldechova, A.: A case for humans-in-the-loop: decisions in the presence of erroneous algorithmic scores. In: Conference Human Factors Computing System – Proceedings (2020). https://doi.org/10.1145/3313831.3376638

5. Hall, M., Mazarakis, A., Chorley, M.J., Caton, S.: Editorial of the special issue on following user pathways: key contributions and future directions in cross-platform social media research. Int. J. Hum. Comput. Interact. 34(10), 895–912 (2018). https://doi.org/10.1080/10447318.2018.1471575

6. Dubrawski, A., Miller, K., Barnes, M., Boecking, B., Kennedy, E.: Leveraging publicly available data to discern patterns of human-trafficking activity. J. Hum. Traffick. 1(1), 65–85 (2015). https://doi.org/10.1080/23322705.2015.1015342

7. Ulges, A., Stahl, A.: Automatic detection of child pornography using color visual words. In: 2011 IEEE International Conference on Multimedia and Expo, pp. 1–6 (2011). https://doi.org/10.1109/ICME.2011.6011977

8. Wendlandt, L., Mihalcea, R., Boyd, R.L., Pennebaker, J.W.: Multimodal analysis and prediction of latent user dimensions. In: Ciampaglia, G.L., Mashhadi, A., Yasseri, T. (eds.) SocInfo 2017. LNCS, vol. 10539, pp. 323–340. Springer, Cham (2017). https://doi.org/10.1007/978-3-319-67217-5_20

9. Hashemi, M., Hall, M.: Identifying the responsible group for extreme acts of violence through pattern recognition. In: Nah, F.H., Xiao, B. (eds.) HCI in Business, Government, and Organizations. HCIBGO 2018. Lecture Notes in Computer Science, vol. 10923, pp. 594–605. Springer, Cham (2018). https://doi.org/10.1007/978-3-319-91716-0_47

10. Hashemi, M., Hall, M.: Detecting and classifying online dark visual propaganda. Image Vis. Comput. 89, 95–105 (2019). https://doi.org/10.1016/j.imavis.2019.06.001

11. Dowthwaite, L., Seth, S.: IEEE P7003 TM Standard for Algorithmic Bias Considerations. In: 2018 IEEE/ACM International Workshop on Software Fairness (FairWare), pp. 38–41 (2018)

12. Dressel, J., Farid, H.: The accuracy, fairness, and limits of predicting recidivism. Sci. Adv. 4(1), eaao5580 (2018)

13. Khosla, A., Zhou, T., Malisiewicz, T., Efros, A.A., Torralba, A.: Undoing the damage of dataset bias. In: Fitzgibbon, A., Lazebnik, S., Perona, P., Sato, Y., Schmid, C. (eds.) ECCV 2012. LNCS, vol. 7572, pp. 158–171. Springer, Heidelberg (2012). https://doi.org/10.1007/978-3-642-33718-5_12

14. Raghavan, M., Barocas, S., Kleinberg, J., Levy, K.: Mitigating bias in algorithmic hiring: evaluating claims and practices (2020)

15. Obermeyer, Z., Powers, B., Vogeli, C., Mullainathan, S.: Dissecting racial bias in an algorithm used to manage the health of populations. Science (80-.) **366**(6464), 447–453 (2019). https://doi.org/10.1126/science.aax2342

16. Caliskan, A., Bryson, J.J., Narayanan, A.: Semantics derived automatically from language corpora contain human-like biases. Science (80-.) **356**(6334), 183–186 (2017). https://doi.org/10.1126/science.aal4230

17. Caton, S., Haas, C.: Fairness in machine learning: a survey. arXiv, October 2020

18. Oulasvirta, A., Hornbæk, K.: HCI research as problem-solving. In: ACM Conference on Human Factors in Computing Systems, CHI 2016, pp. 4956–4967 (2016). https://doi.org/10.1145/2858036.2858283

19. Derrick, D.C., Ligon, G.S., Harms, M., Mahoney, W.: Cyber-sophistication assessment methodology for public-facing terrorist web sites. J. Inf. Warf. **16**(1), 13–30 (2017)

20. Nelson, R.: A Chronology and glossary of propaganda in the United States, Annotated (1996)

21. Bolognesi, M., Pilgram, R., van den Heerik, R.: Reliability in content analysis: the case of semantic feature norms classification. Behav. Res. Methods **49**(6), 1984–2001 (2016). https://doi.org/10.3758/s13428-016-0838-6

22. Alom, Z., et al.: The history began from AlexNet: a comprehensive survey on deep learning approaches (2018). https://doi.org/10.1016/S0011-9164(00)80105-8

23. Muñoz, S.R., Bangdiwala, S.I.: Interpretation of Kappa and B statistics measures of agreement. J. Appl. Stat. **24**(1), 105–112 (1997). https://doi.org/10.1080/02664769723918

A Bibliometric Analysis of Intelligent Agent Researches During 2010–2020 Based on VOS Viewer

Yu Liu, Yaqin Cao[⊠], Yi Ding, and Yun Zhang

School of Economics and Management, Anhui Polytechnic
University, Wuhu, People's Republic of China

Abstract. This paper is aimed uses VOS viewer to evaluate the history, current and future of publications regarding intelligent agent. Intelligent agents are sometimes called bot, short for robot. With the rapid development of communication technology and network information technology, the characteristics and functions of intelligent agent technology have been constantly expanded. In the paper, VOS viewer was used to identify and summarise the publicaitons of intelligent agent researches in Web of science from 2010 to 2020. Publication source, publication organization, authors, country, citation of articles, citation of country and organization were recorded and analyzed. Bibliometric maps of authorship, citation, co-citation and network of co-occurrence of keywords were drawn. 7378 articles and 10792 cited references were analysed. Nowadays, intelligent agent was mainly used in the research and development of intelligent search agent, digital library, e-commerce and distance education. As for researchers and practitioners, this paper suggests an analysis of integrated visualization in terms of the knowledge and innovation based on the area of Intelligent agent or virtual agent.

Keywords: Intelligent agent · Virtual agent · Bibliometric · Vos viewer

1 Introduction

Nowadays, intelligent agent has been widely used in the research and development of intelligent search agent, digital library, e-commerce and distance education. Some agents can also personalize information on the site based on registration information and usage analysis. Other types of agents include spot monitoring, waiting for websites to update or find other things, and analytics agents not only collect information, but also organize and provide information for you [1]. In Wan JF's article in 2016, intelligent factory is proposed to realize flexible and reconfigurable manufacturing system and classify intelligent objects into different types of agents.we provide a classification of the smart objects into various types of agents and define a coordinator in the cloud. The autonomous decision and distributed cooperation between agents lead to high flexibility [Wan JF, 2016]. Hayers Roth of Stanford University believes that "intelligent agents continuously perform three functions: perceiving dynamic conditions in the environment, Execution affects the environment, Reasoning to interpret sensory information, solving problems,

© Springer Nature Switzerland AG 2021
V. G. Duffy (Ed.): HCII 2021, LNCS 12778, pp. 208–219, 2021.
https://doi.org/10.1007/978-3-030-77820-0_16

generating reasoning and determining actions." In his opinion, agents should reason and plan in the process of action selection. In general, intelligent agents in a broad sense include humans, mobile robots in the physical world, and software robots in the information world. In the narrow sense, intelligent agent refers to the software robot in the information world. It is a mobile computing entity that performs a group of operations in the way of active service on behalf of users or other programs [2]. Active service includes active adaptability and active agent. In a word, an intelligent agent is a program that collects information or provides other related services. It can perform the required functions on time without the need for immediate human intervention. Intelligent Agent is a dynamic distributed directory service, which provides the functions used by both the client and the server. The intelligent agent must be started on at least one host in the local network. When a client invokes the bind method of an object, it automatically queries the intelligent agent and the intelligent agent looks up the specified implementation, thereby establishing a connection between the client and the implementation. Communication with the intelligent agent is completely transparent to the client program. If the POA has the persistent policy set and uses the Activate object with ID method, the smart agent registers the object or implementation so that it can be used by the client, and when the object or implementation is frozen, the smart agent removes it from the list of available objects. Like the client program, the communication with the intelligent agent is completely transparent to the object implementation [3]. With the rapid development of communication technology and network information technology, the characteristics and functions of intelligent agent technology have been constantly expanded, and it is mainly used in the research and development of intelligent search agent, digital library, e-commerce and distance education.

Today, intelligent agents have come into my life, integrated into every aspect of our lives. An intelligent agent is a set of software that assists and acts as their representative. People can conduct online transactions with the help of an intelligent agent. People can obtain a lot of information through intelligent agents, and through real-time access to information, we can more accurately and clearly accomplish the established goals. An intelligent agent can be thought of as using sensors to sense the environment and using effectors to act on any entity in the environment.

The general intelligent agent has the following four characteristics: agent, intelligence, mobility and individuation. First of foremost, Agent rationality mainly refers to the autonomous and coordinated working ability of the intelligent agent. It is manifested as the degree of automation of the intelligent agent's behavior, that is, the operation behavior can leave the intervention of human or agent program. But agents in their systems must be controlled by operational behavior, and when other agents make a request, only the agents themselves can decide whether to accept or reject the request [4]. Secondly, Intelligence refers to the reasoning and learning ability of an agent. It describes the ability of an intelligent agent to accept the user's target instructions and complete tasks on behalf of the user, such as understanding the user's demand for information resources and computing resources expressed in natural language. Help users to overcome the language barrier of information content to a certain extent, and capture users' preferences and interests. Presuming the user's purpose and acting for them, etc. Then,

Mobility refers to the ability of an intelligent agent to migrate between networks. Operational tasks and processes can be run from one computer to another. When necessary, intelligent agents can communicate with other agents and people, and they can all carry out their own operations and help other agents and people. Lastly, Mobility refers to the ability of an intelligent agent to migrate between networks. Operational tasks and processes can be run from one computer to another. When necessary, intelligent agents can communicate with other agents and people, and they can all carry out their own operations and help other agents and people. In addition, intelligent agents have personalization, through personalized rendering and personalized Settings. The user will be in the process of browsing products, gradually increase the desire to buy [5]. If the intelligent agent technology is applied to the electronic commerce system. Intelligent agent can an provide a global user without time and space restrictions trading place.

Creation of Expert and Intelligent Dialogue or Virtual Agent (VA) that can serve complicated and intricate tasks (need) of the user related to multiple domains and its various intents is indeed quite challenging as it necessitates the agent to concurrently handle multiple subtasks in different domains [6].

Among them, distributed intelligence systems (DIS) occur where natural intelligence agents (humans) and artificial intelligence agents (algorithms) interact, exchange data and make decisions, and learn how to evolve to higher quality solutions. The network dynamics of distributed natural and artificial intelligence agents lead to new complexities that differ from those previously observed [7]. Intelligent agents gather information and perceive semantics within the environments before taking on given tasks. The agents store the collected information in the form of environment models that compactly represent the surrounding environments. The agents, however, can only conduct limited tasks without an efficient and effective environment model. Thus, such an environment model takes a crucial role for the autonomy systems of intelligent agents [Kim, UH; Park, JM; Song, TJ; Kim, JH; 2019].

Therefore, it is significant to bibliometrically evaluate the research output of intelligent agent at large over the latest decade. The bibliometric analysis method can be used to survey the quantity and quality of a research discipline [Lee, & Hew, 2018], and has advantages to handle a large number of articles compared to traditional literature review method [Hew et al., 2019; Wang et al., 2017]. Articles related to intelligent agent has attracted a larger quantity of interest mainly in the last several years [8]. Thus, under different perspectives in the past decade, this article aims to delve into provide a comprehensive and objective analysis on simultaneously intelligent agent.

2 Methodology

This study used the data from Web of Science, which is the most important and frequently used scientific database in many research fields [Pan, Jian, & Liu, 2019]. The Web of science has more than 15,000 journals containing the fields of natural science, engineering technology, biomedicine, social science, art and humanities et al., which indexes the highest quality of articles [Hew et al., 2019; Pan, Jian, & Liu, 2019]. Hence, article indexed to the Web of science core collection were included. Search terms "intelligent agent" or "virtual agent" in title, abstract, keywords were searched on the Web of science, all data is available online from January 2010 to February 2020. reviews, book reviews, Journal articles and conference proceedings have already been recorded. In the period from 2010 to 2020, there were 7378 articles after overlapping records retrieved from both sources that were downloaded and recorded from the databases.

A bibliometric analysis was performed using Vos Viewer 1.6.14. The Vos Viewer, developed by Van Eck and Waltman, is a powerful piece of software for building and visualizing bibliometric networks, with keyword emergence, that can process large amounts of items or data extracted from well-known databases such as Scopus and Web of Science [van Eck and Waltman, 2017].

3   Results

3.1   Co-author's Country or Region Analysis

Figure 1 shows the annual publications of total (red solid line) and top 4 most productive countries from 2010 to 2020. The number of articles had a narrow range increment at 2015 from total and China. Many researchers pointed out that new fields of research and development in digital libraries, e-commerce and distance education at home and abroad have led to small fluctuations in the total number of articles and the number of Articles in China in recent years [9]. Due to the decline in 2020 was incomplete data. China (3674), USA (2368), UK (1121), and India (959) are the top 4 most productive countries since 2010, followed by Spain (693), Germany (630), Italy (571), and France (451). The citation of countries can show the quality of publications of each country. And the results show that the top 10 cited countries are China (3674), USA (2368), UK (1121), India (959), Spain (693), Germany (630), Italy (571), France (451), South Korea (426), and Canada (395).

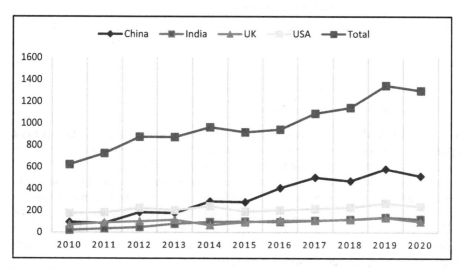

Fig. 1. The numbers of annual publications of total and top 4 most productive countries in intelligent agent from 2010 to 2020.

We also analysed the most productive institution. Obviously, the principal research institutes are mainly from USA, China, India, and UK. In the United States, University of California System, Harvard University, University of Texas System, State University System of Florida, etc., are the main institutes. In the following China, the most productive institutes are University of Chinese Academic of Sciences, Shanghai Jiao Tong University, Fudan University and Zhejiang University, Tsinghua University, etc.; In the India, they are Council of Scientific Industrial Research CSIR India, Indian institute of technology system IIT system, etc.; In the UK, University of London, Imperial College London, University of Cambridge, University of Oxford, etc. Table 1 shows the main distribution of production facilities. There are 291 published articles in University of Chinese Academic of Sciences, ranking first, and the second is University of California System with 272 published papers [10]. We can see from the results that most of the productive institutes are from China, USA, UK and Indian. In the Intelligent agent the highly cited organizations are the University of Chinese Academic of Science (562), University of California System (319), Indian Institute of Technology System IIT (186), Shanghai University (153), Sichuan university (136), Harvard University (124), University of London (122), University of Texas System (78).

Table 1. The top 8 most productive institutes.

Total publications	Institutes	Total publications	Institutes
562	University of Chinese Academic of Science	136	Sichuan University
319	University of California System	124	Harvard University
186	Indian Institute of Technology System IIT	122	University of London
153	Shanghai University	78	University of Texas System

3.2 Co-authors, Citations and Journals

This study has further analysed the co-authorship at the level of author. Top twenty most productive authors (based on number of publication) were acquired from the search results. Figure 2 shows the co-authorship network of productive authors. Every node is made representing one author. The identical colour means that there exists co-authorship between each author. The distance between two circles is conversely corresponding to the cooperation between each author. The larger the circle, the more productive the author. Table 2 gives the top twenty main productive authors. Corchado JM is the most productive author with 63 publications. Most of the authors contribute to this field, such as Zhang, N, Liu, Y, Chen, Y, Wang, Y etc. [11].

It can be seen that Wan, JF (2016) article was quoted 391 times, which indicated it to be the most significant article. In this paper, we present a smart factory framework

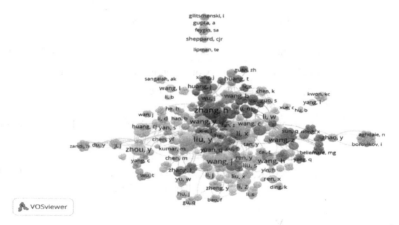

Fig. 2. Co-authorship network of productive authors.

Table 2. The top 20 most productive authors.

Total publications	Author	Total publications	Institutes
63	Corchado, JM	25	Liu, J.
37	Liu, Y.	25	Zhang, L.
36	Zhang, N.	24	Wang, L.
34	Chen, Y.	23	Zhang, X.
32	Wang, Y.	21	Zhang, J.
30	Li, X.	19	Chen, LJ
30	Wang, J.	19	De Paz, JF
28	.Li, J.	19	Julian, V.
28	Bajo, J.	19	Li, D.
28	Wang, H.	19	Wang, Z.
25	Li, Y.	18	Wang, X.

that incorporates industrial network, cloud, and supervisory control terminals with smart shop-floor objects such as machines, conveyers, and products. Then, we provide a classification of the smart objects into various types of agents and define a coordinator in the cloud [12]. The autonomous decision and distributed cooperation between agents lead to high flexibility. In Table 3, Scassellati, B's paper (2012) had been cited for 350 times, ranking second. This paper discussed the past decade's work in SAR systems designed for autism therapy by analysing robot design decisions, human-robot interactions, and system evaluations. We conclude by discussing challenges and future trends for this young but rapidly developing research area. Chen, B's paper (2010) for 286 times ranking third. This paper examines an agent-based approach and its applications in different modes of transportation, including roadway, railway, and air transportation.

Table 3. Top 10 highly cited articles.

Cited frequency	Cited article	Source	Volume	Page
391	Wan, JF, 2016	Computer networks	101	P168
350	Scassellati, B, 2012	Annual review of biomedical	14	P294
286	Chen, B, 2010	IEEE transactions on intelligent transportation systems	11	P497
249	Nunna, HSVSK, 2013	IEEE transactions on intelligent transportation systems	60	P1687
223	Cheng, WM 2017	Fuel	210	P835
211	Logenthiran, T 2011	Electric power systems research	81	P148
193	Logenthiran, T 2017	IEEE transactions on smart grid	3	933
185	Xu, LD, 2011	International journal of production research	49	P198
171	Borras, J 2014	Expert systems with applications	41	P7389
165	Klein, L, 2012	Automation in construction	22	P536

This paper also addresses some critical issues in developing agent-based traffic control and management systems, such as interoperability, flexibility, and extendibility [13]. Finally, several future research directions toward the successful deployment of agent technology in traffic and transportation systems are discussed. Chen B's (2010), Nunna, HSVSK's (2013), Cheng WM's (2017), Logenthiran's (2011), Xu, LD's (2011), Borras, J's (2014) and Klein, L (2012) articles significant in the area of intelligent agent.

The dedication of journals was also analysed. The top 10 highly cited journals are "Expert Systems with Applications", "IEEE Access", "Biomaterials", "Sensors", "Sensors Basel Switzerland", "Colloids and Surfaces B Biointerfaces", "Journal of Materials Chemistry B", "Materials Science and Engineering Materials for Biological Applications", "Acta Biomaterialia" [14].

3.3 Co-citation Network

In a specific scientific activity, co-citations of reference are one of the most significant method to analyse and reflect the evolutionary process. Figure 4 shows the mapping on co-citation of references. The 254 points represent the 254 cited reference. The identical colour shows that the cited reference is from the same cluster the point's size repre-sents the citation the paper's frequency. The connection between two points represents that both of articles had been cited in one paper. On the contrary, the distance between two points is corresponding to the closer between each paper. The conclusion is that two clusters were obtained. The first cluster contained 165 articles, mainly investigated intelligent agent in network communication, software, robot and other aspects of appli-cation innovation. The second cluster included 89 publications, and mainly focused on intelligent agent in biology, medicine and other aspects of the main research applications [15]. Figure 6 the articles showing all of the intelligent agents in the Web of Science are divided into two clusters (Fig. 3).

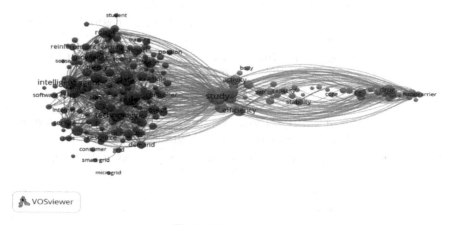

Fig. 3. Two clusters.

Table 4 displays the co-citation of authors. considering the large quantity of cited authors, the minimum number of citations of an author was set 30, of the 12148 authors, and 146 met the threshold. 146 points represent the 146 authors [16]. The authors were divided into four clusters (i.e., four colours). Points size indicates the citation frequency of the author. The link between two point represents both authors had been cited in one article. The distance between two points is conversely corresponding to the closer between each author. Wan JF, Scassellati, Chen Y, Nunna HSVSK, and Cheng WM are the top co-cited authors, whose research are representativeness and authority [17].

Table 4. Top 10 highly co-cited articles.

Co-Cited frequency	Cited article
391	Wan, JF2016, Computer networks, V101, P168, Doi10.1016/j. comnet2015.12.017
350	Scassellati, 2012, Annual Review of Biomedical Engineerging, https://doi.org/10.1146/annurev-bioeng-071811-150035
286	Chen, B 2010, IEEE Transactions on Intelligent Transportation, V11, P497, https://doi.org/10.1109/TITS.2010.2048313
249	Nunna, HSVSK 2013, IEEE Transactions on Industrial Electronics, V60, P1687, https://doi.org/10.1109/TIE.2012.2193857
223	Cheng, WM 2017, Fuel, V210, P835, https://doi.org/10.1016/j.fuel.2017.09.007
211	Logenthiran, T 2011, Electric Power Systems Research, V81, P148, https://doi.org/10.1016/j.epsr.2010.07.019
193	Logenthiran, T, 2012, IEEE Transactions on Smart Grid, V3, P933, https://doi.org/10.1109/TSG.2012.2189028
185	Xu, LD 2011, International Journal of Production Research, V49, P198, https://doi.org/10.1080/00207543.2010.508944
171	Borras, J 2014, Expert Systems with Applications, V41, P7389, https://doi.org/10.1016/j.eswa.2014.06.007
165	Klein, L 2012, Automation in Construction, V22, P536, https://doi.org/10.1016/j.autcon.2011.11.012

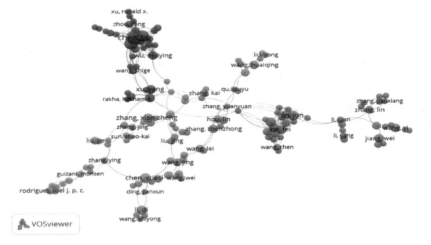

Fig. 4. Author co-citation.

3.4 Hotspots of Papers Related to Intelligent Agent

Figure 5 and 6 show the co-occurrence of author keywords by VOS viewer. The minimum number of occurrences of a keyword was set 20, of the 108359 keywords, and 856 keywords were divided into four clusters. Cluster 1 consisting of 453 keywords, are mainly about classification of Intelligent agent. Cluster 2 consisting 253 items and are mainly about influence of Intelligent agent. Cluster 3 consisting 86 items and are mainly about cognition of Intelligent agent. Cluster 4 consisting 33 items and are mainly about other cognition of Intelligent agent. The latest keyword "dialogue management" appeared in 2020. Other relative new keywords include "agent" "behaviour" "paper" "multi agent system" [18].

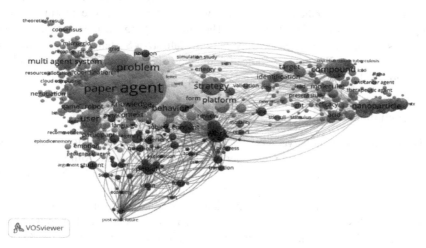

Fig. 5. Network visualization of co-occurrence of keywords.

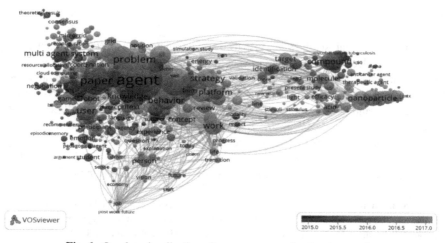

Fig. 6. Overlay visualization of co-occurrence of author keywords.

4   Discussion

4.1   Research Trends Related to Intelligent Agent

Form the annual publications of total and top 4 countries, we can see that there is a growing trend both in published articles and research interest in this field since 2010, China leads both in the publications and citations [19]. The ranks of USA, Indian, and UK are relatively lower than that of total publications and citations of USA, indicating that the quality of studies of these countries are relatively low and need improvements [20].

University of Chinese Academic of Science, University of California System, Indian of Institute of Technology System IIT and Shanghai University are the most productive institutes in the world, indicating researchers who are interested in false information may cooperate with these organizations [21]. The most cited organizations are University of Chinese Academic of Science, University of California System, Indian Institute of Technology System IIT and etc., indicating the most significant studies are more likely to be published in these institutes.

4.2   Limitations

This study uses a quantitative and visual method to evaluate the history, current and future of publications regarding intelligent agent and virtual agent. Although relatively objective and comprehensive, there are some limitations in this study. First, extensive databases containing other languages should be considered. Second, predefined terms are used which may make some publications ruled out. Third, bibliometric data are dynamic, but this analysis is based on a static data. Hence, some newly published and outstanding articles may not be cited much times but with a rapid increase. On this condition, bibliometric analysis may not reflect the truth.

5   Conclusion

This bibliometric analysis showed a visual and scientometrics review of Intelligent agent in detail by collecting every related paper from Web of science from 2010 to 2020. China dominates the research in Intelligent agent, followed by USA, Indian, and UK. University of Chinese Academic of Sciences, University of California, and CNRS from China, Indian, and USA are the stop 3 productive institutes related to Intelligent agent. *Expert System with Applications, IEEE Access* and *Biomaterials* are the mainly sources of publications related to Intelligent agent. All the summarise of this study mainly depends on databases from Web of science, extensive literature should be collected. Few conclusions may be one-sided. Hence, study should be updated in the future.

Acknowledgements. This work was supported by National Natural Science Foundation of China (Grant No. 71701003, 71801002, 71802002), the Ministry of Education Industry-University Cooperation Collaborative Education Project (Grant no. 201901024006), and the University Natural Science Research Key Project of Anhui Province (Grant no. KJ2017A108).

References

1. Wang, S.Y., Wan, J.F.: Towards smart factory foe industry 4.0: a self-organized mutil-agent system with big data base feedback and corrdination. https://doi.org/10.1016/j.comnet.2015. 12.017.
2. Scassellati, B., Admoni, H., Mataric, M.: Robots for use in autism research (2012). https://doi.org/10.1146/annurev-bioeng-071811-150035
3. Chen, B., Cheng, H.H.: A review of the applications of agent technology in traffic and transportation systems, vol. 11 (2010). https://doi.org/10.1109/TITS.2010.2048313
4. Nunna, H.S.V.S.K., Doolla, S.: Multiagent-Based distributed-energy-resource management for intelligent microgrids (2013). https://doi.org/10.1109/TIE.2012.2193857
5. Cheng, W.M., Hu, X.M., Xie, J., Zhao, Y.Y.: An intelligent gel designed to control the spontaneous combustion of coal: fire prevention and extinguishing properties (2017). https://doi.org/10.1016/j.fuel.2017.09.007
6. Logenthiran, T., Srinivasan, D.: Multiagent system for real-time operation of microgrid in real-time digital simulator. https://doi.org/10.1109/TSG.2012.2189028
7. Borras, J., Moreno, A., Valls, A.: Intelligent tourism recommender systems: a survey, vol. 41, 7370–7389 (2014). https://doi.org/10.1016/j.eswa.2014.06.007
8. Klein, L., Kwak, J.Y.: Coordinating occupant behavior for building energy and comfort management using multi-agent systems, vol. 22, 525–536 (2012). https://doi.org/10.1016/j.autcon.2011.11.012
9. Arel, I., Liu, C., Urbanik, T.: Reinforcement learning-based multi-agent system for network traffic signal control, vol. 4, 128–135. https://doi.org/10.1016/j.jmsy.2020.06.018
10. Niazi, M., Hussain, A.: Agent-based computing from multi-agent systems to agent-based models: a visual survey (2011). https://doi.org/10.1007/s11192-011-0468-9
11. Wang, L.F., Wang, Z., Yang, R.: Intelligent multiagent control system for energy and comfort management in smart and sustainable buildings, vol. 3, 605–617 (2012)
12. Chen, J.Y.C., Barnes, M.J.: Human-agent teaming for multirobot control: a review of human factors issues, vol. 44, 13–29 (2014)
13. Zhang, Y.F., Qian, C., Lu, J.X.: Agent and cyber-physical system based self-organizing and self-adaptive intelligent shopfloor. https://doi.org/10.1109/TII.2016.2618892
14. Kantamneni, A., Brown, L.E., Parker, G.: Survey of multi-agent systems for microgrid control, vol. 45, 192–203 (2015). https://doi.org/10.1016/j.engappai.2015.07.005
15. Zhou, X.J., Xu, Y., Li, Y.F.: The state-of-the-art in personalized recommender systems for social networking (2012). https://doi.org/10.1080/00207543.2010.508944
16. Bernardini, S., Porayska-Pomsta, K.: ECHOES: an intelligent serious game foe fostering social communication in children with autism, vol. 264, 41–60 (2014). https://doi.org/10.1016/j.ins.2013.10.027
17. Poria, S., Cambria, E., Hussain, A.: Towards an intelligent framework for multimodal affective data analysis. https://doi.org/10.1016/j.neunet.2014.10.005
18. Nunamaker, J.E., Derrick, D.C., Elkins, A.C.: Embodied conversational agent-based kiosk for automated interviewing, vol. 28, 17–48 (2011)
19. Wang, X., Khemaissia, I.: Dynamic low-power reconfiguration of real-time systems with periodic and probabilistic tasks, vol. 12, 258–271 (2014)
20. Yu, L.A., Yue, W.Y.: Support vector machine based multiagent ensemble learning for credit risk evaluation, vol. 37, 1351–1360 (2010).https://doi.org/10.1016/j.eswa.2009.06.083
21. Ganapathy, S., Kulothungan, K.: Intelligent feature selection and classification techniques for intrusion detection in networks: a survey (2013). https://doi.org/10.1186/1682-1499-2013-271

What if: Human Rights vs Science – or Both?

An Unusual Argument from a Disability Perspective

László Gábor Lovászy$^{(\boxtimes)}$

University of Public Service, 2 Ludovika tér, 1083 Budapest, Hungary
Lovaszy.Laszlo.Gabor@uni-nke.hu

Abstract. The author examines the social, economic and political consequences to human rights in terms of modern ICT technologies and biotechnology advances (CRISPR-Cas9) as well as newly developed medical-based rehabilitation techniques. In addition to the benefits of newer technologies, the author offers a recognition and understanding of the hidden risks and their possible long-term consequences when it comes to human rights. The author, who has been a member of the UN CRPD, the human rights committee on the rights of the persons with disabilities for 8 years, puts whether human rights or science and scientific innovation takes precedence. Both artificial intelligence and biotechnology together with invasive solutions (implants) face a number of ethical issues that still remain unanswered. The author also presents the socio-political and legal aspects that arise in connection with the latest developments (see Elon Musk's brain implant project). Moreover, the author also introduces a new term, *homo sapiens correctus*, pointing out that we can speak not only of a correction in relation to modern rehabilitation, but also directly of an upgrade, leading to unpredictable social consequences. This process will also lead us to *'post-Renaissance polymaths'*, which will revolutionize the world of work and education.

Keywords: Rehabilitation · Biotechnology · CRISPR · Implants · Invasive devices · Wearable devices · Artificial intelligence · Post-renaissance polymaths · Homo sapiens conrectus · Corporate individualism · Productivity · Digitalisation · Disability · UNCRPD · Robotics · EU charter of fundamental rights · Eugenics · DARPA · Triple revolution · Asymmetric technological singularity

1 Introduction – A Personal Point of View with Background

The 15th anniversary of the UN Convention on the Rights of Persons with Disabilities (CRPD) will be held in 2021, which instrument was called by the United Nations as the very first human rights convention of the 21st century. [1] Actually, this is the first comprehensive international human rights agreement to have recognised technology as an opportunity and, at the same time, by the experts of its committee (UNCRPD), as an indirect threat, too. In this paper, my aim is to scrutinise the basic question whether we must make a choice between human rights and science.

Why? Fifteen years after the Convention was adopted, we are beginning to realise entirely new topics that, apart from the most talented and respected science-fiction

© Springer Nature Switzerland AG 2021
V. G. Duffy (Ed.): HCII 2021, LNCS 12778, pp. 220–238, 2021.
https://doi.org/10.1007/978-3-030-77820-0_17

writers, no one could have thought of and that are completely uncovered by it, while technology and science have been developing at an incredible speed.

I believe that issues such as robotics, biotechnology, and DNA-related scientific breakthroughs are not only becoming especially high-profile and will be industrialized for everyday consumers very soon, but the consequences are practically unknown to even the most competent decision-makers and the scientists in charge of these innovations, not to speak of ordinary citizens. The recent articles and columns of the Economist, Newsweek and Scientific American published almost every week clearly indicate how something has changed, something very profound and irrevocable.

To begin with a personal note, when I was born, my parents were depressingly told that I would have the life of a disabled person being seriously hearing impaired and I would have to face that condition all my life. But what if that were not true anymore? What if my disability will not be significant in the future and my hearing capacity (or its alteration) could be corrected or even somehow restored? Or even upgraded? [2] As the first hearing-impaired UN human rights expert at the UNCRPD Committee (2012–2020), I am convinced that this kind of personal experience can contribute to further consideration and analysis.

Why? At the time of my birth, there was no synthetic, artificial gene, and it did not occur that a child could genetically have up to three biological parents. Today, biotechnology is an enormous business: it is expected to cost nearly $750 billion by 2025, [3] and it is no coincidence that dozens of biotechnology solutions – like different vaccines for the same cure – would be produced in less than one year for the coronavirus epidemic. By comparison, the total global pharmaceutical industry is worth $1,300 billion. [4] Thus, biotechnology – and at the same time bioethics as a field of science – is becoming one of the most important human rights issues.

Again, why? After all, according to David Eagleman's findings, [5] our brains can learn and understand any kind of information eventually, regardless of the source of the input on condition that the input structure is stable and structured. Very soon, as Eagleman noted, based on new biotechnological innovations, we may be able to understand and rely on information that is currently exclusively available to animals. This therefore follows that mankind could soon be able to re-design itself biotechnologically.

In addition to bioethics, another issue that has a significant impact on human rights is the increasingly important spread of artificial intelligence and robotics already permeating everyday life. When the UN Convention was adopted, no one expected that the world of artificial intelligence and increasingly intelligent, more independent robots could come so soon and already become available to market so quickly that they should be treated as a social issue, or even more: a challenge.

Why? Because we are already developing new generations of artificial intelligence with the brain capacity of hundreds or even thousands of people, at least in terms of speed of calculation and communication. These innovations – like intelligent services for independent living scheme, supported decision-making process, artificial (avatar) sign language interpreters, effectively communicating household devices will definitely ease the burdens of, among others, persons with mental and/or sensory disabilities. As to persons with limited mobility, the area of 3D printing technology or newer generations of exoskeleton is also promising. Producing tools and replacing missing or paralyzed body parts for a person with a disability may soon become commonplace, and even more, the replacement parts could make that person stronger or more efficient than ever – see the case of Paralympic Oscar Pistorius who, in 2008, had to undergo a complex examination to see whether his artificial legs do not give him unacceptable advantage when competing with non-disabled athletes. (Eventually he was restricted to certain types of legs.) [6] Pistorius's case clearly shows that people equipped with artificial body parts or with upgraded tools leading to newly integrated and intelligent skills, extra sensory abilities included, could be in a stronger and more competitive position to secure advantage or even better-paid jobs than those who have no such access to these technologies.

Perhaps in a few decades, looking back on today, we will confirm that in 2012 humanity has entered a new era of civilization that may have determined its own evolution. The 2010s not only brought earthquake-like changes in politics (global financial and economic crisis, which also brought unorthodox fiscal and central bank policy or led to the referendum on Brexit, the election of Donald Trump and the introduction of modern Chinese Silk Road), but also new revolutions began in the field of science. We may even be able to identify a specific year, which could be the opening of a new era in history: 2012. In that year, there were two revolutionary events: artificial intelligence was introduced to consumers and entered the field of the Internet as well as there was a breakthrough in genetic modification affecting humans based on CRISPR-Cas9. The consequences of these milestones are still unpredictable.

Finally, in this paper we will examine the following main narratives, backgrounds and correlations of five more or less combined and interrelated technological phases and aspects in connection with the issue of disability and technology which topic is profoundly influencing science today:

- wearable medical devices (e.g., smartwatches and home medical smart tools, monitoring applications built into mobile phones);
- invasive devices (e.g., implants and 3D-printed body parts - more than 300,000 cochlear implants [7] (devices that create a hearing experience for the deaf) have been installed in the world so far and the referred case of Oscar Pistorius is also relevant here);
- robotics (e.g., introduction of humanoid machines for nursing care – see the New Robot Strategy [8] adopted in Japan in 2015 and hundreds of thousands of robots lifting patients will be installed in hospitals within a few years);
- artificial intelligence (e.g., supporting decision-making and alerting functions, or education tools for the individual development of mental-emotional abilities (e.g., autism); and finally
- genetic engineering, i.e., the so-called CRISPR technology.

2 Bioethical Aspect: Can a Disability Be 'Fixed'?

Although a body of experts in the field of bioethics has been operating at UN level under the auspices of UNESCO [9] since 1993, little is known about their work and technology is now evolving much faster than (international) law could follow. As I pointed out, from a legal point of view, one of the largest biotechnology events took place in 2012: the so-called CRISPR technology was patented in the United States, which is nothing but a revolutionary new method of genetic modification, in fact a kind of the Swiss Army knife of genetic engineering, which is particularly inexpensive and therefore easy to use and disseminate. (Although Jennifer Doudna and Emmanuelle Charpentier [10] won the 2020 Nobel Prize in Chemistry, they are still fighting in a bizarre way in despair for their own patent.) [11].

With this procedure, it will be possible to eliminate severe, incompatible with life disabilities during pregnancy as scientists have already been able to modify the monkey genome with a 40% success rate in recent years and, by 2015, it will already have taken another 20 monkey embryos to also survive. However, experts foresee we may be only 20 years away from an even more improved technology. [12] Partly due to this development, more than a hundred children have already been saved in this way since 2017. According to Newcastle's Wellcome Trust Centre for Mitochondrial Research, about 1 in 6,500 children are thought to develop a serious mitochondrial disorder, and the Newcastle team aims to offer treatment for up to 25 women a year affected by mitochondrial disease. [13] (However, ethical issues still remain with the success of the procedure, but more on that later in this paper.) In addition to that, since 2016 the creation of a human-pig hybrid embryo [14] has also become possible for organ transplantation, in order to reduce growing waiting lists as well as to potentially reduce illegal and brutal organ trafficking business [15].

Genetics is nowadays facing unpredictable changes not only because serious diseases and inherited disabilities can be avoided, but even entirely new abilities or additional skills or features can be constructed. In relation to the human-pork embryo, another breakthrough occurred in April 2016: scientists of the University of Washington and Microsoft were able to store 10,000 gigabytes of digital data in a single pencil tip of natural DNA. [16] Recent research and successful experiments with mice have also made it possible to erase certain memories in the brain with a special light therapy procedure to allow the patient to recall memories considered "lost" associated with Alzheimer's disease. (This milestone is extremely important in terms of research on aging as well.) [17, 18].

Moreover, there was another, even more controversial breakthrough in 2019: Chinese scientists modified human embryos to make them more resistant to AIDS, but also reported that the IQ of children is also thought to have increased as an unintended consequence. However, as a kind of collateral damage, they were also expecting shorter lifespan. [19] This is particularly challenging given that this technology may soon possibly modify an estimated 10,000 disability-related genes as well [20].

In addition, the activities of the scientific community and the transparency of research are becoming less and less assured. If we look back for a moment, we can see that 10 years ago there were only 30, and in 2018, there were more than 7,000 registered so-called CRISPR-patents - and their number is constantly growing ever since. [21] Meanwhile, researchers working on the CRISPR-Cas9 gene editing process have become divided on the issue of human genetic modification. [22–24] In addition, we might note cultural-civilizational reasons for this argument, as both the US, the EU and Asian countries have different images of people and society. These areas have a completely different socio-organizational and demographic perception, whether it is to maintain competitiveness focusing on issues like robotics, artificial intelligence or to keep the (aging) population at a certain level with issues like artificial insemination, slowing down aging, immigration – or with their combination as a result. As it is well known, international and ratified conventions do not define the nature or concept of a person or a family. The lack of definitions could be a burning issue within a few years. Why?

Well, since 2015 the scientific publishers like *Nature* and *Science* have not been publishing several cases of ethically questionable (Chinese) research findings concerning the editing of the human genome, including those which later turned out to be milestones. [25] This also has the implication that, in practice, 99.99% of people do not know what kind of research and "social engineering" opportunities are actually already available. Perhaps this is the best indication that science has also found itself in a critical position in some respects, as society may lose control of scientific research, which may raise increasingly serious ethical issues and affect society in the longer term, not to speak of the unique responsibility of the international scientific community.

In addition, the EU prohibits the "development" of the human genome, i.e., eugenics, in the EU Charter of Fundamental Rights – partly due to the Holocaust. [26] Most recently, the World Health Organization set up the WHO Expert Advisory Committee on Developing Global Standards for Governance and Oversight of Human Genome Editing [27] last March, which have presented a draft for a comprehensive regulatory concept [28].

And now let's look at what specific issues might arise, especially for persons with disabilities, who make up 5–6% of the population. Well, it all started with the idea that genetic engineering researchers wanted to eliminate congenital and often life-incompatible, inherited disorders, even in an embryonic phase. It follows that this is now increasingly technically available and may also help reduce the number of abortions, since this aspect is a registered factor (3%), and even a more significant one when it comes to rape in the USA in terms of abortions [29].

This aim was also important for the Conservative British Prime Minister, David Cameron when, with his support, a law was passed in 2015 to allow the existence of genetically three-parent babies where the mother's egg is dysfunctional. The personal background to this was that his little son had died at the age of 6 from an illness that might have been prevented by such a (then non-existent) procedure [30].

The issue, on the one hand, is also complicated by the fact that 90% of children with disabilities are born to non-deaf parents [31] who usually turn to science even more for help. On the other hand, no matter how incredible it may sound, there is also the challenge of whether a parent with a disability can demand that his or her child has a right (obligation) to inherit his or her disability ("genetic inheritance") or whether the "interest" of the child or society contradicting that of parents is stronger.

In addition, there are growing indications that the prevalence of hearing loss in old age, which will be the most common disability due to aging after 2020, will also be linked to dementia, which is also spreading rapidly and generates huge costs. [32] In spite of all these, the processes also mean that the concept of aging is being re-evaluated in such a way that the level and duration of activity and thus productivity can be further increased for those who have access to these solutions. Therefore, it is a fundamental national (economic) investment interest to invest in health care in terms of active aging.

As a significant part of diseases and disabilities in old age are related to the brain, brain research projects are – correctly – increasingly being identified as a national economic interest; see the good practice of Hungary: the creation and running of the National Brain Research Program (NAP) was an important research investment of the government starting in 2013. (The NAP's leader is Dr Tamás Freund, Brain Prize holder and the newly elected President of the Hungarian Academy of Sciences from 2020.) [33] This impetus is indeed significant since the one of the biggest challenges of aging is the deterioration of brain functions and cognitive, mental performance. In addition, I also see a huge opportunity to "humanize" and to make a close link between brain research and artificial intelligence.

So, the evolution of DNA-related technologies, gene-editing CRISPR-Cas9 in particular, could be relevant for legislation not only in terms of prevention, which is not the topic of the UNCRPD Convention, but also for adults with disabilities – see the recent legislation on the so-called three-parented babies in the United Kingdom in which fertility-disabled women can have access to fertile donors' eggs. It follows that the time will soon come when checking the balance between the medical aspect of disability and (re)habilitation would be a critical issue in light of the human rights-based model in accordance with the Convention. Why? Around 100 years ago hundreds of scientists and politicians explored and argued the results and expected outcomes of eugenics based on then popular methodology of designing desired genetic traits and sexual reproduction approaches. (Eugenics as a movement began in the US and became popular in the Western societies in 1910–1920s.). [34] Today gene-editing is a hard fact and more or less a reality. Modern, as well as scientifically developed societies have an important responsibility to handle this technology in a much more responsible and socially sustainable way because it will have an effect on almost everything we know in terms of social behaviour and drivers, not to mention social mobility.

3 The Renaissance of Medical Rehabilitation – Are Human Rights Pushed into the Background?

From the second half of the 20th century onwards, thanks to technological advances, not only passive diagnostic and medical devices but also increasingly advanced IT monitoring equipment improve the quality of health service, and invasive devices implanted in the human body (e.g., pacemakers, cochlear implants) have also been developed. Since the 2010s, medical devices and services (applications) worn on the body have begun to spread via new generations of smart phones, smart bracelets and smart watches. Through the digitization of health data, algorithms based on increased artificial intelligence are also contributing to the toolbox of health diagnostics as well as to a wider use and application of medical and surgical robots. It follows that there are countless new directions in terms of the application of increasingly intelligent and flexible robots, including nanoscale devices and even tiny DNA robots that move in the human body and intervene in physiological processes with a defined program and some of them are even thought-driven [35].

At the same time, a completely new direction appeared: the renaissance of medical rehabilitation. As part of this, there are already mobile-controlled or thought-driven artificial limbs, and even a successful invention that makes the artificial limb feelable by its owner. [36] Moreover, the limbs to be replaced may slowly be replaced by a "better" item in the future. This could also mean that the device replacing the disabled body part may lend a more competitive advantage to its owner – see the case of Oscar Pistorius mentioned earlier.

The first breakthrough of a new generation of rehabilitation, the direct brain-internet ("brainternet") connection took place in September 2017; this may also open up unpredictable prospects. [37] The improved person, in other words, individuals with 'enhanced skills', are a new development to which there is currently no social and political response, as it may essentially call into question the human rights aspect of disability in the longer term (i.e., who will be considered disabled and who receives care). It also indicates the risk that disability will become an even greater risk of poverty due to limited or non-existent access to increasingly modern (but still very expensive) medical and technological features and solutions. In addition, another question is whether the safety of these (biologically integrated) devices and (implanted) invasive peripherals can be guaranteed. Neither just a question of external threats to the user, i.e., legal and effective guarantees against hacker attacks, nor just a matter of "hacking" open-source devices at home are important, but also the issue is quite relevant whether the user can be protected sufficiently to deal with or understand his own health risks when accessing to these technologies.

What do I mean? Today's digital hearing aids can now be controlled by a single phone, and there are currently no built-in and flexible safeguards or "fuses" that would prevent further hearing loss when using excessive volume. Another aspect that is worth mentioning here is the issue of implants, which they not only rehabilitate but make the user part of an integrated system leading to a situation where the consumer becomes a passive, adaptive subject of an ecosystem. Moreover, these devices, as it looks, will not be platform independent; it will even be an asset for a kind of caste as different devices can be accessed with different, limited options and can be controlled remotely with restricted access. At the same time, we also need to talk about whether closed systems have an advantage: they can be more effectively guaranteed to protect the interests of consumers because in the event of internal failure of such products provided for hundreds or thousands of people (mass health damage), the liability of manufacturers can be more easily defined.

When it comes to rehabilitation, huge advances in previously inaccurate, non-invasive devices are also expected as now there are "caps" with sensitive sensors that can measure and accurately locate activities in the brain, enabling people with severe disabilities to live a fuller, and more importantly, a more independent life. [38] This also means that these tools will fundamentally change a person's thinking and communication (and its speed), as there will be no barriers to the integration of digitized information, which, when networked, can be transmitted and interpreted even faster for the brain.

So, if we think of the evolution of wearable devices, hearing aids and exoskeletons included, we have to realise that these items and tools are going to be an everyday issue and experience. We also have to scrutinize aspects relevant to privacy, accessibility, interoperability as well as affordability, otherwise persons with disabilities could be excluded. At this point, in light of interoperability and conformity, we have to emphasise that the State parties have an obligation to make sure customers can have access to those products and services without interference problems. When it comes to the evolution of the so-called invasive devices (e.g., cochlear implants for the deaf), including brain and computer interfaces, these could also be part of our life to a much greater extent, which also raises interesting aspects such as the integrity of person as well as autonomy, liability and responsibility for their decisions. Not to mention who shall bear the consequences of hacking and other malicious activities and to what extent? As to competitiveness and employment, we also have to identify and handle the weak points of technology in terms of ethical issues and fairness at social level.

4 Artificial Intelligence: Can a Revolution in Independent Living and Post-renaissance Polymaths Come?

The world's most successful mobile phone maker, US-based Apple made its own artificial intelligence-based virtual assistant service, Siri, available on all mobile devices in 2012. According to Andreessen Horowitz, the total performance of iPhones sold on the weekend when releasing them is 20–30 or even more times that of all personal computers in the world in the 1990s. [39] Soon, thanks to intelligent facial recognition technology, we will be able to communicate and shop with our (micro) facial expressions [40] but in the meantime, we already reveal a lot about ourselves, almost everything from sexual orientation to many other qualities and conditions, including the expression of guilt; however, although science still questions the results of algorithms developed by the largest firms. [41] At the same time, it is undeniable that the importance of the so-called behavioral economics is growing, most recently one of its most prominent representatives, Richard H. Thaler, received the Nobel Prize in Economics in 2017.

At the end of November 2017, according to *Science*, two artificial intelligence algorithms learned to translate individually from two languages independently in one (!) day through neural networks without human intervention, which was unthinkable even a few years ago. The essence of the method is based on two steps. In the first step, it creates a dictionary based on the two languages (e.g., French and English) and then translates back and forth until the translations are perfect [42].

Elon Musk, head of Tesla, himself is mobilizing vast resources for research and development related to artificial intelligence and, in parallel, building artificial neural networks. [43] Musk stated in early 2017 that implants are also expected that would be able to rehabilitate certain neurological and brain diseases (e.g., Parkinson's disease), sensory injuries (e.g., blindness, deafness) that are still considered severe disabilities today. [44] Moreover, according to a November 2017 issue of *Nature*, the U.S. military, through its research-science company DARPA, is treating veterans to control their mood swings and certain mental illnesses (depression and epilepsy) by developing a brain implant for happiness and well-being in order to help them to lead a more independent life by raising serious ethical issues, too [45].

We can make even greater progress with further development of artificial intelligence in terms of health care. This is especially true for people with disabilities, as a smart device or a health care service application based on AI can greatly improve the quality of their independent living. For example, blind people can use smartphones excellently or artificial limbs based on brainwaves connected to computers for the severely disabled may soon become available; not to mention other apps that help people with autism or deaf persons. These perspectives are already incomprehensible when it comes to the evolution of AI: in January 2018, in one of the most complex ancient games of Chinese origin, go, Google's software had almost completely defeated in each and every game not only the European but also the world champion [46].

Notwithstanding, artificial intelligence may still be better able to answer "how" than "what." Sticking to the example of the go game: although the machine is able to win the match, it does not "inherently" aim to win because solving the challenges of the game is only a task that has been programmed into it. An increasing number of analyses suggest that, due to the self-learning process of machines, the word "impossible" should be forgotten in the foreseeable future in terms of replacing certain knowledge-based jobs. Humans will be organically integrated in an environment maintained by AI, where people's individual physical and certain mental-cognitive abilities are constantly degraded as time goes by. In this way, human abilities are increasingly becoming a "disability", which is not a tragedy because disability itself will become less and less relevant in society and social relationships as well. See e.g., the centuries-old history of eyewear and contact lenses - wearing "old-fashioned" eyewear is now rather a fashion-related custom as more people can choose laser treatments.

But at the same time this means that our way of life is radically changing. Europe will perhaps be a bit of an exception, as the countryside is already liveable and the more developed countries have higher population densities and much better infrastructure (public services, road network, etc.) than the developing countries now. However, global trends indicate the emergence of megacities: half of the Earth's population already lived in cities in 2007. With the advancement of giant cities, it is worth seeing that in 1950 there was only one such city (i.e., where more than 10 million people lived): New York City. Today, their numbers are around 30 and by 2030, their numbers will grow rapidly, mainly in Asia [47].

Therefore, predictable, stable energy consumption and electricity-based infrastructure, which will be used by an increasing and aging number of people, will be essential. Thus, conscious urban planning, including accessibility, is also becoming increasingly important. Again, for the sake of the whole picture: energy demand in the world has doubled since 1990 and this demand will continue to grow as we use more and more electric devices, not to mention the coming advent of electric vehicles. In addition, computing, and in particular artificial intelligence, are increasingly being used to operate these infrastructures and services, especially due to the growing number of smart cities [48].

Few people actually know that, according to MIT Technology Review, teaching algorithms also requires enormous amount of energy consumption: deep learning has an incredibly large carbon footprint. Training a single AI model can emit as much carbon as five cars in their lifetimes, says Karen Hao, indicating that a human life as a person's carbon footprint benchmarks is 11,023, whilst a transformer (213M parameters) with neural architecture search is 626,155 per year in lbs of CO_2 equivalent. In addition to that, perhaps one of the most important developments is that, next to tourism and travel, communications, i.e., mobile devices and Internet-related products and services, which make life easier for people with disabilities, are also a very heavy burden on nature [49, 50].

As market analysts predict, tens of billions of products (from washing machines to cars) will be connected to the internet in years to come. [51] Let us also not forget that the first mobile phone, which already had Internet access, appeared not so long ago, in 1996 to be more precise, when only less than 5% of the world's population had access to the Internet. [52] Today, that number is almost over 60% [53] and there are more than 3,5 billion mobile users worldwide. [54] At the same time, compared to 1996, the price of mobiles with 4G access dropped roughly to one-fifth. [55] Therefore, even in much less developed areas, mobile penetration is growing rapidly, and in many cases, it happens without the construction of new jobs and social infrastructures that used to be the source of the wealth of the middle class in Europe once, for example, as you can see in the banking system in many areas in Africa as branches of banks are also disappearing due to automation and mobile technology. [56] In terms of travel and mobility, we can see that the EU has the highest use of cars in the world as a proportion of the population - this will be interesting for self-driving vehicles, especially in an aging EU, since the number of accidents caused by older drivers is also increasing as disabilities become more and more a part of everyday life. As far as disability is concerned, this issue is also linked to the safety of invasive (e.g., surgically inserted) devices built into or connected to nervous systems (see next section), as more recently the challenge of cyber-terrorism has emerged in terms of the use of non-self-driving means of transport for terrorist purposes (see terrorist attacks in Germany in 2020).

These issues will be even more important very soon. Why? Because we are living in an era of 'Great Acceleration', with temperatures, population that increases by about one billion on Earth every 15 years, migration, carbon emissions, GDP, the mass extinction of animal species, the sharp decline in human fertility in developed countries, the overuse of fresh water and the depletion of fertile lands, not to mention the garbage and pollution in the seas. With all these changes it means an even bigger change—especially in the shorter run—in terms of accelerating the development of artificial intelligence. This also means that more and more practical and flexible, say, 'post-Renaissance polymaths' will be needed in the future who are ready and able to continuously learn, innovate and work with artificial intelligence. What does it mean? Currently important qualities, previously attributed to young people (speed, load capacity, endurance, etc.), are devalued or underrated in some respects. Employment statistics support a spectacular increase in the employment of older people in developed countries, as experience, human capital and proficiency in organizational cultures become increasingly important in companies as well. Even more, workers in general will be more flexible and, in a way, greatly enhanced in terms of production. Individuals in the open labour markets will be able to perform like whole companies many decades ago in terms of productivity. This 'corporative individualism' will change the face of capitalism itself, too. [57] At the same time, it will be critical which society has the needed level of digitization capacity because these processes will affect each country differently. China, as well as South Korea, which ranks first in the world in the field of robotics, and Japan, which ranks fourth, want to deal with their own demographic crisis in part with robotics (see: manufacturing industry-related robot density, 2019). [58] Moreover, China, that is facing perhaps the greatest challenge of ageing in the world, is also developing this area at a rapid pace and will invest nearly $60 billion in the development of artificial intelligence by 2030, [59] whilst the EU (European Commission) will invest only a fraction of that [60].

So, the evolution of Artificial Intelligence-related services, applications and products built on them are going to be extremely useful not only for people looking for comfortable solutions but persons with limited mobility and/or multiple disabilities, the blind, the hearing impaired, as well as persons with mental disabilities and autism based on virtual assistants and avatars, which will create an entirely new momentum in modern societies in terms of independent living with less demand for human caretakers and helpers by mitigating the shortage of social workers. Not to mention the possibility of early recognition and intervention services for disabled children at home in terms of health care. It also follows that this aspect of technological evolution will possibly ease the burdens of all – persons with disability, families, professionals, taxpayers – even in education. When it comes to education, our children will not only learn about facts to be memorized but also how to organize and synthetize those facts and data by triggering upper levels of skills in synthesizing and cooperation for further specialization of knowledge based on individualised method of learning supported by AI. The latter (individualised learning methods) is the source of the education of disabled children, which will be an asset and innovation for all non-disabled children in the foreseeable future either, leading to an indeed inclusive education for all.

As to the evolution of robotics, it will also change everything that we believe in when it comes to societal consequences. According to estimates published in TIME, within years millions of care robots at home will be deployed worldwide. Based on the forecast of the International Federation of Robotics, the market for social robots is expected to grow 29% annually from 2019 and 2022, and in the same period the figure for rehab robots is projected to grow 45% per year. [61] It follows that independent living and inclusive education (by stemming from the successful methods provided for disabled students) will also have an entirely different approach when it comes to humanoid robots and smart toys with emotions and programmed educational attitudes, as well as robot caregivers in elders' institutions and at home. It will also transform the customs and habits of families and the current approaches towards work-life balance as well as human rights.

5   Brain-Machine Implants: Is 'Cybernation' Coming?

The current speed of communication and processing of the human brain is increasingly lagging behind that of accelerating machines. According to Kurzweil, it was identified a difference of 1:3,000,000 between the speed of thought and the speed of interactions between the circuits of machines in favour of machines. It means that the speed of electrochemical signals of mammalian brains is about one hundred meters per second, which is in fact negligible compared to the near speed of light of signals in machines [62].

In the fall of 2020, Elon Musk unveiled his new research and development concept, an implant that can be inserted into the brain, which is a brain-computer interface (BCI). [63] Even though, there has not been much talk about exactly what this technology would be, providing a direct connection between the brain and the prosthesis to improve the quality of life for people with disabilities, especially those with reduced mobility, can be key to independent living. In fact, Musk's new announcement was not a surprise to the researchers at all, since the head of Tesla has been working on this project for three years. Musk, who has now a flagship of private spacecraft (see SpaceX project), also in early 2017 that revolutionary medical implants are expected to appear soon, which will also treat some neurological and brain diseases (e.g., Parkinson's disease), sensory disabilities (e.g., blindness, deafness). Musk indicated that these tools will be able to rehabilitate not only severe, but currently incurable disabilities and make the lives of those affected and their families better. [44] In addition, there can be much more exploitable areas in almost all sectors of the economy to improve productivity with a brain implant. Almost the only question is where the border is and where to draw the line as none of the most advanced economies has yet reached the potential level of full digitalisation. [64] In relation to this, the billionaire entrepreneur of Tesla also remarked in his own way, semi-funnily, that in the future, even Tesla vehicles will be able to be thought-driven [65].

Coincidentally or not, also in 2017, the renowned American scientific journal Nature reported that the U.S. military, through its development company DARPA, already had veterans to control mood swings and certain mental illnesses (major depression and epilepsy) by developing implants. [66] Moreover, there are indications that the BCI presented by Musk is still under development, especially targeting computer game users and media consumers. [67] (Musk informed the public about monkeys using implants when playing videogames in February 2021.) [68] At the same time, it is worth knowing that, both the entertainment industry and the social community have transformed to such an extent that the market capitalization (value) of IT companies is currently hitting historic stock markets' peaks, [69, 70] which in fact questions traditional social institutions such as (indirect) elections or ownership of and press freedom from editors, or even public education.

Qualitatively, this will be a completely new direction in history, as humans themselves are integrated into an information technology system, rather than the "dumb" devices adapting to man as they have so far. Just to remember, a proclamation signed by hundreds of scientists, referring to the dangers of the 'cybernation', was published in 1964. Its title was Triple Revolution, which also visioned mass unemployment and explosive poverty. Even though they thought of silent and relatively simple but efficient machines endangering humans' jobs, whilst standards of living have increased significantly over time, today we face entirely different challenges as in terms of poverty mankind has improved and many developing nations were also able to lift hundreds of millions out of poverty. As international law does not have a definition of the human race, nor does about family, whilst many countries that are at the forefront of technological innovation have not already acceded to various human genetic and human rights conventions and agreements, this challenge not only opens up but practically directly hints at the possibility of the coming of 'Homo sapiens conrectus', i.e., 'the improved man', and raises a number of other ethical questions, such as the goals of the transgender community, which is at the forefront of changing the human body, and the consequences of recognizing entirely new rights. It means that technology respects fewer and fewer social boundaries and today it can present unimaginable perspectives. Would all this be impossible? Let's see how much of a difference there can be between man and man: there are still fishing-gathering, spear-hunting tribes living today, with low life expectancy and their disadvantages and almost unimaginably large falling behind compared to the average person in New York using a smart phone and communicating with a headset.

Therefore, this phenomenon could be described as an asymmetric technological singularity, which could definitely become increasingly obvious and problematic in more and more areas of life and among individual social entities, especially in the areas of productivity, individualized – inclusive – education, employability and active aging. This kind of asymmetry will also be relevant in terms of geographical distribution. This process clearly showed the nature of presented changes even in the area of coronavirus vaccines when access to vaccines indicated asymmetric geographical distribution of the first wave of vaccines against coronavirus [71].

6 Conclusions

According to Kurzweil, as widely cited, the next 100 years could bring at least as much of a technological-biotechnological leap as has happened in history over the past 10,000 years, meaning that humanity is still facing an evolving singularity. Just as a reminder, the transition to farming may have taken place only ten thousand years ago, however, we cannot know this for sure since the oldest written clues to this are barely 5–6000 years old. In comparison, the (first phase) of the Industrial Revolution took place over virtually more than 80 years (1770–1850) in the world. And the computer revolution took only a few decades, starting in the 1980s. Biotechnology is also facing tremendous development, as human DNA can already be modified through the CRISPR-Cas9 patented in 2012. These technologies also raise a number of additional ethical issues, as they may mean the emergence of animal skills (e.g., night vision, super-hearing, etc.), which, however, may also bring a special advantage in the global labour market leading to a complete reinterpretation of anti-discrimination law in the future.

It is also indisputable that biotechnology can hold great potential even in the field of adult rehabilitation - presumably the hope of Formula 1 ex-pilot Michael Schumacher is also based on this. However, no matter how much technology develops, the rehabilitation period itself can hardly be shortened, as, for the time being, the learning process of the brain cannot be greatly accelerated. We currently can learn our physical functions in the same way (slowly) in childhood as we need to learn them again after an accident.

The future direction of technological development is always only one out of many options. It is worth remembering that major technological innovations have not spread in the past as previously predicted, so prophetic predictions should always be treated with caution. Nevertheless, it is interesting that as early as 1930, John M. Keynes addressed in *Economic Possibilities for our Grandchildren* the potential and mass unemployment effects of a higher level of technological advancement on society. [72] According to Keynes, technological advancement could reach a level where less living labour force will actually be needed. We are not here yet, as automation is currently dominant in certain sectors and areas only, and its further spread depends on many other things: wages, labour market size, robot developmental costs, logistics, position of companies and national banks, role of central government in the economy, political trends, etc. In addition, state-of-the-art technological innovation and solutions often only leak to the level of SMEs over many years or decades. Although there is a change here as well, as not only production cycles and innovation-driven adaptations are shortened, but individual production and service scales can be continuously expanded to increase consumption in order to resize companies by accelerating the socialization of innovations as presented by KPMG-Harvard's research on SMEs adaption. [73] Where will we be in 10 years from now, and will Keynes really be right by 2030?

Perhaps in a few decades, looking back today, we would say that in 2012 humanity has indeed entered a global crisis of global civilization. It seems that several insoluble contradictions are developing in parallel in our world because overpopulation and accelerated productivity occur at the same time, whilst a dramatic drop happens in controllability and sustainability in one part of the world as the exact opposite happens in another.

To sum up, we have arrived at the gates of a new world. The UNCRPD Convention [74] itself supports that more attention shall be paid to innovations and research. At the same time, we also have to protect the rights of persons with disabilities and even more: that of all persons. We therefore need a fine-tuned as well as twin-track approach for all people' sake with legal and real safeguards via human rights, based on universal freedom while freedom of science should also be respected at the same time in terms of protecting personal liberty as well as preserving the drive of innovation. It follows that the UN convention is not about preserving a right to remain disabled, but about providing choices and opportunities science can ensure for all by respecting individual identity and free choices as well as by maintaining an anti-discriminatory approach when it comes to services and built environment. These are the safeguards of democracy in terms of wider context.

We all have to recognize and acknowledge the fact that innovation stems from finding solutions to a specific, even personal purpose or problem, related to disability in many cases. The UNCRPD Convention is about dignity, diversity and human rights. As the Convention claims and cites, we have to make more efforts in terms of research and innovations; [74] however, I am always of the opinion that at the same time we also have the obligation based on our inherent interest to cherish the value of freedom, competition and diversity in technological development and services on the grounds of reasonableness and fairness.

Why? Because evolution of technology must also serve a wider purpose of finding and meeting the different needs of our very diverse humanity via reasonable conditions. This perspective is, however, based on societies' different developments and situations, which could provide us with flexibility and affordability in accordance with the given economic performance. It follows that we must not shut the door on new, even unusual solutions to special personal needs. We therefore must not curb innovation meaning freedom and more importantly, motivation in science; however, science and technology should serve the society itself, too. In relation to this, we cannot neglect those with special, even extreme needs, either. As already stated, in the future everybody might be somehow and to some extent disabled in one way or another when it comes to intelligent and smart software and services. In this sense, we are talking about a kind of evolution of disability itself by covering even healthy people, too.

In our age technology plays an enormously significant role as we have seen in the presented cases and argument; however, technology is not the purpose but always a means in the hands of humans. Human rights or science, you may ask. I firmly say: both. Both, because even the most developed societies can witness an evolving concept of disability as technology itself also evolves and the nature of disability changes as well. Although one of the most famous Hungarian atomic scientists, Ede Teller once said: "Two paradoxes are better than one. They may suggest a solution", [75] our real solution is to leave all options open and to accurately identify our own social values and, along these, to set goals that also guarantee our own national, community and human rights.

It will not be easy – but the key to our success as the guarantee of survival of mankind is human rights *and* science.

References

1. United Nations, Department of Economic and Social Affairs Disability: Convention on the Rights of Persons with Disabilities. https://www.un.org/development/desa/disabilities/convention-on-the-rights-of-persons-with-disabilities.html. Accessed 11 Feb 2021
2. Lovaszy, L.: What if my disability will not be relevant in the future?: On the occasion of the 10th anniversary of the united nations cinvention on persons with disabilities. IEEE Technol. Soc. Mag. **36**(1), 16–17 (2017). https://technologyandsociety.org/what-if-my-disability-will-not-be-relevant-in-the-future/. Accessed 11 Feb 2021
3. Polaris Market Research: Biotechnology Market Share, Size, Trends & Industry Analysis Report 2020–2026 (2020). https://www.polarismarketresearch.com/industry-analysis/biotechnology-market. Accessed 11 Feb 2021
4. Fortune Business Insights: Pharmaceuticals Market to Reach USD 1,310.0 Billion in 2020; Eruption of the COVID-19 Pandemic to Accelerate the Demand for Effective Treatments and Drugs Worldwide: Fortune Business Insights. GlobeNewswire (2020). https://www.globenewswire.com/news-release/2020/04/27/2022157/0/en/Pharmaceuticals-Market-to-Reach-USD-1-310-0-Billion-in-2020-Eruption-of-the-COVID-19-Pandemic-to-Accelerate-the-Demand-for-Effective-Treatments-and-Drugs-Worldwide-Fortune-Business.html. Accessed 11 Feb 2021
5. Eagleman, D.: The Brain – The Story of You, pp. 81–82. Pantheon, New York (2015)
6. BBC: Pistorius eligible for Olympics, 16 May 2008. http://news.bbc.co.uk/sport2/hi/olympics/athletics/7243481.stm. Accessed 11 Feb 2021
7. National Institute on Deafness and Other Communication Disorders (NIDCD): Cochlear Implants. https://www.nidcd.nih.gov/health/cochlear-implants. Accessed 11 Feb 2021
8. The Headquarters for Japan's Economic Revitalization: New Robot Strategy – Japan's Robot Strategy (2015). https://www.meti.go.jp/english/press/2015/pdf/0123_01b.pdf
9. UNESCO: International Bioethics Committee (IBC). https://wayback.archive-it.org/all/20091111091254/http://portal.unesco.org/shs/en/ev.php-URL_ID=1879&URL_DO=DO_TOPIC&URL_SECTION=201.html. Accessed 11 Feb 2021
10. The Nobel Prize: Press release: The Nobel Prize in Chemistry 2020, 07 October 2020. https://www.nobelprize.org/prizes/chemistry/2020/press-release/. Accessed 11 Feb 2021
11. Reader, R.: 2 women won the Nobel for CRISPR, but the battle for its patent rages on. Fast Company, 10 October 2020. https://www.fastcompany.com/90561762/nobel-prize-jennifer-doudna-emmanuelle-charpentier-crispr-patent-lawsuit. Accessed 11 Feb 2021

12. Regalado, A.: Engineering the Perfect Baby. MIT Technol. Rev., 05 March 2015. https://www. technologyreview.com/2015/03/05/249167/engineering-the-perfect-baby/. Accessed 11 Feb 2021

13. Masters, J.: 'Three-parent' babies approved in the UK. CNN, 15 December 2016. https://edi tion.cnn.com/2016/12/15/health/babies-three-people-embryos/index.html. Accessed 11 Feb 2021

14. Wu, J. et al.: Interspecies Chimerism with mammalian pluripotent stem cells. Cell **168**(3), 473–486 (2017). http://www.cell.com/cell/fulltext/S0092-8674(16)31752-4. Accessed 11 Feb 2021

15. Reardon, S.: Hybrid zoo: introducing pig–human embryos and a rat–mouse. Nature (2017). https://www.nature.com/news/hybrid-zoo-introducing-pig-human-embryos-and-a-rat-mouse-1.21378. Accessed 11 Feb 2021

16. Langston, J.: UW team stores digital images in DNA—and retrieves them perfectly. University of Washingon News, 04 July 2016. https://www.washington.edu/news/2016/04/07/uw-team-stores-digital-images-in-dna-and-retrieves-them-perfectly/. Accessed 11 Feb 2021

17. Clements-Cortes, A., et al.: Short-term effects of rhythmic sensory stimulation in Alzheimer's disease: an exploratory pilot study. J. Alzheimer's Disease **52**(2), 651–660 (2016). https:// pubmed.ncbi.nlm.nih.gov/27031491/

18. Klein, A.: Lasers reactivate 'lost' memories in mice with Alzheimer's. New Scientist, 25 July 2017. https://www.newscientist.com/article/2141677-lasers-reactivate-lost-memories-in-mice-with-alzheimers/. Accessed 11 Feb 2021

19. Cyranoski, D.: The CRISPR-baby scandal: what's next for human gene-editing. Nature, 26 February 2019. https://www.nature.com/articles/d41586-019-00673-1. Accessed 11 Feb 2021

20. Shwartz, M.: Target, delete, repair – CRISPR is a revolutionary gene-editing tool, but it's not without risk. Stanford Medicine, 20–27 (Winter 2018). https://stanmed.stanford.edu/2018wi nter/CRISPR-for-gene-editing-is-revolutionary-but-it-comes-with-risks.html. Accessed 11 Feb 2021

21. Statista: Total number of CRISPR patent applications worldwide per year from 1984 to 2018. https://www.statista.com/statistics/975117/total-number-of-crispr-patent-applications-worldwide/. Accessed 11 Feb 2021

22. Cyranoski, D.: Ethics of embryo editing divides scientists – Researchers disagree over whether making heritable changes to human genes crosses a line. Nature, 18 March 2015. https://www.nature.com/news/ethics-of-embryo-editing-divides-scientists-1. 17131. Accessed 11 Feb 2021

23. Cyranoski D.: Scientists sound alarm over DNA editing of human embryos. Nature, 12 March 2015. https://www.nature.com/news/scientists-sound-alarm-over-dna-editing-of-human-embryos-1.17110. Accessed 11 Feb 2021

24. As early as 1975, there was a scientific debate on DNA modification in the United States within the Life Sciences of the National Academy of Sciences, more: Berg, P. et al.: Summary Statement of the Asilomar Conference on Recombinant DNA Molecules. Proceedings of the National Academy of Sciences **72**(6), 1981–1984 (1975). https://www.ncbi.nlm.nih.gov/pmc/ articles/PMC432675/pdf/pnas00049-0007.pdf. Accessed 11 Feb 2021

25. Retraction Watch: Controversial gene-editing study flagged by Nature journal. https://retractio nwatch.com/2016/11/29/controversial-gene-editing-study-flagged-nature-journal/. Accessed 11 Feb 2021

26. See Article 3 of Charter of Fundamental Rights of the European Union (2012/C 326/02)

27. World Health Organization: Advisory Committee on Developing Global Standards for Governance and Oversight of Human Genome Editing - call for contributions. https://www.who. int/ethics/topics/human-genome-editing/consultation-2020/en. Accessed 11 Feb 2021

28. Human Genome Editing: A Draft Framework for Governance, 03 July 2020. https://www.who.int/docs/default-source/ethics/governance-framework-for-human-genome-editing-2nd onlineconsult.pdf?ua=. Accessed 11 Feb 2021

29. U.S. Abortion Statistics. Facts and figures relating to the frequency of abortion in the United States. https://abort73.com/abortion_facts/us_abortion_statistics/. Accessed 11 Feb 2021

30. Chorley, M.: Three-parent babies is not 'playing God', says Cameron as MPs vote to legalise IVF technique in Britain. Daily Mail Online, 03 February 2015.https://www.dailymail.co.uk/news/article-2937254/Cameron-set-vote-yes-three-parent-babies-Britain-country-world-approve-IVF-technique.html. Accessed 11 Feb 2021

31. Feher-Prout, T.: Stress and coping in families with deaf children. J. Deaf Stud. Deaf Educ. 1(3), 155–165 (Summer 1996). https://pubmed.ncbi.nlm.nih.gov/15579820/. Accessed 11 Feb 2021

32. Chadha, S., et al.: Global hearing health: future directions. Bulletin of the World Health Organization, p. 146. (2018). https://www.who.int/bulletin/volumes/96/3/18-209767/en/. Accessed 11 Feb 2021

33. National Research, Development and Innovation Office: National Brain Research Program to be continued, 05 September 2017. https://nkfih.gov.hu/english-2017/news-of-the-office/national-brain-research. Accessed 11 Feb 2021

34. Bouche, T., Rivard, L.: America's Hidden History: The Eugenics Movement. Nature, 18 September 2014. https://www.nature.com/scitable/forums/genetics-generation/america-s-hidden-history-the-eugenics-movement-123919444/. Accessed 11 Feb 2021

35. Arnon, S., Dahan, N., Koren, A., et al.: Thought-controlled nanoscale robots in a living host. PLoS ONE 11(8) (2016). http://journals.plos.org/plosone/article/file?id=10.1371/journal.pone.0161227&type=printable. Accessed 11 Feb 2021

36. Creighton, J.: Bionics: the astonishing future of the human body. Futurism, 12 February 2015. https://futurism.com/images/bionics-the-astonishing-future-of-the-human-body/. Accessed 11 Feb 2021

37. Wits University: Biomedical engineers connecting a human brain to the internet in real time. Medical Xpress, 14 September 2017. https://medicalxpress.com/news/2017-09-biomedical-human-brain-internet-real.html. Accessed 11 Feb 2021

38. NBC Learn: Mysteries Of The Brain: Brain-Computer Interface (video). NBC, 04 May 2020. https://www.youtube.com/watch?v=p1XQ4uxqxZI. Accessed 11 Feb 2021

39. Evans, B.: Mobile is eating the world, 2015. Andreessen Horowitz, 19 June 2015. https://a16z.com/2015/06/19/mobile-it-changes-everything/. Accessed 11 Feb 2021

40. Roberts, J.: Walmart's Use of Sci-fi tech used by Walmart to spot shoplifters raises privacy questions. Fortune, 09 November 2015. http://fortune.com/2015/11/09/wal-mart-facial-recognition/. Accessed 11 Feb 2021

41. Vincent, J.: AI 'Emotion recognition' can't be trusted. The Verge, 25 July 2019. https://www.theverge.com/2019/7/25/8929793/emotion-recognition-analysis-ai-machine-learning-facial-expression-review. Accessed 11 Feb 2021

42. Hutson, M.: Artificial intelligence goes bilingual – without a dictionary. Science – AAAS, 28 November 2017. http://www.sciencemag.org/news/2017/11/artificial-intelligence-goes-bilingual-without-dictionary. Accessed 11 Feb 2021

43. Loria, K.: Elon Musk wants to link computers to our brains to prevent an existential threat to humanity. Business Insider, 17 June 2017. http://www.businessinsider.com/elon-musks-neuralink-artificial-intelligence-2017-6?IR=T. Accessed 11 Feb 2021

44. Statt, N.: Elon Musk launches Neuralink, a venture to merge the human brain with AI. The Verge, 27 March 2017. https://www.theverge.com/2017/3/27/15077864/elon-musk-neuralink-brain-computer-interface-ai-cyborgs. Accessed 11 Feb 2021

45. Reardon, S.: AI-Controlled brain implants for mood disorders tested in people. Nature, 22 November 2017. http://www.nature.com/news/ai-controlled-brain-implants-for-mood-disorders-tested-in-people-1.23031. Accessed 11 Feb 2021
46. Le Roux, M., Mollard, P.: Game over? New AI challenge to human smarts. Phys.org., 08 March 2016. https://phys.org/news/2016-03-game-ai-human-smarts.html. Accessed 11 Feb 2021
47. United Nations: The World's Cities in 2018, Data Booklet (2018). https://www.un.org/en/events/citiesday/assets/pdf/the_worlds_cities_in_2018_data_booklet.pdf. Accessed 11 Feb 2021
48. Hao, K.: Training a single AI model can emit as much carbon as five cars in their lifetimes. MIT Technol. Rev. 06 June 2019. https://www.technologyreview.com/2019/06/06/239031/training-a-single-ai-model-can-emit-as-much-carbon-as-five-cars-in-their-lifetimes/. Accessed 11 Feb 2021
49. United States Environmental Protection Agency: Greenhouse Gas Emissions. Sources of Greenhouse Gas Emissions. https://www.epa.gov/ghgemissions/sources-greenhouse-gas-emissions. Accessed 11 Feb 2021
50. Belkhir, L., Elmeligi, A.: Assessing ICT global emissions footprint: Trends to 2040 & recommendations. J. Clean. Prod. **177**, 448–463 (2018). https://www.sciencedirect.com/science/article/abs/pii/S095965261733233X. Accessed 11 Feb 2021
51. Statista: Internet of Things (IoT) active device connections installed base worldwide from 2015 to 2025. https://www.statista.com/statistics/1101442/iot-number-of-connected-devices-worldwide/. Accessed 11 Feb 2021
52. Mobility Arena: The First Mobile Phone with Internet Capabilities – Authoritative Mobile History. https://mobilityarena.com/first-mobile-phone-with-internet-access/. Accessed 11 Feb 2021
53. Statista: Global digital population as of October 2020. https://www.statista.com/statistics/617136/digital-population-worldwide/. Accessed 11 Feb 2021
54. Statista: Number of smartphone users worldwide from 2016 to 2021. https://www.statista.com/statistics/330695/number-of-smartphone-users-worldwide/. Accessed 11 Feb 2021
55. Dudley, D.: The Evolution of Mobile Phones: 1973 to 2019. Flaunt Digital, 07 November 2018. https://flauntdigital.com/blog/evolution-mobile-phones/. Accessed 11 Feb 2021
56. Ekekwe, N.: What Africa's banking industry needs to do to survive. Harv. Bus. Rev. 28 July 2016. https://hbr.org/2016/07/what-africas-banking-industry-needs-to-do-to-survive. Accessed 11 Feb 2021
57. Lovaszy, L.: Corporate individualism – changing the face of capitalism. IEEE Technol. Soc. Mag., December 2015. https://ieeexplore.ieee.org/stamp/stamp.jsp?arnumber=7360305. Accessed 11 Feb 2021
58. Statista: Manufacturing industry-related robot density in selected countries worldwide in 2019. https://www.statista.com/statistics/911938/industrial-robot-density-by-country/. Accessed 11 Feb 2021
59. Laskai, L.: Beijing's AI Strategy: Old-School Central Planning with a Futuristic Twist. Council on Foreign Relations, 09 August 2017. https://www.cfr.org/blog/beijings-ai-strategy-old-school-central-planning-futuristic-twist. Accessed 11 Feb 2021
60. Statista: Projected artificial intelligence spending in Europe in 2019 and 2023. https://www.statista.com/statistics/1115464/ai-spending-europe/. Accessed 11 Feb 2021
61. Purtill, C.: Stop Me if You've Heard This One: A Robot and a Team of Irish Scientists Walk Into a Senior Living Home. Time, 04 October 2019. https://time.com/longform/senior-care-robot/. Accessed 11 Feb 2021
62. Kurzweil, R.: The Singularity Is Near: When Humans Transcend Biology. Pengiun Books, London (2006)

63. Crane, L.: Elon Musk demonstrated a Neuralink brain implant in a live pig. New Scientist, 29 August 2020. https://www.newscientist.com/article/2253274-elon-musk-demonstrated-a-neuralink-brain-implant-in-a-live-pig/. Accessed 11 Feb 2021

64. European Investment Bank: Who is prepared for the new digital age? (2020). https://www.eib.org/en/publications-research/economics/surveys-data/eibis-digitalisation-report.htm. Accessed 11 Feb 2021

65. Vanian, J.: Elon Musk shows off Neuralink brain implant technology in a living pig. Fortune, 29 August 2020. https://fortune.com/2020/08/28/elon-musk-neuralink-brain-implant-livestream/. Accessed 11 Feb 2021

66. Reardon, S: AI-controlled brain implants for mood disorders tested in people. Nature, 22 November 2017. https://www.nature.com/news/ai-controlled-brain-implants-for-mood-disorders-tested-in-people-1.23031. Accessed 11 Feb 2021

67. Dujmovic, J.: Opinion: Facebook passes its first hurdle on a brain-computer interface. MarketWatch, 08 August 2019. https://www.marketwatch.com/story/facebook-passes-its-first-hurdle-on-a-brain-computer-interface-2019-08-08. Accessed 11 Feb 2021

68. Stevenson, R., Davis, R.: Elon Musk Says He Wired Up a Monkey's Brain to Play Video Games. Bloomberg, 01 Feb 2021. https://www.bloomberg.com/news/articles/2021-02-01/elon-musk-wired-up-a-monkey-s-brain-to-play-videogames. Accessed 11 Feb 2021

69. Statista: Market capitalization of selected U.S. tech and internet companies in 2006 and 2020. https://www.statista.com/statistics/216657/market-capitalization-of-us-tech-and-internet-companies/. Accessed 11 Feb 2021

70. Levy, A.: Tech's top seven companies added $3.4 trillion in value in 2020. CNBC, 31 December 2020. https://www.cnbc.com/2020/12/31/techs-top-seven-companies-added-3point4-trillion-in-value-in-2020.html. Accessed 11 Feb 2021

71. Furlong, A.: The ultimate geopolitical game – distributing a coronavirus vaccine. Politico, 27 July 2020. https://www.politico.eu/article/the-ultimate-geopolitical-game-distributing-a-coronavirus-vaccine/. Accessed 11 Feb 2021

72. Keynes, J.M.: Economic possibilities for our grandchildren. In: Keynes J.M. (ed.) Essays in Persuasion. Palgrave Macmillan, London (2010). https://doi.org/10.1007/978-1-349-59072-8_25

73. Harvard Business Review Analytic Services – KPMG: Embracing Disruption With Innovation (2016). https://hbr.org/resources/pdfs/comm/kpmg/EmbracingDisruptionWithInnovation.pdf

74. UN Convention on the Rights of Persons with Disabilities: Article 4, General obligations, point f). https://www.ohchr.org/EN/HRBodies/CRPD/Pages/ConventionRightsPersonsWithDisabilities.aspx#4. Accessed 11 Feb 2021

75. Teller, E., Teller, W., Talley, W.: Conversations on the Dark Secrets of Physics, p. 135. Springer, New York (1991). https://doi.org/10.1007/978-1-4899-2772-9

Sources of Risk and Design Principles of Trustworthy Artificial Intelligence

André Steimers[(⊠)] and Thomas Bömer

Institute for Occupational Safety and Health of the German Social Accident Insurance,
Alte Heerstrasse 111, 53757 Sankt Augustin, Germany
andre.steimers@dguv.de

Abstract. The importance of artificial intelligence is constantly increasing due to ongoing research successes and the implementation of new applications based on it. It is already described as one of the core technologies of the future. This technology is also increasingly being applied in the field of safety-related applications, which enables the implementation of innovative concepts for novel protection and assistance systems. However, for this to lead to a benefit for human safety and health, a safe or trustworthy artificial intelligence is required. However, the increasing number of accidents related to this technology shows that classical design principles of safe systems still need to be adapted to the new artificial intelligence methods. On the one hand, this requires a basic understanding of the components of trustworthy artificial intelligence, but on the other hand, it also requires an understanding of AI-specific sources of risk. These new sources of risk should be considered in the overall risk assessment of a system based on AI technologies, examined for their criticality, and managed accordingly at an early stage to prevent later failure of the system.

Keywords: Trustworthy artificial intelligence · Safety · Risk · Machine learning

1 Introduction

1.1 Artificial Intelligence

Artificial intelligence (AI) methods are mainly used to solve highly complex tasks, such as processing natural language or classifying objects in images. They not only allow significantly higher levels of automation to be achieved, but also open up completely new fields of application.

Today, the term artificial intelligence is mainly used in the context of machine learning, such as in neural networks, decision trees or support vector machines, but also includes a variety of other applications such as expert systems or knowledge graphs.

A common property of all these methods is the ability to solve problems by emulating concepts that are generally associated with intelligent behavior. Thus, by using artificial intelligence, concepts such as learning, planning, perceiving, communicating, and cooperating can be applied to technical systems. These capabilities enable entirely

© Springer Nature Switzerland AG 2021
V. G. Duffy (Ed.): HCII 2021, LNCS 12778, pp. 239–251, 2021.
https://doi.org/10.1007/978-3-030-77820-0_18

new intelligent systems and applications, which is why artificial intelligence is often seen as the key technology of the future.

By using artificial intelligence, concepts such as learning, planning, perception, communication and cooperation can be transferred to technical systems. These capabilities enable completely new intelligent systems and applications, which is why artificial intelligence is often seen as the key technology of the future.

1.2 Current Status and Forecast Potential

Today, advanced industrialized countries allocate significant sums of money in the order of billions to research and development in AI, with the United States leading the way, closely followed by China and Israel [1]. For example, the estimated strategic funding for the sector in China is in the hundreds of billions. This funding sum is composed of various national but also municipal funding programs. For example, the investments of the city of Shanghai already amount to 15 billion Euros or those of the city of Tianjin 13 billion euros.

Due to the increasing importance of artificial intelligence, the EU Commission has therefore also decided to strategically promote this area and is providing 1.5 billion euros in the "Horizon 2020 Research and Development Program". Furthermore, the European Innovation Council will provide another 2.5 billion euros for the promotion of innovative AI projects. There are also funding programs of the individual countries, such as France with 1.5 billion euros until 2023 or Germany with 3 billion euros until 2025 [2].

The consulting firm PwC forecasts that due to the accelerated development and spread of artificial intelligence, global gross domestic product will be up to 14% higher in 2030, which would correspond to an increase of an additional 13.3 trillion euros. The largest increases here would be expected for China at 26% and the USA at 14.5% [3]. In these forecasts, the economic impact of artificial intelligence is based on the following three assumptions:

1. productivity gains by companies automating processes (including the use of robots and autonomous vehicles).
2. productivity gains from companies augmenting their existing workforce with AI technologies (assisted and augmented intelligence).
3. increased consumer demand due to the availability of personalized and/or qualitative AI-enhanced products and services.

In particular, the ongoing automation expected as a result of artificial intelligence will inevitably have an impact on the labor market and make simple production tasks obsolete. On the other hand, its use will create new jobs that will not only be reserved for experts and proven specialists. For example, the acquisition and preparation of the training data required for machine learning processes is very labor-intensive and generally represents a rather simple activity. For this reason, some forecasts suggest that as many jobs will be created as eliminated through the use of artificial intelligence [4].

1.3 Areas of Application and Sample Applications

Devices based on artificial intelligence methods can solve even complex problems with a high degree of accuracy and are already encountered in a variety of applications.

For example, one of the most frequently used applications on a daily basis are virtual assistants. Cortana (Microsoft Inc.), Google Assistant (Google Inc.), Siri (Apple Inc.) and IBM Watson (IBM Inc.) represent the most popular digital personal assistants today. They all have in common that they can process instructions in natural language, making them very easy to use. The user's voice instructions are executed after processing and acknowledged by feedback, which is also provided by a voice message.

Chatbots are another way to take advantage of advances in natural language processing driven by artificial intelligence. For example, chatbots can handle a large proportion of basic customer service queries in first-level support, helping to free up call center staff to answer more complex questions. Many chatbots can also be found in the area of customer service. For example, large German companies such as Commerzbank, Lufthansa, Telekom and BMW have also been successfully using chatbots in this area for many years.

Today, we mostly encounter self-driving vehicles in the form of driverless transport vehicles, but some of them are already on the road. Tesla, for example, offers driver assistance in its vehicles that realizes some elements of a self-driving vehicle. Since 2015, for example, the Tesla Model S has been able to drive autonomously on highways. The driver does not have to operate the steering wheel, the gas pedal or the brake. It is difficult to make a statement about the quality of the self-driving vehicles currently being tested, as there are no standardized metrics or data. However, the annual figures published by the California Department of Transportation, which not only list the mileage of test vehicles in California by manufacturer, but also indicate how far these vehicles were able to drive independently without the intervention of a test driver, provide an indication. Even though other manufacturers have since caught up to Waymo, this list has been topped for years by this subsidiary of the Alphabet group of companies, which includes Google. The figure for 2019 for this company was a distance of 21,151 km without the intervention of a test driver [5].

Artificial intelligence can also support a wide range of activities that previously required experts. For example, the analysis of CT, MRI, or X-ray images is a much-discussed and often mentioned possibility in the media to support doctors in their diagnosis.

Another possibility is the automated verification of contracts. In 2018, for example, a study investigated the possibility of verifying non-disclosure contracts using artificial intelligence. In this study, the results of 20 lawyers were compared with those of an artificial intelligence-based algorithm. The algorithm achieved an average accuracy (F1-score) of 94%, whereas the average accuracy of the lawyers was only 85%. In terms of speed, the algorithm with a processing time of only 26 s naturally beat the lawyers' average of 92 min as well [6].

Artificial intelligence can also be used in various ways in the area of occupational safety and health.

Protection and control devices based on artificial intelligence already enable not only fully automated vehicles or robots, but also the avoidance of accidents through assistance systems that recognize hazardous situations.

Examples include two projects by Microsoft Corp. and Skanska AG in collaboration with Smartvid.io Inc. that aim to provide comprehensive monitoring of construction sites and storage areas. With the help of special software, not only can construction progress be documented automatically, but the use of personal protective equipment such as helmets, safety vests and gloves can also be monitored. It can also detect and warn of hazards such as hot machines or leaking hazardous liquids. In addition, the software also allows dynamic warning of a shift in the hazards that mainly occur on the construction site.

2   Trustworthy Artificial Intelligence

The previous section shows that the use of artificial intelligence offers many opportunities and can promote new innovations in many respects. However, the use of systems, especially machines, based on AI processes can also change the physical and mental strain on employees. In order to exclude new hazards from the use of this technology or to reduce them, trustworthy AI is required.

The concept of trustworthiness goes far beyond that of security and includes the following fundamental properties:

- **Reliability**
  The system or application must maintain proper function under specified environmental conditions and provides consistent output. The limits of the system both in terms of its functionality but also in terms of environment are thereby defined by the system specification.
- **Robustness**
  The system or application must maintain its function or transition to a safe state under all conditions. These conditions include deviations from the system specification, especially from the defined environmental conditions, but also external and internal disturbances as well as defects.
- **Resiliency**
  Describes the ability of the system or application to return to normal operation as quickly as possible after a disruption.
- **Security**
  The system or application must be protected against external attacks.
- **Data security**
  The data and privacy of all stakeholders must be protected at every stage of the lifecycle.
- **Transparency**
  The actions and results of the system or application must be transparent. For this, the data, features, learning algorithm, but also the model must be available for inspection by a human.

- **Explainability**
  The actions and results of the system or application must be understandable and comprehensible. For this purpose, the model must be described or prepared in such a way that it can be interpreted by a human being.
- **Verifiability**
  In a verifiable AI system, the process that led to a specific result of the AI system can be repeated under the same conditions with the same result.
- **Controllability**
  The user of an AI system, can take control from and/or over the AI system at any time.
- **Predictability**
  In a system with high reliability, the accuracy of the results, in terms of a desired system behavior, is within predetermined limits. A high degree of predictability is especially relevant for systems that interact or cooperate with humans.
- **Security against misuse and misapplication**
  The system or application must be protected against foreseeable misuse or misapplication of operators.

Due to the high importance of this topic, there are currently a number of international standardization projects dealing with individual aspects of a trusted AI. The already published Technical Report ISO/IEC TR 24028 "Information technology - Artificial intelligence (AI) - Overview of trustworthiness in artificial intelligence" gives a good overview of this topic. More information on specific aspects of the robustness of a trustworthy AI system can be found in the Technical Report ISO/IEC TR 24029-1 "Information technology - Artificial Intelligence (AI) - Assessment of the robustness of neural networks - Part 1: Overview".

3   AI Characteristics with an Impact on Trustworthiness

It is necessary for an AI system that claims the notion of trustworthiness to have a variety of relatively different characteristics. Many of these characteristics are known from general security technology and are also considered a general benchmark for the development of secure systems. Other properties only acquire a special relevance due to the specific characteristics of AI-based systems. Thus, it remains to be clarified which special characteristics of AI-based systems influence the various properties of a trustworthy AI system and what special attention should be paid to during its development.

A few of those relevant characteristics can for example be found in the Technical Report ISO/IEC TR 24027 "Information technology - Artificial Intelligence (AI) - Bias in AI systems and AI aided decision making" or the International Standard ISO/IEC IS 23894 "Information Technology - Artificial Intelligence - Risk Management". The following list represents a compilation of various specific AI characteristics that have an impact on the trustworthiness of such a system. These characteristics should also be taken into account when preparing risk assessments for systems of this type.

3.1   Degree of Automation and Control

The degree of automation, which is often also referred to as the degree of autonomy, describes on the one hand the extent to which an AI system can operate independently of human supervision, but also its independence from human control. It thus determines not only how much information about the behavior of the system is available to the operator, but also defines the control and intervention options of the human. On the one hand, it must be assessed how high the degree of automation must be for the respective application, but on the other hand, it must also be assessed whether the human is adequately supported by the AI application and is given appropriate room for maneuver in the interaction with the AI application.

Systems with a high degree of autonomy may exhibit unexpected behavior that can be difficult to detect and control. Highly automated systems can thus pose risks in terms of their reliability and safety.

In this context, several aspects are relevant, such as the responsiveness of the AI system, but also the presence or absence of a human critic. In this context, a critic serves to validate or approve automated decisions of the system. Such a critic can be realized by technical control functions in the system or be present in the form of a human whose task it is to intervene in critical situations or to acknowledge system decisions. Furthermore, the adaptability of the AI system has to be considered. Here the question arises whether or to what extent the system can change itself. Especially systems that use continuous learning or reinforcement learning change their behavior over time. This has the advantage that these systems can acquire new functions or adapt to changing environmental conditions via feedback loops or an evaluation function. The disadvantage of such systems, however, is that they can deviate from the initial specification over time and are difficult to validate.

3.2 Degree of Transparency

The degree of transparency determines how much information about the internal processes of an AI system is available to the operator. In particular, information about the model underlying the decision-making is relevant here. Often, aspects of comprehensibility, explainability, reproducibility and general transparency are summarized under this term. Thus under this aspect usually the evaluation of the general function takes place, with which it is examined whether information about this is present in a sufficient extent and is comprehensible both for experts and the user. Furthermore, it depends on this aspect whether results of the system can be reproduced. The question of whether an AI system is recognizable as such to a user is also answered under this point.

Systems with a low degree of transparency can pose risks in terms of their fairness, security and accountability. On the other hand, a high degree of transparency can lead to confusion due to information overload. It is important to find an appropriate level of transparency to provide developers with opportunities for error identification and correction, and to ensure that a user can trust the AI system. A high level of explainability protects against unpredictable behavior of the system, but is often accompanied by lower overall performance in terms of quality of decisions. Here, a trade-off must often be made between transparency or explainability and the performance of a system.

In addition, the accuracy of the information about an AI system's decision-making process must be considered in each case. Thus, it is possible for a system to provide clear and coherent information about its decision-making process, but for that information to be inaccurate or incomplete.

1. explainable:
   The system provides clear and coherent explanations.
2. articulable:
   The system is able to extract the most relevant features and roughly represent their interrelationship and interaction.
3. comprehensible:
   The system is not capable of providing real-time explanations of system behavior, but these are at least verifiable after the fact.
4. black box:
   No information is available about how the system works.

3.3 Intended Operating Environment

The complexity of the intended use environment of an AI system determines the full range of possible situations that an AI system, when used as intended, must handle. Since it is not possible to create an exact and fully complete system specification, especially when used in complex environments, the actual operational context during operation will deviate from the specified limits. As a general rule, more complex environments can quickly lead to situations that were not considered in the design phase of the AI system. Therefore, complex environments can introduce risks with respect to the reliability and safety of an AI system.

For this reason, an AI system must have the ability to still provide reliable results even under small changes in input parameters. Although it is often not possible to predict all possible states of the environment that an AI system may encounter during its intended use, efforts should be made during the specification phase to gain an understanding of the intended use environment that is as complete as possible. In doing so, knowledge about the input data underlying the decision-making and the sources used to obtain it, such as the sensor technology used, should also be obtained and taken into account. Important aspects here are the questions whether the system is fed with deterministic or stochastic, episodic or sequential, static or dynamic and discrete or continuous data.

3.4 Development Process

The development process includes the lifecycle phases of specification, design, implementation, and verification/validation of the AI system. Inappropriate or inadequate methods and processes applied in each of these phases can lead to low-quality and thus unsafe or unreliable AI systems.

The specification phase is of particular importance here, since errors arising from this phase have an immediate effect on all further phases of the lifecycle and can only be remedied with difficulty or not at all in these phases. For example, a faulty or inadequate design process may result in insufficient description and specification of the contexts in which the AI system is to be used, which will lead to later unexpected failure of the finished AI system.

When planning the design and architecture of the system to be implemented, it is important to ensure that the complexity of the application and the future operating environment is kept to a minimum. In general, an increase in complexity always increases the risk that the system will exhibit unexpected behavior in its use. In this context, we often speak of an apparent non-determinism of the AI system. However, this term is critical in that even complex AI systems will always produce deterministic results at an arbitrarily granular point in time. This is especially true for systems based on machine learning. Only in the case of systems that continue to learn should it be noted that changes in the model on which the decision is based occur over time (model drift). However, if this process is interrupted and only a static point in time is considered, these systems also deliver deterministic results. Increasing complexity leads to an increase in the stochastic state space in which the system moves, which increases the probability that the system will encounter situations that lie outside the specified range.

In the implementation phase, the system is built according to the requirements of the specification. For this purpose, the specification is usually analyzed and interpreted by a development team in order to create a strategy for the technical realization of the system. This strategy and the associated design should again be kept as simple as possible in order to reduce the complexity of the system and increase its transparency. This applies in particular to the hardware and software architecture as well as the selection of the AI methods to be used. The implementation strategy is of great importance here, as it can have an immense impact on the design. For example, a requirement can often be paraphrased in such a way that it is still fulfilled semantically, but its technical implementation can be significantly simplified. As an example, consider the simple requirement for a collaborative robot arm that should not reach for a human. This function can already be implemented relatively reliably using deep learning methods, but it is a very complex task for a technical system because the possible state space for the object "human" is very large. If, however, this requirement is formulated in such a way that the robot arm may only grip a certain selection of workpieces, the original goal of the basic requirement is likewise fulfilled, but now represents a fairly easy output for the technical system to handle, since the object "workpiece" can be completely specified and thus spans a very small state space.

Another special feature of AI systems based on machine learning methods is the basic implementation process. In classical software development, the specification is interpreted by the development team and implemented accordingly. In machine learning systems, which are trained with the help of an algorithm on the basis of data, however, the mental concept of the specification must be described implicitly by the database. Thus, the composition of the database as well as the general data quality is of immense importance. Beyond that the training algorithm does not always find the best possible solution, why here usually much work must be invested into the optimization of the resulting model and it is usual to accomplish many training runs with different parameterization, in order to receive a model as good as possible.

Reusing existing components, modules, trained models or complete systems in a new application context can lead to problems due to the different requirements between the specified context and the new context. For example, the use of a system designed to identify people in photos on social networks will not be easily used to identify people in the context of an assistance system in a work environment. This is partly due to the different state spaces of the applications, so the system may not be able to recognize workers in their personal protective equipment because there was no data to train the model for this, but also because of the higher precision required for the latter application. This shows that even a transfer to new environments, for example other industries, is not easily possible.

In the verification and validation phase, difficulties arise especially in the verification of non-transparent systems and systems that continue to learn, which are not easy to handle. In the case of systems that continue to learn, one is confronted with the circumstance that the model of the AI system on which the decision-making is based changes constantly over time and thus a stable final version of this model and thus of the system never exists. This would require a dynamic verification, validation and release process. This can be based on a combination of continuously running automated internal tests and regularly recurring or continuously running external tests at the manufacturer. The fundamental problem of testing complex and thus non-transparent systems must be countered by an appropriate scope of verification and validation activities. Statistical, formal and empirical methods are generally available for this purpose. It is advisable to exploit their bandwidth as fully as possible, but at least to use a high degree of statistical and empirical methods. In particular, empirical methods, such as extensive field testing, falsification testing, actively exploring the limits of the AI system, or the application of metamorphic testing methods, which allow a better erudition of the stochastic state space, are effective means here.

3.5 System-Hardware

AI technology is increasingly dependent on custom ASIC chips rather than commodity hardware. This can lead to new security risks, especially in context where access to hardware for training machine learning is given to external users (such as cloud computing applications). Users with access to accelerator chips can potentially exploit this access to hijack the system, steal intellectual property, or damage the hardware.

If hardware-related errors occur during the training phase or during the operation of an AI system, they can negatively affect the correct execution of the algorithm or even prevent it altogether.

In general, hardware-related failures can be divided into three groups. The first group refers to classical hardware errors that are based on defective components. Examples are short circuits or interruptions of single or multiple memory cells, defective bus lines, drifting oscillators, stuck-at errors or parasitic oscillations at the inputs or outputs of integrated circuits. The second group of errors are so-called soft errors. Soft errors are unwanted temporary state changes of memory cells or logic components, usually caused by high-energy radiation. The last group consists of faulty drivers and, if used, faulty modules of the application software of the hardware used.

The relevance of the different fault models depends on the system architecture used. When using cloud or edge computing, for example, it is particularly important to perform an analysis of the possible errors of the network architectures used.

For example, an error model for different networks includes communication errors such as data corruption, unintended repetition of messages, incorrect sequencing of messages, data loss, unacceptable delays, message insertion, masking, and different addressing problems. On the other hand, thread scheduler errors and memory errors play a special role when GPUs are used.

Besides that, the asymmetry of machine learning algorithms can also be another cause of errors. This asymmetry means that in the training phase, the amount of data and computational power needed to calculate the coefficients by a machine learning algorithm is very high, while in the application phase, less computational power is needed. However, there are some difficulties in transferring the training results from a GPU, edge, or cloud system to an embedded system because many AI frameworks use Python as the description language, while the control program of an embedded system is usually in C or C++. In addition, incompatibilities between the memory management of the different systems as well as different accuracies are also a cause of errors.

3.6 Technological Maturity

Technological maturity describes how mature and error-free a particular technology is in a particular application context. If less mature and new technologies are used in the development of the AI system, they may harbor risks that are still unknown or difficult to assess. For mature technologies, on the other hand, a greater variety of experience data is usually available, making risks easier to identify and assess. However, with mature technologies, there is a risk of risk awareness decreasing over time, so that the positive effects depend on constant risk monitoring and appropriate maintenance.

The maturity of a technology for implementing an AI system can be classified as follows:

1. emerging:
   Being researched and tested for possible future use.
2. strategic:
   Is likely to be operational only in the medium to long term.
3. limited:
   Is already operational for the implementation of a limited number of applications.
4. preferred:
   Is already preferred for the implementation of most applications.
5. current:
   Is currently supported and in use.
6. out of service:
   On the verge of no longer being used.

3.7 Privacy

Due to the central importance of training data in AI systems based on machine learning methods, data protection also plays an important role in both the development and operation of an AI system. Care must be taken to protect sensitive data, such as personal data but also trade secrets, at every stage of the lifecycle. Especially when cloud systems are used to train the models and these are not under the control of the own organization, the question of data protection comes to the fore. At the same time, however, care must be taken to ensure that measures to guarantee data protection do not affect the quality of the trained models. For example, it can have negative effects if a model for person recognition is trained on data in which persons have been anonymized by pixelating their bodies.

3.8 Fairness

Fairness means that the AI application treats all users and affected parties equally fairly. This is achieved when no group is more adversely affected by a decision than another. Fairness is related to the creation and operation of decision systems. A fair system treats all people, without undue preference or bias. Wherever possible, it excludes or appropriately controls for the influence of variables such as sensitive characteristics or demographic categories when they are not relevant to the proper performance of the task or when their use would result in or exacerbate unfair outcomes.

Unfair bias usually occurs when data about individuals are processed by a machine learning model and bias in the design process has negatively affected the quality of human-computer interaction. In a symbolic AI system, it usually arises from the bias in specified knowledge or when data about individuals are not processed directly, but individuals or groups of individuals are affected indirectly.

Typical sources of discrimination represent unbalanced training data or even statistical underrepresentation of minorities, which in consequence can lead to poorer functional quality of the application for these user groups.

4 Measures

The field of risk control is strongly characterized by safety-related systems as well as protective and assistance systems. The development of such systems usually takes place in a regulated context on the basis of international standards, which place requirements on the quality of such systems, but also on the design of the development of such systems. The interpretation and implementation of such normative requirements requires not only a broad, but also in-depth background knowledge, but above all experience in this field. Technical measures are based on the four pillars of inherently safe design, safety margins, fail safe and safety-related measures. In the field of artificial intelligence, however, these have some special features to which attention must be paid.

4.1 Inherently Safe Design

In machine learning, the quality of the result depends to a large extent on the quality of the training data. If the training data does not cover the complete variance of the test data or contains errors, the model will generate an equally erroneous algorithm. If a very complex model was used, it is very difficult to understand the decision making of the algorithm and thus to identify faulty parts of the program. Consequently, it is advantageous to choose models of low complexity, which can be interpreted by humans and thus also be checked and maintained. In this way, features that do not contribute a causal relationship to the result and would thus lead to erroneous results can be removed manually. A disadvantage of interpretable models, however, is that their simplicity is often accompanied by a lower quality in the sense of the probability of a correct result.

4.2 Safety Margins

If we consider a mechanical system, for example, there is a point at which a load will cause the system to fail. Since this point can usually only be determined within a certain tolerance range, these systems are operated well below these limits by introducing a certain safety margin or safety factor.

Such uncertainties can also be identified in machine learning. For example, there is uncertainty about whether the learning data set fully covers the distribution of the test data, or even in the instantiation of the test data. To the extent that this uncertainty is captured, a safety distance or safety boundary can also be defined for an algorithm that sufficiently delineates the areas of a reliable decision from those in which uncertainty exists. Therefore, models that can algorithmically calculate a measure for the uncertainty of their prediction are to be preferred.

For classification problems, for example, the distance from the decision boundary can be used, where a large distance means an increase in the reliability of a prediction. At the same time, however, it is important to note that this only applies to areas where there is a high number of available training data and therefore where the probability density is high. The reason for this is that in areas with a low probability density, there is usually little or even no training data available. This leads to the fact that there the decision boundary is determined by inductive errors and thus a high epistemic uncertainty and thus the distance from this boundary has no meaning for the reliability of the prediction.

4.3 Fail Safe

One of the most important safety engineering strategies is the fail safe principle. Again, it is important to have a measure of the uncertainty of the prediction. If this is relatively high, the system could request further verification by a human. In the case of a collaborative robot, however, this would also mean that the robotic arm must first and foremost assume a safe state.

4.4 Safety-Related Protective Measures

Safety-relevant protective measures can be implemented in a variety of ways and cover a broad spectrum from external protective devices to quality-assuring processes for error minimization. The development process of software in the safety-related environment is described by a multitude of regulations and standards. The IEC 61508 series of standards "Functional safety of safety-related electrical/electronic/programmable electronic systems", in particular Part 3 "Requirements for software", is a good example of this. This standard also contains a large number of methods to be applied to avoid and reduce systematic errors during software development. This development process is embedded in the Functional Safety Management (FSM), which, among other things, describes the entire lifecycle of the system in Part 1. In addition, there are some software-related requirements in Part 2 of this series of standards, which must also be taken into account. However, to date there are no regulations that clarify the relationship between functional safety and artificial intelligence or describe special measures for AI systems in a safety-related environment. At the international level, initial activities have been underway since 2020 to describe requirements for the use of artificial intelligence in the context of functionally safe systems.

5 Conclusion

Artificial intelligence already has many fields of application today and is a rapidly growing market. It is to be expected that artificial intelligence processes will increasingly contribute to the realization of new innovative applications in the future and will thus find their way permanently into various domains. However, especially in order to ensure safety and health at work, this development can only take place in compliance with fundamental principles of developing safe systems within the framework of trustworthy artificial intelligence. This requires a precise understanding of the specific aspects of the individual artificial intelligence processes and their impact on the overall quality of the system in general and its safety in particular.

References

1. Delponte, L.: European Artificial Intelligence leadership, the path for an integrated vision. Policy Department for Economic, Scientific and Quality of Life Policies, European Parliament, Brussels (2018)
2. European Commission: Communication on Artificial Intelligence for Europe. European Commission, Brussels (2018)
3. PwC: Artificial intelligence in HR: A no-brainer. PwC (2018)
4. PwC: AI will create as many jobs as it displaces by boosting economic growth. PwC (2018)
5. DMV: Autonomous Vehicle Disengagement Report 2019. State of California Department of Motor Vehicles (2019)
6. LawGeex: Comparing the Performance of Artificial Intelligence to Human Lawyers in the Review of Standard Business Contracts. LawGeex (2019)

Analysis of the Application of Artificial Intelligence in the Creative Space

BeiLe Su[✉]

School of Art, Shandong Jianzhu University, No. 1000, Fengming Road, Licheng District, Jinan 250101, Shandong, China

Abstract. Artificial Intelligence (Ai intelligence) abbreviated for AI. It is a science and technology to study and develop theories, methods, techniques and application systems for simulating, extending and expanding human intelligence. With the progress of science and technology, artificial intelligence has become the development strategy of many countries, countries gradually integrate artificial intelligence into all areas of society. As a new place for technological innovation activities in recent years, the open, shared, innovative and democratic nature of the creative space has given it a very wide range of development prospects.

The application of artificial intelligence in the creative space can realize the intelligent management process, intelligent business operation, intelligent online communication, intelligent material management, intelligent personalized information push service, environment and order maintenance intelligence, aiming to create a new type of creative space, further attract creative talents from all walks of life and develop into high-quality creative and entrepreneurial distribution center.

The information age environment has provided unprecedented new opportunities and challenges for the creative space. To realize the intelligence of the creative space, we need to do a good job in the following four aspects of the response. First of all, the development of creative space should focus on and break through the key technologies of AI, combine with the needs of users, combine the technological achievements of external artificial intelligence, give full play to artificial intelligence talents and technological advantages, and tap the greatest value of the creative space. Secondly, the foundation and core of the creative space service is all kinds of raw materials, tools and resources of innovative products, and the use of artificial intelligence technology should also serve the resource construction and management of space. By integrating the tool materials required by the founders with modern intelligent analysis, we continue to enrich the variety of materials and lay the resource base for enhancing the creative services of the genesis space. Third, artificial intelligence technology is a new technology, in order to ensure that artificial intelligence technology in the creative space services play a real role, we must strengthen the construction of human resources, the introduction and training of high-end talent has become a new need for intelligent applications. In addition, we can use advanced artificial intelligence equipment to optimize the space planning and management of the Creative Space. Space design should be reasonable science, intelligent space and intelligent products combined, hardware equipment to meet the needs of big data, can support big data storage and computing services and operating systems, etc.

V. G. Duffy (Ed.): HCII 2021, LNCS 12778, pp. 252–262, 2021.
https://doi.org/10.1007/978-3-030-77820-0_19

In order to adapt to the development and application of artificial intelligence, we should do a good job in artificial intelligence technology, resource intelligent management technology, related personnel integration, intelligent space re-engineering four aspects of the response measures. Increase investment in construction, as soon as possible to apply artificial intelligence in the creative space, in order to provide the founders with a better quality of modern creation.

Keywords: Artificial intelligence · Creative space · Application

1 Introduction

With the progress of science and technology, countries are scrambling to lay out artificial intelligence development strategies, and gradually integrate artificial intelligence into all areas of society. Facing the new opportunities and challenges brought about by the development of artificial intelligence, the creative space can be intelligent through the use of artificial intelligence, so as to better serve the creation of space.

2 Artificial Intelligence and Creative Space

Artificial Intelligence, abbreviated as AI. It is a science and technology to study, develop the theory, method, technology and application system for simulating, extending and expanding human intelligence. Artificial intelligence is a multi-sphere comprehensive science, which covers a wide range of knowledge, including computer science, mathematics, logic, psychology, biology, neuroscience, bionics, statistics, economics, linguistics and philosophy and other related scientific content. Artificial intelligence is a branch of computer science that can highly simulate human consciousness and thought processes, and the core of research is how to enable machines to handle highly complex tasks like humans. The continuous iteration and innovation of artificial intelligence enables it to integrate more widely into many areas of human society.

There is a close relationship between artificial intelligence and creative space. Genesis Space was originally moved to China from the United States, and its corresponding English is Hackerspace, which translates directly as Hackerspace, which is called The Creative Space because of differences in language and social environment. Refers to the organization of diversified activities, such as salons, training, competitions and other activities, is committed to helping creators to interact, exchange circle construction, to enable entrepreneurs in the common environment to help each other.[1] People see the creative space as the democratic embodiment of innovation, the existence of the creative space, so that everyone has a low-cost opportunity to personally participate in design, engineering, manufacturing, learning and other activities, which greatly enhances the creative passion of ordinary people. Therefore, from this point of view, the maker space embodies democracy in design, engineering, manufacturing and education. From

---

[1] Liu wei. Create new driving back scene under the big school students create a new industry education carrier construction Study - to Tianjin City High School public creating space as an example of the example of the city of Tianjin. Did not come and develop,2018,042(09):94–99.

the development trend, as a new place for technological innovation activities in recent years, the creative space will become a place for technological innovation activities and academic exchanges and accumulation, and will also become a space for creative generation and realization and trading, and then gradually form an entrepreneurial distribution center, its openness, sharing, innovation and democracy have given it a very broad development prospects (Fig. 1).

In January 2015, for example, Premier Li Keqiang visitedChaihuo Maker, Shenzhen'sfirst creative space, and signed on the membership card, has since entered a period of rapid development in China's creative space (Fig. 2).

Public libraries with innitable advantages have naturally joined the boom in creative space. This kind of creative space usually has good hardware and software equipment, digital technology and mobile Internet technology and other technologies parallel huge database, spacious experimental space, these all provide a good basis for the development of artificial intelligence technology, and the development of artificial intelligence can be faster and better conversion applications, for the transformation and innovation of creative space services to provide strong technical support, promote the creative space to intelligent, sustainable direction. The interaction between the two is very close. In recent years, many colleges and universities in China have set up corresponding disciplines and specialties around the field of artificial intelligence, trained a number of high-quality professionals, and set up a special guest space in public libraries. Such as Wuhan University Library held the "Creative Carnival", innovation and entrepreneurship contest, such as Shanghai Jiaoxuan University Library held 3D printer pioneer competition (Fig. 3).

Thus, artificial intelligence has a unique advantage in the creative space, whether it is application research and development, practice or post-maintenance.

3   The Application of Artificial Intelligence in the Creative Space

Artificial intelligence in the creative space through the implementation of management process modules and business operation modules, mainly using the Internet, big data, artificial intelligence technology and cloud computing, based on the actual situation of the operation of the creative space business, to achieve the creative space resources construction and management of intelligent, spatial circulation management, creative services and spatial reference consulting and other services intelligent process.

3.1   Intelligent Management Processes

The construction of creative space resources is mainly to do a good job in the compilation of space professional resources. Genesis space professional resources to be selected, ordered and accepted three stages, need a lot of manpower, financial resources and time. Artificial intelligence in the creative space should be used, can optimize the resource screening process, resource demand and procurement laws analysis, combined with user needs to develop procurement lists, develop scientific procurement plans and processes, the creation of relevant information and demand analysis, targeted procurement. The creative space screening work, under the artificial intelligence technology can automatically process the resource type, automatically generate the order catalog, the post-acceptance

Fig. 1. Creative space

Fig. 2. Wood-burning creative space

work can also be completed in bulk. The construction of creative space resources can also use artificial intelligence technology for the classification and protection of professional resources. It is possible to introduce advanced artificial intelligence technology and means to class out the professional resources of the creative space and realize the security protection of the resources.

Fig. 3. Smart Creater Library

Fig. 3. (*continued*)

3.2 Intelligent Material Management

Artificial intelligence to achieve the creative space resources collection circulation management services intelligent, including self-help loan also creater tools circulation services, intelligent access services, tool information automatic finishing services. Self-service loan also circulation service using automatic loan robot real tool resources to borrow also automation, through the robot automatic identification tool bar code, to achieve the purpose of automatic loan tool. At the same time, automatic loan robot can also be based on the type of bar code identification tools, through the pre-installed mobile device, the tool transport to the identified area, reduce the intensity of the work of tool managers, improve the efficiency of the creation of resources sorting. Artificial intelligence uses sophisticated positioning technology for open reading and service of electronic data resources in the open shelf access service of the genesis space, and integrates remote positioning technology, face recognition technology, accurate positioning of users, and organizes the record of the access of the pioneering data in order to provide intelligent open-shelf access services for them. The application of artificial intelligence in the creation of space data collection mainly involves the collection of electronic data, shelf, sorting and other work. Artificial intelligence robot can replace the operator to complete the heavy electronic data collection and sorting work, improve the speed of data on the shelf, and thus improve the data flow rate.

3.3 Intelligent Online Communication

The purpose of online communication services is to provide a platform for businesses in different fields. Through the online communication system established by artificial intelligence, the integration, analysis and human-machine dialogue of multidisciplinary and multi-disciplinary knowledge are realized, real-time interaction with the founders is realized, and the child-based and intelligent work of the creation data search, basic consulting, communication and other work is realized, and on this basis, the behavior of the pioneers is analyzed and summarized, prompted and informed in advance when the creation of customer consultation questions, and the establishment of a creative exchange platform in the same field. At the same time, the creative space can also make full use of virtual reality technology, online and offline and other ways to implement intelligent interactive robot real-time consulting services.

3.4 Intelligent Operation of the Business

The creative space has a large number of paper resources and digital resources, the creation of a large number of resources to retrieve their own information needs there are certain difficulties. The introduction of artificial intelligence into resource retrieval can make the retrieval process fast and accurate, improve the accuracy rate of information effectively, and make corresponding suggestions for errors. Artificial intelligence technology can use computers to simulate the human brain, and combined with the user's retrieval process, the use of neural network algorithms to speculate on the user's needs, filter out more in line with the user"s needs of the resource information and provide to the user, which greatly improves the efficiency and accuracy of spatial retrieval, and thus improves the utilization of space resources and user service satisfaction.

3.5 Personalized Information Push Service Intelligence

Artificial intelligence makes personalized, customized applications the norm, enabling the space network to push the information it needs to users more proactively, intelligently, in a timely and accurate manner. Through artificial intelligence, the use of large data, intelligent analysis, Internet technology, such as the construction of creative space intelligent analysis system, rapid collection, sorting, analysis and processing of data information, comprehensive collection, analysis and processing of creative behavior information, tool circulation information, a comprehensive grasp of the personal habits of the creation of customers, access to the flow of data tools, for the creation of personalized information information push services, to achieve personalized intelligent customized services, and video transmission of data resources display, improve the efficiency and quality of creative space services.

3.6 The Maintenance of the Environment and Order is Intelligent

Artificial intelligence and the Internet of Things deep integration, linked to artificial intelligence computer vision recognition technology and video surveillance means, can build a creative space intelligent online monitoring system, to achieve the monitoring and management of tool resources, access control system of personnel access control management, seat reservation system seat reservation management, environmental health monitoring and management, to achieve the positioning, tracking, management and monitoring of space personnel, the use of language communication ability robot supervision space order, discourage the creation of uncivilized behavior, maintain a good environment in space.

4 The Response of Creative Intelligence in Creative Space Applications

The development of artificial intelligence has provided unprecedented new opportunities and challenges for the creative space, and in order to realize the intelligent space of the creative space, we need to do a good job in the following four aspects of the response.

4.1 Technical Support

The development of creative space should focus on and break through the key technologies of AI, combine with the needs of users, combine the technological achievements of artificial intelligence outside, give full play to the talents and technological advantages of artificial intelligence, make full use of space big data analysis, mining, all-round expansion of services, tap the greatest value of the creative space.

4.2 Resource Security

The foundation and core of the creative space service is the various tools and professional materials of the creative space, and the use of artificial intelligence technology should first serve the resource construction of the space. Through artificial intelligence technology, the development of modern space resources construction program, the use of the Internet's huge information network, and constantly excavate interview information, the construction of digital information service platform. Through the integration of traditional offline tool resources and modern online resources, and constantly enrich space resources, in order to enhance the creative space intelligent services to lay a resource base.

4.3 Talent Protection

Creator space can provide entrepreneurs with free and adequate product display space, and in many activities, creators can carry out projects, product visual display.[2] Artificial intelligence technology is a new technology, in order to ensure that artificial intelligence technology in the creative space services play a real role, we must strengthen the construction of human resources. It is possible to set up scientific and reasonable organization to ensure the effective application and orderly implementation of artificial intelligence technology. In order to introduce and train high-end talents, the application of artificial intelligence technology needs big data technology, computer technology, scientific computing decision-making, etc., to introduce and train a group of high-end talents with practical ability in order to ensure that artificial intelligence technology is effectively applied in the creative space. We should strengthen the re-training and re-education of space management and service personnel, constantly adapt to the rapid development of science and technology, and promote the deep integration of artificial intelligence and space management services.

4.4 The Re-creation of Intelligent Space

Creative space can use advanced artificial intelligence equipment to improve space planning and management. Space design should be reasonable science, intelligent space and intelligent products, hardware equipment to meet the needs of big data, can support big data storage and computing servers and operating systems. The combination of artificial intelligence and the creative space is an important witness of the deepening of the application scope of artificial intelligence, through artificial intelligence, the creative space in the electronic data resource construction, circulation service management, reference consulting, information retrieval, personalized information services, environment and order maintenance and other aspects to achieve intelligence, so as to provide more quickly and perfectly to the creation of a variety of support and services, to achieve efficient and intelligent operation of space.

5 Conclusion

To sum up, the construction of creative space is not only an important means to promote the development of China's entrepreneurial cause, but also one of the main ways to improve the overall innovation and creative consciousness. In this regard, it is necessary to fully grasp the existing problems in the construction of the creative space, combined with the implementation of the above-mentioned measures to promote the long-term development of the creative space. In order to adapt to the development and application of artificial intelligence, Creator Space should increase investment and construction in artificial intelligence technology, resource intelligent management technology, related talent integration, intelligent space re-engineering, etc., and apply artificial intelligence to The Creator Space as soon as possible, so as to better provide more high-quality and convenient services for Creators.

---

[2] Chen Dejin. Create space for allDevelopment Model Comparison and Propulsion Strategy Research... Straits Section学,2016(05):3–5.

References

1. Xin, G.: The application of artificial intelligence in university libraries. Inside Outside Lantai **7**, 47–49 (2020)
2. Liu, W.: Create a new driving back scene under the university students create a new industry education building research - to Tianjin City High School public creating space as an example... not come and develop. **042**(09), 94–99 (2018)
3. Chen, D.: Comparative and Propulsion Strategy Research on the Development Model of Crowd-Creative Space, Straits Science (05), 3–5 (2016)

Benchmarking Robots by Inducing Failures in Competition Scenarios

Santosh Thoduka$^{(\boxtimes)}$ and Nico Hochgeschwender

Department of Computer Science, Hochschule Bonn-Rhein-Sieg,
53757 Sankt Augustin, Germany
{santosh.thoduka,nico.hochgeschwender}@h-brs.de

Abstract. Domestic service robots are becoming more ubiquitous and can perform various assistive tasks such as fetching items or helping with medicine intake to support humans with impairments of varying severity. However, the development of robots taking care of humans should not only be focused on developing advanced functionalities, but should also be accompanied by the definition of *benchmarking protocols* enabling the rigorous and reproducible evaluation of robots and their functionalities. Thereby, of particular importance is the assessment of robots' ability to deal with failures and unexpected events which occur when they interact with humans in real-world scenarios. For example, a person might drop an object during a robot-human hand over due to its weight. However, the systematic investigation of hazardous situations remains challenging as *(i)* failures are difficult to reproduce; and *(ii)* possibly impact the health of humans. Therefore, we propose in this paper to employ the concept of scientific robotic competitions as a benchmarking protocol for assessing care robots and to collect datasets of human-robot interactions covering a large variety of failures which are present in real-world domestic environments. We demonstrate the process of defining the benchmarking procedure with the human-to-robot and robot-to-human handover functionalities, and execute a dry-run of the benchmarks while inducing several failure modes such as dropping objects, ignoring the robot, and not releasing objects. A dataset comprising colour and depth images, a wrist force-torque sensor and other internal sensors of the robot was collected during the dry-run. In addition, we discuss the relation between benchmarking protocols and standards that exist or need to be extended with regard to the test procedures required for verifying and validating conformance to standards.

Keywords: Robotics competitions · Benchmarking · Assistive robots

1 Introduction

The Multi-Annual Roadmap for robotics in Europe identifies healthcare as one of the domains in which robotics is expected to play a significant role [7]. Assistive robotics, which is seen as one of the sub-domains along with clinical and rehabilitation robotics, is concerned with providing assistive aid to care givers or to

© Springer Nature Switzerland AG 2021
V. G. Duffy (Ed.): HCII 2021, LNCS 12778, pp. 263–276, 2021.
https://doi.org/10.1007/978-3-030-77820-0_20

persons with physical, sensory or cognitive impairments. Their acceptability and impact on such users is increasing, though most robots are still in the research phase [10, 22]. The challenges identified for deploying robots include updating safety standards to ensure a certain level of robustness [22]. Research is also ongoing in areas such as designing the robots to cater to user needs [23], and assessing the impact of personality factors on the acceptance of socially assistive robots [25].

Typical tasks for such robots include fetching items, engaging in conversation, assisting with medicine intake, monitoring a person's activity, etc. They work in close proximity to humans, with some tasks such as object handovers requiring close contact. Therefore the robots must be guaranteed to perform their activities in a safe manner before they can be deployed in care facilities or in homes.

The evaluation of functionalities developed for these robots is often performed in laboratories or in a limited number of settings. Developing benchmarking protocols will enable a more rigorous evaluation of such robotic systems, ensuring that the functionalities of the robot are reproducible in various environments, and repeatable across several trials. Benchmarking is also one of the ways in which the conformance to standards can be improved. The standard ISO 13482 [15], which provides requirements and guidelines for designing personal care robots, requires that all "performance values related to safety of the robot shall be verified and validated." Some of the methods listed for achieving this is through testing the various performance values of the robot under normal and abnormal conditions, injecting faults during tests, endurance tests and observation during operation. The standard ISO 12100 [14], which provides guidelines for risk assessment and risk reduction in machinery, requires the estimation of the probability of occurrence of identified hazardous events. Since the estimation is typically based on historical and statistical data, this is a challenge for robots that have not been put through rigorous testing yet. Several functionalities of assistive robots are still in the research phase; therefore there is a lack of data concerning the likelihood of failure of different components such as perception or grasping. Additionally, since the likelihood of failure is often a function of the robot's morphology and sensor configuration, it is hard to share data between different robots types.

It is even more challenging to quantify failures in the case of functionalities which require interaction with humans or the environment. A failure, leading to a hazardous event, could be caused by several factors, including the behaviour of the human. For example, during a robot-to-human handover, the robot might release the object shortly after feeling a pulling force, but the human might also release the object immediately if they feel the robot is not releasing the object. This would result in a potentially hazardous event (such as a knife falling down), but identifying the exact cause of the failure and estimating the likelihood of the event is a challenge.

Hence, incorporating failures and hazardous events in the benchmarking process is necessary to fully evaluate a robotic system and is a step towards ensuring compliance with standards for safety and risk reduction.

In the context of scientifically and rigorously evaluating assistive robots, we attempt to answer the following questions:

1. *How should benchmarking protocols for social and physically assistive robots be defined?* We propose employing scientific competitions as the means to benchmark functionalities and task execution of robots, which has been shown to be a viable method in prior work such as RoCKIn [4]. We elaborate on this in Sects. 2 and 3.
2. *What is the methodology to define benchmarks which incorporate failure conditions in the interaction between robots and humans?* We propose a procedure which defines the expected function and corresponding failure modes, and incorporates these as independent variables in the experiment design. Failure modes which involve interaction are induced by the human volunteer participating in the experiment. We discuss this with the help of a use case in Sect. 4.
3. *How can benchmarking robots with this methodology help them conform to existing standards?* In Sect. 5, we discuss existing standards which define safety guidelines and risk assessment and reduction procedures and how they relate to the methodology discussed.

2   Related Work

Benchmarking in robotics is an active field of research, whether focused on benchmarking complete systems [21,29], benchmarking tasks such as pick-and-place [24,28] and navigation [26], or benchmarking hardware components such as end-effectors [11]. Typically, they define a benchmarking framework by specifying the task, environment and evaluation metrics, allowing users to replicate the setup in their own facilities. In the case of [29], the authors develop a simulation-based benchmarking platform using software containers to enhance reproducibility.

Benchmarking has also been carried out through robotic competitions. The DARPA robotics challenge [1], RoboCup [3] and World Robot Challenge [6] are all robotics competitions which target robot applications in different domains such as rescue, agile manufacturing, service robotics, etc. More recently, projects such as RoCKIn [4] and RockEU2 [5], which have now been brought under the umbrella of the European Robotics League [2], have brought competitions closer to scientific experiments by comparing the performance of robots in certified test beds such that the results are reproducible and repeatable [8]. They target three domains, namely, domestic service robots, industrial robots working in a smart factory environment and rescue robots. Benchmarks for domestic service robots include functionalities such as object recognition and navigation, and tasks such as *Getting to know my home, Catering for Granny Annie's comfort,* in which the robot is operating in the home of *Granny Annie* performing various domestic tasks [9].

RoCKIn [4] introduced the concept of functionality and task benchmarks, separating the evaluation of standalone functionalities and complete tasks which require the integration of several functionalities. This was a differentiating factor from previous competitions, which typically evaluated robots on their performance in a complete task. By introducing the benchmarking of standalone functionalities, the evaluation is more fine-grained, while limiting the influence of one functionality on another. However, while these competitions evaluate functionalities of service robots, there is no explicit benchmarking of factors such as safety and resilience to failures. Unsafe actions such as collisions result in a penalty or disqualification, but is not the focus of the benchmarks.

Safety and autonomy are two of the benchmarks proposed in [12] for evaluation socially assistive robots, amongst others such as scalability, privacy, impact on user's care etc. The authors regard both safety of the robot itself, and ensuring safety of the user as important factors. Autonomy is considered from the viewpoint of whether the robot can effectively perform its tasks, and whether the user can trust the robot to perform them. Resilience to failure conditions or unexpected situations is therefore a crucial aspect of autonomy.

Tolmeijer et al. [27] propose a taxonomy of failures which affect trust during human-robot interaction. Four failure types are identified: (i) design: failures caused by the robot performing as designed, but not as expected by the user, (ii) system: failures caused by the robot not performing as designed, (iii) expectations: similar to the design failure except that the behaviour of the robot is still considered correct, and the user's expectations should be corrected to mitigate the failure, and (iv) user: failures caused by actions by the user which were not expected by the robot. Several mitigation strategies are suggested for regaining trust of the user, such as apologizing, proposing alternate actions, or asking the user for a justification of their behaviour.

Using competitions as a means to benchmark robots has been shown to be successful. However, in particular for assistive robots, they must be updated to incorporate aspects such as resilience to failure, trust, safety, etc. We utilize the benchmarking procedures from RoCKIn [4] and extend it to explicitly include failure conditions as part of the variability of the benchmark.

3   Scientific Competitions for Robot Benchmarking

The domestic service robotics competitions in RoboCup, RoCKIn, and RockEU2 target robots operating in a home environment performing various domestic tasks, including iteracting with people. Assistive robots in healthcare environments are closely related but with the additional caveat that they could interact with persons with impairments. This makes safety a crucial aspect in designing the robots, and by extension competitions, and benchmarking protocols.

3.1   HEART-MET: Healthcare Robotics Technologies - Metrified

The METRICS project[1] aims to address the need for benchmarking robots in the four priority areas healthcare, inspection and maintenance, agri-food and agile

---

[1] https://metricsproject.eu/.

production by organizing robotics competitions in the four areas under a common evaluation framework. The healthcare competition, Healthcare Robotics Technologies - Metrified (HEART-MET), targets assistive robots which perform care-related tasks by benchmarking typical tasks in a care facility or private home. Since the tasks involve the robot operating in dynamic and unstructured environments, and interacting with older adults with physical, sensory and cognitive impairments, it is necessary to validate the safety of the robot. The HEART-MET evaluation plan [13] describes the competition in more detail and includes definitions of various functionality and task benchmarks.

The competitions are of two types: (a) field evaluation campaigns (FEC), in which robots compete at a certified physical test bed; and (b) cascade evaluation campaigns (CEC), which are online competitions evaluated on datasets. The datasets for the cascade evaluation campaign are collected from robots competing in the field evaluation campaigns. The CEC thus allows teams to improve specific functionalities which do not require the use of a robot, but nevertheless benefit from realistic datasets which have been generated by several different robot platforms.

Following the benchmark types introduced in RoCKIn [4], the FEC comprises of two types of benchmarks: (a) functionality benchmarks (FBM), which evaluate individual functionalities of the robot; and (b) task benchmarks (TBM), which evaluate the execution of a complete task. Functionality benchmarks include object detection, human recognition, activity recognition, human-to-robot and robot-to-human handover, task-oriented grasping, opening a cupboard etc. Task benchmarks include the delivery of a requested item to a person, preparing a drink, and assessing the activity state of a person. Robots are expected to run multiple trials, particularly for FBMs, and are evaluated based on aggregated metrics (such as true positive rate) over all trials. In benchmarks where quantitative metrics are not applicable, scoring is based on intermediate achievements during the trial. For example, for item delivery, intermediate achievements include navigating to the pickup location, detecting the item, grasping the item, etc.

For both FBMs and TBMs, there is a special emphasis on the feature variations introduced for each trial. Some variations are simply the configuration of the task, such as the object to be detected, location of the task, or the person involved in handover task. Some variations are introduced to evaluate the resilience of the robot to unexpected situations. This applies in particular to tasks which involve interaction of the robot with a human or the environment. For example, while opening a cupboard, the robot might encounter a stuck door, or items could fall out of the cupboard.

3.2 Defining a Benchmark

In order to specify the benchmarking procedure for a given functionality or task, we first identify and specify several aspects of the benchmark, i.e. *(i)* define the objective of the benchmark, *(ii)* identify dependent and independent variables, *(iii)* identify failure modes associated with the execution of the benchmark, *(iv)*

specify evaluation metrics (or achievements for non-quantitative evaluation), and
(v) specify minimum data sources to be recorded.

An example of this process for the activity recognition benchmark can be
seen in Fig. 1.

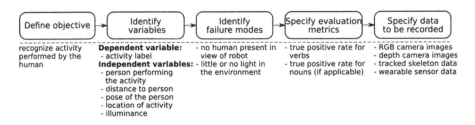

Fig. 1. Procedure for defining a benchmark using activity recognition as an example

The objective must concisely state the desired objective of the robot when
performing the benchmark. This is later used to identify failure modes by considering different aspects of the objective which are not able to be fulfilled.

Variables for the benchmark include the dependent variables (i.e. those which
are the target of the benchmark), and independent variables which are varied
across trials. The failure modes are a particular type of independent variable,
which present the robot with some type of abnormal condition. In the example
shown in Fig. 1, the robot does not interact with a human or environment,
hence the failure modes correspond to the configuration of the environment.
The absence of a human renders the objective of the benchmark unachievable
while a low light environment possibly makes the objective unachievable for most
robots. Failure modes can also be caused internal hardware and software faults
(such as a broken camera), but our focus here is on failure modes arising from
external factors (i.e. through configuration of the scene, or behaviour of humans
during interaction). When such a situation is encountered during the execution
of a benchmark, the robot scores an achievement if it is able to identify that it
is an abnormal condition.

The final step is to identify data which is to be recorded during the execution
of the benchmark. The actual data recorded may differ based on the robot platform and available sensors. Recording the right data is important since it will
allow the careful design of challenges for the cascade campaign, which target the
same benchmark (e.g. activity recognition in the case of Fig. 1), or challenges
that address the detection of failure conditions (as in the case for handovers
described in Sect. 4).

3.3   Execution and Dataset Collection

The execution of trials is controlled using a referee box, which communicates
with the robot by sending a start signal and type of benchmark to be executed.

The robot sends back the result of the trial once it has completed. For example, for a trial of the activity recognition FBM, the robot is placed near a person, and the referee box sends a start signal. The person is instructed to perform the activity specified by the referee box, which the robot recognizes and finally returns a result message with the recognized activity.

Collecting data during the execution of a benchmark serves two purposes: *(i)* it serves as a method of recording the test conditions, including available sensors on the robot, a third-person view of the functionality, and results, all of which can be analyzed at a later time; and *(ii)* it aids in the creation of realistic datasets which can be used for improving the performance of algorithms related to that benchmark. In HEART-MET, data collected during the execution of a benchmark in a FEC will later be labelled and used as test sets in the CEC. The recorded data can include sensors on the robot (such as cameras, force-torque sensors, laser scanner etc.), external cameras, smart home sensors, wearable sensors etc. For each trial, the robot begins recording internal sensor data in the form of ROS bagfiles when triggered by the start signal from the referee box, and stops once the trial is complete. The recorded data, result messages, and trial configurations on the referee box are collated to form a partially labelled dataset. For some FBMs, such as object detection, additional annotation of the recorded data is needed to create a fully labelled dataset.

4   Use Case: Handover FBM

In this section, we use the robot-to-human and human-to-robot handover as a use case to describe the benchmark specification process in more detail and to exemplify the data collection process which includes interaction failures. Receiving and giving objects are essential skills for an assistive robot. Several challenges exist, including variablity in the type of objects, coordinating the interaction with the human in a natural manner, and ensuring a safe and fault-free execution. In defining the benchmark for the handover functionality, we focus primarily on evaluating the robot's capability of handling failure scenarios. We follow the procedure defined in Sect. 3.2 to define the benchmarking protocol for this functionality.

Objective. The objective of the handover functionality is to safely transfer an object from the giver to the receiver. *"Safely"* refers to ensuring the safety of the robot itself, the human, the object being handed over and the surrounding environment. An additional requirement is that the handover occurs in a manner that is intuitive to the person, which includes executing the handover at a comfortable position between the human and robot, comfortable grasp pose on the object and timely release or grasp of the object. These additional requirements are subjective and require feedback from the persons involved for evaluation. We focus here on the primary objective, though the subjective requirements can be included in the benchmarking protocol using the same process.

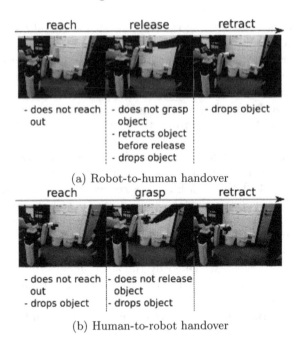

(a) Robot-to-human handover

(b) Human-to-robot handover

Fig. 2. The phases and interaction failure modes caused by the human for (a) robot-to-human and (b) human-to-robot handover

Variables. The location, time of day and lighting conditions are variables common to several benchmarks, and are included for this benchmark as well. For this benchmark, the object, the person and the person's pose (such as sitting, standing, or laying) are specified as independent variables as well.

Failure Modes. Figure 2 illustrates the phases and the associated failure modes for both handover functionalities. The failure modes do not indicate the *cause* of the failure, but simply the type of failure that can occur. For example, for the failure mode *does not grasp object*, the cause could be that the human no longer wants the object, the object is too far away, or that there is no suitable grasp position available. For the purposes of benchmarking, we are currently only interested in the failure mode, and not the causes. Once the failure modes are enumerated, they are used to generate variations in the benchmark trials by instructing the human to either behave nominally or to induce one or more of the failure modes. Some sample trial configurations for a robot-to-human handover benchmark are shown in Table 1. The volunteer receives an instruction for each phase of the handover.

Evaluation Metrics. The evaluation of this benchmark is based on intermediate achievements. In the nominal case, the achievements are successfully reaching

Table 1. Sample trial configurations for a robot-to-human handover with instructed behaviour for the human volunteer

No.	Object	Location	Time	Reach	Release	Retract
1	Bottle	Kitchen	Morning	Reach out	Grasp object	-
2	Towel	Bedroom	Evening	Do not reach out	-	-
3	Pill box	Living room	Afternoon	Reach out	Do not grasp object	-
4	Book	Living room	Morning	Reach out	Grasp object	Drop object

out, grasping or releasing the object, and retracting. In the case where a failure mode is induced, the robot instead scores an achievement if it detects the failure mode. For example, if the human drops the object during the handover, the robot scores an achievement if it detects that the object has dropped.

Fig. 3. Trials the handover functionalities consist of successful handovers, failed trials including unreleased objects, dropped objects, and ignoring the robot (top to bottom)

The trial configurations, each of which consists of an instantiation of the defined variables, are fixed beforehand, and all teams must execute all trials. Some variants, such as the lighting conditions, are difficult to reproduce for all teams, but a best effort is made to achieve uniformity in such cases. The failure modes are easily induced by instructing the human volunteer to behave in a certain way for a particular trial.

Data. The data collected during this benchmark will be used for improving the detection of the failure modes. Therefore, any available sensors that the robot might use for detecting the failures are recorded. Figure 3 shows a subset of the frames captured from the robot's camera during several trials, in which the volunteers completed the handover successfully, did not release the object, dropped objects and did not respond to the robot. Other data recorded includes depth images, RGB images from the end-effector camera, force-torque sensor at the wrist, and proprioceptive sensors of the joints. Figure 4 shows force measurements by the force-torque sensor and corresponding image frames from a second camera on the robot. The force caused by the interaction is evident in the top plot at the start of the *release* phase, and the reduced downward force once the object leaves the robot arm is visible in the bottom plot towards the end of the *release* phase.

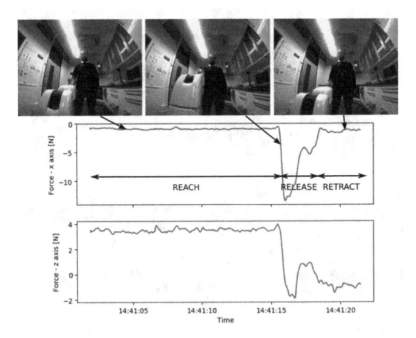

Fig. 4. Force measurements from the wrist force-torque sensor during a robot-to-human handover

The videos and other sensor data are extracted and labelled with the outcome of each phase of the handover. Since the handover functionality cannot be evaluated in a cascade campaign, the dataset recorded during the field campaign is used to create two related dataset challenges: *(i)* to detect whether the handover was successful or not; and *(ii)* to detect the failure mode if the handover was unsuccessful. During a dry-run of the field evaluation campaign conducted in our lab, 150 trials of the robot-to-human handover and 144 trials of the human-to-robot handover were executed with nine volunteers, of which 93 and 117 trials respectively resulted in a failure. Since the robot was not equipped with the functionality to detect certain failures, it only achieved points for successful handovers and for detecting when a person did not respond to the robot. However, the dataset will enable the development of functionality to detect dropped objects and unreleased objects for future campaigns.

The benchmark protocol defined here and the data collection process can be easily replicated and extended by the community. A tool which coordinates execution of the benchmark, and generates trial configurations based on the variations defined for the benchmark has also been made available[2].

5   Related Standards

Benchmarks and standards are closely related since benchmarks can provide a means for measuring the conformance to standards. In defining the benchmarking protocols, we want to identify synergies with existing benchmarks and ways to define them in such a way that they can be used as verification and validation procedures required by standards.

The International Organization for Standardization (ISO) has defined several standards for safety of machines. ISO 12100:2010 [14] provides a framework for designing safe machines, including guidelines for risk assessment and reduction. The process of risk assessment and reduction begins by identifying limits of the machine and identifying the risk of potential hazards and the likelihood of their occurrence. Removing the hazard, or reducing the risk of the hazard is performed by incorporating protective measures. The standard is applicable to all machines, and hence to robotic systems as well. Benchmarking protocols will primarily aid in the development of risk reduction strategies and to some extent help in estimating the likelihood of the occurrence of hazards.

The technical committee ISO TC/299 is concerned with standards related to robotics including safety, performance criteria and test methods. Among the standards developed by this committee is the safety standard ISO 13482 [15], which provides requirements and guidelines for designing personal care robots. It defines safety requirements for hazards caused by robot motion, a charging battery, environmental conditions, localization errors etc., and guidelines for protective measures against each type of hazard. Following ISO 12100, these requirements are to be used to perform a risk analysis of the robot, with the application of protective measures if necessary. Several options for verifying and

---

[2] https://github.com/HEART-MET/metrics_refbox.

validating that the robot conforms to the requirements are also specified. For example, for hazards due to incorrect autonomous decisions and actions, the verification and validation methods are practical tests, measurement, observation during operation, examination of software and review of task-based risk assessment. Practical tests and observation during operation both involve subjecting the robot to abnormal conditions in addition to normal operating conditions. ISO/TR 23482-1 [19] defines test methods that can be used ensure compliance with ISO 13482, and ISO/TR 23482-2 [20] provides additional guidelines to design robots according to ISO 13482. Similarly, ISO 18646-1 and ISO 18646-2 [17,18] define several performance characteristics of the locomotion, and navigation of service robots, such as rated speed, stopping characteristics, turning width etc., along with recommendations on how to test them. They include specific details of the recommended test facility, test procedure and reported results for each of the performance characteristics. ISO 15066:2016 [16] is concerned with safety requirements for collaborative robots and identifies the collaboration types safety-rated monitored stop, hand guiding, speed and separation monitoring, and power and force-limiting. For tasks which involve a physical interaction between the robot and human, the power and force-limiting collaboration type is most applicable since intentional or unintentional contact with the robot is expected.

Our goal in defining benchmarking protocols is to enhance and extend the test procedures already defined, with a focus on robot-human interaction. We define the test facility (a certified test-bed), test procedure incorporating the failure modes, and the evaluation metrics to report results for each benchmark. The manner in which the robot responds to failure conditions is also an aspect which can benefit from standardization. Even though some standards have similar activities which can be found in the proposed benchmarking protocols (e.g. defining the scope and task as defined in ISO 12100) the existing standards lack, to the best of our knowledge, test procedures to assess the failure conditions occurring in human-robot interaction tasks such as object handover.

6   Conclusions

In this paper we proposed scientific competitions as a means to benchmark functionalities for assistive robots with a particular focus on failure modes, especially in tasks that involve human-robot interaction. The process for defining a benchmark comprises of defining the objective, identifying the variables and failure modes, and specifying the evaluation metrics and data to be recorded. We demonstrated the feasibility of the proposed approach with the help of a handover use-case, which incorporates several failure modes associated with the interaction between the human and the robot. While related standards share several activities as those included in the benchmarking protocol the investigation of failure conditions are not yet present in robotic standards. For the future we aim to establish further synergies and harmonize the activities between standards and benchmarking protocols developed in competitions as both share the common goal to systematically assess the performance of robotic systems.

Acknowledgement. This project has received funding from the European Union's Horizon 2020 research and innovation program under grant agreement No. 871252 (METRICS).

References

1. Darpa Robotics Challenge. https://archive.darpa.mil/roboticschallenge/. Accessed Jan 2021
2. European Robotics League. https://www.eu-robotics.net/robotics_league/. Accessed Jan 2021
3. RoboCup. https://www.robocup.org/. Accessed Jan 2021
4. Robot Competitions Kick Innovation In Cognitive Systems and Robotics. http://rockinrobotchallenge.eu/. Accessed Jan 2021
5. Robotics Coordination Action for Europe Two. https://www.eu-robotics.net/eurobotics/about/projects/rockeu2.html. Accessed Jan 2021
6. World Robot Challenge. https://worldrobotsummit.org/en/wrs2020/challenge/. Accessed Jan 2021
7. Robotics 2020 Multi-Annual Roadmap for Robotics in Europe. Technical guide, SPARC - Partnership for Robotics in Europe (2016)
8. Amigoni, F., et al.: Competitions for benchmarking: task and functionality scoring complete performance assessment. IEEE Robot. Autom. Mag. **22**(3), 53–61 (2015)
9. Basiri, M., Piazza, E., Matteucci, M., Lima, P.: Benchmarking functionalities of domestic service robots through scientific competitions. KI - Künstliche Intelligenz **33**(4), 357–367 (2019). https://doi.org/10.1007/s13218-019-00619-9
10. Cavallo, F., et al.: Robotic services acceptance in smart environments with older adults: user satisfaction and acceptability study. J. Med. Internet Res. **20**(9) (2018)
11. Falco, J., et al.: Benchmarking protocols for evaluating grasp strength, grasp cycle time, finger strength, and finger repeatability of robot end-effectors. IEEE Robot. Autom. Lett. **5**(2), 644–651 (2020)
12. Feil-Seifer, D., Skinner, K., Matarić, M.J.: Benchmarks for evaluating socially assistive robotics. Interaction Stud. **8**(3), 423–439 (2007)
13. Hochgeschwender, N., Thoduka, S., Dragone, M., Caleb-Solly, P., Bellamy, D., Cavallo, F.: HEART-MET Evaluation Plan (2020). https://metricsproject.eu/healthcare/. Accessed February 2021
14. Safety of machinery – General principles for design – Risk assessment and risk reduction. Standard, International Organization for Standardization (2010)
15. Robots and robotic devices - Safety requirements for personal care robots. Standard, International Organization for Standardization (2014)
16. Robots and robotic devices – Collaborative robots. Standard, International Organization for Standardization (2016)
17. Robotics - Performance criteria and related test methods for service robots – Part 1: Locomotion for wheeled robots. Standard, International Organization for Standardization (2016)
18. Robotics - Performance criteria and related test methods for service robots – Part 2: Navigation. Standard, International Organization for Standardization (2019)
19. Robotics – Application of ISO 13482 – Part 1: Safety-related test methods. Standard, International Organization for Standardization (2010)
20. Robotics – Application of ISO 13482 – Part 2: Application guidelines. Standard, International Organization for Standardization (2010)

21. Kimble, K., et al.: Benchmarking protocols for evaluating small parts robotic assembly systems. IEEE Robot. Autom. Lett. **5**(2), 883–889 (2020)
22. Kyrarini, M., Lygerakis, F., Rajavenkatanarayanan, A., Sevastopoulos, C., Nambiappan, H.R., Chaitanya, K.K., Babu, A.R., Mathew, J., Makedon, F.: A Survey of Robots in Healthcare. Technologies **9**(1), 8 (2021)
23. Lin, C.-C., Liao, H.-Y., Tung, F.-W.: Design guidelines of social-assisted robots for the elderly: a mixed method systematic literature review. In: Stephanidis, C., et al. (eds.) HCII 2020. LNCS, vol. 12425, pp. 90–104. Springer, Cham (2020). https://doi.org/10.1007/978-3-030-60128-7_7
24. Morgan, A.S., et al.: Benchmarking cluttered robot pick-and-place manipulation with the box and blocks test. IEEE Robot. Autom. Lett. **5**(2), 454–461 (2019)
25. Rossi, S., et al.: The role of personality factors and empathy in the acceptance and performance of a social robot for psychometric evaluations. Robotics **9**(2), 39 (2020)
26. Sprunk, C., et al.: An experimental protocol for benchmarking robotic indoor navigation. In: Hsieh, M.A., Khatib, O., Kumar, V. (eds.) Experimental Robotics. STAR, vol. 109, pp. 487–504. Springer, Cham (2016). https://doi.org/10.1007/978-3-319-23778-7_32
27. Tolmeijer, S., et al.: Taxonomy of trust-relevant failures and mitigation strategies. In: Proceedings of the 2020 ACM/IEEE International Conference on Human-Robot Interaction, pp. 3–12 (2020)
28. Triantafyllou, P., Mnyusiwalla, H., Sotiropoulos, P., Roa, M.A., Russell, D., Deacon, G.: A Benchmarking Framework for Systematic Evaluation of Robotic Pick-and-Place Systems in an Industrial Grocery Setting. In: 2019 International Conference on Robotics and Automation (ICRA). pp. 6692–6698. IEEE (2019)
29. Weisz, J., Huang, Y., Lier, F., Sethumadhavan, S., Allen, P.: Robobench: towards sustainable robotics system benchmarking. In: 2016 IEEE International Conference on Robotics and Automation (ICRA), pp. 3383–3389. IEEE (2016)

Fairness and the Need for Regulation of AI in Medicine, Teaching, and Recruiting

Laila Wegner[iD], Yana Houben[iD], Martina Ziefle[iD], and André Calero Valdez[⊠][iD]

Human-Computer Interaction Center, RWTH Aachen University, Campus Boulevard
57, 52076 Aachen, Germany
laila.wegner@rwth-aachen.de
yana.houben@kpnplanet.nl
{ziefle,calero-valdez}@comm.rwth-aachen.de

Abstract. The connections between the perception of trust, fairness, and regulatory needs regarding artificial intelligence have not been sufficiently investigated, yet. We address this research gap and analyze the role of trust, acceptance, and confidence in technology use towards the need for regulations and perceptions of fairness of artificial intelligence. A quantitative questionnaire (n = 103) was used to empirically and deductively study the aforementioned research question and established hypotheses. Overall, the results suggest most importantly trust has an impact on assessing the fairness of AI, and that it correlates with regulatory needs. Furthermore, we found that trust and a lack of regulatory needs predict the assessment of perceived AI fairness, explaining 41% of the variance. We also found that the usage context has a significant impact on perceived fairness and regulatory needs. Interestingly, teaching showed the highest need for regulation of all our contexts and showed the lowest perceived fairness.

Keywords: Fairness · Regulatory needs · Artificial intelligence · User study · AI in teaching · AI in medicine · AI in recruiting · Trust in AI · Contextual AI · Technology acceptance

1 Introduction

Artificial intelligence is one of the major topics of our time. Scientific discussions occur in a variety of disciplines, from the perspective of computer scientists to technical feasibility to philosophical and psychological elaborations of social consequences. The prominence of artificial intelligence is also growing in public discourse, and many headlines circle around the topic. For example, "ZEITonline," a German news magazine, reports: "Congratulations, you have convinced the AI! - When it is a matter of who is hired or promoted, prejudices also influence us. Should difficult decisions rather be made by a computer? [...] **Fairness through algorithms—that sounds too good to be true.** Unfortunately, it is. It has become common knowledge that algorithms can also discriminate.

© Springer Nature Switzerland AG 2021
V. G. Duffy (Ed.): HCII 2021, LNCS 12778, pp. 277–295, 2021.
https://doi.org/10.1007/978-3-030-77820-0_21

One case that has gained unfortunate notoriety comes from the field of criminal justice: [...]" [10]

The social context that artificial intelligence can change has long been recognized. Initial use is already being tested in some fields of application. Because the technology is in the development phase, it currently carries some risks. As the quote from DIE ZEIT makes clear, **fairness in the use of artificial intelligence is one of the central aspects in the public discourse**. The above quote has a very negative connotation and provides an example of the fears when it comes to evaluation by algorithms.

The topic of fairness is also already being considered in science. In the following chapter, we look at the state of research, which types of artificial intelligence exist, and how the aspects of fairness are evaluated. As O. Renn points out in his essay, the **establishment of new technologies is closely linked to their societal acceptance** [18].

However, the correlations between the social perception of the fairness of artificial intelligence, technology acceptance, and the establishment of artificial intelligence have not yet been sufficiently investigated. The goal of this elaboration is to be able to make statements about these interrelationships, and to this purpose, the following question is examined: *What is the effect of technology acceptance and trust in technology on the need for regulation to ensure the fair use of artificial intelligence?*

We derive five hypotheses to answer this research question. To be able to test the hypotheses, we conduct an empirical and quantitative survey. The survey works with the evaluation of different application scenarios. More details regarding the method follow in chapter four. To be able to place the survey responses in a broader context, the sample description follows in the fifth chapter. In the results chapter, the relationships established in the hypotheses are analyzed using the statistical programming language R.

To analyze the results in the context of the research proposal, they are contrasted with the expectations derived from the state of research in the following sections. The research question is answered with the help of our findings.

Out of five hypotheses, three could be accepted. We could confirm that strong trust in AI leads to low regulatory needs. Furthermore, a significant impact of trust and distrust in technology on the need for regulation was shown. The need for regulation for three scenarios was compared and it could be confirmed that they differ depending on each scenario. However, we could not confirm that there is a correlation between technology affinity and the need for regulation in AI. We also were not detecting any effect of injustice sensitivity on the expected fairness of AI. The meaning of these findings as well as the importance for the fair use of artificial intelligence is presented in the conclusion.

2   Related Work

As mentioned at the beginning, artificial intelligence is a technology with interdisciplinary relevance. The research area that has emerged is correspondingly large. To be able to classify the current state, some basics and development trends of artificial intelligence are considered in the following. The main focus here is on the different types of artificial intelligence and its proliferation. Subsequently, this chapter is dedicated to the previous discussions of ethical challenges to be able to delimit which scientific findings have been gained on the fair use of artificial intelligence. To accomplish this, some specific use cases are also discussed thereafter. Finally, some findings from acceptance research and the influence of certain personality traits are considered.

2.1   Trends in Artificial Intelligence Development

A clear definition of the term artificial intelligence (AI) is sometimes difficult to delineate. According to McCharty in 1955 artificial intelligence are machines that behave as if they have human intelligence [12]. However, because human intelligence is also difficult to define, this definition is appropriately abstract. More recent definitions instead work with degrees of intelligence. Mainzer, for example, provides the following working definition in his book "Künstliche Intelligenz – Wann übernehmen die Maschinen"[1]: "A system is called intelligent if it can solve problems independently and efficiently. The degree of intelligence depends on the degree of self-reliance, the degree of complexity of the problem, and the degree of efficiency of the problem-solving procedure (translated from German)." [13]

These different degrees are also reflected in the distinction between strong and narrow (or weak) AI. Narrow AI is an expert in one single area; abstraction into other contexts is not possible. Whereas in the development of strong AI, the goal is for the AI to acquire the same intellectual capabilities of a human. With the current state of the art, all existing systems belong to the category of narrow AI [20]. Furthermore, emotions or empathy cannot be reproduced by an AI, only simulated. However, it is possible to program ethical behavior based on rules and machine learning [9]. One trend that can currently be observed is the spread of ambient intelligence. This describes the networking of sensors, radio modules, and computer processors that are integrated into everyday life and serve to improve it [6].

2.2   Addressing Ethical Challenges

Artificial intelligence is thus gradually spreading into all areas of society. This includes high-risk areas (such as medicine), increasing the relevance that AI must be designed to be fair and transparent. Unforeseen and collateral cultural impacts cannot be ruled out [5]. The development of AI creates new opportunities for the economy. On the one hand, new products and services are conceivable, as they provide an enormous increase in productivity. On the other hand, though, the increased use of AI can also lead to increased unemployment and greater wealth disparities than before [14]. Many commentators, academics, and

---

[1] Artificial Intelligence - When machines take over.

policymakers are therefore calling for ensuring that algorithms are transparent, fair, and accountable [16]. One possible solution comes from Iyad Rahwan. He demands the regulation of AI and proposes the "programming of an algorithmic social contract". Here, the characteristics of successful algorithmic regulation are based on O'Reilly. These require a deep understanding of the desired outcome; real-time measurement to determine whether that outcome is being achieved; algorithms (i.e., a set of rules) that make adjustments based on new data; and periodic, a deeper analysis of whether the algorithms themselves are correct and working as expected.

Recent policy decisions such as the GDPR[2] in Europe show that the need for action is recognized. These laws provide the initial legal basis to address impacts from AI on society. The focus is on the fair processing of personal data [2].

2.3 Current Use Cases

As mentioned, artificial intelligence is spreading into many different areas. Some use cases are being tested and analyzed. The following briefly outlines three significant use cases, which will also be addressed in the empirical survey.

- **Medicine**: In medicine, AI has the potential to optimize the care pathway for chronically ill patients. Artificial intelligence can be used to plan precise therapies for complex diseases, reduce medical errors, and improve enrollment of subjects in clinical trials. Although absolute confidence in the diagnostic performance of artificial intelligence has not yet been established, the combination of machines and physicians reliably improves system performance [15].
- **Human resource management**: If a new employee is sought, the support of artificial intelligence is possible. This supports the decision through prepared analyses of video interviews. However, in addition to supporting the goal of finding the optimal employee, the use of AI in the HR management process also brings the potential for discrimination. Moreover, potential legal and ethical consequences must be considered [7].
- **Teaching**: In teaching, the increasingly widespread use of eLearning portals can be observed. Acceptance and success of this medium can only be achieved if the systems act as helpful assistants and are not designed to be too complex. Intelligent guidance and situational support for the students are necessary for this. In addition, adaptivity for individual use of the portal is an essential feature [11].

2.4 Acceptance Research

As mentioned at the outset, the spread of new technologies is closely linked to their acceptance. Artificial intelligence is a relatively new phenomenon on which there is still little comprehensive research. However, acceptance research has been conducted in numerous disciplines and some findings can be applied

---

[2] General Data Protection Regulation.

to the subject area of this study. The strong influence of acceptance on the diffusion of new products lies on the one hand in the fact that the absence of resistance follows from acceptance, and on the other hand in the fact that acceptance leads to active participation and willingness to act. Therefore, **acceptance research also results in approaches for successful technology implementation** [22]. In addition to the usefulness of new products, product acceptance, as well as ethical and moral attitudes and widespread thoughts and beliefs about humanity, also play a central role in the perception of consumers today. Products such as artificial intelligence, which lead to strong individual and social change, can only be realized with broad acceptance [22].

If acceptance is to be promoted, innovation faces the challenge that acceptance is a subjective variable and cannot be enforced. However, it is possible to contribute to an increase in acceptance by tailoring technology to the respective target group and implementing it competently. The measures to achieve this should be aimed at reducing the perceived costs of the technical innovation and increasing the benefits. Recommendations from the literature are based in part directly on the object of acceptance and focus on an adapted design of the new technology [22]. This approach is pursued in the context of this elaboration. By asking potential users about their regulatory needs, it is possible to use the insights gained to adapt the regulations of artificial intelligence and thus increase acceptance.

Trust in technology is also an influential factor. If a potential consumer distrusts a new product, their perception focuses on the risks. With trust, on the other hand, the consumer relies on the satisfaction of their expectations [8].

2.5   Personality Characteristics

As the previous section made clear, acceptance is a subjective factor. Thus, individual personalities also influence the perception of new techniques. Since the focus of this paper is the fairness of artificial intelligence, we analyze the participants' sensitivity to unfairness. It is known from research that different perceptions and reactions to unfairness can be identified. These differences can be generalized across different unfair situations [21].

3   Research Question and Hypotheses

To answer the overarching question in this article we propose the following research question: *RQ: What is the effect of technology acceptance and trust in technology on the need for regulation and how does it impact the perception of fairness of artificial intelligence?* To answer this research question (see Fig. 1), five hypotheses were derived from the state of the art research, which will be answered throughout the paper using the survey. In the following, the established hypotheses are stated and the justified expectations are outlined.

H1: People Who Generally Show Low Technology Affinity Exhibit a High Need for Regulation of AI. This hypothesis focuses on the relationship between technology

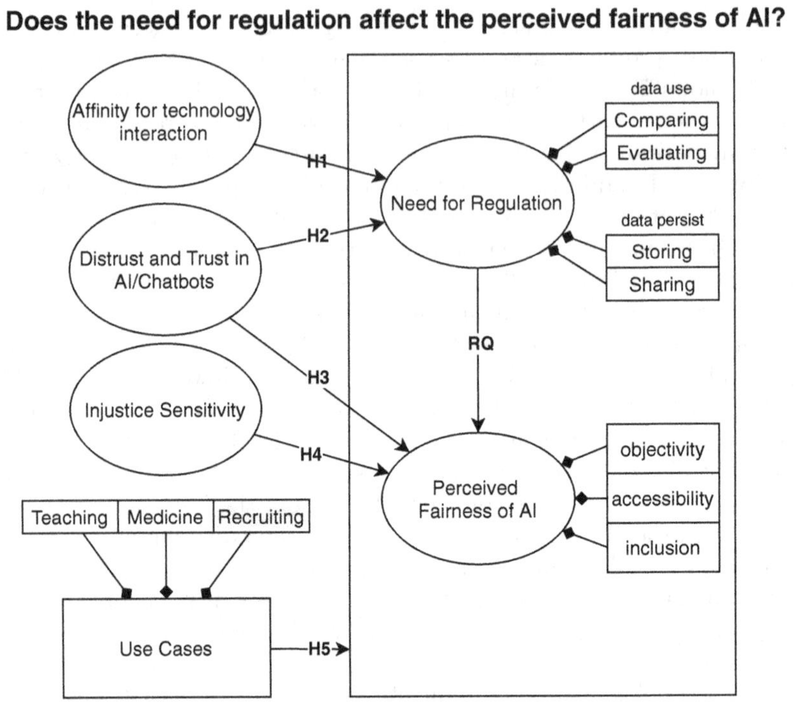

Does the need for regulation affect the perceived fairness of AI?

Fig. 1. The proposed research model of this article including hypotheses and measurement model.

acceptance and the need for regulation. From acceptance research it became clear that only accepted products are used, if this acceptance is missing this leads to restrictions in the willingness to use. Therefore, the expectation is: those who are generally not open to new technologies are also averse to artificial intelligence. As a consequence, restrictions on the unaccepted product follow through regulation.

H2: People Who Exhibit Strong Trust in AI Have Low Regulatory Needs When Using AI. The second hypothesis analyzes the factors of technology trust and the need for regulation. Acceptance research indicates that distrust focuses on risks, whereas trust relies on the occurrence of expectations. To manage the risks, regulations would be a possible solution. If trust dominates, this solution is not needed because the risks are not the focus. The expectation is therefore that there is a negative correlation between trust in artificial intelligence and the need for regulation.

H3: Trust and Distrust in Technology Play a Significant Role in the Perceived Fairness of AI. The third hypothesis assumes the perception of fairness of AI can not yet have been established from real interactions, or if so only to a small degree. Therefore, we hypothesize that the attitude towards AI, in this case, trust or distrust, plays a large role in how the fairness of AI is evaluated.

H4: People Who are Highly Sensitive to Justice are Critical of the Fairness of Artificial Intelligence. The fourth hypothesis addresses the fairness aspect of artificial intelligence. As was shown from the research on unfairness sensitivity, differences in sensitivity can be generalized across different situations. The resulting expectation is that this generalization can also be applied to new technologies (such as artificial intelligence).

H5: The Required Need for Regulation Varies Between the Different Use Cases. The research question considers the use of AI. Different application scenarios have already been studied in the literature, and different benefits and risks have been identified in different application scenarios. However, a comparison of user acceptance across application scenarios has not been extensively researched. Therefore, it is of interest whether findings on user acceptance from individual application areas can be abstracted to other areas. Since the benefits and risks have different consequences per use case, the expectation is that the need for regulation will vary depending on the scenario.

4 Method

After the literature review, the research question and five different hypotheses were formulated. With the help of these hypotheses, it should be possible to answer the research question at the end of this quantitative study. Empirical data collection was conducted with the help of a questionnaire to afterward deductively investigate the previously formulated research question and established hypotheses.

Next, we present the designed survey questionnaire, the used scales, as well as the statistical procedures in this study.

4.1 Materials and Survey Design

The questionnaire consists of some demographic questions and three scenarios, with questions on fairness and regulatory needs for each. The order of the scenarios is randomly assigned and all items that should not be sorted were additionally randomly presented to avoid effect errors. The questionnaire contains an introduction as well as a message of gratitude at the end. Participants were informed that data is gathered anonymously and voluntarily.

Before the data were collected, the questionnaire was administered in a pretest with three participants. The time required was recorded. After the questionnaire was improved, data collection was started. A within-subject design was used as the experimental design, which means that each subject had to answer questions on all scenarios, albeit in randomized order. Participants were acquired using a mix of methods between self-selection, snowball effect, and a deliberate selection process. On June 5th 2019, participants were personally contacted by their circle of acquaintances via social media. On June 18th 2019, the questionnaire was closed.

4.2   Description of Measurement Instrument and Scenarios

In the questionnaire, which can also be viewed in the OSF repository, three scenarios are compared. Introductory texts are presented here, translated into English. Original texts are available in the OSF repository as well.

Medicine Scenario. The first scenario, Medicine, is defined as follows:

Imagine an artificial intelligence that you can contact with medical questions. Here, natural written or verbal communication (via keyboard or telephone) with the artificial intelligence is possible. It can answer questions about health and make diagnoses based on the chat or conversation with the patient. For the latter, it is able to ask specific queries. In addition, appointments for a possible subsequent doctor's visit are coordinated by the AI.

Teaching Scenario. The second scenario teaching is introduced with the following text:

Imagine you are a student at a language school. An artificial intelligence that understands natural languages accompanies the lessons. It can respond to the individual knowledge levels of the learners and answer follow-up questions from the students. In addition, it can act as a training partner and apply various pedagogical concepts.

Recruiting Scenario. The third scenario is human resource management, defined by the following description:

Imagine HR management processes at work being supported by an AI. The AI analyzes and evaluates your application documents. In addition, the AI summarizes all the data for the HR manager. In the end, the AI coordinates the interviews, and a chatbot is used to communicate with the applicants.

Regulatory Needs and Fairness. After each scenario, the regulatory needs, adapted to the scenario, are asked by using six-point Likert scales. Fairness was measured on a six-point bipolar scales with textual opposing anchors for levels one and six. Participants are asked to indicate their personal opinion for each regulatory need and for each fairness item. In total, there are five different regulatory needs and three different fairness items per scenario.

The first **regulatory requirement** for each scenario describes data storage. The second regulatory requirement focuses on the comparison of personal data with other users and the third focuses on the analysis of the data. The last regulatory requirement deals with the transfer of data.

The different **fairness** items ask whether users expect to be treated equally or whether they believe that certain groups are expected to be disadvantaged. Next, we ask whether the AI is expected to function safely or whether it can be manipulated and is faulty. The third queried expectation is whether disclosure of information will lead to improvements or to disadvantages for the user. The fourth contrasts adequate evaluation competence by AI against lack of inclusion of individual evaluation aspects, and the last question compares whether benefits by AI are accessible to all users versus benefits are not accessible to all user groups.

4.3 Data Analysis and Statistical Procedure

After the survey, the analysis of the data took place. The data set was reduced to rows of data with at least 50% of the data present. After the incomplete cases were taken out, all items were renamed to prepare for further analysis. All statistical procedures were conducted R Version 4.0.2. All data manipulations were conducted using the `tidyverse` [24]. All procedures are available on a GitHub Repository[3]. Data and supplementary materials are available at an OSF repository[4]. Supplementary materials are created using several R-packages [1,25].

We first verify the internal consistency of existing scales using Cronbach's α. For item sets designed for this study, we use exploratory factor analysis to determine the internal structure of these item sets. Both methods were taken from the R `psych` package [19]. We verify assumptions to factor analysis using Bartlett's test of sphericity and the Kaiser-Meyer-Olkin criterion of sampling adequacy.

Factor calculation was done using the `hcictools` package [4]. Descriptive analysis of relevant variables was conducted using the `psych` package [19].

We tried testing our proposed model using a partial least squares structural equation model from the `seminr` package [17]. However, measures of reliability were not sufficient for our data. The efforts to model our data using `seminr` are available in the supplementary materials.

Next, we conducted correlation analysis with Pearson moment correlation for the variables in question using tools from the `hcictools` package. We used repeated-measures ANOVA and multiple linear regression from the `jmv` package [23].

In general, we assume a level of significance of $\alpha = .05$, meaning that when findings are significant, there is a 5% change that our data could have been observed given the null-hypothesis is true. We use non-parametric tests when we have reason to assume that underlying population data would not be normally distributed.

5 Results

Using the aforementioned statistical methods, we now describe our findings in three sections. First, we describe the data set using descriptive statistics. Next, we test our hypotheses using correlation analysis and repeated-measures ANOVA. Lastly, we use multiple linear regression to determine the impact of our variables on our target variable perceived fairness of AI.

---

[3] https://github.com/Sumidu/AIFairnessPaperHCII2021.

[4] https://osf.io/54fjy/.

5.1 Sample Description

In any study, both different and similar characteristics of the subjects are of concern. It is useful to list the samples in order to be able to compare the data with the samples afterward.

In total, there were 136 participants in the survey, of which 103 completed more than half of the questionnaire. The mean age is rather young with M=33. The youngest participant is 14 years old and the oldest participant is 77. Out of 103 participants, 58 are women and 45 are men.

School-leaving qualifications were asked and it is shown that most of the respondents have completed at least the vocational diploma (German: Fachabitur/Abitur), so the educational level of the respondents is comparatively high. One person has no school-leaving qualification, one mentions the Certificate of Secondary Education (German: Hauptschulabschluss), two mentions the General Certificate of Secondary Education (German: Realschulabschluss, there were 48 answers with vocational diploma, 15 times vocational training and 36 times university degree.

In Table 1 an overview with the mean of our main variables is shown. With M=3.72, the respondents show a rather high level of trust in AI. Furthermore, with M=3.77, the need for regulation in the use of data is also rather high. It is striking that the need for regulation in data persistence is noticeably lower with M = 2.81.

Table 1. Descriptive overview of our main variables

Variable	n	mean	sd	se
Age	103	33.16	15.43	1.52
Affinity towards technology	103	3.04	1.11	0.11
Injustice sensitivity	103	3.25	0.93	0.09
Need for regulation - data use	103	3.77	1.08	0.11
Need for regulation - data persist	103	2.81	0.98	0.10
Trust in AI	103	3.72	0.77	0.08
Distrust in AI	103	3.57	0.77	0.08

5.2 Hypotheses Tests

In the following section, we will test our hypothesized associations in our model by applying correlation analysis. We assume normality on all scales with more than three items and thus use Pearson's moment correlation for analysis. For our first four hypotheses, we test the effect of our independent variables and the respective dependent variable for all scenarios in a single measure as the single measure achieved the highest reliability and factor analysis often did not yield strong enough variation to assume multiple factors.

H1: People Who Generally Show Low Technology Affinity Exhibit a High Need for Regulation of AI. The need for regulation was measured on two scales. We see no significant correlation of affinity towards technology (ATI) with a need for regulation regarding the use of data ($r(101) = .06, p > .05$). This means that the need for regulation when it comes to using data in all our scenarios does not depend on the individual's affinity towards technology. The same is true for a need for regulation regarding the persistence of data ($r(101) = -.15, p > .05$).

H2: People Who Exhibit Strong Trust in AI Have Low Regulatory Needs When Using AI. Our trust-related items showed an interesting two-factor structure meaning that trust in AI and distrust in AI are not complete opposites on the same scale. Exploratory factor analysis yielded two factors that are negatively correlated on their primary axes ($r = -.424$). The scores themselves, as expected, also show a negative correlation ($r = -.33$)

With this, it is interesting to see that trust plays a larger role in the need for regulation than distrust in our sample (see Fig. 2). We see no correlation between distrust and both measures for the need for regulation ($|r| < .13, p > .05$). Meaning that a general distrust in AI does not translate to a stronger need for regulation directly. However, trust is correlated with both measures. It is weakly correlated with the need for regulation regarding data persistence ($r(101) = -.22, p < .05$), meaning that the higher the users trust in AI the less they are concerned about data storage. This effect is even larger for data usage ($r(101) = -.31, p < .01$). Here, a medium effect is seen, meaning that the more a user trusts AI in general the less they are worried about the use of data by AI.

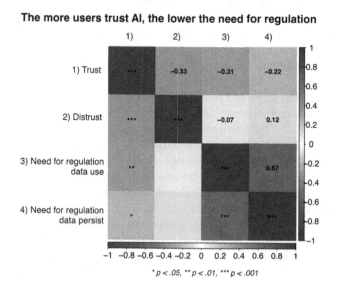

Fig. 2. Evaluating how users perceptions of AI related to the need for regulation.

H3: Trust and Distrust in a Technology Play a Significant Role in the Perceived Fairness of AI. As trust towards a trusted subject is associated with fair behavior we also test whether trust in AI plays a role in the perceived fairness of AI. Indeed we find that trust is positively associated with perceived fairness $(r(101) = .41, p < .001)$. This means that users that show high trust in technology also expect AI to be fairer than users that show lower trust in technology. Interestingly, the inverse measure—distrust—is also correlated with fairness, yet at a lower effect $(r(101) = -.26, p < .01)$.

H4: People Who Are Highly Sensitive to Justice Are Critical of the Fairness of Artificial Intelligence. One of our assumptions was that the perception of fairness of AI would also be connected to a general sensitivity towards injustice. If a person is more aware of injustice by being more sensitive, they should also be more attuned to detecting injustice and thus the lack of fairness in an AI system. However, this association is only very weak $(r(102) = -.16, p > .05)$ and not statistically significant. We must assume that participants that are more sensitive to injustice do not expect AI to be more unfair—in our scenarios at least.

H5: The Required Need for Regulation Varies Between the Different Use Cases. Although factor analysis did not reveal a clear factor structure in our dependent variables from all three scenarios, we still can investigate differences in means between the different scenarios. The resulting short scales also show high reliability, but they are highly correlated. A shift in average evaluation between scenarios is still imaginable and thus tested here.

We use a repeated-measures ANOVA to test for differences between scenario choices and both fairness and need for regulation (both scales combined).

For fairness, we see that the ANOVA yields significant differences between contexts $(F(2, 204) = 6.75, p < .001)$. Post-hoc Tukey corrected tests show that there is only a difference in means between the teaching and the recruiting scenario $(t(204) = -3.64, p < .001$, see supplementary materials for the full ANOVA tables). The expected fairness is highest in recruiting $(M = 3.52, SE = 0.104)$, and lowest in teaching $(M = 3.14, SE = 0.104)$. The expected fairness is on a medium level for the medicine scenario $(M = 3.38, SE = 0.104)$. It is important to note that the overall fairness is rather low (below or near the scale mid-point of 3.5). For visual inspection, we plotted the means and the Cosineau-Morey within-subject confidence intervals (95% CIs) in Fig. 3.

For the need for regulation (both scales combined) we also significant differences between usage scenarios $(F(2, 204) = 37.4, p < .001)$. Here, all scenarios show different means when looking at Tukey-corrected p-values (all $p < .05$). Interestingly, the need for regulation in medicine scores lowest $(M = 2.92, SE = 0.09)$, while the need for regulation in teaching scores highest $(M = 3.57, SE = 0.09)$. Recruiting is in the middle place with a mean of 3.16 $(SE = 0.09)$.

How fair is AI and how large is the need for regulation?

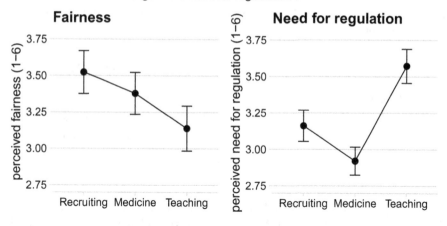

Error bars denote Cosineau–Morey within–subject 95% CIs.

Fig. 3. Comparing perceived fairness and the need for regulation between contexts.

When viewed together with the fairness findings it is interesting to see that teaching plays a different role in the evaluation of fairness and the need for regulation.

5.3   Main Research Question

The main research question of this article was whether the need for regulation impacts the perceived fairness of AI in different contexts. We have already seen that the teaching context might be peculiar in our data, and therefore resort to investigate this effect using the combined factor scales for fairness and the two scales for the need for regulation. We use multiple linear regression to test whether the other correlated variables (trust, injustice sensitivity) also impact the perceived fairness. We do this by using the enter method and comparing three models.

The first mode uses both regulatory needs as predictors. The second model adds trust as a predictor and the third adds injustice sensitivity. The multiple regression analysis showed that the initial two-predictor approach was sufficient in explaining 37% of the variance in the perceived fairness ($F(2, 100) = 29.6, p < .001$). Adding trust into the equation increases the explained variance only to 43% ($F(3, 99) = 25.7$), but at the same time causing the 0 to inside the 95% confidence interval for the coefficient of data use regulatory needs. Adding injustice sensitivity did not make two predictors become not significant.

Therefore, we also tested a model that uses data persistence and trust to predict fairness. This model able to explain 41% of the variance ($F(2, 100) = 36, p < .001$, see Table 2). The need for regulation had a standardized coefficient of −0.51, while trust had a standardized coefficient of 0.3.

Overall, we can say that the perceived fairness of AI is thus strongly influenced by the need for regulation regarding data persistence and weakly influenced by a general trust in AI.

Table 2. Linear regression table for perceived fairness of AI

Variable	B	SE	Stat	t	p
(Intercept)	3.66	0.42	8.80	8.80	<.001
Need for regulation - data persist	−0.45	0.07	−6.54	−6.54	<.001
Trust in AI	0.33	0.09	3.84	3.84	<.001

We can also look at the individual fairness ratings for each context (see Fig. 4). Here, we look at whether to mean rating of a value is significantly different from the scale mean of 3.5. We can see that our participants do believe that AI is able to assess personal skills more objectively, while at the same time thinking that the evaluation of soft skills was maybe insufficient. In the medical scenario, users are afraid that data is used to their disadvantage from insurance companies and that AI might make incorrect diagnoses from data. However, they do think AI can help in making better and fairer appointment schedules for patients. In the teaching scenario, participants do believe that the quality of teaching will improve fairly and that an AI system will be able to evaluate learning progress more objectively.

6 Discussion

After presenting our findings, we contextualize our results in light of other research. We first look at the individual hypotheses before discussing the implications of the findings regarding the main research question.

6.1 Discussion of the Hypotheses

The first hypothesis *People who generally show low technology affinity exhibit a high need for regulation of AI* was not found to be true and could therefore be rejected. According to the state of research, only accepted products are used. If this acceptance is missing, this leads to restrictions in the willingness to use. This leads to the expectation that people who are generally not open to new technologies will also be negative towards artificial intelligence and that this will result in restrictions on the unaccepted product through regulation. Since the hypothesis could be rejected, the result does not match the expectation derived from the current state of research. One possible reason that technology acceptance has no influence on regulatory needs is that the respondents assess technology acceptance based on current technical products and therefore cannot directly imagine artificial intelligence as a technical product and there is, therefore, no correlation

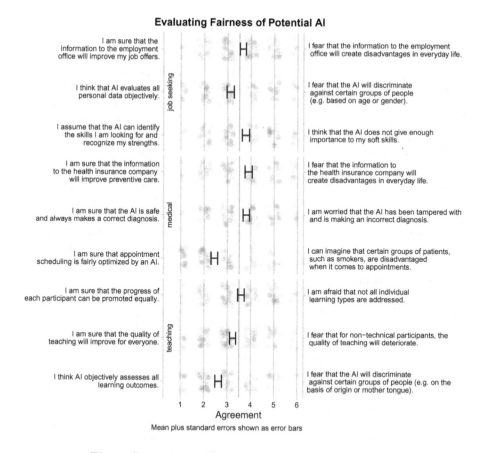

Fig. 4. Comparison of fairness evaluations for all contexts

between the two variables. To confirm or re-examine this, another study should be conducted in the future that examines the acceptance of artificial intelligence and not only the general acceptance of technology.

According to the state of research, for people with low trust in technology, regulating AI is a possible solution to improve their trust in AI. As an expectation, it follows that there is a negative correlation between trust in AI and desired regulatory needs, as well as fairness.

The second and third hypotheses *People who exhibit strong trust in AI have low regulatory needs when using AI and perceive AI as more fair* were found to be true. Thus, the result is consistent with the expectation.

Interestingly, we found that trust and distrust towards AI are not full antonyms using factor analysis. This indicates the multi-faceted nature of AI and that future evaluation should focus on more detailed aspects of AI when evaluating trust and distrust. Moreover, it is recommended to study the general propensity to trust both individuals and technology as possible confounds in future research.

Unexpectedly, we found that the persistence of data played a larger role in determining the fairness of AI than the use of data. Other studies in the field of privacy research have found conflicting evidence for this finding [3]. Here, secondary use is considered particularly harmful for acceptance. However, we did not ask for "secondary" use, but for primary use, which could explain the increased importance of data persistence in our scenarios.

Another expectation based on the current state of research was that injustice sensitivity can be generalized to different situations and that this generalization can also be applied to new technologies such as artificial intelligence. The fourth hypothesis *People who are highly sensitive to justice are critical of the fairness of artificial intelligence* followed from this expectation and could not be found to be true and therefore is rejected. This means that the expectation is not consistent with the hypothesis. One possible reason for this would be that respondents do not (yet) associate injustice sensitivity with technical situations. For example, people could not be able to imagine different ways that AI can treat users unfairly. This lack of "negative creativity" could have caused users with higher injustice sensitivity to react similarly to users with lower injustice sensitivity. At the same time, it would be possible that people find it difficult to imagine AI and thus evaluate the trust in AI, the fairness of AI, and the desired need for regulation with the same tendency every time.

Furthermore, another expectation derived from the state of research was that the desired regulatory needs differ between different application areas or scenarios. The fifth hypothesis *The required need for regulation varies between the different use cases* was found to be true, as there was at least one significant difference. Thus, the result is in line with the expectation.

This study shows that there is a difference between the scenarios and further research should investigate which regulatory needs differ in the different scenarios and which regulatory needs are valued the same in each scenario. For a future study, it would therefore be interesting to investigate which regulatory needs are labeled as primary (in each scenario) and which regulatory needs are labeled as secondary (different in scenarios). A possible conjoint study could help identify the relative strengths of individual regulatory needs depending on the different types of benefits AI could provide.

6.2 Answering the Research Question

To answer the research question *RQ: What is the effect of technology acceptance and trust in technology on the need for regulation and how does it impact the perception of fairness of artificial intelligence?*, five different hypotheses were formulated and examined. The first hypothesis was rejected, but findings for the general research question show that the evaluation of the fairness of AI is influenced by the desired regulations. We proposed that the perceptions of fairness are determined by the perceived need for regulation. However, it is equally valid, to assume this association going the other way. With larger samples and using structural equation modeling, the direction of this association could be identified more clearly. We intend to investigate this relationship in more detail in later research.

According to the second hypothesis, there is a negative correlation between technology trust and the need for regulation, where the third hypothesis assumed a positive correlation between trust and perceived fairness. Both were confirmed. The fourth hypothesis was rejected and tells us nothing about the research question. The fifth hypothesis describes that there is an additional difference in regulatory needs between the scenarios of medicine, teaching, and human resource management.

Overall, it follows from the results that technology trust has an influence on the evaluation of the fairness of AI and that technology trust correlates with regulatory needs. In addition, the evaluation of the fairness of AI and the regulatory needs influence each other. According to this study, technology affinity does not correlate with regulatory needs. For further research, it would be interesting to investigate how people generally accept AI and what influence this AI acceptance has on the regulatory needs, and the evaluation of the fairness of AI. In addition, it would be interesting to investigate which regulatory needs are designated as primary and secondary and which other characteristics besides technology trust have an influence on the desired regulatory needs and on the evaluation of the fairness of AI.

7   Conclusion

This paper opened with the observation that fairness in the use of artificial intelligence is one of the central aspects of the public discourse. With the help of a survey, the regulatory needs and expectations for fairness were queried based on concrete scenarios. This study has attempted to answer the question *RQ: What is the effect of technology acceptance and trust in technology on the need for regulation to ensure the fair use of artificial intelligence?*

We confirmed an influence of technology trust on low regulatory needs as hypothesized. Furthermore, it is crucial for the participants to which scenario the need for regulation refers to. It is also interesting to note that the influence of technology trust on the regulatory need for data use was more pronounced than on the regulatory need for data persistence. Based on the results, however, the hypotheses that a high injustice sensitivity leads to a critical evaluation of the fairness of AI and that a low affinity towards technology leads to a high need for regulation had to be rejected.

The reason for the different impact of technology trust compared to technology affinity on regulatory needs should be investigated in further studies. Further results from acceptance research specifically focused on AI are also needed. Different application scenarios are evaluated differently, with high relevance for the practical development of AI. For further research, it is recommended to explore more details about these assessments and to divide the regulatory needs into primary and secondary requirements.

The establishment of new technology depends on the assistance and acceptance of consumers. This study is a first step in understanding the influences on the requirements for fair AI in more detail and can serve as a starting point for further research.

Acknowledgements. This research was supported by the Digital Society research program funded by the Ministry of Culture and Science of the German State of North Rhine-Westphalia. We would further like to thank the authors of the packages we have used.

References

1. Allaire, J., Iannone, R., Presmanes Hill, A., Xie, Y.: distill: 'R Markdown' Format for Scientific and Technical Writing (2020). https://CRAN.R-project.org/package=distill, r package version 1.1
2. Butterwoth, M.: The ICO and artificial intelligence: The role of fairness in the GDPR framework. Comput. Law Secur. Rev.: Int. J. Technol. Law Practice (2018)
3. Calero Valdez, A., Ziefle, M.: The users' perspective on the privacy-utility trade-offs in health recommender systems. Int. J. Hum Comput Stud. **121**, 108–121 (2019)
4. Calero Valdez, A.: hcictools: Tools for data analysis in psychological surveys (2021), r package version 1.1.2
5. Cath, C.: Governing artificial intelligence: ethical, legal and technical opportunities and challenges introduction. Philos. Trans. Roy. Soc. A: Math. Phys. Eng. Sci. **376**(2133) (2018)
6. Cook, D., Augusto, J., Jakkula, V.: Ambient intelligence: technologies, applications, and opportunities. In: Pervasive and Mobile Computing, pp. 277–298 (2007)
7. Fernandez, C., Fernandez, A.: Ethical and legal implications of AI recruiting software. In: ERCIM News, pp. 22–23 (2019)
8. Fuchs, G.: Vertrauen in technische Systeme ist eine Voraussetzung, um Risiken zu bewältigen. https://www.ingenieur.de/karriere/bildung/weiterbildung/vertrauen-ersetzt-wissen/. Accessed 08 July 2019
9. Haladjian, H.H., Montemayor, C.: Artificial consciousness and the consciousness-attention dissociation. Elsevier Inc. (2016)
10. Herzog, L.: Glückwunsch, sie haben die ki überzeugt! https://www.zeit.de/arbeit/2019-05/kuenstliche-intelligenz-arbeitsplatz-fairness-algorithmen-diskriminierung. Accessed 08 July 2019
11. Jantke, K.P.: Informatik und künstliche intelligenz-beiträge zur adaptivität einer kommenden generation intelligenter elearning-systeme. In: eLearning in der Sportwissenschaft: Strategien, Konzeptionen, Perspektiven (eLearning in sports science: Strategies, conceptual design, prospects), pp. 49–70 (2005)
12. Schäffer, U., Weber, J.: Künstliche Intelligenz. Controlling Manag. Rev. **65**(2), 3–3 (2021). https://doi.org/10.1007/s12176-021-0370-0
13. Mainzer, K.: Künstliche Intelligenz - Wann übernehmen die Maschinen?. Springer, Heidelberg (2016)
14. Makridakis, S.: The forthcoming artificial intelligence (ai) revolution: Its impact on society and firms. In: Futures (2017)
15. Miller, D., Brown, E.: Knowing what we know: supporting knowledge creation and sharing in social networks. Am. J. Med. **131**(2) (2018)

16. Rahwan, I.: Society-in-the-Loop: Programming the Algorithmic Social Contract. Springer, Netherlands (2017). https://doi.org/10.1007/s10676-017-9430-8
17. Ray, S., Danks, N.P., Calero Valdez, A.: seminr: Domain-Specific Language for Building and Estimating Structural Equation Models (2021). r package version 2.0.0
18. Renn, O.: Akzeptanzforschung: Technik in der gesellschaftlichen Auseinandersetzung. Chem. unserer Zeit **20**(2), 44–52 (1986)
19. Revelle, W.: psych: Procedures for Psychological, Psychometric, and Personality Research. Northwestern University, Evanston, Illinois (2020). https://CRAN.R-project.org/package=psych, r package version 2.0.12
20. Scherk, J., Pöckhacker-Tröscher, G., Wager, K.: Künstliche Intelligenz - Artificial Intelligence. BMVIT, Bereich Innovation (2017)
21. Schmitt, M., Baumert, A., Fetchenhauer, D., Gollwitzer, M., Rothmund, Schlösser, T.: Sensibilität für ungerechtigkeit. Psychologische Rundschau **60**(1), 8–22 (2009)
22. Schäfer, M., Keppler, D.: Modelle der technikorientierten Akzeptanzforschung - Überblick und Reflexion am Beispiel eines Forschungsprojekts zur Implementierung innovativer technischer Energieeffizienz-Maßnahmen. Zentrum Technik und Gesellschaft (2013)
23. Selker, R., Love, J., Dropmann, D.: jmv: The 'jamovi' Analyses (2020). https://CRAN.R-project.org/package=jmv, r package version 1.2.23
24. Wickham, H., et al.: Welcome to the tidyverse. J. Open Source Softw. **4**(43), 1686 (2019). https://doi.org/10.21105/joss.01686
25. Xie, Y., Dervieux, C., Riederer, E.: R Markdown Cookbook. Chapman and Hall/CRC, Boca Raton, Florida (2020). https://bookdown.org/yihui/rmarkdown-cookbook, ISBN 9780367563837

Digital Human Modeling in Product and Service Design

Research on Tourism Marketing Based on Community E-commerce

Wei Feng[✉] and Feng Liu

Shandong College of Tourism and Hospitality, 3556, East Jingshi Road, Jinan, Shandong, China

Abstract. Modern and fast-paced life makes people reluctant to and cannot spend too much time choosing. What users need is efficient, accurate and affordable marketing that is convenient to the naked eye. Convenience, affordability and profitability are in great demand for both the customers and the business. It relies on companies' ability to catch users' psychology accurately, to determine their needs and provide complementary products. Community e-commerce applies to all population clusters, and the future is promising as long as a business model suitable for local conditions and regional characteristics is used. As community e-commerce penetrates deeper and deeper in life, it will gradually shift from mainly selling Fast Moving Consumer Goods (FMCG), especially fresh goods, to a full range of products. The tourism industry is looking forward to recovery after the Novel Corona Virus Pandemic and we should innovate the tourism marketing in the latest period based on better user experience, take the strengths, complement the weaknesses, and make cross-border integration.

Keywords: Community e-commerce · Tourism marketing

1 Introduction

In recent years, community e-commerce has been rapidly promoted and popularized in China, which is inseparable from the rapid development of the Chinese Internet and consumer psychology changes. As of December 2020, the size of Chinese Internet users reached 989 million, the size of mobile Internet users reached 986 million, and the Internet penetration rate reached 70.4%. Meanwhile, advanced 5G devices have been rolled out to the most remote locations in China. It can be said that fast Internet access can be achieved anywhere in China. Community e-commerce is an online transaction behavior for users with community attributes in counties, villages, towns and communities, etc. It provides a more convenient way to sell goods online, with a significant user scale, good experience, fast&direct access, low cost, and high user stickiness. Meanwhile, the tourism industry, which was hit hard by the global outbreak of COVID-19 in 2020, is looking forward to recovery. In the post-epidemic era, the tourism industry should integrate across borders with a development perspective and develop more suitable marketing methods for travelers and tourism enterprises.

© Springer Nature Switzerland AG 2021
V. G. Duffy (Ed.): HCII 2021, LNCS 12778, pp. 299–309, 2021.
https://doi.org/10.1007/978-3-030-77820-0_22

2   Community E-commerce

2.1   Community E-Commerce Overview

Community e-commerce is a sinking market for traditional e-commerce based on the fission of community group buying. It is a model of e-commerce + social + group buying, "an online trading behavior for users with community attributes and community as the basic unit, and it provides a more convenient way to sell goods online" [1]. In China, community e-commerce is a large market of 2–3 trillion, but the market is relatively fragmented. In addition to the first and second-tier cities, the layout of low-tier cities is relatively blank; besides, the continued epidemic objectively let the industry on the cost of user habits cultivation significantly reduced, especially to pry the original penetration of difficult sinking market demand, which gives new entrants to the opportunity. More importantly, there are many big V involved, such as Alibaba Group, JD.COM, Meituan, and other e-commerce giants incubated brands. However, community e-commerce is a local life class warehouse with all the differences, and quality control is more complex than before. There is a dependence on local offline physical stores, the distinction is not apparent, "winner takes all" situation is difficult to form in the short term, there is The opportunity for new entrants with strength is still there, which is why major Internet companies are joining the competitive queue one after another. Community e-commerce is not only a promising business model, and it is a better way for users to experience shopping: faster, more efficient, and more direct.

2.2   The History of Community E-commerce in China

"The opportunity for the development of Internet Electronic Commerce (IEC) first appeared in the 1990s. After U.S. President Clinton raised concern about the development of e-commerce at the fifth APEC informal summit (APEC) at the end of 1997, internationally renowned information technology vendors such as IBM, HP and Sun declared 1998 year of e-commerce" [2]. In March 1998, China's first Internet online transaction was successful. With the popularity of the Internet, the continuous increase of national income, and the continuous improvement of technologies related to electronic commerce (EC - Electronic Commerce), e-commerce in China has developed rapidly. Some data show that in 2019, China's e-commerce transactions reached 34.81 trillion yuan.

In the author's view, the development of e-commerce in China has experienced two major turning points: First, in 2003, due to the impact of SARS, online shopping began to enter the public eye. Alibaba Group, founded in 1999, created Taobao in May 2003 and launched a third-party payment tool called Alipay in October of the same year. In October of the same year, it launched Alipay, a third-party payment tool with a "secured transaction model," which led to a significant transaction volume increase. JD.COM, formerly founded in 1998, started its involvement in e-commerce in January 2004 and has grown into a large e-commerce platform with a scale of several hundred billion dollars and continues to fracture; secondly, the community closure policy based on containing the spread of COVID-19 from late 2019 to early 2020 has disrupted cross-territory express logistics, and people are starting to choose more local network-based community e-commerce. Opt for community e-commerce based on local networks. The community e-commerce model began to take shape in China in 2014, but it was not until 2017 that it gradually reached various residential communities in the city, but it has been lukewarm. With the outbreak of COVID-19, the community closure policy has led to the rapid entry of community e-commerce to community residents, allowing them to experience a convenient, fast and efficient shopping experience fully. Community e-commerce applies to all population clusters, and the future is promising as long as a business model suitable for local conditions and regional characteristics is used.

2.3 Community E-commerce Business Model Analysis

Community e-commerce complete transaction chain consists of e-commerce management, suppliers, e-commerce platform (generally based on the WeChat applet), head, and group members. Traditional e-commerce has various business models such as B2B/B2C/C2C, but the author believes that community e-commerce is closer to the new B2B2C or B2T model. "The first B refers to the seller in a broad sense (i.e., finished products, semi-finished products, material providers, etc.), the second B refers to the trading platform, which provides a platform for the seller to connect with the buyer, while providing additional quality services, and C refers to the buyer. B2T, originally the definition of "group purchasing," i.e., Business To Team, is for a team to purchase from a merchant" [3]. The popularity of the Internet has made group purchasing a consumer revolution in which many Chinese people are involved. Consumers who initially did not know each other, using the opportunity to live in a similar geographic area, the community shopping organizer (head) organized as many community members as possible to place orders for pre-sold goods, increasing the negotiating power of the merchant to get the best price. Although the emergence of online group buying has only been a few years, it has become a trendy new consumption way. It is worth noting that the e-commerce trading platform (e.g. WeChat-based applet, which plays a crucial role in the community e-commerce transaction chain), simultaneously undertakes multiple functions such as placing orders, making payments, soliciting leaders, and soliciting goods, and consequently provides a convenient and efficient channel to expand more communities and various goods in the process of transactions. Currently, there are many community e-commerce business platforms with similarities and differences and different business models. Community e-commerce is a shopping model of e-commerce + social + group buying, all starting from the proximity of community network socialization, gradually completing the shopping process, and generally relatively low. This is the similarity between them.

(1) Different operating methods

From the author's personal experience and research for more than two years, it is clear that the difference is mainly the difference in arrival time, which is more typical of the two ways of next day delivery and daily delivery. The next day that the community members through the shopping applet the same day & the next day before the afternoon order, pre-sale goods to the community on the third day; daily that the community members through the shopping applet the same day order, pre-sale goods to the community the next day.

(2) Differences in main products

The next-day delivery method is diversified and currently mainly involves Fast Moving Consumer Goods (FMCG) such as vegetables, fruits, eggs, milk, laundry detergent, toilet paper, and other types of products, as well as home department stores such as underwear, shoes and socks, hangers, dishes, and other items; Daily Delivery is more focused on FMCG products and is more affordable.

Even if there are many competitors, a mature system has not yet emerged in this field. It provides space for new entrants to explore. Compared to traditional e-commerce, community e-commerce involves new categories, sources, warehousing, logistics system are different, sources, new categories are complex, the origin is more scattered, warehousing and logistics, new e-commerce is exceptionally dependent on the front warehouse, the offline network requirements are high. Nevertheless, the other side of the difficulty is the huge demand potential and industry value. There are many pain points for consumers when purchasing in community retailing system, which covers fresh food most of the time, namely, the standardization of new food categories, the convenience of shopping and the richness of products. As a result, different experiences appear among consumers in different areas. Good news is that these pain points can be solved by increasing the penetration and enormous consumer potential will be released. That is why community e-commerce is widely favored.

3 Current Status of the Tourism Industry

3.1 Tourism in the Post-epidemic Era

Affected by COVID-19, compared with the rapid development of tourism before 2019, countries around the world have generally seen a sharp decline in the annual income of tourism-related industries, with the United Nations World Tourism Organization data showing that the global tourism revenue loss in the past year reached the order of trillions of dollars. The tourism industry in various countries has stagnated inbound and outbound travel, a large number of tourism enterprises have closed down, and many tourism workers have changed jobs or lost their jobs. With data suggesting that more than 100,000 tourism businesses, large and small, China is no different, will close between the end of 2019 and mid-2020. However, data shows that by mid-February of 2021, nine provinces and cities have generated more than 10 billion yuan in tourism revenue during the Spring Festival, the most important traditional Chinese holiday, although the government advocates "spending the Chinese New Year in place," and "enjoying a local Spring Festival". We can see that the epidemic is under continuous and effective control and a full recovery in tourism is within reach. The World Tourism Organization (UNWTO) and the Chinese travel industry predict that tourism will fully recover by 2022. The tourism industry belongs to the category of high-end services, and with China's large population, abundant tourism resources, and the continued growth of people's income and strong desire to travel, the trend is for tourism to continue to develop at a high quality and rapid pace.

The China Tourism Research Institute released a report at the end of 2020, predicting that a large domestic tourism market with an annual average of 10 billion travelers and a 10 trillion yuan consumption scale is expected to form in the next five years.

3.2 Commodity Properties of Tourism Activities

Tourism activities are composed of various aspects such as food, accommodation, transportation, tourism, shopping, and entertainment. Each element has commodity properties and can be circulated as long as it is a commodity. This chain of tourism has made numerous tourism enterprises. Tourism is the synthesis of various economies, and it has a robust driving effect on related industries. Someone once joked that tourism from a certain point of view is the activity of a person who is tired of staying in his living environment and looking for freshness in another living environment where others are tired of staying. Thus it can be seen that the essence of cross-regional tourism activities is to experience life.

3.3 Tourism Marketing Trends

After COVID-19 in 2020, the trend of Chinese national tourism activities has changed significantly. In the past, when people used public holidays to go out, they usually chose places that were usually difficult to reach, such as outbound trips, or geographic areas that were completely different from the local flavor, such as from the south to the north, feeling that this would make the tourist activity worthwhile. The scenery around people can be seen at any time and can go back later. Due to various factors such as national conditions and transportation, people are starting to change their mindset and relax, friends and family travel together to become mainstream, and peripheral tours, rural tourism, and B&Bs become hot spots of concern. These local characteristics, non-famous district attractions, and B&Bs do not have marketing advantages in OTAs or large travel agencies. Local tour operators should seize the opportunity to take advantage of the location and look around. As long as they are good at discovery and management, there will be a diverse landscape around them. Research proves that tourism recovery should start from suburban and peripheral tourism, play the familiar scenery and style of the characteristics, dig the local niche attractions, and promote the recovery of tourism has become a top priority.Besides, new tourism supply methods will drive new tourism demand and tourism growth points, such as self-guided travel for small groups of family and friends, cultural and creative travel, study tours, rural folklore tours, etc. The evolution and alienation of cell phones have made life easier and faster and created various tourism marketing possibilities.

Moreover, the tourism industry's recovery is bound to trigger a strong rebound of retaliatory travel activities. On one side is the people's strong willingness to travel, on the other side is the OTA digging the design of long and short travel programs and push, the lack of useful links in the middle, travel companies should also consider expanding channels, change passive push to active strike, this channel is the pain point.

4   Tourism Marketing Based on Community E-commerce

Every new social form has its justification for existence, and at the same time, has unknown risks and challenges. The interdisciplinary integration of professions and the cross-border integration of industries must find the right combination to achieve the effect of $1 + 1 > 2$. As community e-commerce penetrates deeper and deeper in life, it will gradually shift from mainly FMCG, especially fresh goods, to a full range of goods. Then, it will face is in the 35 trillion yuan of e-commerce market discourse. The traditional travel agency, OTA, modern short video, live are not to achieve the precise positioning of tourism marketing, inconvenient, too passive, these ways rely on the initiative of potential tourists, be mobilized, belong to the half-hearted marketing methods and ways, the conversion rate can be how much? This is precisely where the strength of community e-commerce lies. We should be based on a better user experience, take the strengths and complement the weaknesses, cross-border integration, innovation in the new era of tourism marketing methods.

4.1   Tourism Goods and Community E-commerce

There are single-factor products and combination products, single-factor products are separate travel goods, such as tickets, beds, food, etc…, while combination products are group goods, such as airline tickets + beds + breakfast, visa + airline + beds, etc. Community e-commerce currently operates mainly in FMCG (Fast Moving Consumer Goods) products, and from the perspective of source channels and product attributes, single-factor travel products are more suitable for sale in community e-commerce platforms at the beginning of marketing. When selling travel goods in community e-commerce, separate FMCG,or single-factor product, would be a must in the initial stage. The product characteristics should be focused on travel products that are easy to reach, low cost, temporary substitution and with family leisure, or even a trip without plan. Consumers in community are price-sensitive and longing for high quality. Single-factor products can be sold in a faster speed and the quality is easier to be monitored and controlled. Once the popularity is gathered, a combination of products can be gradually launched. In the view of industry insiders, China's community e-commerce is still in the stage of platform promotion to seize the market, and user word-of-mouth is significant. In this case, pre-sales and after-sales issues need to invest in human resources to solve. The major e-commerce platforms mainly focus on the formation of offline teams and the expansion of purchasing channels, and the categories of products they operate are relatively concentrated, with less attention paid to the expansion of product categories. At present, the primary community e-commerce business is focused on fresh and household goods and almost no travel goods. This is an opportunity.

Community e-commerce operations success stories are mainly characterized by the head of the affinity and patience, flexible and accessible business hours and pick-up locations, open channels of rights, a variety of business commodities, are essential goods, timely delivery, etc., which greatly enhance the stickiness of community e-commerce users. At the same time, community e-commerce sellers have collected various strategies to increase user residence time and enhance user stickiness. For example, they will declare in advance to postpone the delivery time of some popular and quality goods, two intervals for instance, to lengthen the time-line. The user is free to choose, to wait or quit. If buyers can not resist the temptation, a period of shopping will be extended to a equivalent two periods of time. It also works well in tourism goods marketing. Whether it is tourist cultural and creative products, or scenic spot tickets, performances, B&B inter-nights, or even short-term travel routes, the same operation can be carried out. Community e-commerce also has a unique community e-commerce culture. Users gradually form public order and self-governance conventions based on value recognition in participating in community e-commerce, with a high degree of inclusiveness and firm exclusion, and prone to the agglomeration effect in shopping. Modern, fast-paced life makes people not want to and cannot spend too much time choosing what they need are more efficient and accurate marketing and naked-eye benefits and convenience.

4.2 Tourism Marketing Based on Community E-commerce

In summary, community e-commerce and tourism marketing integrate across borders and are mutually fulfilling relationships. By analyzing community e-commerce operations' characteristics and incorporating tourism commodity information, successful tourism marketing can be achieved. Tourism-related goods generally do not need to be stored and do not occupy space; they are less risky to use or trade and are easier to maintain; they are FMCG goods with fast circulation and high customer loyalty and relevance.

(1) Advantages of community-based e-commerce for tourism marketing

The community mentioned here, i.e., it can be a residential community or an administrative community, including school campuses, and the clustering of people with needs can be regarded as a community, which has an extensive outreach. Cross-border integration should be based on the needs and recognition of the audience. The ultimate goal is to achieve a win-win or even multi-benefit. This marketing approach involves multiple disciplines, tourism, psychology, marketing, ergonomics, quality control, and after-sales are more accessible to grasp than fresh and can be said to have a hundred benefits without harm. The main advantages are the following.

Faster, direct access and larger mass of users. Take a shopping platform's community e-commerce group as an example, a group of 500 people, a city has as many communities as there are such groups, the author's city has about nearly six hundred communities to join this shopping platform. After research and access to information, China's first and second-tier cities in the community e-commerce group situation are the same and continue to radiate and promote. Simultaneously, community e-commerce members' conversion rate when shopping is much higher than that of users of large e-commerce platforms such as OTAs because large e-commerce platforms are passively waiting for customers, while community e-commerce platform users are actively placing orders. It achieves user reachability, changing passive waiting to active, short arrival cycles, and a large group portfolio base. If people look at each community as a point, the community marketing model is multi-point with a surface. It is not an exaggeration to say that community e-commerce can even pry the epidemic that hinders the entire tourism industry from moving forward. The vast community and the base population in the community provide us with a vast space for research.

Relatively stable clientele and accurate marketing. Modern, fast-paced life makes many people have a phobia of choice, and precisely targeted marketing is more suitable for establishing a stable customer base while building intimate social relationships, which we can call group-buying social or community e-commerce social. Tourism companies can provide both package and sell tourism lines in the community e-commerce platform, such as suburban leisure tours; and they can split the tourism lines and contact each link for wholesale sales, such as hotel inter-nights, tickets to scenic spots or shows, or even transportation charters & tickets. This flexible sales approach into the community with community e-commerce as the entry point can involve multiple parties, benefit multiple parties, and be very accurate and stable. In the post-epidemic era, the community e-commerce platform can achieve precise targeting marketing to the customer base and combined with the people's strong willingness to travel. It can lead to a rapid recovery of the tourism industry.

Unnecessary e-tourism products storage. For example, tickets to attractions, accommodations, etc., are digital tourism goods that do not require storage space and are shipped quickly and easily. Digital tourism products are completed as a pre-sale of goods because they can be shipped at any time, without the quality control risks and storage needs of general fresh goods; at the same time, the user of this product is first identified with the product, unless it is force majeure, there is no risk of after-sales. Both sides of the transaction can agree in advance on the validity period of the goods, beyond the deadline, no consumption can be returned to the customer 80%, the other 20% as the user consumption records occupy the server storage operating costs deducted, people can also agree to exempt customers from liability for 100% refund of extraordinary circumstances, attributed to force majeure. This point can be borrowed from the airline's liability-free refund clause. It is also possible to open channels for early replacement of the next stage of travel products.

Effective triage and risk avoidance. Local tourism enterprises' geographical advantages are not easily replaced, so tourism marketing by local tourism enterprises based on community e-commerce can avoid the vicious competition between regions to a certain extent. Tourism enterprises can also form a regional cooperation relationship with each other for mutual tourism distribution and agency of products and grow together. In this way, once there is a public crisis, each region is relatively independent and can spread the risk, and after the crisis is lifted, this cooperative relationship can also help tourism enterprises quickly revitalize. Community-based e-commerce tourism marketing can help the sales of tourism products and form a safety net. Tourism has a strong dependence on a stable social environment, and whether it is an epidemic or war, whether it is a natural disaster or a human factor, it can hit the tourism industry hard. How to avoid risks is a topic worth studying. The question of how to achieve steady developments and relieve the worries of tourism practitioners and tourism enterprises is well worth exploring.

(2) Approaches to E-tourism implementation

Community-based e-commerce tourism marketing is relatively easy to achieve. Due to the different personalities and travel needs of people and scattered locations, it is not easy to achieve precise targeting of tourism marketing worldwide or in a particular country or region, while there are many competitors. If the target group of tourism marketing is divided into groups organized in communities, precise marketing becomes relatively easy. Three approaches are listed below to enhance implementation of E-tourism marketing.

To divide the area and plan multi-point attacks. Community e-commerce must be carried out in a community. The community mentioned here, that is, can be a residential community, can also be the administrative community, including school campuses, etc., there is a demand for the settlement of people can be seen as a community; it is a vast extension. There are many communities in a city in China, which are relatively independent and have different needs and characteristics. If a tourism company wants to carry out community-based e-commerce tourism marketing, it should first conduct research and gain a deeper understanding of the community and then cooperate. This can start with the communities where members of the tourism business live. Communities in China will commonly have online community groups, and community members who join the community group may not know each other. However, they will help each other by exchanging and communicating through this group about life issues, property problems, difficulties they encounter, good content sharing, etc. It is also possible to get in direct contact with the head of the community e-commerce, who will assist in tourism marketing activities. As mentioned earlier in this article, in order to avoid vicious competition, an e-commerce platform in a community will only arrange ahead, so as long as people can reach a cooperation agreement with this head, tourism marketing activities are almost half successful, the other half, of course, depends on the quality of tourism products. The head of the group is a rebate in the community e-commerce operation process, which needs to be well researched in advance. Even members of the tourism business themselves can apply to become community e-commerce leaders so that both can better avoid the risk of unemployment. School campuses are also good community options, and tourism enterprises can conduct tourism research and tourism promotion and marketing through student unions, which will not be repeated here.

To establish long-term partnerships with community e-commerce platforms. Tourism enterprises can establish a two-way communication channel by establishing long-term partnerships with community e-commerce platforms for tourism marketing activities. This can be understood in two ways: on the one hand, through the e-commerce platform to push marketing objectives or tourism products to the head of its multiple communities, through the head of tourism product marketing and tourism activities organization, it is characterized by the ability to implement corresponding marketing strategies for the needs of users in diverse communities; on the other hand, it can also provide only tourism products to the e-commerce platform directly to the users for sales. Tourism enterprises can choose flexibly according to the enterprise's specific situation and the characteristics of tourism products.

The advantage of this method is that it is simple and straightforward, and it also provides direct access to the sales data of each community's tourism goods in the region. The disadvantage is that it is more dependent on e-commerce platforms and has certain risks.

To discover highlights and improve tourism products. No matter who the target is, cooperation is only one aspect. Want to make tourism marketing successful, the quality of tourism products is another aspect and the core issue. An ancient Chinese saying - "wine is not afraid of the alley," tourism products stand the test, tourism marketing will eventually be successful. Community-based formation of a very stable customer base, especially after a period of operation, based on community e-commerce social relations and family and friends' synergy, community tourism marketing target customers will establish a solid social network between them, spontaneous formation of an interrelated travel team. This is entirely different from the ad hoc travel groups organized by travel agencies. They are like-minded and very close, and even over time, this network becomes larger and larger. Of course, this marketing process can also feed the tourism enterprise. Travel companies can analyze the large amount of data generated during the travel marketing process, helping them discover users' preferences and characteristics and find the uniqueness and attractiveness of travel products. Therefore, in the process of tourism marketing based on community e-commerce, tourism enterprises should be good at finding the highlights, paying attention to collecting feedback from community members, analyzing sales data, continuously developing and improving tourism products with more uniqueness and attractiveness, and organizing colorful tourism activities, so as to have a long-term and stable customer population. As long as the community does not disperse, marketing is eternal.

4.3 Big Data Analysis in Community E-commerce

Community e-commerce sales data is easy to collect, less invalid data, easy to analyze, and accurate targeting. A large amount of data is automatically generated in community e-commerce activities, authentic and valid, and can be used directly as the primary data for data analysis without even data cleaning. Data is the most valuable resource in the digital age, and its value is incalculable. Of course, this requires much research data and sales data, such as the community's district, the age & gender composition of users, whether they are working, economic level, travel mode, destination selection preference, travel partners, etc. A rich enough data sample can help travel companies make decisions for different user characteristics. It is not just the number of collections that matters here, but the nature and richness of the data at all levels and the fact that this data can only be obtained through an authentic community marketing process.

5 Conclusions

Looking back, we found that very few platforms in the Internet era started and grew with an apparent goal of making profit, although the ultimate goal of everyone is to be profitable. The essence of internet commodities is to create value, but it is based on mobile phone traffic and data. Tourism can both be classy and close to life at the same time, so tourism enterprises should give up the negative attitude of waiting for chances and become active to strike at the right time. Modern and fast-paced life makes it hard for ordinary people to spend too much time choosing. What users need most are products that are efficient, convenient and affordable with accurate marketing. The achievement of convenience, affordability and corporate profitability relies on companies' ability to understand users' psychology accurately, that is to say, to analyze and catch their needs, and provide complementary products. As a quotation from Auguste Rodin, the French sculpture artist says: "The world never lacks beauty, but lacks the eyes to find it." What tourism marketing lacks is never the source of visitors and attractions but the wide dissemination of tourism information and accurate digital marketing channels. It is well known that we are in an era of rapid development with sufficient opportunities and challenges for everyone and every industry, resulting in a win-win cross-border integration and mutual achievement business for both sides. As long as we face the chance in front bravely, respond and take actions promptly, unlimited possibilities will be created in the moment of crisis with the help of high-tech tools and good user experiences. It is time to face the present squarely and embrace the future tightly.

References

1. Li, X.: An empirical study of community e-commerce based on social network analysis. Knowl. Econ. **2**, 87+89 (2018)
2. Ma, Z.H., Huang, Y.: Study on the current situation of e-commerce development in China. Leadersh. Sci. Forum **7**, 21–23 (2014)
3. Zhang, Y.: Research on reverse logistics network construction of B2C in electronic commerce. North China University of Electric Power (Beijing),10 (2016)

An Empirical Study of the Influencing Factors on User Experience for Barrage Video Website — A Case Study of Bilibili

Weilin Liu[✉], Zhaoshuang He, and Mengxin Liu

School of Management Engineering, Qingdao University of Technology, Qingdao, China

Abstract. According to the recent study, barrage video website gradually spreads throughout people's lives. This research analyzes the influencing factors of the user experience of barrage video website in order to provide basis and reference for improving user experience and increasing the attractiveness of the website. A conceptual model of the influential factors of the user experience for barrage video website was constructed based on UTAUT and APEC theories. Taking Bilibili as a case study, user experience data was collected by a questionnaire. The data was then used to quantitatively analyze the impacts of factors on user experience by the regression analysis. The results show that the variables including content and function of barrage video website significantly impact the user experience. User's emotion has a partial mediating effect in the relationship between content and user experience, and has a full mediating effect in the relationship between function and user experience. But the influence of environment and website interaction design on user experience is not significant.

Keywords: User experience · Barrage video website · Influencing factors · Bilibili

1 Introduction

Barrage video website is a subcategory of network video sharing sites. Compared with general video sharing sites, users can post some instant thoughts on this type of site, and the site will record these comments in this video. When other users watch this video, the recorded comments can float horizontally across the screen like captions and users can discuss what happened at this time together, thus increasing the interaction between the audience [1]. According to "The 46th China Statistical Report on Internet Development" issued by China Internet Network Information Center (CNNIC), as of June 2020, the number of Internet users in China has reached 940 million, and the scale of video websites has also developed rapidly with the development of China's network environment. The number of online video users in China has reached 888 million, accounting for 94.5% of the total Internet users [2]. At present, almost all mainstream video websites have launched the barrage function, which have become barrage video websites in a broad sense. Researches have showed that the user experience of website can greatly affect

© Springer Nature Switzerland AG 2021
V. G. Duffy (Ed.): HCII 2021, LNCS 12778, pp. 310–321, 2021.
https://doi.org/10.1007/978-3-030-77820-0_23

users' memory of website content [3] and the choice of website [4], and it is also a key factor affecting customer loyalty [5]. Thus, finding out the main factors that affect the user experience of the barrage video website and analyzing the relationship between them will play a positive role in the design and operation of the barrage video website.

Because the barrage video website is different from the general website in the way of use and use environment, its user experience and influencing factors will also have its own characteristics and require specific analysis. Bilibili is one of the well-known barrage video websites in China. In 2019, the number of its daily active users reached 37.9 million, and it was an increase of 41% year-on-year. The scale of users continued to expand, especially among young people. It has become the most concentrated video community for young people in China [6]. Based on many researches about Internet user experience, this study constructed a comprehensive user experience model for barrage video website to discuss the impacts of the influencing factors on the user experience, which can be used to reveal the occurrence mechanism of the user experience for barrage video websites. Bilibili was taken as a case study. The research conclusions can provide a reference for the user experience design of barrage video websites, help them improve the design quality, and then enhance the market competitiveness.

2   Related Researches

User experience was first proposed by Norman, who pointed out that a successful user experience design must first meet the needs of users without harassing and annoying users. Second, the products provided should be simple and elegant to make users happy. In addition, to be able to bring additional surprises to users [7]. With the development of the theory of user experience, the connotation of user experience is constantly expanded, but the essence of its "user-centered" design has not changed.

Different researchers had different opinions on user experience, and different research models of user experience had also been proposed. Davis proposed the TAM model (Technology Acceptance Model), which analyzed the cognitive process of the user experience about the information system, and pointed out that the actual use of the information system was determined by user's behavioral intention, while the human behavioral intention was co-determined by user's attitude and user's cognition of the system [8]. Perceived usefulness and perceived ease of use were two key factors in this model. Perceived usefulness referred to the degree to which the system could help users improve work efficiency, and perceived ease of use referred to the degree to which the system could be mastered by the user. From a website design perspective, the two factors mainly show the interaction design, content design and function design. Venkatesh et al. proposed the UTAUT model (Unified Theory of Acceptance and User of Technology) [9]. In the study of Venkatesh et al., the measurement items used for UTAUT model verification also revealed that functional design, interaction design, and content design were key factors that affected website user experience. Vyas, Gerrit, and Vander proposed the APEC model of user experience for interactive systems, pointing out that the use of a system was a complex, changeable, interactive, and feedback process. When users experienced a system, the system's interaction, appearance and functional design would affect user experience (aesthetic, practical, emotional & cognitive), which in turn affected user's behavior and the system's feedback to users [10]. Garrett designed a five-level model of the user experience of the website. The five levels were the presentation layer including the visual design, the frame layer with the interface and navigation design, the structural layer of interaction and information architecture design, the scope layer including function and content design, and the strategic layer including product goals and user needs [11]. It's not difficult to see that interaction design, content design and function design are the key factors affecting the user experience of the website.

At present, the researches on barrage video websites mainly focus on operation, management mode, audience analysis and so on. From the perspective of user experience, there are few researches that comprehensively consider the relationships among human cognition, environmental factors, and the design of the barrage video website (one special system) to guide the optimization design of the barrage video website. With the continuous increase in the number of users of barrage video websites, it is necessary to study the user experience for barrage video websites.

3   Research Hypotheses and Conceptual Model

Based on the UTAUT model and APEC model, this research takes three design dimensions that can affect the user experience, i.e., the interaction, function and content of the barrage video website, as the system factors. The influence of emotion on user experience is based on the design of the information system itself, so emotion is often placed at the center of many empirical studies related to user experience [12]. This research assumes that emotion has a mediation effect between user experience and the system factors and it can also directly affect the user experience. In addition, the existing studies have verified that the personal characteristics of users such as age and gender will affect user experience when users are using the website [13, 14]. Considering the large number of users and user diversity of barrage video websites, this research considers multiple variables including user's usage characteristics and demographic characteristics as the main content of environmental factors. Taking these variables mentioned above, i.e., system factors, user emotion and environmental factors, as the influencing factors, this research studies the impacts of the influencing factors on user experience. Thus, the conceptual model of the influential factors of the user experience for barrage video website is construct, as shown in Fig. 1.

According to the research model and the relationships between constructs, the following research hypotheses are proposed:

H1: Interaction has a significant impact on user experience.
H2: Content has a significant impact on user experience.
H3: Function has a significant impact on user experience.
H4: Emotion has a significant impact on user experience.
H5: Interaction has a significant impact on emotion.
H6: Content has a significant impact on emotion.
H7: Function has a significant impact on emotion.
H8: Emotion plays a mediating role in the relationship between interaction and user experience.

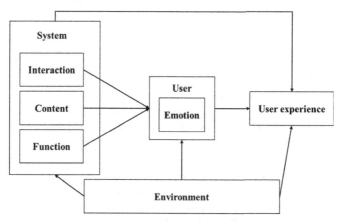

Fig. 1. Conceptual model of the influential factors of the user experience for barrage video website

H9: Emotion plays a mediating role in the relationship between content and user experience.

H10: Emotion plays a mediating role in the relationship between function and user experience.

H11: Environment has a significant impact on user experience.

4 Research Method

4.1 Data Acquisition and Sample Statistics

Data for analysis was collected through questionnaire survey, and the corresponding questionnaires were designed according to the influencing factor model of user experience. The questionnaire consists of three parts: ① One question "Have you ever used Bilibili ?" used to screen out subjects who are the effective subjects; ② Basic user information survey to measure the construct of "Environment". Five one-choice items were used as shown in Table 1. ③ Twenty-one items used to measure the other constructs, i.e., measuring "Interaction", "Content", "Function" and "User Experience" with four items respectively, and measuring "Emotion" with five items, as shown in Table 1. The twenty-one items were all based on previous researches, and they were screened and adjusted appropriately to ensure the validity of the questionnaire. Subjects were invited to evaluate the questionnaire using a Likert five-point scale, with a score ranging from –2 (completely disagree) to + 2 (completely agree).

Questionnaires were distributed on the online questionnaire survey platform "wenjuanxing". The main respondents were college students. After data cleaning and processing, 166 valid questionnaires were collected. In the effective samples, the proportions of men and women were 48.19% and 51.81%, respectively. Students accounted for 89.76% and non-students accounted for 10.24%. In terms of age, the general age distribution was mainly concentrated in the 19–24 years old range, accounting for 90.36%, 7.83% for 25 years old and above, and only 1.81% for 18 years old and below. In terms of using time, respondents having used Bilibili for one year, 1 to 2 years and more than 2 years

Table 1. Constructs and items

Variable types	Constructs	Number	Items	Main literature
Independent variable	Interaction	A101	It is simple to use	[15–17]
		A102	It's easy to find the function you are looking for	
		A103	The operation is relatively smooth, not stuck	
		A104	There are few black screens and flashbacks	
	Content	A201	The quality of video resources is excellent	[5, 18]
		A202	Video resources are rich	
		A203	Video resources are updated timely	
		A204	There are video resources you like or useful to you	
	Function	A301	Video playback and related functions can meet your own needs for video browsing	[19, 20]
		A302	Barrage evaluation function can meet your needs for video evaluation and communication	
		A303	Recommendation function can recommend content that is suitable for you	
		A304	Special functions such as interactive videos are attractive	
Mediating variable	Emotion	A401	Bilibili is interesting	[21, 22]
		A402	Bilibili can give you satisfaction	
		A403	Bilibili can make you happy	
		A404	The popularity of Bilibili is high	
		A405	You can find potential contacts by Bilibili	
Dependent variable	User experience	A501	Overall, the user experience of Bilibili is satisfactory	[20, 23]
		A502	You will recommend Bilibili to others	
		A503	Bilibili is useful for you	
		A504	Bilibili is easy to use	
Environment variable	Environment	A601	What's your gender?	
		A602	How old are you?	
		A603	How well do you know it?	
		A604	When did you start using Bilibili?	
		A605	How often did you use Bilibili?	

accounted for 31.93%, 19.88% and 48.19% respectively. In terms of use frequency, respondents who use it almost every day accounted for 38.55%. 33.13% of respondents used it 1 to 3 times a week, and 28.31% used it rarely.

4.2 Data Analysis and Results

Reliability Analysis. SPSS 20.0 was used to analyze the reliability of Interaction, Content, Function, Emotion and User Experience. The results (Table 2) show that the Cronbach's α coefficients of each influencing factor and user experience are all greater than 0.8, indicating that the reliability of the questionnaire is good. At the same time, the total correlations of corrected items are all greater than 0.4, indicating that there is no need to delete any item, and the deletion of any item does not greatly improve the Cronbach's α coefficient. Therefore, the quality of the questionnaire is good and the questionnaire data can be used for further analysis.

Table 2. Results of reliability analysis

Constructs	Items	Corrected item-total correlation	Cronbach's α if item deleted	Cronbach's α
Interaction	A101	0.727	0.791	0.848
	A102	0.693	0.805	
	A103	0.633	0.834	
	A104	0.702	0.800	
Content	A201	0.453	0.846	0.806
	A202	0.653	0.741	
	A203	0.691	0.724	
	A204	0.727	0.711	
Function	A301	0.660	0.752	0.811
	A302	0.597	0.777	
	A303	0.652	0.753	
	A304	0.617	0.768	
Emotion	A401	0.777	0.885	0.907
	A402	0.785	0.883	
	A403	0.795	0.880	
	A404	0.696	0.901	
	A405	0.786	0.882	
User experience	A501	0.750	0.878	0.897
	A502	0.747	0.890	
	A503	0.836	0.842	
	A504	0.805	0.859	

Validity Analysis. In SPSS 20.0 software, the factor analysis method was used for validity analysis. First, KMO value and Bartlett sphericity test were used to determine whether the data was suitable for factor analysis. The results (Table 3) show that the KMO value of each construct is greater than 0.7, and the significance probability of Bartlett's sphericity test is less than 0.01, indicating that the data is suitable for factor analysis. Then, factor analysis was performed. The results (Table 3) show that the factor loading of each item is greater than 0.6, and the interpretation level of each construct is higher than that of the 30% standard of social science research. In summary, the questionnaire has good validity.

Table 3. Results of validity analysis

Constructs	Items	Factor loading	Eigenvalues	KMO value	% of variance	Sig. of Bartlett sphere test
Interaction	A101	0.862	2.767	0.752	69.164	.000
	A102	0.842				
	A103	0.786				
	A104	0.834				
Content	A201	0.639	2.595	0.778	64.884	.000
	A202	0.830				
	A203	0.859				
	A204	0.872				
Function	A301	0.821	2.565	0.782	64.132	.000
	A302	0.777				
	A303	0.818				
	A304	0.787				
Emotion	A401	0.861	3.655	0.877	73.107	.000
	A402	0.868				
	A403	0.875				
	A404	0.801				
	A405	0.868				
User experience	A501	0.859	3.114	0.830	77.856	.000
	A502	0.855				
	A503	0.916				
	A504	0.898				

Correlation Analysis. The Pearson correlation was used to measure the linear relationship between the constructs. The results (Table 4) show that Interaction, Content, Function and Emotion are all significantly related to User Experience. In detailed, the correlation coefficients of Content, Function, Emotion and User Experience are above 0.6, and the correlation coefficient between Emotion and User Experience is 0.8. Combined with the results of previous user interviews, it can be preliminarily judged that Emotion plays an intermediary role in the relationships between Interaction, Function, Content and User Experience.

Regression Analysis. Park et al. found that the simple linear model could be used to obtain relatively stable results of quantitative analysis of user experience [21], so the linear regression analysis was used to study the relationship between influencing factors and user experience and three linear regression models were established. Model 1 was

Table 4. Results of correlation analysis

Constructs	Mean	Standard deviation	Interaction	Content	Function	Emotion	User experience
Interaction	4.012	0.702	1				
Content	4.208	0.549	0.348**	1			
Function	4.051	0.581	0.262**	0.655**	1		
Emotion	4.258	0.615	0.303**	0.714**	0.706**	1	
User experience	4.258	0.625	0.303**	0.708**	0.611**	0.800**	1

Note: ** represent the correlation is significant at the 0.01 level (2-tailed).

established to test the impacts of Interaction, Content and Function on Emotion in the certain Environment. Model 2 was used to test the impacts of Interaction, Content and Function on User Experience in the same Environment, and Model 3 was used to test the impact of Interaction, Content, Function, and Emotion on User Experience in the same Environment.

The specific linear regression models are as follows:

$$Y_{Emotion} = \alpha_1 + \beta_1(Interaction) + \gamma_1(Content) + k_1(Function) + \theta_1(Gender)$$
$$+ \lambda_1(Age) + \varphi_1(\text{Degree of Understanding}) + \omega_1(\text{Use Time}) + \sigma_1(Use\ Frequency) + \varepsilon_{1i}$$

$$Y^1_{User\ Experience} = \alpha_2 + \beta_2(Interaction) + \gamma_2(Content) + k_2(Function) + \theta_2(Gender)$$
$$+ \lambda_2(Age) + \varphi_2(\text{Degree of Understanding}) + \omega_2(\text{Use Time}) + \sigma_2(Use\ Frequency) + \varepsilon_{2i}$$

$$Y^2_{User\ Experience} = \alpha_3 + \beta_3(Interaction) + \gamma_3(Content) + k_3(Function) + \mu_3(Emotion)$$
$$+ \theta_3(Gender) + \lambda_3(Age) + \varphi_3(\text{Degree of Understanding}) + \omega_3(\text{Use Time}) + \sigma_3(Use\ Frequency) + \varepsilon_{3i}$$

According to the three models, stepwise linear regression analysis is performed on the above linear model in three steps. Put the result data of the questionnaire survey into the model, and get the regression results. See Table 5.

Table 5 shows that the adjusted R-squares of the three models are 0.631, 0.564, and 0.692 respectively, and the goodness of fit is acceptable. According to the regression results of Model 1, both Content and Function have significant impacts on Emotion, but Interaction and Environment (at the significance level of 0.01) don't. The results of Model 2 show that Content and Function also have significant impacts on User Experience, while Interaction and Environment (at the significance level of 0.01) have no significant impact on User Experience. In the previous correlation analysis, it was concluded that the correlations between Interaction and Emotion or User Experience were both significant. This paradox between correlation analysis and regression analysis may be interpreted that the relationships between Interaction and Emotion or User Experience are mainly caused by the correlation between Interaction and Content or Function, so once controlling the Function and Content, the net correlation between Interaction and Emotion or User Experience are not significant. In model 3, Emotion and Content have significant impacts on User Experience, and Emotion has a greater impact on User Experience. Because of

Table 5. Regression analysis results of the three models

Independent variables	Dependent variable: emotion			Dependent variable: user experience					
	Model 1			Model 2			Model 3		
	SE	SC	Sig	SE	SC	Sig	SE	SC	Sig
(Constant)	0.357	—	0.004	0.394	—	0.244	0.34	—	0.453
Interaction	0.045	0.029	0.576	0.05	0.031	0.573	0.042	0.014	0.759
Content	0.077	0.362	0	0.085	0.444	0	0.078	0.23	0.001
Function	0.068	0.425	0	0.075	0.267	0	0.071	0.016	0.814
Emotion	—	—	—	—	—	—	0.074	0.593	0
Gender	0.061	0	0.995	0.067	0.034	0.533	0.057	0.034	0.462
Age	0.045	−0.073	0.133	0.049	0.053	0.315	0.042	0.096	0.032
Degree of understanding	0.057	0.034	0.603	0.063	0.046	0.521	0.053	−0.066	0.272
Use time	0.026	−0.039	0.513	0.029	0.043	0.51	0.025	0.066	0.228
Use frequency	0.031	0.211	0.011	0.034	0.166	0.016	0.03	0.041	0.486
Adjusted R^2	0.631			0.564			0.692		

Note: SE represents Standard Error. SC represents Standardized Coefficients.

the involvement of Emotion, the impact of Function on User Experience becomes no longer significant, and Interaction and Environment (at the significance level of 0.01) neither show significant impacts on User Experience.

In the three models, the regression coefficients of Interaction are all small, and the significances are all greater than 0.01. It shows that Interaction has no direct significant impact on User Experience, and Emotion does not play the mediating role in the relationship between Interaction and User Experience. The results of Model 2 and Model 3 show that the impacts of Content and Function on User Experience changed after adding the variable Emotion, i.e., the impact of Content on User Experience is reduced, while Function has no impact on user experience. Therefore, Emotion has a partial mediating effect in the relationship between Content and User Experience, and a full mediating effect in the relationship between Function and User Experience.

5   Conclusions and Suggestions for Improvement

5.1   Research Conclusions

Based on the above data analysis, the verification of the hypotheses is summarized as shown in Table 6.

Table 6. Hypothesis testing results

Hypotheses	Results
H1: Interaction has a significant impact on user experience	Not support
H2: Content has a significant impact on user experience	Support
H3: Function has a significant impact on user experience	Support
H4: Emotion has a significant impact on user experience	Support
H5:Interaction has a significant impact on emotion;	Not support
H6: Content has a significant impact on emotion	Support
H7: Function has a significant impact on emotion	Support
H8: Emotion plays a mediating role in the relationship between interaction and user experience	Not support
H9: Emotion plays a mediating role in the relationship between content and user experience	Support
H10: Emotion plays a mediating role in the relationship between function and user experience	Support
H11: Environment has a significant impact on user experience	Not support

Except for H1, H5, H8, and H11, other hypotheses are supported. The research conclusions are as follows:

1. Function and content are the two main factors that affect user experience, and content has a greater impact on user experience than function. This shows that most users are more concerned about the video resources of barrage video websites. The better the video resources are, the better the user experience is. After considering the function and content, the interaction does not show a significant impact on the user experience, indicating that the interaction cannot directly affect the user experience. The interactivity of the website can be experienced after users are satisfied with the function and the presentation of the content, which in turn affects users' emotion and the user experience.

2. Emotion has a significant mediating effect on the relationship between the system (function, content) and user experience. Emotion has a completely mediating role in the relationship between function and user experience, and has a partially mediating role in the relationship between content and user experience. Based on this, it can be inferred that good functional design and high-quality content are the foundation of high-quality user experience on barrage video websites. Users pay attention to the both firstly when using Bilibili. If users' needs are met, users will have better emotional cognition, which in turn will help produce a high-quality user experience.

3. In terms of environmental variables, including users' gender, age, etc., they have no significant impact on emotion and user experience. It shows that users with different backgrounds do not have many differences in user cognition and experience about Bilibili, one of the barrage video websites.

5.2 Suggestions for Improving the User Experience of the Barrage Video Platform

According to the above research results, suggestions for improving the user experience of the barrage video platform are as follows:

1. Because content and function are the two key factors that can directly affect the user experience and the users' emotion, we can start with enhancing the richness of the website's content and the usability of its functions to improve the user experience of the barrage video website. Through the improvement of website resources and functions, the website can more directly meet users' needs and increase user stickiness, which is also conducive to improving website reputation. The effective improvement of a single website will also cause healthy competition in the market, which will help promote the upgrading and improvement of the video industry.
2. Interactivity is the foundation of the website, which can affect users' perception of the content and function of the barrage video website. Although the interaction doesn't significantly affect the user emotion and user experience, it does have a high relevance with user emotion and user experience. The website needs to have a friendly interactive design to be convenient for users.

6 Limitations

Although we try our best to be scientific and rigorous in this research, there are still some limitations. First, due to the impact of Covid 19, we have not carried out large-scale user surveys on the basis of ensuring certain research reliability and validity. The accuracy of the research results needs to be improved. Second, the measurement of environmental factors is not detailed enough, such as age, which is only divided into three categories, so the analysis of the relationship between environment and emotion or user experience is not accurate enough. Finally, this research uses Bilibili as the research object, which can't represent all the barrage video websites, so the universality of the research conclusion needs to be improved.

Acknowledgments. This work is supported by the First Batch of 2020 MOE Industry-University Collaborative Education Program (No. 202002035012, Kingfar-CES "Human Factors and Ergonomics" Program), Comprehensive, Designed and Innovative Experimental Teaching Project in 2020 of Qingdao University of Technology (No. ZSC2020013), and Shandong Provincial Natural Science Foundation of China (No. ZR2018PG001).

References

1. Baidu Encyclopedia: Barrage Video Website. https://baike.baidu.com/item/%E8%A7%86%E9%A2%91%E5%BC%B9%E5%B9%95%E7%BD%91%E7%AB%99/4254693?fr=aladdin. Accessed 25 Dec 2020
2. China Internet Network Information Center: http://www.cnnic.cn/hlwfzyj/hlwxzbg/hlwtjbg/202009/P020200929546215182514.pdf. Accessed 29 Sep 2020

3. Liu, W., Liang, X., Liu, F.: The effect of webpage complexity and banner animation on banner effeceiveness in a free browsing task. Int. J. Hum. Comput. Interact. **35**(11–15), 1192–1202 (2019)
4. Chang, S.H., Chih, W.H., Liou, D.K., Hwang, L.R.: The influence of web aesthetics on customers' PAD. Comput. Hum. Behav. **36**, 168–178 (2014)
5. Loureiro, S.M.C., Roschk, H.: Differential effects of atmospheric cues on emotions and loyalty intention with respect to age under online/offline environment. J. Retail. Consum. Serv. **21**(2), 211–219 (2014)
6. Huajing Information Network: https://www.huaon.com/story/520575. Accessed 23 March 2020
7. Norman, D.A., Miller, J., Henderson, A.: What you see, some of what's in the future, and how we go about doing it: HI at Apple computer. In: Katz, I., Mack, R., Marks, L. (eds.) CHI 1995: Conference Companion on Human Factors in Computing Systems, Association for Computing Machinery, New York, NY, United States, pp.155–155 (1995)
8. Davis, V.F.D.: A theoretical extension of the technology acceptance model: four longitudinal field studies. Manage. Sci. **46**(2), 186–204 (2000)
9. Venkatesh, V., Morris, M.G., Davis, G.B., Davis, F.D.: User acceptance of information technology: toward a unified view. MIS Q. **27**(3), 425–478 (2003)
10. Vyas, D., Gerrit, C., Van Der, V.: APEC: A framework for designing experience. https://www.researchgate.net/publication/251990033. Accessed 25 Dec 2020
11. Garrett, J.: The Elements of User Experience, 2nd edn. New Riders Press, Indianapolis (2010)
12. Agarwal, A., Meyer, A.: Beyond usability: evaluating emotional response as an integral part of the user experience. In: CHI EA 2009: CHI 2009 Extended Abstracts on Human Factors in Computing Systems, Association for Computing Machinery, New York, NY, United States, pp. 2919–2930 (2009)
13. Etcheverry, I., Terrier, P., Marquie, J.C.: Assessing web interaction with recollection: age-related and task-related differences. Comput. Hum. Behav. **28**(1), 11–22 (2012)
14. Wang, H.F.: Picture perfect: girls' and boys' preferences towards visual complexity in children's websites. Comput. Hum. Behav. **31**, 551–557 (2014)
15. Peng, A., Xia, L.: Research on the influence factors of effect of university library micro-services from the perspective of user perception. Libr. Inf. Serv. **62**(17), 33–43 (2018)
16. Guan, L.: Research on users' continuance use intention of academic library website—based on integration model of user experience, TAM and ECM. Libr. Work. Study **1**(2), 48–59 (2020)
17. Lee, D.Y., Lento, M.R.: User acceptance of youtube for procedural learning: an extension of the technology acceptance model. Comput. Educ. **61**, 193–208 (2013)
18. Floh, A., Madlberger, M.: The role of atmospheric cues in online impulse-buying behavior. Electron. Commer. Res. Appl. **12**(6), 425–439 (2013)
19. Chen, W.: Research on Danmu video sites and users—Taking Bilibili video as an example (2016). https://www.ixueshu.com/document/79da8b70f0a1bdbac4ee3675a2dff96d3189 47a18e7f9386.html. Accessed 25 Dec 2020
20. Chen, J., Zhong, Y., Deng, S.: Analysis and empirical study on the influencing factors of user experience of mobile social networking platform: take WeChat as an example. Inf. Theory Pract. **39**(01), 79+99–103 (2016)
21. Park, J., Han, S.H., Kim, H.K., Moon, H.: Modeling user experience: a case study on a mobile device. Int. J. Ind. Ergon. **43**(2), 187–196 (2013)
22. Deng, L., Poole, M.S.: Affect in web interfaces: a study of the impacts of web page visual complexity and order. MIS Q. **34**(4), 711–730 (2010)
23. Du, H.: The user experience research for SNS website (2013). https://www.ixueshu.com/document/2a3852453088c5d1318947a18e7f9386.html. Accessed 25 Dec 2020

Application of Design Thinking in the Education Segment, Regarding the Human-Computer Interactions

Vanda Orbulov[(⊠)] [iD]

Faculty of Economic and Social Sciences, Department of Ergonomics and Psychology, Budapest University of Technology and Economics, Műegyetem rakpart 3, Budapest 1111, Hungary
orbulov.vanda@gtk.bme.hu

Abstract. After having a short overview of the new approach, the paper will introduce the possible future of design thinking and launch its opportunity, especially in the organizations dedicated not as primarily profit-oriented, like the state-maintained educational segment. The paper offers an insight into the practical application of today's design thinking approach, covering its main background and observes its methods and tools in the pragmatic operation involving segment fields like education. Paper introduces the design process with diverse characteristics from the former project management processes, highlighting the significance of covering all the segments and activities applied to design thinking. Moreover, the paper aims to provide a detailed research plan including research fields for demonstrating the optional change of the stakeholders' attitude, opinion, and customer satisfaction among students caused by the measurements due to COVID pandemic, closely related to the digital transformation in a sense and higher level of human-computer interaction's need.

Keywords: Service design · Educational design · Design thinking

1 Introduction

The paper intends to introduce the application possibilities of the design thinking mindset in an education service segment. The paper aims to highlight the design thinking mindset's role in a segment where profitability is not the key driving force through its advantages and future potentials. Design thinking as an innovative mindset [1] appeared in many organizations; also, ones are in particular situations: they are state-maintained, so they are not primarily similar to the profit-oriented business organizations. The observation of framing and the novel, innovative process intended to call attention to the examined mindset's usability, effectiveness, and competitiveness [2, 3]. The paper focuses primarily on the state-maintained higher education segment, given the unique features the examined service has in Hungary. After discussing the design thinking mindset and its role and place in organizations, businesses, and education, the research method's planned research fields are detailed. Countries are nowadays actively reorganizing their pedagogical, educational models, moving away from standardized approaches and "a

© Springer Nature Switzerland AG 2021
V. G. Duffy (Ed.): HCII 2021, LNCS 12778, pp. 322–331, 2021.
https://doi.org/10.1007/978-3-030-77820-0_24

one-size-fits-all experience" toward new and individualized learning modes based on what students learn rather than on their time in a classroom [4].

Furthermore, the research aims to approach the question, if the players are aware of being service providers and customers, or the operation follows other principles. The author intends to reconsider the traditional concept created for education and bring a new perspective by defining the higher education segment's relevance to having the characters similar to the examined Hungarian one. The paper focuses on determining and evaluating the design thinking mindset as a service development method and not covering the aspects for teaching design thinking, so the new mindset's education is out of scope in this research. Moreover, the aim is to discover how the current pandemic situation influenced decision-makers' thinking can have an impact on the application of the design thinking mindset. The research consisted of two phases. First, discovering the design thinking mindset as a critical driver of the innovation, parallel with highlighting the examined service segment's unique features. Paper summarizes main findings, including the literature reviews, and points out the research plan for a future conclusion stems from qualitative data.

2 Literature Review, Innovation in Designing Process

Design thinking can be described in diverse ways as having significantly various relations with today's research and practical expert fields. Design research started in the '60s and has a broad role and application within innovation, society, and industry [5]. Design fields have become cross-disciplinary and multi- faceted [4]. Cross highlighted the main essence of design: the appropriate design methods are modeling, pattern-formation, synthesis, while the values of design are practicality, ingenuity, empathy, and concern for "appropriateness" [6]. However, there are some differences in explaining the design thinking approach; the paper focuses on their similarities and points out the relevancies for businesses and the education segment. Today, the design has presumably become a complicated way of thinking and guiding principles that concern all life situations [7]. The differences are possible based on the actual focus of the approach, the type of segment researchers is examining at that time, or the type of the product, experts tend to apply any practical methods of the approach. In an age of mass production greater understanding of the people is demanded by those who practice design and more insight into the design process by the public, according to Victor Papanek [8]. Understanding and applying the way of thinking was mainly used successfully by tangible product designers in the past. Definition of design thinking similar to the historical focus points may vary in the literature, but they have similar points for expressing its essence. The design profession and the context for design practice have changed relevantly over the past 50 years [9]. Design thinking can be defined as a mindset, approach, or even a discipline, method, and toolkit; it is also determined as a mix of different thinking [10]. According to Norman [11], attention must be paid to the entire experience, which means the aesthetic of form and interaction quality. The point is to determine that the focus is always on creating solutions by contacting a problem, defining that, and finding solutions creatively by involving people who affect the phenomenon put into the focus. As having a comprehensive understanding of design, the designer's name is also applied for all the researchers and experts develop any processes regarding this mindset in this paper. Some universities, organizations, and institutions started to create in-depth research about and establishing related programs and schools for design thinking [9, 12]. Facilitating the more in-depth understanding and spread of the mindset into many segments. The other crucial point is discovering the highlighted role of customers and stakeholders in how designers intend to find the right solutions to the carefully defined problems. Understanding and a clear definition of problems and needs from a customer-aspect are critical factors in the design thinking mindset [11]. As Norman determined, "good design starts with an understanding of psychology and technology" [11]. The human-centered and iterative characteristic of the design thinking let researchers concentrating on the stakeholders, discovering the needs and frustrating issues concerning the examined process. The final goal of the process is to create a product, service, process, or experience that people need, have real potential to become useful, and quickly or conveniently be built in terms of technology [13]. Moreover, design thinking is about learning, putting in the right effort and learn from the mistakes, lead to success. Over the ergonomics, the culture and the context are as relevant as the physical aspects. In order to create a long-term relationship with the stakeholders, designers should be aware to involve partners actively instead in a passive way. Author introduces the design process with diverse characteristics from the former mindsets and development processes, highlighting the significance of covering all the segments and activities applied to design thinking. Instead of pre-defined series and phases, the design process can be interpreted as a creative, human-centered discovery process followed by iterative prototyping cycles, testing, and refinement [13]. One of the special features that it moves along iterative, circular processes, instead of the traditional linear process. The iterative, circular feature of the mindset's practical application ensures the continuous learning and therefore, the correction and perfection of a human centered solution, based on an emphatical attitude. A deep understanding of the people may be affected by the product or process designers intend to make any developments is crucial, as unless they have a clear vision about the design process, so the design thinking mindset cannot drive success. In an organization the place and role of the design thinking mindset and so the designers are significant, as unless creating a strategic importance of the mindset integrated into the strategic implementation, the right success and results are not achievable. The involvement of stakeholders interested by the approach, collaboration of diverse professional and scientific fields is essential. Design thinking is a mindset to address wicked problems with multidisciplinary and cross-functional innovation teams [1]. Multi-professional' designers and planners are needed whose intuitive leaps are informed by knowledge and experience of change at all levels from community action to component design [14]. Unless creating a wide range of perspectives derives from diverse professional background, additional value of the design thinking mindset could not validate the right and special effect that makes it different from other process development methods. Individual designers have to collaborate for designing a unified whole: foreign circumstances and experts from different cultures with disparate ways of thinking and working increase the ambiguity [15]. Norman described the Iterative Cycle of Human-Centered Design in the '80s contains phases as observation, ideation, prototyping, and testing [11]. Before creating of the stages described by Norman, the artificial intelligence and cognitive science researcher, Simon defined seven phases in

1969, as the definition, the researching, the ideation, the prototyping, choosing, the implementation, and the learning [16]. Paper aims also to point out the learning process provided by the design thinking mindset. "Designing is thus not something one is instructed how to do, but something one learns how to create" [14]. The design process in case of products and services also covers the emphasizing phase according to another model [17] followed by the definition, where framing gets a special attention. Designers often deal with complex and, sometimes wicked problems. The challenge of managing these open problems leads to a particular interest in the ways they construct 'frames' and how to design organizations deal with frames in their field of operation [10]. Framing is an applied term for creating a new outlook and how designers can manage a complex problem or a situation that tends to be solved [18]. Throughout the observation phase, empathy had a crucial function. Empathy and design are in compelling combination; Cross [6] defined empathy as a critical value of design. The ideation stage of process needs an open creative mindset for discovering and expressing all the optional solutions suitable for the well-defined problems. Designers should build deeper impressions, so prototyping so getting feedback from users as testing [19].

3 Design Thinking in Organizations

Design is not just successfully acceptable for creating material, along physical aspect, but the thinking perspective, itself, the way designers come closer, and define problems were more relevant. This mindset flowed into new segments and sectors like the businesses by discovering the advantages of the promising and practical approach in the physical product developments and designing artistic and technical artifacts. A designer can transform the way team develops products, services, processes, and even strategy [13]. Design thinking can be defined as a fresh new approach enough infiltrating into the businesses and public services having the courageous and dynamic engagement for creating some more efficient, creative and profitable solutions both in the present activities and the innovation field desired by the market players, customers, and concerned stakeholders. Design thinking is a stimulating and exciting new paradigm for dealing with problems in many professions, like IT and business [10]. To understand the main points of the approach in businesses and management, managers suggested adopting the growth mindset drawn up by Carol Dweck [20]; this kind of mindset as effort plus learning equals growth and success. By coming to the business world as a new approach, the managers reason mostly in an inductive or deductive way, having an analytical thinking instead of intuitive one [21], and waited at the same time for any kind of advantages can be expressed in a monetary unit for proving its real importance similar to all other performance indicators. The management and the customers' expectations are diverse: the board prefers to have loyalty, trust, and high customer lifetime value, while the customer needs a smooth, customized, and fast solution. However, organizations strive for innovation, managers and decision-makers rely incomparably on analytical thinking, which slightly improves current information and knowledge, creating modest improvements to the status quo [21]. According to Martin [21], the competitive advantage is achievable by applying a kind of thinking: how knowledge advances from one step to another-from mystery to heuristic to the algorithm, which is a predictable key for creating an answer giving to the mystery question. Design can be profitable for organizations. On the one hand, design thinking determined as a simple, temporary, and passing new wave in the product- and service development; on the other hand, we can observe a brand-new aspect having a relatively profound impact on all of the affected organizational units from the strategic level through the employees finally, until the customers, stakeholders, involving all of them into the creation of a more valuable future cooperation, together with the environment in a broad sense.

3.1 Design Thinking in the Education

The paper intends to introduce the possible future of design thinking and launch the design thinking's opportunity, especially in the organizations dedicated not as primarily profit-oriented, like the state-maintained educational segment. Design thinking extends for segments, activities, and processes beyond the businesses targeting the increasing profits, incomes, and market shares along with providing the mindset, methods, and toolkit for meeting the real needs of services' stakeholders not necessarily or primarily connected to the revenue-expenditure-profit "triangle." Moreover, the author offers an insight into the practical application of today's design thinking approach and observes its methods and tools in the practical application involving segment fields like education. Their introduction is provided by a research plan containing the targeted methods for evaluating the future research questions. Trends can indicate significant future challenges and areas of benefits. Education has a crucial role in all societies concerning all directly or indirectly. The examined higher-educational segment can cover state-maintained, not primary profit-oriented institutions. The profit-oriented institutions are out of the scope of this research. However, the situation, opportunities, and discipline of players in higher education show a varied picture worldwide; the author focuses on the ones maintained by the state and offers technical or economic studies for students on all levels. State-maintained higher education is defined as all the services offered for the graduated and undergraduate students, in this case, covering all the processes, activities, and stakeholders impacting the services themselves. It is crucial to consider its features, highlighting the possibilities and advantages from a design thinking aspect. Over the last two decades, the popularity of design thinking in higher education for undergraduates, managers, and executives has grown worldwide [10, 22]. The idea's promotion stems from using the perspective of design for problem-framing and problem-solving in large multinational companies. They argue in favor of the design thinking mindset as a driver of innovations. Examples listed by de Figueiredo are the American design company IDEO and the books published by its CEOs, and the inspiration from celebrated designers' work, the architect Frank Gehry [22]. Design education has diversified and developed considerably in the art academies, and increasingly in universities and technical education [9].

4 Research Fields

Research questions cover the three main fields suspected to achieve relevant findings and further developments. Research fields are equaled research questions. The first field to be improved is the innovation's design thinking approach, qualitative research about what decision-makers think of design thinking, including assessing the knowledge about and the attitude and conditions for integrating the mindset into the everyday operation, in a whole or part. The design thinking-led process makes the problem definition and the team collaboration more impactful, affecting the development process's final output. The observation and understanding of possible barriers influence the mindset's integration as a research question as to the second field. The second research question includes the intended determination of possibilities can provide a more straightforward intention for being open to accepting and understanding its advantages, especially in the educational sector. To draw appropriate conclusions from the difference between the results derived in the case of questioned people from the business segment and the ones belong to the educational segment, the author plans to make comparative analyses. The third research question aims to provide a detailed research plan for demonstrating the optional change of the customer satisfaction among stakeholders of the education segment caused by the measurements due to the COVID pandemic, closely related to the digital transformation in a sense and higher level of human-computer interaction's need. Table 1 gives a summary of the leading research fields.

Table 1. Main fields of research

Filed of research	Business relevant question	Educational relevant question
Basic background	Educational and demographical background	Academical background
Attitude and motivation	Attitude of working	Motivation, research fields
Currently applied methods	IT systems and	Educational systems, infrastructure for teaching
Problem-solving techniques	Methods for cooperating in projects	Methods for creating new subjects, courses
Decision-making	Process of decision-making and information about decisions	Process of decision-making and information about decisions
Involvement of stakeholders	Partners, customers, employees, stockholders and other companies	Students, offices, partners, Significant relationships, and cooperations
Digital transformation	Opinion about pandemic changes in business, profitability and human resource questions	Opinion about pandemic changes, educational needs and transformation
Customer complaint management	CRM systems	Student offices and other contacts
Visions	Short- and long-term vision of the organization	Short- and long-term vision of the organization

The author designed an investigation to connect these challenging fields, the user-centered design, with the opportunity-driven technology-based innovation. The purpose for clarifying the research questions is twofold; firstly, to explore in a controlled research environment how innovative and exact results can be created for the research fields, and secondly, how new knowledge or a deeper understanding of design thinking can be gained for the invited stakeholders participated in the research.

4.1 Education as a Service

The research tends to apply the suitable design thinking methods for precise and profound observation and examination, especially in the education segment, from relevant stakeholders' and customers' aspects, i.e., from the teacher to the management students' perspective. First of all, a relevant question should be answered at the beginning of the research. Is education a service? What is the opinion of the critical stakeholders about? Services cover a massive variety of different and often very complex activities. In time, a broader association emerged, captured in the dictionary definition of "the action of serving, helping, or benefiting; conduct services contrasted them against goods and described services as "acts, deeds, performances, or efforts" and argued that they had different characteristics from goods in services. The word service was originally associated with the work tending to the welfare or advantage of another" [23]. Today, our thinking has advanced and focuses on the lack of ownership transfer when buying a service. Education as a service aims to meet the need for studying, acquiring knowledge-providing an intangible benefit and skills, produced with the guidance of a set of tangible infrastructure, where the customer of the service does not get any ownership [24], similar to services, in general.

5 Research Method

Research starts with defining and understanding the problem. The required goal is to choose tools for understanding to help discover the problem's meaning in this phase.

Effective design practice is based not on widespread problem analysis but adequate 'problem scoping' and a focused or directed approach to gathering problem information and prioritizing criteria [25]. Therefore, the opening point of designing is the dilemma itself, i.e., designers do not have a ready solution or ready plan.

5.1 Market Analysis

The market analysis includes interviews and field research. In the part of the market analysis, 30 face-to-face or online interviews are planned to be conducted. For an in-depth understanding, it is crucial to invite people who use and provide services. In one-half of the personal interviews, the business segment's participants: experts and managers, will be interviewed who mostly perform innovative and development tasks. The author will discover their official duties, communication, devices applied, working method, and environment. In the other half of the interviews, decision-makers, stakeholders, and customers will be interviewed from the education segment about the aspects they have about the provider and customer relation, how they judge the service innovation option and the opinion. During the interviews, design thinking methods will be applied, as the mom test. The method is about having real conversations with people and draw feedback from there [26]. Moreover, both interviewed groups will have questions regarding the new situation: changes reasoned by COVID pandemic, therefore the impact of the digital transformation in the segment. Interviews will be followed by field research at workplaces and educational or research institutions and customer attitude surveys.

5.2 Field Research

Field study belongs to the observation design phase. Design research varies from scientists' research. It occurs directly at the users themselves to have a clear picture of their needs, interests, motives, and understanding of the real situations they face, not some actual separate experiences [11]. In this phase, empathy has a significant role in imagining the observed people's situation with all the feelings and thoughts. The author tends to conclude field research for discovering the circumstances of the working methods, environment, and possible cooperation among the different expert fields. Moreover, design empathy is thought being taken to improve by certain types of methods such as research techniques for setting contact between users and designers, procedures for reporting findings of user studies to design teams like the storytelling, or the ideation methods to evoke a designer's own experiences in a field connected to the user [6]. By taking a "people first" strategy, designers can imagine constitutionally acceptable answers and meet specific unknown needs [13].

5.3 Mapping

The visualization is a crucial element of the design thinking mindset for clarifying the discovered connections, roles, and essential details. Synthesis maps mix examination data and information, system expertise, and design schemes into visible stories. These narratives encourage interaction and decision-making among stakeholders. Synthesis mapping is a method that promotes learning, description, and discussion of views, actors, and links in compact system challenges. Synthesis maps combine knowledge from research cycles and iterative sensemaking to establish a consistent design story, represent relationships among parts. Its mission is to support shared understanding while exploring the design options available in these systems [27]. The author prefers to create visualization by applying two maps followed by the researches because the research fields are instead referred to as a complex system challenge than a dedicated service description.

6 Expected Research Benefit

To create a transparent service offer from a process-approach supported by the design thinking mindset, the paper intends to determine key performance indicators (KPIs) related to the research results. Measurable value demonstrating how effectively an organization is achieving its key business, social, environmental, and other relevant objectives. As the social and ecological advantages for any organization, the monetary units for the getting to know, the implementation, and applying the design thinking mindset are quite a challenge as proving its ability to return. Famous business metrics concentrate on the performance, measured quantitatively and accurately, based on stockholders' and stakeholders' interests and aspects. The truth is that business indicators can follow the customer experience by a time-shift, providing a late interruption into affected processes. Evaluation of customer experience might be based on reference points incorporated in the customer journey covering the total numbers and types of interaction between the customer and representatives of the product or the service provider. Metrics specialized to brand loyalty, and customer satisfaction can optionally be applied; organizations also can create their metrics-system for evaluating customer experiences.

7 Conclusion, Findings and Limitation

Design thinking is a holistic, integrated mindset, having a clear place among mindsets present in the businesses and the educational segments. Design Thinking mindset might be the most relevant differentiating factor in the next years. Whether they are profit-oriented companies or non-business ones, organizations are indifferent to the sector they operate in; pursuing an approach of customer-oriented focus will have a clear competitive advantage. Researches are planned to be concluded, followed by a detailed evaluation of all the types of analysis and research. The research is planned to be conducted from a process-oriented view to gain new insights into a new way of thinking. Questions of the exploratory analysis are also determined by this aspect, reflected in the process of innovation. Throughout the entire process, the user-centered approach is remaining in focus, involving them in all the phases, was as close to them as possible for exploring and answering the real problem. The project had not covered the implementation phase, though, put into vision, results would have been the real consequence could be further developed, refined, and finalized before a transformation into a final evaluation and conclusion. The next step is to examine the results and findings. A significant result is the literature review and former findings for the examined research fields, including methodologies. The relevance of the participatory design, the cooperation, and multidisciplinary are crucial elements of the research as having particular importance of innovation of participants into the operation. The concept is expended for proposals for the optional application of the design thinking methods in the public sector, particularly regarding an organizational transformation brought by the new means of this aspect and even for the educational field having strong constraints. Finally, the research draws up the advantages and further opportunities of the design thinking mindset based on the former experiences and researches, especially for the educational segment.

References

1. Hasso, P., Christoph, M., Leifer, L.: Design Thinking Research Making Design Thinking Foundational. Springer, Heidelberg (2016)
2. McDonnell, J.: Design roulette: a close examination of collaborative decision-making in design from the perspective of framing. Des. Stud. **57**, 75–92 (2018). https://doi.org/10.1016/j.destud.2018.03.001

3. Dorst, K.: Frame Innovation: Create New Thinking by Design. MIT Press, Cambridge (2015)
4. Pontis, S., van der Waarde, K.: Looking for alternatives: challenging assumptions in design education. She Ji J. Des. Econ. Innov. **6**, 228–253 (2020). https://doi.org/10.1016/j.sheji.2020.05.005
5. Cooper, R.: Design research – its 50-year transformation. Des. Stud. **65**, 6–17 (2019). https://doi.org/10.1016/j.destud.2019.10.002
6. Cross, N.: Designerly ways of knowing. Des. Stud. **3**, 221–227 (1982). https://doi.org/10.1016/0142-694X(82)90040-0
7. Géczy, N.: Design. Scolar, Budapest (2019)
8. Papanek, V.J.: Design for the Real World: Human Ecology and Social Change. Pantheon books, New York (1972)
9. Voûte, E., Stappers, P.J., Giaccardi, E., Mooij, S., van Boeijen, A.: Innovating a large design education program at a university of technology. She Ji J. Des. Econ. Innov. **6**, 50–66 (2020). https://doi.org/10.1016/j.sheji.2019.12.001
10. Dorst, K.: The core of 'design thinking' and its application. Des. Stud. **32**, 521–532 (2011). https://doi.org/10.1016/j.destud.2011.07.006
11. Norman, D.: The Design of Everyday Things. Basic Books, New York (2013)
12. Pennock, G.R.: Professor Bernard ("Bernie") Roth – His journey from kinematics to design thinking. Mech. Mach. Theory. **125**, 146–168 (2018). https://doi.org/10.1016/j.mechmachheory.2017.10.001
13. Brown, T.: Design thinking. Harv. Bus. Rev. **86**(6), 84–92 (2008)
14. Redström, J.: Certain uncertainties and the design of design education. She Ji J. Des. Econ. Innov. **6**, 83–100 (2020). https://doi.org/10.1016/j.sheji.2020.02.001
15. Stompff, G., Smulders, F., Henze, L.: Surprises are the benefits: reframing in multidisciplinary design teams. Des. Stud. **47**, 187–214 (2016). https://doi.org/10.1016/j.destud.2016.09.004
16. Simon, H.A.: The Sciences of the Artificial. MIT Press, Cambridge (1996)
17. Doorley, S., Holcomb, S., Klebahn, P., Segovia, K., Utley, J.: The Design Thinking Bootcamp Bootleg. Presented at the (2018)
18. Schön, D.A.: The Reflective Practitioner: How Professionals Think in Action. Temple Smith, London (1983)
19. Degen, H., Yuan, X.: Design thinking. In: UX best practices - How to achive more impact by User experience? McGrow-Hill Education, New York (2011)
20. Dweck, C.: Mindset: Changing The Way You think To Fulfil Your Potential. Robinson, London (2017)
21. Martin, R.L.: Design of Business: Why Design Thinking is the Next Competitive Advantage. Harvard Business Press, Boston (2009)
22. Dantas de Figueiredo, M.: Design is cool, but … a critical appraisal of design thinking in management education. Int. J. Manag. Educ. **19**, 100429 (2021). https://doi.org/10.1016/j.ijme.2020.100429
23. Lovelock, C.H., Wirtz, J.: Services marketing - people, technology, strategy. Harvard Business Review, Brighton (2010)
24. Kalenskaya, N., Gafurov, I., Novenkova, A.: Marketing of educational services: research on service providers satisfaction. Procedia Econ. Financ. **5**, 368–376 (2013). https://doi.org/10.1016/S2212-5671(13)00044-0
25. Cross, N.: Expertise in design: an overview. Des. Stud. **25**, 427–441 (2004). https://doi.org/10.1016/j.destud.2004.06.002
26. Fitzpatrick, R.: The Mom Test: How to talk to customers & learn if your business is a good idea when everyone is lying to you. CreateSpace Independent Publishing Platform (2013)
27. Jones, P., Bowes, J.: Rendering systems visible for design: synthesis maps as constructivist design narratives. She Ji J. Des. Econ. Innov. **3**, 229–248 (2017). https://doi.org/10.1016/j.sheji.2017.12.001

Learning Effectiveness Evaluation of Lesson Plan on Streamline in Model Design Course

Meng-Dar Shieh[1]([⊠]), Jia-Lin Tsai[1], Chih Chieh Yang[2], and Fang-Chen Hsu[2]

[1] Department of Industrial Design, National Cheng Kung University, Tainan City 70101, Taiwan, ROC

[2] Department of Multimedia and Entertainment Science, Southern Taiwan University of Science and Technology, Tainan City 71005, Taiwan, ROC

Abstract. The purpose of this study is to tailor a "streamline design lesson plan" for students of design departments in the hope of promoting it in the design-related courses of various universities. The lesson plan is based on the Revised Bloom's Taxonomy (RBT). The subjects came from industrial design departments (The first teaching course) as well as multimedia and computer entertainment science departments (The second teaching course), both of which received a pre-test and post-test.

Three professors from the industrial design department and two designers were appointed to grade the pre-test and post-test works of the students. Five scoring criteria were obtained: drag value, smooth, dynamic, speed, and flow. After modifying the first lesson plan (p-value > 0.05), the second experiment was carried out. Since the number of student samples ($n < 30$) did not conform to the normal distribution, the one-sample sign test of nonparametric methods was adopted. Students' learning results (p-value $= 0.006363$) < 0.05 indicated that the overall learning effect of students had significantly improved.

In order to explore the overall learning effect of the second lesson plan, this study selected five students with the highest scores in the post-test evaluated by the five experts to build 3D models. Ten models were built for the pre-test and post-test, combined with SolidWorks software computational fluid dynamics (CFD) to analyze the air resistance and wind drag coefficient of the streamline. Finally, the satisfaction questionnaire designed with RBT was discussed and the feedback of students showed a high degree of satisfaction.

Keywords: Streamline · Aerodynamics · Design education · Modeling design · CFD

1 Research Background and Motivation

The streamline design started in the 1930s when Raymond Loewy applied streamline design to product and transportation vehicle design, which were well-received by entrepreneurs and consumers, and officially made him an industrial designer. At the end of 1980, the first generation of Ford Taurus became the best-selling car in the United States.

© Springer Nature Switzerland AG 2021
V. G. Duffy (Ed.): HCII 2021, LNCS 12778, pp. 332–347, 2021.
https://doi.org/10.1007/978-3-030-77820-0_25

Streamlining has become one of the key modeling styles. Therefore, it is mentioned in the art classes of high schools, design groups of higher vocational colleges, in design departments of universities. Unfortunately, it is not explained in-depth, which makes it difficult for students to grasp the requirements of streamlining, and they generally cannot understand the concept correctly. Especially in the design of transportation tools, many students cannot properly combine the streamline concept with the functions. This problem often occurs in cross field cooperation, for example, the National College SAE (Society of Automotive Engineers). It requires students to think about how to reduce friction loss and improve energy efficiency based on the same power unit, so as to reduce energy consumption and thereby win the competition. In addition to reducing the power consumption, students should also consider the body styling design and how to meet the aerodynamics needs for reducing wind drag while designing a streamlined result with pleasing aesthetics.

2 Instructional Design

Instructional design is also called lesson planning. Instructional design has significance in two aspects: the first is the mode of teaching to be followed; the second is teaching prescription, which selects specific methods, contents, and strategies according to specific objects and objectives.

2.1 Instructional Structure

There are six levels of progressive requirements in Revised Bloom's Taxonomy (RBT). The design should help students learn interdisciplinary knowledge, cultivate their innovative ability, and improve their knowledge acquired rather than just accept the knowledge. Therefore, "learning" and "creative" production are necessary (Koh et al. 2015). The first is the Remembering (LV. 1); it requires students to remember what they have learned, then Understanding (LV. 2) and being able to Apply (LV. 3) what they have learned, Analyzing (LV. 4) the concepts learned and learning to Evaluate (LV. 5) the good streamlined design. Finally, students should be able to Create (LV. 6) their own design.

Instruction of the Course

Streamline of Creatures. Biological streamlining can basically be described as clean modeling in aerodynamics. Take birds as an example: the head, neck, and feet cause turbulence. If they are retracted close to the body, the outer layer of smooth feathers can form a good streamline. In that case, an estimated wind drag coefficient of nearly 0.08 indicates that the bird body has a good streamline shape (Pennycuick et al. 1996). Examples of Good Streamline Profile, one is the Isurus oxyrinchus and Tursiops truncates in the sea, because they display the streamlined, so they can get high swimming speed. Another is Thrush Nightingale and Peregrine Falcon in the sky.

Streamline Shape and Design. Geddes's expanded his new direction in the late 1920s and started his career in industrial design. He promoted the streamline design concept through his book Horizons. This book focuses on the visual streamline design of streamlined coach cars, trains, airplanes, ships, and automobiles (Brunswik and Kamiya 1953).

Geddes' speech at stage design mentioned that streamline is the beauty of motion and dynamics. It applies speed and power to the visual reference of living and inanimate objects. In terms of living objects, historians point out that the development of modeling is influenced by evolution (Cogdell 2003).

To this day, the most effective and best design is still observed and discovered in nature. Many scientists and engineers have succeeded in transferring natural phenomena to design via science and technology. The aerodynamics of traditional automobiles combined the background of human and engineering, organized in body engineering or the vehicle engineering group. Designers provide aerodynamic forms or styles for aesthetic pleasure and introduce aerodynamics (Le Good et al. 2011).

2.2 Topic of Test

SAE Supermileage Competition. SAE Supermileage Competition provides a challenging design project for engineering and technology students. In this paper, SAE Supermileage Competition is classified into low-level and high-level courses. The curriculum is planned for one year and is divided into two groups: the body and frame group, and the engine and drive system group. Here we will only focus on the body (Hardin 2006).

The body design is mainly shifted from human prediction to CFD calculation. This literature-related course is designed as a one-year course, but according to the experience of the university in this study, it took two weeks to develop and revise the concept of body design, and a month to reach a consensus with the mechanical department and finalize the design. The problems of SAE and the external factors of the above-mentioned vehicles and other wheeled vehicles with experts, the experts thought that in order to implement the specialized study on streamline modeling design, it is necessary to reduce the generation of complex factors as much as possible. Therefore, it is not recommended to use wheeled transport vehicles, nor to use the SAE Supermileage Competition as the theme of the lesson plan design.

Aircraft. As for the revision of the topic, the experts suggested two kinds of transport vehicles as references for the design of the topic. The expert replied: "it is aircraft and ships that exclude the physical phenomena generated by wheels. It will be simpler for the aircraft against air and the ship against water. The concept of streamlined design based on aircraft only has to conform to streamline, interpret streamline, combine appearance streamlined with aerodynamics, focus on the theme, and exclude functional factors. For example, the engine, motor and other mechanical power are hidden within the shape, and the shape should be simplified to the optimal extent (Maeda 2006), as it is more suitable to study streamline design. "Finally, this study will only discuss whether the air resistance and wind drag coefficient for air and the design can be reduced as verification.

An introduction to the aircraft that have been discussed and experimented on many times academically. There are two types of aircraft: the first is the type with a cockpit, and the second is the straddle and riding type. The first one is Cockpit Type Aircraft.

Its cruise speed is 180 km/h, which is equal to 50 m/s. The total length of the aircraft is 6000 mm, the width without wings is 1600 mm, and the width with wings is 8200 mm (Rajashekara et al. 2016) with a single-seat; the second one is Straddle, Riding Type Aircraft. After comparing the two aircraft, Malloy Aeronautics and Hoversurf, the data on Malloy Aeronautics were selected as the parameter setting of CFD for analyzing students' works.

The CFD analysis here is operated by this study and will not be included in the lesson plan. The reason is that after asking the experts of mechanical engineering whether the students of design department need to learn CFD analysis, the experts replied, "No, they don't, because it is too professional and complicated, and that is why we need the division of labor among different departments." Therefore, this part is only used to verify the effectiveness of the resistance effect of students' works; it will not be helpful for students to learn how to use SolidWorks Flow Simulation to operate CFD in the experiment.

2.3 Learning Satisfaction

In the selection of student learning questions, Paechter et al. (2010) classified the online course satisfaction questionnaire into five major items, each with three to five related questions. His research proved that these questions are the best predictive indicators, so this study will continue to use his question structure in the questionnaire on learning satisfaction. In addition, by interviewing relevant education experts, we can use their teaching experience and the difficulties encountered by students or what they have to learn to formulate questions. Academia generally believes that feedback is an essential part of the learning cycle, which can provide reflection and development (Weaver 2006). When students fill in the learning satisfaction questionnaire, it is also a kind of feedback. It not only tells the teacher what needs to be strengthened but also reminds students whether they have learned something.

Likert Scale. The Likert scale is a psychological response scale, which classifies the opinions on each question from very negative to very positive; it is widely used in research. The use of the Likert scale is like: Totally Agree scores 5 or 7 points; totally disagree is 1 point. Therefore, attention should be paid to the narration to see if it is in positive narration or the reverse narration before the subsequent operation. Considering the reliability of the subjects' responses, the scale items defined by the survey structure were selected. The 7-point scale provides more choices, thus increasing the possibility of being in line with people's real situation, so it could really stimulate the "rational ability" of the subjects (Joshi et al. 2015). Some scholars have sorted out various forms of Likert's options, such as acceptability, probability level, importance level, difficulty level, etc., which can be used directly together with the 3-point scale, 5-point scale, and 7-point scale (Vagias 2006). This method was applied to the learning satisfaction questionnaire and the expert grading questionnaire. The Likert 5-point scale was used in the learning satisfaction questionnaire, and the Likert 7-point scale was used in the expert questionnaire.

3   Research Methods

3.1   Statistical Methods

Normal distribution: a convenient mathematical model (Hogg et al. 2005). The mean value of the probability density function of the normal distribution is μ, the variance is σ^2, and the standard deviation is σ:

$$f(x) = \frac{1}{\sqrt{2\pi}\sigma} \exp\left\{-\frac{(x-\mu)^2}{2\sigma^2}\right\}, \quad \text{for } -\infty < x < \infty \tag{1}$$

σ(sigma) is the standard deviation, which measures the dispersion of a group of values in probability statistics. The research uses the Randomized Complete Block design (RCBD).

Nonparametric methods: nonparametric statistics is particularly suitable for the analysis of qualitative data. The categorical data (nominal scale) and sequential data (ordinal scale) usually do not belong to the normal distribution but rather to the multiple distribution types. Therefore, the data cannot obtain the population parameters (parameters) such as mean value and variation number, so it is more suitable for statistical analysis without parameters rather than those with parameters (normal distribution). The research uses the One sample sign test referring to the book (Daniel 1978).

3.2   Computational Fluid Dynamics (CFD)

$$C_D = \frac{\frac{D}{A}}{\frac{1}{2}\rho v^2} \tag{2}$$

C_D is the wind drag coefficient (dimensionless quantity). D is the air resistance, also known as the shape resistance (N, N = kg $\cdot$ m/s^2). A is the orthographic area (m^2). ρ is the air density of 1.29 kg/m^3, and V is the velocity (m/s).

The orthographic area (A) means the cross-sectional area under the action of the air resistance (D). Generally speaking, the wind is flowing from the X direction to the object. Therefore, orthographic projection is selected to calculate the area.

ρ is the density of the fluid or air. In this study, the topic for the students' design was a flying machine, and the flight altitude was set to be below 10 km. Therefore, the air was used as the flow field, and the density of air was about 1.29 kg/m^3. If water was the flow field, the density of water was about 997 kg/m^3 (Blevins 1984).

4   Research Procedures

The research steps architecture is shown in Fig. 1:

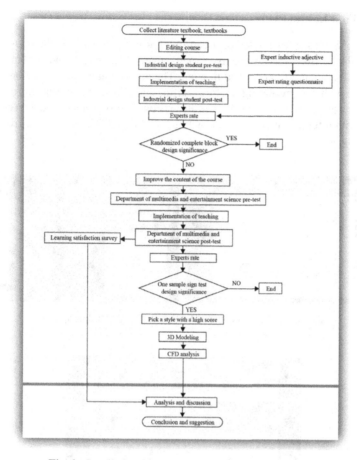

Fig. 1. Detailed architecture of the research procedures

Three professors from the industrial design department and two designers were appointed to grade the pre-test and post-test works of the students (Table 1).

Table 1. Qualifications of the experts

Current occupation	Expertise in design area	Years of service
Professor of the vehicle design group of the department of industrial design	Airplanes, automobiles, motorcycles	Over 30 years
Professor of the vehicle design group of the department of industrial design	Bicycles, motorcycles	Over 30 years
Professor of the vehicle design group of the department of industrial design	Motorcycle, ATV	Over 20 years
Transportation Designer	Automobiles and motorcycle	Over 10 years
Industrial Designer	Golf cart, baby carriage	Over 10 years

4.1   The First Lesson Plan

First of all, the vocabulary related to streamlining was extracted from the relevant literature and books. After interviewing five experts, five scoring criteria were obtained: drag
value, smooth, dynamic, speed, and flowing. The questionnaire was based on a 7-point
Likert scale with 1 representing. Before starting the course, we briefly introduced the
configuration diagram of the SAE Supermileage competition vehicle and then conducted
a pre-test with reference pictures, such as Fig. 2 and Fig. 3. The test paper given was as
shown in Fig. 4.

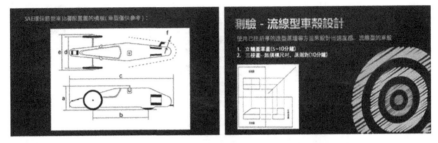

Fig. 2. (a) The template of SAE; (b) the pre-test description

Fig. 3. Reference pictures for pre-test

Finish the pre-test, take back the test paper and start teaching.

Content of the Course. Unit 1, what is streamline? First, the masters and history of
streamline; second, feature recognition of streamlined modeling.

Unit 2 was about the principle of streamline - biological modeling. The first was the
streamline shape of fish; the second was the form of diving animals; the third was the
form of birds; the fourth was the transformation of biological modeling.

The third unit was the principle-bionic design of streamline; the first point was the
patent category of bionic design; the second point was the transformation of animal
modeling. It explained the case of the designer using the bionic streamline design in
transport vehicle modeling and other cases, as well as the conversion process from the
biological modeling of unit 2 to the transport vehicle.

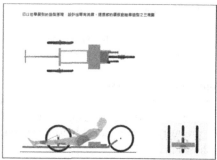

Fig. 4. (a) The stereogram of SAE environmentally-friendly and energy-saving vehicle; (b) the three-dimensional view

Unit 4 was about fluid and aerodynamics; point 1 was the bicycle frame modeling; point 2 was the tail of a racecar; point 3 was the case sharing of the SAE Supermileage Competition.

After the completion of the course, a post-test was carried out. The teaching content and test papers were the same as those of the pre-test.

RCBD Statistical Results

The first lesson plan experiment's p-value > 0.05. It means there was no significant difference, as shown in Table 2. However, the nuisance factor "score difference between experts" in this study was the experts, and p-value (0.00726) < 0.05 means that there was a significant difference. But, the p-value of the target factor excluded the confusing factors, and there was still no significance. Therefore, it could be seen that there may be problems in the lesson plan for the Industrial Design Department, resulting in no significant difference between the students before and after learning. Since the difference was not significant, it was unnecessary to do further computer CFD verification. We discussed the possible causes and tried to solve the problem with experts.

Table 2. RCBD statistical results of the first experiment

SV	SS	df	MS	F	P
Treatment	0.4	1	0.391	0.355	0.56313
Expert	8.5	4	8.502	7.777	0.00726
Residuals	471.2	428	1.101		

4.2   The Second Lesson Plan

The second lesson plan experiment was conducted in the Multimedia and Computer Science and Entertainment Department.

Content of the Course

The first lesson plan was used to revise and solve the problems discussed above. The following is a brief description of the revised course. For details of this lesson plan, The pre-test was conducted before teaching, and the reference pictures were attached, as shown in Fig. 5.

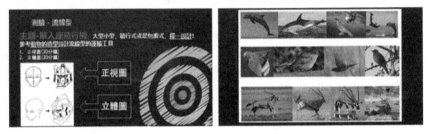

Fig. 5. (a) The description of performing the pre-test; (b) the use of reference pictures for the pre-test

There are the front of the reference drawing and the back of the reference drawing Fig. 6.

Fig. 6. (a) The front of the reference drawing; (b) the back of the reference drawing

After finishing the pre-test, the test paper was collected, and formulating the content of the lesson plan started.

Unit 1: what is streamline? First, the masters and history of streamlining; second, streamline features recognition, 1. visual psychology. 2. Hydromechanics; 3. Q&A.

Unit 2: the principle of streamline, point 1: biological modeling - the sense of speed in nature: 1. the streamline shape of fish; 2. the form of diving animals; 3. the form of birds; 4. Q&A time, learning the sense of speed and hand-painted streamline practice, point 2: conversion of biological modeling: 1. Sketch case; 2. Design application; 3. The practice of the drawing of animal contour (streamline design).

After this part of the teaching was finished, the exercise paper would be given. Its content was the prediction of streamline in the flow field. At the end of the first day's course, two drawings were handed out as homework for students to set up the related concept in a week. Before the second class, we spent an hour discussing homework with 23 students.

Unit 3: bionic design, point 1: industrial design cases sharing; point 2: cartoon concept design case sharing; point 3: Q&A time.

After the above teaching, the same test paper as that of the pre-test was used in the post-test, and the test papers were collected after being finished.

Questionnaire Design Based on Revised Expert Scoring. The requirements for scoring remained the same as those of the first test. After the discussion with several experts, "mobility" was removed because it was too general and not clear enough. The scoring method was changed from a Likert 5-point to a 7-point scale: 7 to 1 for the best to the worst. The purpose of this part was to make it easier for experts to fill in the scoring table and reduce the difficulty of evaluation.

One Sample Sign Test. As the number of samples was insufficient and did not conform to the normal distribution, the one sample sign test of nonparametric methods was used, which could also eliminate the influence caused by the score difference between experts. In other words, if several experts had special scoring ways, only the total number of positive signs (high scores in the post-test) would be considered in this method. Observed value X_i = post-test − pre-test; if it was 0, it would be excluded directly. If the score of the post-test is higher than that of the pre-test, it is a positive sign; otherwise, it is a negative sign. After the analysis of this study, the total effective data calculated was S = 15, with a significant p-value $(0.006363) < 0.05$, which means that the post-test score was better than the pre-test score, that is, the teaching effect was significant, as shown in Table 3.

The purpose of the second lesson plan was to reduce the difficulty without changing the necessary knowledge of the streamlining, and to increase the time for students to interact with the teacher, whether to ask questions or engage in discussions with the teacher; this process is the key to enhancing students' memory and learning motivation.

4.3 CFD Analysis

In order to explore the overall learning effect of the second lesson plan, this study selected five students with the highest scores in the post-test evaluated by the five experts to build 3D models. Their scores in the post-test were 25, 16, 29, 29, and 34, with a full score of 35. Ten models were built for the pre-test and post-test, combined with SolidWorks software computational fluid dynamics (CFD) to analyze the air resistance and wind drag coefficient of the streamline. After CFD, the wind drag coefficients of the students' post-test works were 0.15, 0.20, and 0.19 (the lowest drag is 0 and the highest drag is 1). The post-test results of the three students tended to be 0, belonging to the streamline of low drag. The drag coefficients of the other two students were 0.31 and 0.46, which were relatively mediocre.

Table 3. The score of the post-test of the second lesson plan was better than that of the pre-test.

	pre-test	post-test	+/- [(post-test)-(pre-test)]
	7	13	+
	5	24	+
	18	25	+
Expert 1	13	24	+
	10	10	0
	5	10	+
	10	10	0
Expert 2	5	10	+
	13	29	+
	24	10	-
	26	20	-
Expert 3	22	24	+
	20	21	+
	5	16	+
	11	7	-
Expert 4	27	29	+
	19	27	+
	5	9	+
	14	18	+
Expert 5	20	34	+

4.4 Question Design of the Learning Satisfaction Survey

The questions and details of the first edition after three modifications are as follows:

According to the satisfaction questionnaire, 8 questions were deleted and 12 questions were added as follows.

(1) In this unit, I learned about visual psychology.
(2) I am satisfied with the practice of streamline's streakline and streamline prediction in this unit.
(3) In this unit, I can understand the importance of the direction of visual psychology.
(4) In this unit, I can apply visual psychology to design.
(5) In this unit, I can predict whether my design is a good streamlined one by using streakline and streamline.
(6) From this unit, I can successfully use the designed streamline to complete the conceptual design of a single-seat aircraft.
(7) From this unit, I can analyze whether there is obvious directionality.

(8) From this unit, I can observe the trend of streakline and streamline of aerodynamics.
(9) From this unit, I can observe the outline and characteristics of living things.
(10) I can design streamline with obvious directionality.
(11) I can design streamline with an obvious sense of speed.
(12) I can use streamline to design a single-seat aircraft.

Experts thought that the paper questionnaire was not convenient for students to fill in. Therefore, Google form was used to make the questionnaire.

4.5 Analysis Diagram

After dual verification, students progressed through the lesson plan designed by this study, not only in the streamline design but also in the function. Finally, the satisfaction questionnaire designed with RBT was discussed. The satisfaction questionnaire was designed as a 5-point Likert scale. There was no "very dissatisfied" response received in this questionnaire.

The statistical percentage of students who responded "very satisfied" was 53% in Remembering (LV. 1), 50% in Understanding (LV. 2), 44% in Application (LV. 3), 46% in Analysis (LV. 4), 33% in Evaluation (LV. 5) and 29% in Creation (LV. 6). From Remembering (LV. 1) to Analysis (LV. 4), most responded "very satisfied", and the level receiving most "very satisfied" was remembering (53%). Through the research and analysis, we could know that the former level affected the later one, so if the Application (LV. 3) of the lesson plan could be further strengthened, the learning satisfaction of the latter three levels (LV. 4 to LV. 6) would be improved accordingly, as shown in Fig. 7.

In other words, the learning satisfaction of the self-designed lesson plan in the six levels, after the feedback of students, showed a high degree of satisfaction, of which the contents, test papers, and questionnaires in this study are expected to be used as reference materials for teachers in the future.

4.6 Results

After two experiments, the results were divided into three parts:

1. Regarding the lesson plan after the second modification, if seen from the aspects of expert's score, satisfaction survey, and CFD analysis, its design of the content was suitable for students, and the learning effect was good.
2. Integrating the evolution of "streamline" in nature and the principles of hydromechanics, while referring to the application of design cases, can be integrated into the teaching unit of the lesson plan, which can help students have a structural basis for learning.
3. The lesson plan can help students integrate design and function practically. It could stimulate students' thinking and enable them to analyze and evaluate the streamline relationship between fluid and flow field when designing streamlined vehicles.

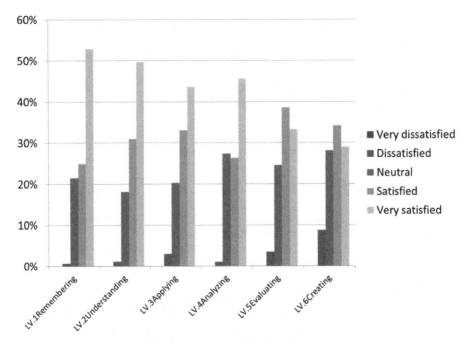

Fig. 7. Learning satisfaction diagram

The most fundamental reason for the failure of the first lesson plan lies in the fact that the students cannot absorb the complex contents with unsuitable topics in a short period of time. However, it is the limitation of time that constrains and affects students' learning. If SAE is used as a streamline design topic, one year's teaching will be needed to achieve the desired effect. Therefore, the second lesson plan focused on simplifying the content, extending the class time, and finding suitable topics. Thus, we can see from the modification part of Chapter 4 Research Steps that the second lesson plan was more cautious and detailed than the first one. The second teaching plan focused on simplifying the content, making it easy to understand, adding cases of industrial design and cartoon. The improvement effect can be seen from the feedback from both students and experts.

In order to enable the students of the Multimedia and Computer Entertainment Science Department to acquire knowledge and apply what they have learned, the second edition also increased the time for hand drawing exercises, so that they could try to make designs in a field they were not familiar with in the past; this was not limited to the transport vehicles that can be seen in the market but included the concept vehicles in cartoon, film, and fantasy with science fiction themes. The lesson plan let students design a single-seat aircraft before the class and kept bringing up this concept until the end of the course, and the cases mentioned were also relevant; this helped students gain a certain understanding of the streamline of the aircraft. They could only focus on streamline design without considering the operation mode and complex structure. While paying full attention to making the whole concept of the aircraft meet the aesthetic requirements of streamline design and the functional requirements of low resistance through the streamlined housing, students could concentrate on learning the core of this study, streamline design.

The experiment of the second lesson plan also met the expectations of this study. Most students (75%) were willing to study hard and cooperated with the teachers' teaching with high participation. For the students who did not learn about streamline or had never heard of streamline in the Multimedia and Computer Entertainment Science Department (there were 23 students of this department participating in the whole teaching process), the teaching content of the second lesson plan was not only simple and easy to understand but also paid attention to the connection and application. As long as the students could learn step by step with clear logic, they performed well in the study and learned to consider the functional conditions. Through the dual tests of experts and CFD, this study can confirm that the students did perform well in learning.

Finally, in the part of the satisfaction, by analyzing the satisfaction and questions of each level, we found that the lesson plan of this study could be further improved in the content of LV. 4 to LV. 6. If this part can be strengthened (for example, LV. 4 can incorporate cases of streamline state of different shapes in the flow field while covering up the real streamline, and let students do analysis exercises), it will certainly help students learn better. On the topic discussion, we can see the distribution of the units with which the students were more satisfied in each level. After analysis, the first unit of the lesson plan "what is streamline?" was the only unit covering LV. 1 to LV. 6, indicating that most students were satisfied with this (what is streamline) unit. Whether it was the lesson plan itself or the ability of students, this study believes that the first unit should satisfy the students so that the subsequent units can be carried out smoothly, which is one of the reasons for the success of the second lesson plan.

5   Conclusions

The purpose of this study is to propose a "streamline design lesson plan" in a design course in Universities. The plan is designed based on the Revised Bloom's Taxonomy (RBT), which has six levels of progressive requirements. The first is the Remembering (LV. 1); it requires students to remember what they have learned, then Understanding (LV. 2) and being able to Apply (LV. 3) what they have learned, Analyzing (LV. 4) the concepts learned and learning to Evaluate (LV. 5) the good streamlined design. Finally, students should be able to Create (LV. 6) their own design. The subjects came from industrial design departments and computer entertainment science departments. They both received a pre-test and post-test. The first teaching was conducted for students in the department of industrial design. The problems were found and improved. After the adjustments, the revised second lesson plan was given to the students of multimedia and computer entertainment science departments to verify the effectiveness.

Three industrial design department professors and two professional designers were appointed to grade the pre-test and post-test works of the students. Five scoring criteria were obtained: drag value, smooth, dynamic, speed, and flow. The questionnaire was based on a 7-point Likert scale. A statistical analysis was conducted after the scoring. The first lesson plan experiment (p-value > 0.05) was modified. The second lesson plan experiment ((p-value $= 0.006363$) < 0.05) indicated that the overall learning effect of students had significantly improved. The purpose of the second lesson plan was to reduce the difficulty without changing the necessary knowledge of the streamlining, and to increase the time for students to interact with the teacher, whether to ask questions or engage in discussions with the teacher. This process is the key to enhancing students' memory and learning motivation.

In order to explore the overall learning effect of the second lesson plan, ten 3D models were built from the students' pre-test and post-test works using SolidWorks software computational fluid dynamics (CFD) to analyze the air resistance and wind drag coefficient of the streamline. After dual verification, students progressed through the second lesson plan designed by this study, improved not only in the streamline design but also in the function design. Finally, the satisfaction questionnaire designed with RBT was discussed. The satisfaction questionnaire was designed as a 5-point Likert scale. There was no "very dissatisfied" response received in this questionnaire. The statistical percentage of students who responded "very satisfied" was 53% in Remembering (LV. 1), 50% in Understanding (LV. 2), 44% in Application (LV. 3), 46% in Analysis (LV. 4), 33% in Evaluation (LV. 5) and 29% in Creation (LV. 6). From Remembering (LV. 1) to Analysis (LV. 4), most responded "very satisfied", and the level receiving most "very satisfied" was remembering (53%). Through the research and analysis, we could know that the former level affected the later one, so if the Application (LV. 3) of the lesson plan could be further strengthened, the learning satisfaction of the latter three levels (LV. 4 to LV. 6) would be improved accordingly. In other words, the learning satisfaction of the self-designed lesson plan in the six levels, after the feedback of students, showed a high degree of satisfaction, of which the contents, test papers, and questionnaires in this study are expected to be used as reference materials for teachers in the future.

References

Blevins, R.D.: Applied Fluid Dynamics Handbook, p. 568. Van Nostrand Reinhold Co., New York (1984)

Brunswik, E., Kamiya, J.: Ecological cue-validity of 'proximity' and of other Gestalt factors. Am. J. Psychol. **66**(1), 20–32 (1953)

Cogdell, C.: Products or bodies? Streamline design and eugenics as applied biology. Des. Issues **19**(1), 36–53 (2003)

Daniel, W.W.: Applied Nonparametric Statistics. Houghton Mifflin, Boston (1978)

Hardin, J.M.: 2006–1983: vertical-integration framework for capstone design projects. Doctoral dissertation, Virginia Military Institute (2006)

Hogg, R.V., McKean, J., Craig, A.T.: Introduction to Mathematical Statistics. Pearson Education, London (2005)

Joshi, A., Kale, S., Chandel, S., Pal, D.K.: Likert scale: explored and explained. Br. J. Appl. Sci. Technol. **7**(4), 396 (2015)

Koh, J.H.L., Chai, C.S., Wong, B., Hong, H.-Y.: Design thinking and education. In: Design Thinking for Education, pp. 1–15. Springer, Singapore (2015). https://doi.org/10.1007/978-981-287-444-3_1

Le Good, G., Johnson, C., Clough, B., Lewis, R.: The aesthetics of low drag vehicles. SAE Int. J. Engines **4**(2), 2638–2658 (2011)

Maeda, J.: The Laws of Simplicity. MIT Press, Cambridge (2006). N.P. Maffei (2000)

Paechter, M., Maier, B., Macher, D.: Students' expectations of, and experiences in e-learning: their relation to learning achievements and course satisfaction. Comput. Educ. **54**(1), 222–229 (2010)

Pennycuick, C., Klaassen, M., Kvist, A., Lindström, Å.: Wingbeat frequency and the body drag anomaly: wind-tunnel observations on a thrush nightingale (Luscinia luscinia) and a teal (Anas crecca). J. Exp. Biol. **199**(12), 2757–2765 (1996)

Rajashekara, K., Wang, Q., Matsuse, K.: Flying cars: challenges and propulsion strategies. IEEE Electrif. Mag. **4**(1), 46–57 (2016)

Vagias, W.M.: Likert-type scale response anchors. Clemson International Institute for Tourism & Research Development, Department of Parks, Recreation and Tourism Management (2006)

Weaver, M.R.: Do students value feedback? Student perceptions of tutors' written responses. Assess. Eval. High. Educ. **31**(3), 379–394 (2006)

Comprehensive Study of Digital Restoration of Buddha Statues in Qingzhou by 3D Technology

Yunqiao Su$^{(\boxtimes)}$

Shandong College of Arts and Design, No. 1255, College Road, Changqing District, Jinan, China

Abstract. The significance of the digital restoration of the Buddha statue in Qingzhou by three-dimensional technology lies in the use of three-dimensional digital technology to study the style, craft and artistic characteristics of the restoration of the Buddha statue in Qingzhou, and to explore the laws contained therefrom. Thus open up a new horizon of Qingzhou style Buddha statue research and aesthetics, and deepen the research connotation of archaeological disciplines. It not only interprets the overall restoration and beauty of Qingzhou-style Buddha statues from a new perspective, but also explores new integration points between archaeology, science and technology and art.

Keywords: Qingzhou Buddha statue · 3D digitalization · Recovery performance

1 Introduction

Beauty is "a fundamental feature of a work of art, and that is a principle"[1]. We should analyze the artistic value of its own connotation rather than the modern conception "in accordance with the law of beauty". This kind of artistic analysis should naturally include appreciation from an aesthetic point of view. The outstanding feature of beauty appreciation is its entertainment, but also let us from the complicated and boring type of ranking out, into the field of art, with the help of the basic knowledge of art history, to carry out in-depth multi-disciplinary analysis and research.[2]

Compared with the "restoration understanding" of art archaeology analysis, this intuitive aesthetic re-creative understanding is a kind of double artistic understanding, which determines that the restoration understanding of art archaeology should be in-depth from these two aspects: on the one hand, restore its practical function. "Historically, looking at things from a conscious utilitarian point of view has tended to predestined things from an aesthetic point of view." On the other hand, it is possible to restore the original artistic composition of ancient art, including the ability of people's aesthetic re-creation activities at that time. In general, archaeologists pay little attention to this problem. Only the aesthetic re-creation activities of art can produce a certain amount of

---

[1] By Clive Bell, Zhou Jinhuan and Ma Zhongyuan: Art, Chinese Publishing Company, 1987, 129.
[2] By Liu Fengjun Introduction to Fine Arts Archaeology, Shandong University Press, 2002, 101.

© Springer Nature Switzerland AG 2021
V. G. Duffy (Ed.): HCII 2021, LNCS 12778, pp. 348–359, 2021.
https://doi.org/10.1007/978-3-030-77820-0_26

plastic arts, in order to "be people's aesthetic feelings."[3] When people appreciate it for aesthetic purposes, its main function changes to a beauty function, so it becomes a work of art with a practical mechanism.[4]

When an ancient stone statue was placed in front of us, art archaeology considered it to be a practical product with artistic components, and the artist, in addition to understanding the original stone statue, "can't help but" regard "mottled" as an aesthetic value that has nothing to do with the original work. The erosion of a statue due to the wind and rain that has been suffered over time is not the original author's intention, for archaeologists how to protect and strive to restore its original appearance. But the artist can think that this kind of statue after the storm, in the process of aesthetic re-creation of modern people's intuition, can make the senses produce the pleasure of "old-style" and "simple": "If these statues are really preserved like the original, our aesthetic pleasure may be seriously damaged".[5]

The essence of the three-dimensional digital restoration of the Buddha statue in Qingzhou is to summarize the law of programming information processing in the ont body of the restoration object, describe it in computer language, make the computer have the ability of information processing, and complete the three-dimensional restoration work through the information exchange between man and machine under the guidance of the theory of optical research. Through the analysis of the shape, color and material of Qingzhou Buddha statue, this paper studies the three-dimensional digital restoration Buddha statue in detail.

2 Digital Restoration of Buddha-Shaped Systems

2.1 The Expression Element of the Buddha's Image

From the shape of the statue, the Longxing Temple statue mainly has a statue monument, back-screen image, and a single round sculpture like three shapes. The Buddha image is the main element of the spatial form of the restoration work, and also the main body of the restoration work, that is, the ontology. Its surface form directly affects the overall image of the restored work space. The overall shape of Buddha statue refers to the condensation and agassing formed by points, lines, faces and bodies in space.

Point: Of all the graphical elements, points usually refer to the absence of mass size, which is an abstract concept. The point in the shape of the Buddha refers to the structural points on the Buddha's body, such as the forehead, cheekbones, jaws, elbows and other structural points. It has the significance of focus, hint and so on in the facade layout, and can play a relationship with some elements that are related and responsive to each other. Therefore, digital performance, should also pay attention to these details of the portrayn, when the performance, often can play a dragon's eye.

---

[3] By Liu Fengjun Introduction to Fine Arts Archaeology, Shandong University Press, 2002, 107.

[4] Yan Ji-man: "On Archaeology and Identification: Basic Research in the History of Fine Arts", "Art Research", 1988, (3).

[5] (U.S.) E. Pannowski, Fu Zhiqiang translation: The Meaning of Visual Arts, Liaoning People's Press, 1987, 18.

Line: A line is the trajectory of a point. The line in the shape of buddha statue refers to the movement of the image limb, the shape of the garment, the bumpy decorative line, etc., which can make the statue facade into zero, and form a horizontal and vertical direction of the hierarchy changes. Therefore, in the Buddha statue, these lines have the function of dividing, changing the scale relationship, shaping the character and temperament of the image. When digitally restoring an image, the wire is handled properly, which helps to properly express the character characteristics of the image. Such as Qingzhou North Qi single round Buddha statue pay attention to the carving of clothing pattern, body proportion and clothing pattern matching, in the treatment of the tattoo, with a large arc of the shading line to show the image of a thick sense of mass, and a small arc or vertical parallel clitoris to express the body volume of the feeling of tall.

Face: Relatively speaking, it is a relative concept, which can be large or small. Buddha's forehead, cheeks, clothing on the "Fukuda" and so on are the categories of the face, it has the meaning of cohesion and radiation. In the digital performance, the expression of the face has a considerable weight, should cause enough attention.

Body: The body in the shape of the Buddha refers to the overall outline of the image and the local space with independent form. The shape of the body has the function of embodying the whole charm of Buddhist statue.

The head works of the two Buddha statues of the Beiqi period (see Fig. 1, Fig. 2) have the same styling characteristics, but there are obvious differences in the overall charm of the statue. I think this is due to the composition of the head shape in the point, line, surface of the clustering pattern changes and resulting in the final charm of the very different. The sculptors of these works have skilled carving skills, for the shape of the works features in the chest, in the production process, echoing back and forth, the overall air. Realistic art can certainly be more real Linyi nature, the painter's heart is also "like a mirror, their own into the color of the object, and truthfully into the image of all objects in front of them." Beauty is also "completely based on the sacred proportional relationship between the parts", the characteristics "at the same time, in order to produce the viewer often like intoxicated harmonious proportion."[6]

2.2 The Content of Digital Restoration of the Buddha Statue

The digital restoration of Buddha statue is a very complex process, which combines technology and art and requires the operator to make a systematic comprehensive analysis and feasibility study. The restoration of the Buddha image system by the operator generally adopts a combination from the whole to the local, from the internal structure to the outer space.

The contents are as follows:

Buddha preservation environmental analysis: geological conditions, unearthed conditions, preservation status and so on.

Buddha technology analysis: that is, in the production of Buddha body all related technologies, such as structure, materials, tools, workmanship and the corresponding process technical indicators.

---

[6] Dai Ying compiled: "Da Vinci's Paintings", Carrying a stream Such as "Art Characteristics", culture and art publishing Society, 1984, 56.

Fig. 1. Buddha statue head I   **Fig. 2.** North Qi period Buddha statue head II

The spatial analysis of Buddha's mass: that is, the study of the internal and external spatial relations of Buddha statues, from local to overall spatial connections. Because the Buddhist statue in Qingzhou pays more attention to the performance of service system, the mass performance of the Buddhist statue in Qingzhou is not obvious compared with that of India.

Buddha animation route analysis: research according to the characteristics of the Buddha to choose suitable animation methods.

The composition analysis of Buddha statue display: that is, the analysis and research on the spatial combination, space and structure, the law of formal beauty, spatial form processing, group combination, etc.

3   Color Analysis of Digital Restoration of Buddha Statues

In addition to the harmonious appearance of the beauty of the Buddhist statue in Qingzhou, fine painting art is also an important factor. The expression of Buddha image is through color, material, style and process, among which color is one of the most dynamic, visual impact and expressive factors. The use of color not only reflects the human characteristics of the Buddha statue, reflects the style of the times at that time, but also bears witness to the development of history. The color of the Buddha statue can arouse people's association, trigger the aesthetic demand at a higher level, it interacts with many factors, and together affects the expression of the Buddha statue. Therefore, the success of the performance of Buddha color is very critical to the shape of the Buddha statue and even the shaping of the charm.

But in the overall shape, the color must obey the whole, that is, the color and the shape must complement each other, and work together to shape the overall effect of the Buddha statue. The Buddhist statues in Beiqi, Qingzhou, are extremely concise. There are only three kinds of mud strip-shaped folds, shallow folds and no folds on the cursive decoration. After carving the image, and then with red, green, blue, and other colors of the painting of the dragonfly, some of the body without any folds of the image, it is entirely by painting to deal with.[7] Therefore, the colors in the Buddha statue in Qingzhou have the function of strengthening the shape, enriching the shape, perfecting the shape and so on.

3.1 Coloring Technology of Buddha Statues

Unlike the fresco painting on the plane, Longxing Temple is like a stone statue of a round sculpture, using the decorative techniques of painting on the round sculpture, previously only used on the pottery, Dunhuang Mogao Caves, although there are also painted mud statues, but most of them appeared in the Tang Dynasty, slightly later. This decorative technique of coloring stone tires is less common than.[8]

Neolithic pottery in the painting before the general first on the ceramic tire to apply a layer of white clothing, in order to facilitate the painting, Qin Terracotta Warriors before painting also to the pottery tire treatment and dressing, "the surface of the pottery painting process in three steps, that is, raw paint - pig blood - painting.... The ceramic surface can not be directly colored, must be treated first, that is, painted raw paint to fill the loose gap in the surface of pottery products, and can increase adhesion, and then apply a layer of pig blood or bean juice, and then paint, and have before coloring the application of white clothing.[9] The ancient tomb frescoes were first painted with lime, white and other white mineral materials before they were flattened and the wall surfaces trimmed.[10]

Stone tire statue is very smooth, is not conducive to painting and gold attachment, so Longxing Temple statue also exists the problem of stone tire dressing. After careful observation, in the image painting and paste gold partial shedding place, also found a layer of white similar to porcelain on the makeup soil material attached to the image stone tire, must also be used to trim the uneven stone and surface gaps in order to facilitate the color paste gold. The color of the painting attached to the stone tire is still very bright, the particles are not big and delicate and uniform, before the color may have been carefully treated.

---

[7] Xia Famous: "The Artistic Characteristics of the Buddhist Statue of Longxing Temple in Qingzhou", From the Museum of Chinese History, 2000, (1):102.

[8] Li Jia: "The First Study of Buddhist Image Art at Longxing Temple in Qingzhou", Master's degree thesis from Southeast University, 2005, 28.

[9] Wang Xueli: "The Costumes and Paintings of Qin Weiwei's Armor", Shaanxi People's Fine Arts Publishing House, 1990, 312.

[10] Li Jia: "The First Study of Buddhist Image Art at Longxing Temple in Qingzhou", Master's degree thesis of Southeast University, 2005, 28.

3.2 The Mineral Composition of Buddha's Color

We observed the painting decoration effect in the image, and found that its painted colors are: Zhu sand red, peacock blue, stone green, zircon, black, white and other primary colors and modulated meat colors. I roughly divide them into red, cyan, green and black, white and other primary color systems. From the situation of ancient painting can be found, in fact, in Wei Jin and the Six Dynasties, The pigment color system in the frescocreation has been basically complete, and as early as the Qin Dynasty, there were examples of coloring on the statue, although in the history of the time did not make relevant records of the painting pigment, but from the Terracotta Warriors, Dunhuang murals and color plastic, Tang Dynasty tomb frescoes used in some mineral color analysis, can make some measurements, so that the composition of these mineral colors used in the Longxing Temple statue more clearly.

4 Material Analysis of Digital Restoration of Buddha Statues

Qingzhou region has a traditional stone carving technology, and many production of stone. The Buddhist statues unearthed at Longxing Temple are mainly made of locally made limestone, and there are a small number of other materials. According to the different material classification can be divided into the following seven categories. The following table shows:[11]

Dragon Xing Si out Soil Made Like	Limestone statue	About 95% of the stone statues are made locally in Qingzhou
	Han Baiyu statue	The quantity is small
	Granite statue	The quantity is small, the stone is gray-white granite
	Pottery statue	The quantity is very small and the fire waiting is low
	Iron statue	The number is very small, for the small body of the altar-based sitting posture, rust serious
	Mud shapes like	A number of, are color plastic, but because of the long burial time and located at the bottom of the pit preservation is too poor, difficult to clean up
	Wood makes like	The quantity is very small, the wood has decayed, the paint residue can be seen is three layers of linen plus a layer of fine cloth made of ramie the tire on the tire

---

[11] Li Jia: "The First Study of Buddhist Image Art at Longxing Temple in Qingzhou", Master's degree thesis from Southeast University, 2005, 28.

The influence of the natural geographical environment on physical plastic arts in various regions goes far beyond the influence on other arts. Japanese art theorist Takeshi Takei is quite objective in his views on this issue, and he believes that in architecture and sculpture it is subject to the nature of the materials produced by the region. All areas of art can distinguish between "local styles".[12] It can also be said that this "local style" is an inherent and established concept that must exist in all material remains. For example, in a region as rich in fine marble as Italy, it is preferable to use this material and require the production of three-dimensional or embossed human images using engraving methods suitable for the characteristics of the substance.[13]

Proper virtual expression of the color, texture and texture of different materials is also very important. Generally according to the roughness of the surface of the material can be divided into rough, medium and fine three levels, namely, high-brightness material, medium-brightness material and low-brightness material. In the performance of these materials, the surface rough materials, such as pottery, wood, etc. often reflect the texture of the weight, color for the second. This material is insensitive to the surrounding environment, the color change is simple, the transition between cold and warm is regular, often based on the inherent color. Relatively speaking, the surface rough medium material, in addition to reflecting its own characteristics, should also show the impact of the surrounding scene on the object, the intensity of the reaction depends on the smoothness and reflective degree of the material itself. Fine texture or processing of fine material surfaces such as metal, polished stone, etc., mostly very shiny, and reflective, responsive, the surrounding environment has a greater impact on it. The performance of this material to environmental color, light source color-based, inherent color next.

5 The Process of Digital Restoration of Buddha Statues by 3D Technology

5.1 Design Scripts for Simulation and Reproduction of the Buddha Statue

The content of this part mainly shows the delicate degree of the structure of the Buddha statue. Break down the entire simulation process to determine the operating time for each stage of work.

5.2 Collect Footage

The structural data, video materials and features of the statue in Beiqi, Qingzhou, were investigated and collected, including historical documents, photographic materials, video materials, text materials, audio materials, etc.

5.3 Create a Model

According to the characteristics and historical data of the statue geometry, a suitable modeling method is chosen to model and reproduce the objects. The concepts of curves,

---

[12] (Day) Toshio Takeuchi Translation: The Theory of Art, Chinese University Press, 1990, 211.
[13] By Liu Fengjun Introduction to Fine Arts Archaeology, Shandong University Press, 2002, 98.

surfaces, polygons, elements, or objects are common in general moulding systems. The general practice of curves is: to establish splines, circles, ellipses, take boundaries, pan, edit, modify, subdivide, break points, close, join and reverse, etc. Surface operations are: to establish off-the-go surfaces, rotation, fill, sample, stretch, subdivide, disconnect, join, close, reverse, etc. Objects can be surfaces, polydes, or a combination of them. The difference between surfaces and polythymes is that surfaces store less information, only vertes, radii, and so on. Rendering is calculated directly from the equation and is therefore fast. Polyhedrons exist many vertestments, there are points, edges, faces of the order and adjacent relationship, the direction of the face of the main line, and so on, so the storage volume is large: its advantages can be transparent, can interpolate, deformation, can do Boolean operations, calculation is accurate. In general, multi-faceted styling is used where complexity permits, and if the shape is too complex, a portion of the object can be represented by a surface. A key factor to keep in mind during modeling is that the number of polygons and nodes an object contains can have a significant impact on computer resources. During rendering, the more complex the object, the slower the system reacts. It is important to keep the minimum number of faces and nodes in each site scene as much as possible.

There are several ways to keep a small model small: break down large scenes into smaller files, do not create or mount objects that are not visible, determine details based on the resolution of the view, and reduce the number of segments when using basic objects, such as cylinders. When you sample objects, use optimization or appropriate to reduce the number of steps for paths and samples.

3D operations can usually be performed using 3D software such as 3DS MAX and MAYA to form a spatial 3D mesh system according to demand, on the basis of which modeling research is carried out. Let's take the more complex head as an example to parse the modeling steps:

(i)   Select two head images of the North Qi Buddha statue in Qingzhou, one as the front view and the other as the side view, as a reference for the creation of the Buddha statue's head model. The previous view is primary and the side view is complementary, and it is imported into the 3DMAX9.0 3D software, placing the front view of the Buddha statue in the Front window and the side view in the Leaf window (see Fig. 3).

(ii) Create a cube in top window the size of the Buddha's head, edit it to polygon level, subdivide the cube with Smoth, and set the subdivision level value to 2, resize the model to match the size ratio of the Buddha's head in the photo (see Fig. 4).

(iii) The left half of the model may be deleted to reduce the amount of data calculated in the computer, depending on the symmetrical styling characteristics of the Buddha's head as the center axis. Refer to the photo, adjust the Vertex in the head model, appropriately add more structural lines, and produce more Vertex to add more

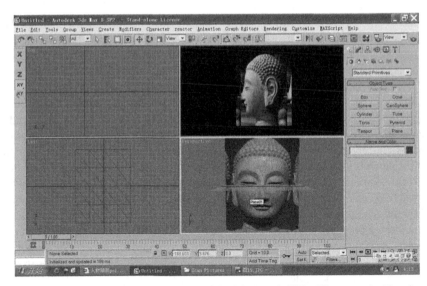

Fig. 3. A diagram of the head-creation model of the North Qi Buddha statue in Qingzhou

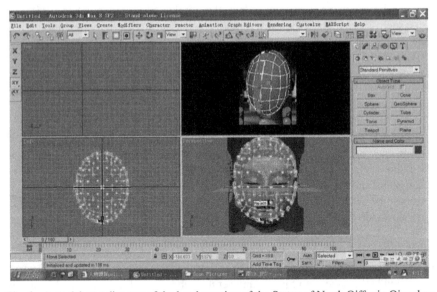

Fig. 4. A model step diagram of the head creation of the Statue of North Qiffer in Qingzhou

detail to the Buddha head model. Adjust the Vertex position on the head model to create a specific position and shape of the pentagon.

(iv) Use Split Polygon Tool to increase the cut line of the nose, create the nose, and use Extrude to adjust the Faces at the bottom of the nose to create nostrils.

(v) Since the muscles around the eye are made up of the surrounding eye cylindrical muscles, the eye model should be modeled with the eye as the center of the ring cut when creating the eye model. Add more detail with Split Polygon Tool, remove the black cut, and use Extrude to make the model's eye socket. Finally, the sphere is used to create a model of the eyeball, with the eye as a reference, adjust the position of the eye Vertex to adjust the shape of the eye, so that the position of Vertex can match the arc of the eye (see Fig. 5).

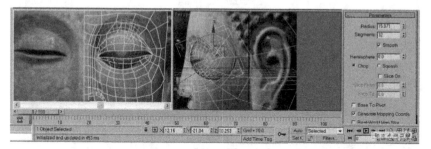

Fig. 5. The North Qi Buddha statue in Qingzhou creates a step diagram of the eye model

(vi) Continuously add new cutting lines on this basis, and then adjust the direction of the cutting lines according to the arrangement pattern of the muscles. Adjust the Vertex position, create a model of the mouth and chin, pay attention to the mouth is made on the same principle as the eyes, with it as the center of the ring cutting modeling.

(vii) Use Extrude to create a model of the neck and finally add ears.

(viii) Copy this half of the Buddha head model along the X axis to the other half, the main parameters are detailed in Fig. 6, select the two halves of the head model, with Merge it with Merge to become a whole, so that the Buddha head modeling is complete. Add the adjustment details as needed.

In the digital restoration performance of Qingzhou Buddha statue, the grasp of the texture of The Buddha statue material is accurate and needs to be complemented by many aspects. In order to express it more accurately in digital restoration, in the process of modeling, we should start with the analysis of the carving process and techniques of the Buddha statue, so as to express the hardness of the material through the knife effect of the carving of the Buddha statue lines, while the nuanced character emoticons can be expressed through the delicate degree of parameter adjustment.

5.4 Lay Out the Scene Lights

After the Buddha statue has built a model, it is necessary to lay out the lights in the scene and lay the foundation for the material design behind it. The environment is different, the method of arranging the light is also different, but basically still using a three-point cloth light method, in this scene is to use a main light to illuminate the entire scene, use

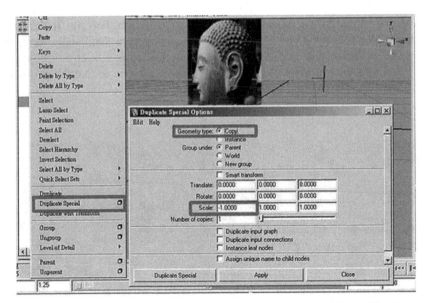

Fig. 6. North Qi Buddha statue in Qingzhou Head creation model step (Fig. 3)

a secondary light to increase the brightness of the local area of the Buddha statue, and then use a backlight to increase the scene contrast. If the size of the scene is large, you can first divide into several areas, and then make a three-point lighting method in each area.

5.5 Define the Material of the Object

In a computer, to represent different materials, you need to define materials and lights. Such as stone, soil, wood and metal and other materials. Defining a material is generally divided into two parts: determining the basic parameters and specifying the map. Basic parameters generally include three basic colors and a thick and light approach. The three basic colors are: the color of the shadow part, the color of the material, the color of the highlight part. Of these three, the material's nature has the most obvious effect and is the easiest to define. The material of the statue of Beiqi Buddha in Qingzhou is locally produced limestone, which sets the material into a real-world color, and sets the color of limestone as a material color. Copy the material's color value to the color of the highlight, and then make the highlight portion more saturated. Finally, concave maps are used to represent the surface effect of the Limestone material of the Buddha statue, resulting in shadows and highlights. The bump map doesn't actually change the geometry, and the unevenness of the Buddha statue is just an effect that simulates highlights and shadows, and it's very effective for textures that produce real effects.

5.6 Define the Decoration of the Buddha Statue

In the 3DSMAX 3D software operation, the original pattern of the Buddha statue model is coated, mainly through 2D map and 3D map technology. The image file is projected directly to the surface of the Buddha statue with a two-dimensional plan map, and the texture is automatically generated by a 3D map, using numerical values to adjust its final effect.

In this case, the key step in defining the decoration is to create a two-dimensional map with the Buddha's own pattern. Through the graphics software Photoshop, draw a fully expanded buddha statue around the pattern, the color of the decoration through multi-point sampling, respectively, set the value of its inherent color, and then, through parameters to adjust the special effects of the decoration. For example, during the process of cellaring for thousands of years, because of the factors that preserve the environment, some colors have changed, the area box of the change can be selected as a selection, through the color adjustment command, so that it produces a realistic color chemical change effect. After being stored in image format, 3DSMAX is introduced through Bitmap and can be used as a map.

For the coloring process of the Buddha statue, synthetic maps are applied here, which can combine multiple map types to produce rich composite effects. A poster will show the white layer of the trimmed Buddha statue stone tire, which is located between the ornament and the stone tire, the upper layer of which places the Buddha statue's ornamental map, in order to truly show the surface thickness effect at its mottled place, the top layer will be placed a bump map, according to the need to adjust its parameters separately.

5.7 Rendering

When the previous work is complete, the image you made is rendered. This is set up differently depending on the situation. If you are simply simulating the appearance of the Buddha statue on your computer, the rendered image should not be too large, it is best not to exceed the resolution of 640×480, and the resulting file format is preferably GPEG image format. If you want to use for paper printing, printing, then it is best to as required, rendered to a resolution of 600×800 or more, the file format is best in TIFF image format. Softimage's famous rendering engine, MentalRay, delivers high-quality visuals.

The general process described above. In real-world production, each stage can be repeated multiple times.

When people express the basic reasons and basic laws in art, they do not use the boring definition that the public cannot understand but only the experts understand, but in a way that is easy to feel, not only to reason, but also to the senses and feelings of the most ordinary people. Art has this characteristic, art is "high-level and popular things, the highest level of content to the public."[14]

---

[14] (Law) Danner, Fu Lei Translation: Philosophy of Art, Anhui Literary Publishing House, 1991, 75.

Influence of the Color and Logo Position of HNB Products on User Experience Based on Eye Tracking

Lili Sun[1], Lizhong Hu[1], Lei Xiang[1], Xiuling Wang[2], Lei Wu[2], and Huai Cao[2(✉)]

[1] Anhui Key Laboratory of Tobacco Chemistry, Anhui Tobacco Industrial Co., Ltd.,
Hefei 230088, People's Republic of China
[2] School of Mechanical Science and Engineering, Huazhong University of Science and
Technology, Wuhan 430074, People's Republic of China
caohuai@hust.edu.cn

Abstract. This paper reports on two experimental psychology studies on influence of the color and logo position in the field of HNB product, which used to measure the user experience. Based on the eye tracking method, we conducted two experimental studies. The independent variables were the different colors and logo position of HNB products. The dependent variables include first fixation time, first fixation duration, total fixation duration, second fixation time and subjective evaluation. A total of 68 people participated in the experiment. The main findings of this study were as follows: (1) In terms of HNB color preference, black and white were the most acceptable colors. (2) In the selection of logo position, the lower right and upper right position were more popular with users. (3) The first fixation time and the second fixation time can reflect the most real inner experience. In addition, this study provides a method for reference value with consumer decision-making for the industrial design optimization in relate consumer electronic product fields.

Keywords: User experience · Eye tracking · Logo position · Color

1 Introduction

HNB product (Heat-not-burn product) are the new type of product made by heating shredded tobacco in low temperature. The advantage of HNB product are as follows: ① no need to burn, greatly reducing the harmful components produced by combustion, and less harmful than traditional cigarettes; ② no second-hand smoke produced; ③ high safety, avoiding the open flame of traditional cigarettes. The most noteworthy aspect of HNB product is its safety features. Various studies have shown that its safety is much higher than traditional cigarettes. In terms of emissions, HNB product account for 5% of traditional cigarettes. From the perspective of cytotoxicity, HNB product are only 14% of traditional cigarettes. How to make HNB products that meet the user needs and improve user experience is new problem that needs to be considered and solved in the related industrial fields.

V. G. Duffy (Ed.): HCII 2021, LNCS 12778, pp. 360–373, 2021.
https://doi.org/10.1007/978-3-030-77820-0_27

User experience is an extension of HCI technology, and the quality of interaction technology is studied from the perspective of considering product construction, product function, users' emotional needs and user experience. Most of the previous researches were based on the internal structure of the product. In this paper, the influence of HNB product color and logo position on user experience is discussed in terms of the external manifestation of the product.

In summary, this research studies the influence of color and logo position in the field of HNB products based on eye tracking technology to measure user experience. The purpose is to better grasp the target consumer's visual preference for HNB products, to grasp the direction of the design, development and upgrade of HNB products. Help companies to better understood the decision making of consumers, and promote sustainable economic development.

2 Literature Review

In the eye tracking evaluation of logo design research field, Gong Yong (2018) used nomenclature and scale rating methods to test the visual complexity, familiarity and semantic distance of 270 icons in order to investigate the influence of cognitive attributes on icon understanding [1]. Xu Zejun (2018) used eye tracking technology to analyze the difference in cognitive tendency of passengers in different culture when watching the subway guide system [2]. Li Hongxia (2018) evaluated the effectiveness of emergency signs in large shopping malls by using eye tracking to solve the problem of whether emergency signs were effective in the emergency safety accident [3]. Zhang Xiongfei (2017) sorted out and summarized the domestic and foreign researches on the complexity of icons through literature analysis, and proposed the possible different dimensions of the complexity of icons [4]. Zhu Zhijuan (2017) used the eye tracking to evaluate the influence of brand logo on people's attention and memory under the conditions of design form, contour, graphic structure and complexity [5]. Gong Yong (2016) studied the effects of color number and consistency on the visual search efficiency of icons [6]. Luo Zhaofei (2015) studied children's visual attention characteristics for warning signs with different shapes of fonts [7]. Niu Guoqing (2014) studied the influence of auxiliary text on the identification of safety signs [8].

In the literature on eye tracking evaluation on food labels and product placement, Denize (2016) conducted eye movement test on label attention of 60 consumers in order to study the differences between ordinary food and functional food labels [9]. Anna (2018) investigated the relative effects of choice labels and traffic light labels on consumers' visual attention and food choices, and found that attention to health labels was not a good predictor of subsequent health choices [10]. Anstrijana (2020) found that front nutrition labeling is gradually becoming an important public policy tool to promote healthy eating [11]. Fu Guo (2018) combined eye tracking and EEG techniques to study the effects of exposure on viewer brand reactions. The results showed that viewers exposed to product placement information disclosure tended to display longer gaze time on placed products [12]. It can be seen from related research that eye tracking technology provides a scientific and objective basis for the directivity of interface identification and food labeling. However, there are few eye tracking evaluation studies on color and logo position of HNB products.

3 Method

This paper explores the influence of different color and logo positions of HNB products on consumers' visual attention and subjective attitudes. In this experiment, Tobii X300 desktop eye tracker was used to record the eye movement of 68 participants when they looked at pictures of HNB products in different colors and different logo positions. The 68 participants were divided into 4 categories according to different attributes: gender, age, occupation and education background. The population distribution and proportion of each attribute were shown in Table 1.

Table 1. The population distribution and proportion of the 68 participants

Gender	Male		Female	
	53 people (77.94%)		15 people (22.06%)	
Age	20–30 years old	30–40 years old	Over 40 years old	
	29 people (42.65%)	24 people (35.29%)	15 people (22.06%)	
Occupation	Corporate management	Professional skill worker	Administration staff	Other
	14 people (20.59%)	42 people (61.77%)	6 people (8.82%)	6 people (8.82%)
Education	Bachelor degree or below	Bachelor degree	Master's degree and above	
	34 people (50.00%)	25 people (36.76%)	9 people (13.24%)	

3.1 Method of Experiment 1

Definitions: to explore the influence of different color of HNB product on consumers' visual attention and decision-making. (a) The independent variable of the experiment was the color of HNB product. (b) The dependent variables of the experiment were eye movement data and subjective score. (c) The control variables are the proportion of shape and the position of logo. The main hypothesis of this study were as follows. H1: The color of HNB product cause significant difference in users' visual attention. H2: Color cause significant differences in participant' subjective attitudes.

Stimuli: six color samples (white, yellow, green, red, blue, black) of the HNB products, as shown in Fig. 1.
Equipment: Tobii X300 desktop eye tracker made in Sweden.
Procedure: present the color sample of HNB product picture, let users observe freely in 15 s, find out their favorite color design, and collect user's eye movement behavior data. Finally, users perform subjective scoring, as shown in Fig. 2.

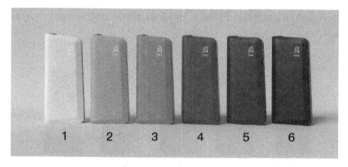

Fig. 1. The experimental stimuli in experiment 1

Fig. 2. Participant in the experiment and the environment of experiment 1

3.2 Method of Experiment 2

Definitions: to explore the influence of different logo positions of HNB product on consumers' visual attention and decision-making. The independent variable of the experiment is the logo position of HNB products. The dependent variables of the experiment were eye movement data and subjective score. The experimental control variables were color. The main hypothesis of this study were as follows: H1: The logo position of HNB products cause significant difference in users' eye movement attention. H2: The logo position of HNB products cause significant differences in participant' subjective attitudes.

Stimuli: The logo position of HNB products divided into five types: respectively upper left, lower right, middle, lower left, upper right, as shown in Fig. 3.

Equipment: Tobii X300 desktop eye tracker made in Sweden.

Procedure: The logo position sample of HNB products is presented as a whole picture, so that users can observe freely in 15 s, find out their favorite logo layout design, and collect user eye movement data. Finally, the user subjective scoring was collected, as shown in Fig. 4.

1   2   3   4   5

Fig. 3. The experimental stimuli in experiment 2

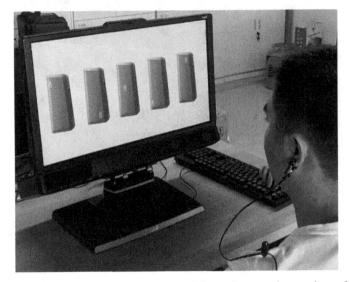

Fig. 4. Participant in the experiment and the environment in experiment 2

4   Result Analysis

4.1   Result of Experiment 1

The heat map mainly used to reflect the situation of users browsing and watching. Red represents the most concentrated area of browsing, and yellow and green represent areas with less gaze. It can reflect the process of information extraction and selection in subtle ways, and can detect the subject's choice of information. The heat maps of the overall 68 people's eye movement data in this experiment. The most focused place on the HNB product is the logo position, which can help researchers understand which features of the product are the most concerned or easily overlooked, as shown in Fig. 5.

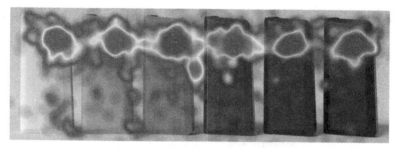

Fig. 5. The heat map visualization in the experiment 1

Experiment 1 studied the influence of color factors on the HNB product. There are 4 main eye tracking parameters studied in this experiment, namely the first fixation time, the first fixation duration, the total fixation duration and the second fixation time. Next, the meaning of different parameters and the data performance under different parameters analyzed in detail.

First fixation time (unit: s): the time taken for the user to first gaze at the area of interest. Figure 6 shows the difference in the first fixation time of 68 participants in color. The first fixation time of 68 participants were as follows: green (0.5415 s), yellow (1.3222 s), red (1.7535 s), blue (2.2731 s), white (2.8457 s), and black (3.3121 s). As can be seen from the data trend, green is the first color to be noticed, and black is the last color to be noticed.

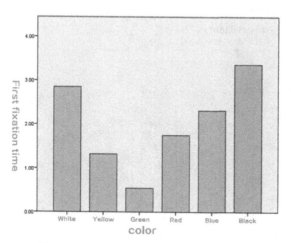

Fig. 6. First fixation time in the experiment 1

First fixation duration time (unit: s): The duration of the first fixation point that the subject appears in the area of interest. Figure 7 shows the overall difference in the first fixation duration time of 68 participants in color. The first fixation duration time of 68 participants were as follows: white (0.2487 s), black (0.2336 s), green (0.2179 s), red (0.1918 s), blue (0.1875 s), and yellow (0.1871 s). As can be seen from the data, among the indicators of the first fixation duration time, white and black are the longest, while yellow is the shortest.

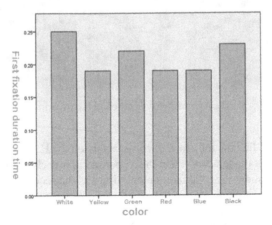

Fig. 7. First fixation duration time in the experiment 1

Total fixation duration time (unit: s): The sum of time spent by the subject at all fixation points in the area of interest. Figure 8 shows the overall difference of the total fixation duration time in color. The total fixation duration time of 68 participants were as follows: green (2.3531 s), red (1.9128 s), yellow (1.8415 s), white (1.6475 s), black (1.6041 s) and blue (1.3238 s). As can see from the data trend, green is the most persistent, while blue is the least persistent.

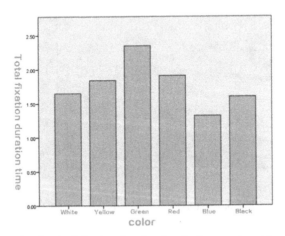

Fig. 8. Total fixation duration time in the experiment 1

Second fixation time (unit: s): The time of the second fixation in the interest area, that is, the duration of the second fixation point. Figure 9 shows the overall difference in the second fixation time in color. The second fixation time of 68 participants were as follows: black (0.2260 s), white (0.1856 s), green (0.1749 s), red (0.1356 s), blue (0.1144 s) and yellow (0.1060 s). As can be seen from the data trend, the duration of the second fixation time parameter is longest in black and shortest in yellow.

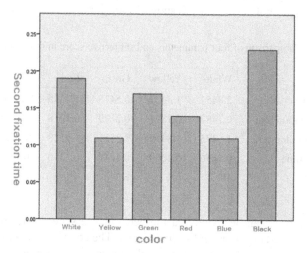

Fig. 9. Second fixation time in the experiment 1

Among the 68 participants' subjective choices, the number of black participants (44.1%) is the largest, followed by white (27.9%), yellow (8.8%), green (8.8%), red (5.9%) and blue (4.4%), as shown in Fig. 10.

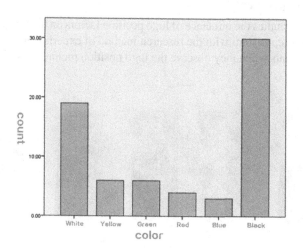

Fig. 10. Subjective score in the experiment 1

The above analysis of the four technical parameters in the experiment and the subjective choice were carried out separately. The first fixation time reflects the unconscious interest area of the subjects to some extent, but the short first fixation time does not mean that the area is positively attractive to the subjects. It may be attracted by the other factors. The research purpose is to dig out the most real psychology of the subjects through the correlation between the parameters. Therefore, this experiment combines various parameters for comparative analysis, as shown in the Table 2.

Table 2. Comparison of four parameters and subjective score in the experiment 1

	White	Yellow	Green	Red	Blue	Black
First fixation time	2.8457	1.3222	0.5415	1.7535	2.2731	3.3121
First fixation duration time	0.2487	0.1871	0.2179	0.1918	0.1875	0.2336
Total fixation duration time	1.6475	1.8415	2.3531	1.9128	1.3238	1.6041
Second fixation time	0.1856	0.1060	0.1749	0.1356	0.1144	0.2260
Subjective score	19	6	6	4	3	30

In the analysis, it can be found that the performance state of the subjects shown by the 4 technical parameters is multi-dimensional. The color that pay attention to first and total fixation duration time is green and the longest first fixation duration time is white, but the longest second fixation time is in black. At the same time, the color that the participants choose the most is also black, which reflects that the participants be attracted by the bright colors in the color observation of HNB products, but in preference is not the bright color. It is consistent with the hypothesis of this experiment.

4.2 Result of Experiment 2

The experiment 2 studies the influence of logo position factors on the HNB product field. The experiment is consistent with the research method of experiment 1. The heat maps of the 68 participants when they observe the logo position picture, as shown in Fig. 11.

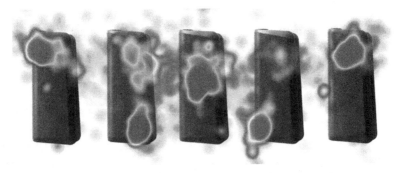

Fig. 11. The heat map visualization in the experiment 2

The first fixation time of the logo position in HNB product were as follows: upper left (3.4647 s), lower right (3.8389 s), the middle (2.2210 s), lower left (4.0838 s), the upper right (4.7120 s). It can be seen from the data trend that from the overall data, it can be concluded that the first place the subjects focused was the middle logo position, followed by the upper left and lower right logo positions, and the last place they attention was the lower left and the upper right logo position, as shown in Fig. 12.

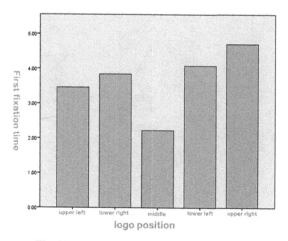

Fig. 12. First fixation time in the experiment 2

The first fixation duration of the logo position was as follows: upper left (0.2974 s), lower right (0.2525 s), middle (0.2649 s), lower left (0.2353 s), upper right (0.4153 s). The longest first fixation duration is the upper right, followed by the upper left, and the position with the shortest duration is the lower left, as shown in Fig. 13.

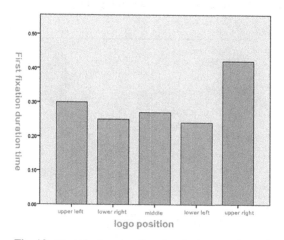

Fig. 13. First fixation duration time in the experiment 2

The total fixation duration time of the logo position of HNB product were as follows: upper left (0.6759 s), lower right (0.8985 s), middle (0.9462 s), lower left (0.5974 s), upper right (0.8166 s). From the data trend, it can be seen that the position with the longest overall fixation duration was the middle, followed by the lower right, and the shortest position was the lower left, as shown in Fig. 14.

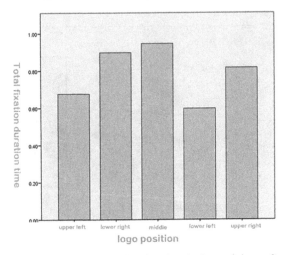

Fig. 14. Total fixation duration time in the experiment 2

The second fixation time of the logo position were as follows: upper left (0.0747 s), lower right (0.0468 s), middle (0.0496 s), lower left (0.0421 s), upper right (0.0693 s). From the data trend, it can be seen that the positions with the longest second fixation duration are the upper left and upper right, followed by the lower right and the middle, and the shortest last is the lower left, as shown in Fig. 15.

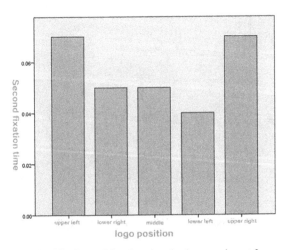

Fig. 15. Second fixation time in the experiment 2

It can be found that among the 68 participants' subjective score, the number of people choosing the logo position in the lower right is the most (44.1%), followed by the upper right (35.3%), and the middle (10.3%), upper left (8.8%), and lower left (1.5%), as shown in Fig. 16.

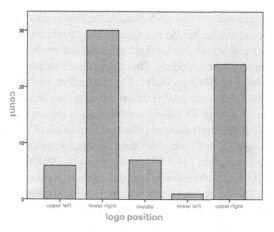

Fig. 16. Subjective score in the experiment 2

The above content is analyzed separately for the data which we can initially find the participant's visual performance in the logo position. The following will combine the experimental data, as shown in the Table 3.

Table 3. Comparison of four parameters and subjective score in the experiment 2

	Upper left	Lower right	Middle	Lower left	Upper right
First fixation time	3.4647	3.8389	2.2210	4.0838	4.7120
First fixation duration time	0.2974	0.2525	0.2649	0.2353	0.4153
Total fixation duration time	0.6759	0.8985	0.9462	0.5974	0.8166
Second fixation time	0.0747	0.0468	0.0496	0.0421	0.0693
Subjective Score	6	30	7	1	24

It can be found the logo position that the participants paid attention first was the middle, and the longest first fixation duration time was the upper right position. In subjective selection, 30 of the 68 participants chose the lower right position, which reflects that when the participants are observing the product, they are easily attracted by the content they are interested in, but on the contrary, it is not true that the attracted area is the user's final choice. It is consistent with the hypothesis of this experiment. Therefore, in the analysis, unilateral data is difficult to feed back the participants' psychology, to combine objective data and subjective data for comprehensive analysis, which is also one of the finding of this experiment.

5   Conclusion

Traditional user testing methods and performance measurements may indicate that the user has a problem or obstacle, but do not explain the "problem of why" or reveal the implicit cognitive process, which eye tracking does. Based on the eye tracking method, we conducted two experimental studies. The independent variables were the different colors and logo position of HNB products. The dependent variables include first fixation time, first fixation duration, total fixation duration, second fixation duration and subjective evaluation. A total of 68 people participated in the experiment.

The main findings of this study were as follows: (1) in terms of HNB color preference, black (44.1%) and white (27.9%) were the most acceptable colors; (2) in the selection of logo position, the lower right (44.1%) and upper right (35.3%) position were more popular with users; (3) the results showed that the subjective choice was correlated with the first fixation time and the second fixation time, the first fixation time and the second fixation time can reflect the most real inner experience.

In this experiment, 77.94% of the participants were male, so the feedback to female users may awaits further research, which is one of the limitations of this study. It is hoped that in the future research, the EEG physiological signal of users for HNB products could be analyzed more comprehensively. In addition, this study provides a method for reference value with consumer decision-making for the industrial design optimization in relate consumer electronic product fields.

Acknowledgments. The research supported by research on quantification analysis technology of eye tracking in user experience of HNB product (project number: 202034000034009).

References

1. Gong, Y., Huo, F., Shen, F.: Analysis and quantitative study of cognitive attributes of icons. Design (07), 54–56 (2018)
2. Xu, Z., Liu, J.: An empirical study on the cross-culture cognition of sign system based on eye tracking data. Packag. Eng. **39**(16), 117–122 (2018)
3. Li, H., He, P.: Application of eye tracking technique in the study of effectiveness of emergency signs. Sci. Technol. Eng. **18**(18), 323–327 (2018)
4. Zhang, X., Xue, C., Shen, Z.: Analysis of icon complexity in human-computer interaction digital interface. Design (19), 119–120 (2017)
5. Zhu, Z., Shen, D.: Research on cognition and memory of brand logo based on eye movement tracking. In: Proceedings on Seminar of Industrial Education of China and International Industrial Design Forum, pp. 21–26 (2017)
6. Gong, Y., Zhang, S., Liu, Z., Shen, F.: Eye movement study on color effects to icon visual efficiency. J. Zhejiang Univ. (Eng. Sci.) **50**(10), 1987–1994 (2016)
7. Luo, Z., Jing, G., Zhang, K.: Analysis of the characteristic features of children's eye movement while watching the warning signs in different aspects. J. Saf. Environ. **15**(5), 151–155 (2015)

8. Niu, G., Cui, C., Zhang, K.: An eye movement study of auxiliary words effect to safety signs' recognition. J. Henan Polytech. Univ. (Nat. Sci.) **33**(04), 410–415 (2014)

9. Oliveira, D., et al.: Consumers' attention to functional food labels: insights from eye-tracking and change detection in a case study with probiotic milk. LWT Food Sci. Technol. **68**, 160–167 (2016)

10. Fenko, A., Nicolaas, I., Galetzka, M.: Does attention to health labels predict a healthy food choice? An eye-tracking study. Food Qual. Prefer. **69**, 57–65 (2018)

11. Gabor, A.M., Stojnic, B., Ostic, D.B.: Effects of different nutrition labels on visual attention and accuracy of nutritional quality perception – results of an experimental eye-tracking study. Food Qual. Prefer. **84**, 103948 (2020)

12. Guo, F., Ye, G., Duffy, V.G., Li, M., Ding, Y.: Applying eye tracking and electroencephalography to evaluate the effects of placement disclosures on brand responses. J. Consum. Behav. **17**(6), 519–531 (2018)

A Study on the Effect of Online Vertical Searching Advertising Presence Towards Customer Behavioral Intentions

Yu Sun[✉]

School of Business Administration, Shenyang University, Shenyang 110044, China

Abstract. Consumers are considered to adopt a higher degree of involvement and a stronger purchase purpose, when they view the vertical searching ads. But the conscious process is still not explored exactly yet. In this paper, the effect of online vertical searching advertising design factors on customer's presence and the relationship between presence and customer's behavioral intentions are found through the eye movement and questionnaire. The data of 30 subjects is collected jointly through the eye-tracking technology and questionnaire survey, including their eye movement toward the different ads, the subjective evaluation of presence, trust, pleasure and behavior al intentions. On this basis, the multivariate analysis of variance method is used to analyze the influence of online vertical searching advertising design elements on user's presence and behavioral intentions. The results show that the vivid model and background picture of vertical searching advertising as well as other consumers' evaluation information listed below can shorten customer's the time and difficulty of advertising information extraction, and improve customer's presence which will affect customer's behavioral intentions through trust and pleasure. The vertical searching advertising with mouse interaction can reduce the difficulty of customer's information extraction, but as the dynamic screen will interfere with customer's continuing browsing, it should be carefully applied. What we've found can be useful in exploring the consumer's conscious process and give a reference for the ads designers on how to attract and persuade consumers to buy through vertical searching ads.

Keywords: Online vertical searching advertising · Presence · Eye-tracking · User experience · Behavioral intention

1 Introduction

Vertical search advertising refers to the ad provided by online shopping websites, such as Amozon, Macy's, Taobao etc. From the perspective of interactive process, vertical search ad can help users in B2C business websites to obtain the information integrating product image, advertising copy, sales and purchase entrance by entering keywords, which thus can help online consumers to make purchase decisions and even complete online purchase. Due to the precise positioning and accurate marketing, this kind of advertisement has been favored by many people since its birth and has a strong development momentum till now. Consumers tend to adopt a higher degree of involvement

© Springer Nature Switzerland AG 2021
V. G. Duffy (Ed.): HCII 2021, LNCS 12778, pp. 374–389, 2021.
https://doi.org/10.1007/978-3-030-77820-0_28

and a stronger purchase purpose, when they view the vertical search ads. As this kind of consumers are always accompanied by time and budget pressure, it has become the first concern of the advertising designers who need to show the users' most concerned information in the limited advertising page, in order to stimulate user' click and help users to make purchase decisions. In addition to general advertising, vertical search ad also needs to consider the virtual nature of the network. As a direct purchase entrance, vertical search ad holds the key to success by creating online environment as field sale and enhancing user's presence experience.

Presence can be illustrated as the individual's perception of the environment (Montes 1992) which can describe the true degree of an individual in a virtual environment, as a sense of "being there" (Peukert et al. 2019). In 2004, Lee divided this sense of presence into three levels, namely physical presence, social presence and self-presence according to the process of human perception. Throughout the current research, most scholars only discuss the sense of presence at one level.

At the physical level, scholars mostly study how products or objects from a remote distance can be vividly presented in front of them through media. As early as 2000, Jahng pointed out that physical presence would bring the "immediate" psychological and physical experience of products to consumers. Fiore (2001) also points out that physical presence can be expressed through rich media, allowing consumers to interact with products' images, so as to achieve users' perception of products' proximity. The presence at this level makes people realize that the vividness and verisimilitude of the product image display will have a positive impact on customers' perception and attitude. At the level of social presence, many scholars have contributed a lot in their researches. Xiaojun et al. (2018), Quesnel and Riecke (2018), De La Rosa and Breidt (2018) all take the social presence as the evaluation index of virtual reality, and adopt the method of questionnaire survey to measure the friendliness and accessibility of a media. Their research results make people realize that in the network, through the shaping of social situations, communicating and sharing with others, the customer's sense of social presence will be enhanced, thus influencing the customer's purchasing intentions. In terms of self-presence, scholars mainly focus on the field of online games and e-commerce. Oatley (1994) pointed out that users can improve their self-presence, understand the purpose of the game and have more fun of the game by imagining themselves as the protagonist. Chuan-Hoo et al. (2012) and Namkee et al. (2010) have also verified through experiments that realistic avatar design and emotional background stories can improve users' sense of self-presence in online games, thus leading to a better task performance. Jeong et al. (2017) combined the sense of self-presence with the sense of immersion and flow experience to illustrate the impact of customers' loyalty on purchasing intentions. The results of these studies showed that the customers who enhanced their self-presence were more immersed in the virtual environment and thus complete the tasks better. In short, presence, as an important factor influencing the interaction between users and virtual environment, has been more and more recognized and valued.

As an engine entrance that can assist customers to complete purchase, vertical search advertising must create presence experience as offline for customers through effective information arrangement, so as to stimulate customers to make purchase behaviors. This paper will make a combination of eye tracking experiment and questionnaire survey, introduce the variable of presence into the evaluation of effect of the vertical search advertising, and analyze the influence of different design elements on users' presence perception. On this basis, further exploration will be made on the effect of presence on users' behavioral intention.

2 Research Model and Research Hypothesis

2.1 Research Model

Morphological analysis method is used to contrast, analyze and filtrate design elements of vertical search advertising. Combined with the samples from seventeen B2C websites, seven design elements which have influences on users' presence were selected, including image display, location, copywriting, sales information, store information, purchase assistance and mouse interaction. Each design element was leveled two, 0 represent a low level of the element, while 1 represents a high level. The specific design elements and their two levels are shown in Table 1.

Table 1. Design elements and their two levels of vertical search ads influencing presence

Design elements	Levels	Levels explanation
A Image display	Product Picture (0)	Only product picture is shown in advertising
	Model and Background Picture (1)	Product, model and background pictures are all shown in advertising
B Location	Not show the location (0)	The location of the product is not shown in this advertising
	Show the location (1)	The location of the product is shown in this advertising
C Copywriting	The copywriting only describes the product (0)	The copywriting only describes the product objectively in advertising
	The copywriting has some subjective assessment (1)	The copywriting not only describes the product but also show some subjective assessment information in advertising
D Sales information	Sales volume (0)	Only sales volume is shown in advertising
	Sales volume and comments (1)	Besides sales volume, the consumers' comments are also shown in advertising
E Store information	Show the basic information (0)	The store image and name is shown in advertising

(continued)

Table 1. (*continued*)

Design elements	Levels	Levels explanation
	Show the detailed information (1)	Besides store image and name, the ratings and credit of the store are also shown in advertising
F Purchase assistance	Without purchase button (0)	Without purchase button, Just click on the picture to enter the product details page
	With Purchase button (1)	Set three buttons to view details, to purchase and to add to favorites
G Mouse interaction	Without mouse interaction (0)	When the mouse is over the product picture, the product picture will not show any reaction
	With mouse interaction (1)	When the mouse is over the product picture, the product picture will pop up big picture to display information

In order to explore the influence of each design element of vertical search advertising on the sense of presence of customers and the relationship between the sense of presence and other variables (emotion, trust and behavioral intention), a theoretical model as shown in Fig. 1 is proposed. The model reflects the relationship among online advertising design, presence, customers' emotional response, and behavioral intention. As can be seen from Fig. 1, online advertising brings different immersive experience to users through different design element combinations. In addition, the sense of presence will affect people's eye movement, pleasure and trust, and further affect the behavioral

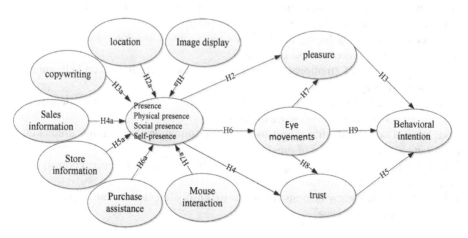

Fig. 1. Theory model

intention of customers. The following will review the research results involved in the theoretical model first and then propose the research hypothesis of this paper.

2.2 Research Hypothesis

Relationship Between Design Elements and Sense of Presence. Combined with the research results of e-commerce and online advertising in recent years, it can be seen that: advertising pictures with characters and social situations can better stimulate customers' sense of social presence and purchase loyalty (Cyr et al. 2007). The closer the geographical distance of the product (for example, in the same city), the more likely the user is to make online impulsive purchase (ZhangXuan 2012). Users' perception of other customers (Wang et al. 2007), store image (Lv 2012), comments of other users or product reputation (Lv 2012; Wen and Sha 2011) on the website all enhance users' sense of presence, thus stimulating users' trust, purchase intention and purchase loyalty. In addition, Shatnawi et al. (2020) found that the level of website interactivity affects the degree of virtual experience (sense of presence) of consumers, that is, the stronger the interactivity, the better the sense of presence experience (Skadberg and Kimmel 2004). Zhao et al. (2014) also found that the interactivity of online stores has a significant positive impact on the formation of consumers' virtual sense of finger-touch (one of the manifestations of presence). Jiang et al. (2014) further divided this online interaction into four dimensions, and found that except the perception of personalization, the other three dimensions of perceived control, perceived response, and perceived mutual assistance all have a significant impact on consumers' sense of presence when they are online purchasing.

Based on the above research results and combined with the specific design elements of vertical search advertising, relevant hypotheses are proposed as follows:

H1a: vertical search ads implanting images that reflect the lifestyle and values of the target users can help to enhance the user's sense of presence.
H2a: vertical search ads display the product's geographical location information, which helps to improve the user's sense of presence.
H3a: the placement of emotional copywriting in vertical search ads can help enhance users' sense of presence.
H4a: the presentation of product sales and comments information in vertical search advertising can improve users' sense of presence;
H5a: vertical search ads that reflect the store's information (e.g. ratings, credits etc.) contribute to the user's sense of presence;
H6a: behavioral assistance (perception mutual assistance and perception control) set in vertical search ads can improve users' sense of presence.
H7a: vertical search ads with mouse interaction (sensory interaction) can help to improve the user's sense of presence.

The Relationship Between Presence and Other Dependent Variables. Many scholars have made research in exploring the influence of presence on customers' pleasure, trust and behavioral intentions. Jahng and Jain (2000) demonstrated that physical presence has a positive impact on users' behavioral intention through different product presentation methods. Sajjadi et al. (2019) studied the positive impact of social presence on users' trust, pleasure and loyalty by implanting a discussion module in the ticket advertisement. Heng et al. (2019) confirmed that social presence has a positive influence on users' pleasure, trust, similarity attraction, perceived usefulness and purchase intention through implanting social clues in clothing websites. Chuan-Hoo et al. (2012) found that by comparing different online chat rooms, the one with self-presence can stimulate users' positive emotions and promote task completion. Namkee et al. (2010) also pointed out that online games with story background can enhance users' sense of self presence and bring better task performance. These results show that physical presence, social presence and self-presence all have an impact on users' emotion, trust and behavioral intention. In view of this, the following hypotheses are proposed:

H2: presence has a positive effect on customer pleasure;
H3: pleasure positively affects customers' behavioral intention;
H4: presence has a positive effect on customer trust;
H5: trust positively influences customer behavior intention.

The Relationship Between Eye Movement Index and Presence and Other Dependent Variables. In addition to the traditional questionnaire survey, the development of eye movement tracking technology makes it possible to evaluate online advertisements objectively. Wedel and Guitart et al. (2019) used the position and duration of the first fixation point to investigate the effect of advertising on people's attention (Guitart et al. 2019). Xu and Wang (2020) used fixation counts, fixation duration and pupil diameter changes to illustrate the consistency between consumers' memory score and their eye movement parameters. According to SOR Model (Mehrabian and Russell 1974), external stimulation can cause changes in physiological and psychological states, and then affect people's behavioral intentions. Similarly, different presence designs of online advertisements can affect people's psychological and physiological responses (Chuan-Hoo et al. 2012; Cyr et al. 2007; Zhaoxiaoyu 2010). However, there is no research on which specific eye movement indicators are used to reflect the sense of presence, but it is generally accepted that pleasant visual stimulation can cause pupil dilation. Furthermore, Van and Mathot (2019) further demonstrated that pupil size can be used to measure emotion (Van Hooijdonk et al. 2019). Based on this, the following hypotheses are proposed:

H6: different sense of presence will lead to changes in customers' eye movement behaviors;
H7: eye movement index can reflect customers' pleasure;
H8: eye movement index can reflect customers' behavioral intention (attention, click and memory).

3   Research Methods

3.1   Experimental Advertising Design

After determining the design elements that affect users' presence, we combined them and created 8 vertical searching advertising samples on clothing through SPSS based on the orthogonal design principle, as shown in Fig. 2.

Fig. 2. Eight experimental treatments obtained through orthogonal experiment

3.2   Selection of Subjects

Thirty subjects (15 males and 15 females) aged between 19 and 45 were selected to participate in this experiment, with an average age of 28.1 years (standard deviation was 6.31). The mean time of exposure to network was 4.58 years (standard deviation was 2.50). All subjects had good physical health, normal vision or corrected vision, and right handedness during the week before and during the test. In the three months prior to the experiment, 93% of the participants had purchased clothes online through a vertical search advertising at least once. It can be seen that the participants of this study are familiar with the vertical searching advertisements on clothes, where their comments on the vertical searching ads are predicable.

3.3   Experimental Equipment, Browsing Task Design and Experimental Process

The RED telemetry eye-movement instrument was used as the experimental equipment, mainly including the iView PC test computer, Stimulus PC image display computer, and two sets of infrared light sources and cameras installed below. The tester controls the contents displayed on the Stimulus PC through the iView PC test computer. The camera installed below the Stimulus PC screen captures the eyes of the subject and sends them to the iView PC test computer to collect and analyze the eye movement data of the subject. The Experiment task was designed by the Experiment Center 2.5 software, the data collection was completed by the iVewX 2.5 software, and the data analysis was completed by the BeGaze 2.5 analysis software.

In order to simulate the purchase behavior of users when they view vertical searching ads in the real world, the task of the following situation was set. As Christmas is approaching, an e-commerce company is preparing to sell sweaters with moose patterns on them. Now there are several advertising designs as follows. Please imagine yourself as a customer with actual purchasing needs and evaluate each advertisement. After seeing each advertisement, fill in the questionnaire to evaluate its sense of presence and your behavioral intention towards it. After all eight ads have been evaluated, select one of them to complete the purchase behavior (adding to the cart is considered as purchase).

The whole experiment was carried out in the eye movement laboratory, with one subject completing the test at a time. Firstly, the subjects were briefly introduced to the experimental purpose, experimental process and matters needing attention, and were asked to fill in a personal information questionnaire. Then, the subjects were seated in a chair in front of the stimulus image display of the eye tracker. The experimenter started the iVewX 2.5 and Experiment Center 2.5 software and calibrated the eye tracker's tracking system through the five-point method. After reaching the experimental requirement of calibration where the accuracy should be less than 0.5, the formal experiment was started. The order of the experimental instructions and the online advertising used in the experiment were designed by the Experiment Center 2.5 software. The eight advertising designs were presented in random order. After viewing one advertisement, the subject clicked the space to switch to another. After seeing all the eight advertising designs, the participants fill in the questionnaire.

3.4   The Selection of Scales and Eye Movement Indexes

In order to evaluate the sense of presence and its impact on visitor's psychology and behavior, the questionnaire includes the items to measure the three different levels of presence, user's trust, pleasure and behavioral intentions. The physical presence was measured from the breadth and depth of vividness. The social presence was evaluated according to Hassanien (2007) and Gefen and Straub (2004) in terms of intimacy, warmth and personal feelings. The items of evaluating self-presence based on Namkee et al. (2010) and make some corresponding adjustments on the content. When measuring the latent of trust, one item was selected for each typical dimension of trust, including goodwill, integrity and ability (Gefen and Straub 2004; Gefen et al. 2003; Wang et al. 2009).

Joyfulness was measured according to the PAD scale and the items that were frequently used, including vitality, comfort, happiness and excitement.

Behavioral intention was measured by typical advertising behaviors, including memory effects, attention and clicks. 7-point Likert scale is adopted for all the above parts, ranging from strongly disagree (1) to strongly agree (7). The detailed item and their reliability test are shown in Table 2 as follows.

Table 2. Items of scale, factor loading and Cronbach's coefficient

Latent variables	Items		Standardized factor loading	Cronbach's α
Presence	Physical presence	This ad is colorful and vivid	0.916	0.966
		The product display in this ad is lifelike	0.913	
	Social presence	This ad is friendly to the customers	0.948	
		This ad is considerate	0.953	
		This ad makes us feel very warm	0.932	
	Self-presence	After watching the advertisement, I temporarily forgot that I was in the laboratory, but felt as if I was in the product scene or advertising scene	0.903	
Pleasure	This ad makes me feel energetic		0.890	0.924
	This ad makes me feel good		0.884	
	After seeing this ad, I feel very happy		0.908	
	After seeing this ad, I feel so excited		0.940	
Trust	I believe that the shop in this ad is kind to customers		0.948	0.939
	I believe the products advertised in this ad are of high quality		0.944	
	I believe the shop in this ad is very professional, and can provide excellent service		0.940	
Behavioral intention	I can easily remember this ad		0.966	0.959
	On the web page, I can see the Ad at a glance		0.959	
	I would like to click on the Ad		0.959	

The selected eye movement indicators include browsing duration, fixation duration, fixation counts, scanning counts, maximum pupil diameter, minimum pupil diameter, average pupil diameter, and first fixation point position etc.

4   Experimental Data Processing, Results and Analysis

4.1   Data Processing

BeGaze 2.5 was used to analyze and export eye movement data. SPSS18.0 software was used to process the subjective questionnaire data. First, the abnormal values were removed according to the frame diagram, followed by the normality test, and then the abnormal data were removed according to 3 times of the standard deviation. The maximum likelihood estimation was used to evaluate the validity of the factor structure of the scale using the AMOS18.0 software. The CFI and SRMR of the test scale were 0.961 and 0.0368, indicating that the model was well adapted (Hu and Bentler 1999). The factor loading of the scale is significant, ranging from 0.884 to 0.966, and the combination reliability is 0.978, indicating that the reliability of the factor is at an acceptable level (Raykov 1997).

4.2   Analysis of the Influence of Advertising Design Elements on the Sense of Presence

In order to study the influence of design elements with different levels of presence on the eye movement indicators, multivariate analysis of variance (MNOVA) were applied, which takes presence (physical presence, social presence, self-presence), browsing duration, fixation counts, saccadic counts and blink counts as the dependent variables, and takes product design elements including image display (A), location (B), copywriting (C), Sales information (D), store information (E), behavior assistance (F) and mouse interaction (G) as the independent variables. The Bonferron post mortem was used to compare pairs of levels of the same design element. The alpha level was set at 0.05 for all statistical analyses.

Table 3. Influence of design elements of vertical searching ad on the indicators of presence

Design elements	Physical presence			Social presence			Self-presence		
	F	p	Partial eta	F	p	Partial eta	F	p	Partial eta
A	175.689	**<0.001**	0.431	316.751	**<0.001**	0.577	128.319	**<0.001**	0.356
B	6.266	**0.013**	0.026	0.622	0.431	0.003	2.435	0.120	0.010
C	0.608	0.436	0.003	0.702	0.403	0.003	0.404	0.526	0.002
D	6.266	**0.013**	0.026	3.697	**0.056**	0.016	4.573	**0.034**	0.019
E	0.487	0.486	0.002	0.087	0.768	0.000	0.030	0.863	0.000
F	0.743	0.390	0.003	0.855	0.356	0.004	2.647	**0.100**	0.855
G	106.093	**<0.001**	0.314	24.305	**<0.001**	0.095	25.867	**<0.001**	0.100

As can be seen from Table 3, when the significance level is 0.05, the design elements that have a significant impact on physical presence include A (image display),

B (geographical location), D (sales information) and G (behavioral assistance). Design elements that have significant influence on social presence include A (image display), G (mouse interaction), and an edge significance ($p < 0.1$) on design element D (sales information). Design elements that have significant influence on self-presence include A (image display), D (sales information), G (mouse interaction), and an edge significance ($p < 0.1$) on design elements F (behavioral assistance).

Vertical searching ad design elements of A (image display), B (location), D (sales information), F (behavioral assistance) and G (mouse interaction) has a significant influence on presence, which means H1a, H2a, H4a, H6a, and H7a hypothesis are verified; Design element C (copywriting) and F (store information) have no significant influence on the sense of presence, that is, H3a and H5a hypothesis are not supported.

4.3 Influence of Presence on Behavioral Intention

After verifying the influence of advertising design elements on the sense of presence, the structural equation model was further used to test the relationship between the sense of presence and subsequent variables. AMOS was used to analyze the data and the following results were obtained, as shown in Table 4.

Table 4. Influence of presence on users' behavioral intention

Hypothesis	Normalized path coefficient	t	Result
H3: presence → pleasure	0.834***	13.135	Support
H4: pleasure → behavioral intention	0.344**	7.814	Support
H5: presence → trust	0.881***	16.308	Support
H6: trust → behavioral intention	0.688***	14.110	Support

4.4 The Influence of Design Elements of Vertical Searching Ads on Eye Movement Index

Table 5 shows the MNOVA results of the influence of vertical searching ads design elements on eye movement indicators.

As can be seen from Table 5, when the significance level is 0.05, advertising design element A (image display) has a significant impact on users' fixation counts, browsing duration and saccade counts. Design factor D (sales information) has an edge significant influence on fixation counts, browsing duration and eye saccade counts ($p < 0.1$). Design factor G (mouse interaction) has a significant impact on fixation duration, and has an edge significant impact on browsing duration, saccade counts and blink counts ($p < 0.1$). Other design factors had no significant effect on eye movement index.

In order to further explore the influence of vertical searching ads with different levels of presence on customers' eye movement behaviors, two extreme advertising samples were selected on terms of the design element ADG, to analyze and make a comparison

Table 5. Influence of design elements of vertical searching ads on eye movement index

Design elements	Fixation counts			Browsing duration		
	F	p	Partial eta	F	p	Partial eta
A	15.798	**<0.001**	0.064	21.059	**<0.001**	0.083
B	0.182	0.670	0.001	0.933	0.335	0.004
C	0.353	0.553	0.002	1.994	0.159	0.009
D	2.571	**0.100**	0.011	3.704	**0.055**	0.016
E	0.113	0.737	0.000	0.439	0.508	0.002
F	0.238	0.626	0.001	1.130	0.289	0.005
G	5.730	**0.017**	0.024	2.652	**0.100**	0.011
Design elements	Saccade counts			Blink counts		
	F	p	Partial eta	F	p	Partial eta
A	16.352	**<0.001**	0.066	1.875	0.172	0.008
B	0.387	0.535	0.002	0.132	0.717	0.001
C	0.666	0.415	0.003	0.750	0.387	0.003
D	2.809	**0.095**	0.012	0.226	0.635	0.001
E	0.316	0.575	0.001	0.413	0.521	0.002
F	0.517	0.473	0.002	0.176	0.675	0.001
G	3.438	**0.065**	0.015	2.906	**0.090**	0.012

of customers' scanning path diagram and hot area map. The scanning path diagram and the hot area map can directly reflect the subjects' overall attention on the advertisement in the experiment.

The scanning path diagram can reflect the position of fixation points, the process of the sight shifting and the duration of each fixation point when browsing the advertisement, so that it can reflect the whole browsing process of the subject on the vertical searching advertisement. Figure 3 (a) and (c) are the scanning path diagrams of two subjects on vertical searching ads in the experiment. The center point of the circle in the figure represents the fixation point of the subject when observing the advertisement, the circle represents the fixation time of the subject when observing the point, the size of the circle is positively correlated with the fixation time, and the line segment represents the route of the subject's gaze shift. According to the scanning path diagram of the subjects, the scanning path of users also presents significant differences in two vertical searching ads with significant differences in design elements A (image display), D (sales information) and G (mouse interaction).

When browsing the vertical searching ads with the design of model display, sales information and mouse interaction, the subject's scanning path is clear and orderly, and their focus stays on the main design elements, which indicates that the subjects can comprehensively read the ads and obtain the advertising information.

When browsing vertical searching ads without the design of model displays, sales information, and mouse interaction, the subject's scanning path is chaotic, with more fixation points but a shorter time on each point. Some fixation points even scattered out of the advertisement, which suggests that when participants watch these ads, they cannot grasp the advertising information effectively, so that this kind of advertising design is difficult to meet the needs of the users when they browse ads to make purchase decisions.

Heat map can vividly reflect the degree of attention paid to different areas of visual stimulation. Different degrees of attention are marked by different shades of color, which makes eye movement data clear. Figure 3 (b) and (d) are the Heat maps superimposing the fixation points of the 30 subjects in two vertical searching ads, where different colors in the map shows the fixation duration of the subjects in the area. The warm area represents the concentration degree of the subject in this area, where the fixation duration is longer. That means the "hot spot", while the cool area has the opposite meaning. It can be seen from the figure that the subjects' attention on vertical searching ads with model display, sales information and mouse interaction is mainly distributed to the key design elements such as advertising images, copywriting and sales information. For vertical searching ads with no model display, sales information, or mouse interaction, the subjects only focused on the pattern of the product, which is just one part of the product.

Thus, it can be seen from the heat map that users' focus areas are concentrated on key design elements when the ad designed with model display, sales information and mouse interaction. While when the ad designed without image display, sales information and mouse interaction, the users' focus areas mainly appeared on the pattern of the product, and the size of the heat is bigger.

It suggests that when the user views the vertical searching ad to complete purchasing task, the ad with model display, sales information and mouse interaction will help users to grasp advertising information and make decisions easily; on the contrary, it is difficult for users to have references from vertical searching ads without these designs. However, driven by tasks, users need information to make decisions. So that users search for information in this ad with low level of design elements constantly, resulting in more fixation points and larger hot areas.

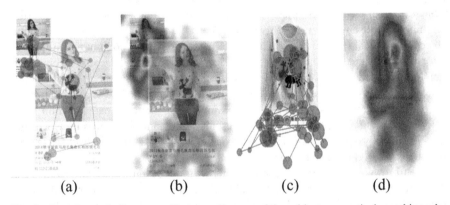

(a)   (b)   (c)   (d)

Fig. 3. Scanning path diagram and hot area diagram of the subjects on vertical searching ads

4.5 The Analysis of the Relationship Between Other Dependent Variables and Eye Movement Indicators

The following results are obtained by one-way anova of each eye movement index on pleasure, trust and user behavior intention. As shown in Table 6, Users' pleasure, trust and behavioral intention can be reflected by eye movement indicators at the significant level of 0.1. The eye movement indicator that reflects pleasure is browsing duration, that reflect trust include average fixation duration and blink counts; and that reflect behavioral intention include average pupil diameter and average fixation duration.

Table 6. Results of one-way Anova of other dependent variables on eye movement indicators

Eye movement indicators	Pleasure		Trust		Behavioral intention	
	F	p	F	p	F	p
Average pupil diameter/mm	0.598	0.916	1.363	0.160	2.083	**0.007**
Fixation/count	1.162	0.288	0.491	0.956	0.991	0.472
Average fixation duration/ms	1.124	0.325	1.955	**0.015**	1.493	**0.094**
Blink/count	1.272	0.196	1.512	**0.092**	0.758	0.747
Saccade/count	1.239	0.221	1.340	0.170	0.943	0.527
Browsing duration/ms	1.797	**0.020**	0.713	0.788	1.103	0.351

This table shows that in the process of viewing vertical searching ads to complete the purchase, users need to draw more mental participate in decision-making due to their strong involvement. Users' eye movement behavior not only reflects obvious psychological feelings such as pleasure and trust, but also reflects users' behavioral intention. Hypothesis H6, H7, H8 and H9 were verified.

5   Conclusion

The development and application of presence technology can help to make up for the lack of interpersonal warmth and cold sense of unapproachable in the network. It can take into account the psychological demands of consumers and thus bring better user experience. In this paper, the influence of presence on the trust, pleasure and behavioral intention of customers is discussed by means of experimental research and subjective and objective measurement, which provides a new perspective for the designers and publishers of online advertisements.

The conclusions of this study are as follows:

1. When a customer checks vertical searching ads to complete the purchase, the ads with model display can help to reduce user's fixation counts, saccade counts, and shorten user's browsing duration, which will greatly improve the efficiency of user's information searching, and bring better user's experience on presence;

2. The behavior-assistance buttons in vertical searching ads can help to improve users' subjective self-presence, but has no significant influence on users' objective eye movement behavior;
3. The mouse interaction function of vertical searching ads can reduce the user's blink counts, illustrating that the interaction function can help users to analyze and extract information easily. However, as the dynamic picture caused an increase of the user's saccadic counts, fixation counts and an extend of the user's browsing duration, this element should be carefully applied in advertising design;
4. Presence positively influences users' behavioral intention through mediating variables of pleasure and trust.

References

Montes, G.L.: Is interaction the message? The effect of democratizing and non-democratizing interaction in video-conferencing small groups on social presence and quality of outcome. Technol.-Mediated Commun. (1), 187–223 (1992)

Peukert, C., Pfeiffer, J., Meißner, M., et al.: Shopping in virtual reality stores: the influence of immersion on system adoption. J. Manag. Inf. Syst. **36**(3), 755–788 (2019)

Jahng, H., Jain, K.T.: Effective design of electronic commerce environments: a proposed theory of congruence and an illustration, systems, man and cybermetics, Part A. IEEE Trans. Syst. Man Cybern. **30**, 456–471 (2000)

Xiaojun, Y., Xiaoxia, C., Zhengcao, C., et al.: Attentional bias towards threatening visual stimuli in a virtual reality-based visual search task. Acta Psychol. Sin. **50**(6), 622–636 (2018)

Quesnel, D., Riecke, B.E.: Are you awed yet? How virtual reality gives us awe and goose bumps. Front. Psychol. **9**(2), 158 (2018)

De La Rosa, S., Breidt, M.: Virtual reality: a new track in psychological research. Br. J. Psychol. **109**(3), 427–430 (2018)

Chuan-Hoo, T., Juliana, S., Chee, W.P.: An empirical assessment of second life vis-a-vis chatroom on media perceptual assessment and actual task performance. IEEE Trans. Eng. Manag. **59**(3), 379–389 (2012)

Namkee, P., Kwan, M.L., Seung-A, A.J., Sukhee, K.: Effects of pre-game stories on feelings of presence and evaluation of computer games. Int. J. Hum.-Comput. Stud. (68), 822–833 (2010)

Jeong, S.W., Chung, J.-E., Fiore, A.M.: The effects of shopping motivation and an experiential marketing approach on consumer responses toward small apparel retailers. Fashion Ind. Educ. **15**(2), 11–24 (2017)

Kaya, B., Behravesh, E., Abubakar, A.M., et al.: The moderating role of website familiarity in the relationships between e-service quality, e-satisfaction and e-loyalty. J. Internet Commer. **18**(4), 369–394 (2019)

Zhong, Q.: The research on Customer's online impulse purchase. Intelligence (21), 209 (2019)

Argo, J.J., Dahl, D.W.: Social influence in the retail context: a contemporary review of the literature. J. Retail. **96**(1), 25–39 (2020)

Jha, S., Balaji, M.S., Peck, J., et al.: The effects of environmental haptic cues on consumer perceptions of retailer warmth and competence. J. Retail. **96**(4), 590–605 (2020). https://doi.org/10.1016/j.jretai.2020.04.003

He, A., Gao, J.: A research on the influence of consumer's goodwill on word-of-mouth communication and negative information avoidance. J. Manag. **16**(1), 123 (2019)

Shatnawi, T., Ashour, L., Kakeesh, D.: Investigating the impact of atmospherics and online flow cues on visiting intentions: the case of Jordan'virtual tourist centre. Int. J. Electron. Mark. Retail. **11**(1), 1–23 (2020)

Zhao, H., Cai, Z., He, S.: A research on online interaction and impulse purchase of online commodity display bases on virtual perspective. J. Manag. **18**(01), 133–141 (2014)

Jiang, C., Zhao, H., Meng, L.: A research on B2C online shopping interaction and consumers impulsive purchas. Explor. Econ. Probl. (5), 64–73 (2014)

Sajjadi, P., Hoffmann, L., Cimiano, P., et al.: A personality-based emotional model for embodied conversational agents: effects on perceived social presence and game experience of users. Entertainment Comput. **32**, 100313 (2019). https://doi.org/10.1016/j.entcom.2019.100313

Heng, S., Zhao, H., Sun, L., et al.: The personification effect of virtual sales agency. Adv. Psychol. Sci. **27**(05), 884–904 (2019)

Guitart, I.A., Hervet, G., Hildebrand, D.: Using eye-tracking to understand the impact of multi-tasking on memory for banner ads: the role of attention to the ad. Int. J. Advert. **38**(1), 154–170 (2019)

Xu, J., Wang, H.: A review of eye tracking studies in readding behavior. Science **28**(2), 52 (2020)

Van Hooijdonk, R., Mathot, S., Schat, E., et al.: Touch-induced pupil size reflects stimulus intensity, not subjective pleasantness. Exp. Brain Res. **237**(1), 201–210 (2019)

Gefen, D., Straub, D.W.: Consumer trust in B2C e-commerce and the importance of social presence: experiments in e-products and e-services. Omega **32**(6), 407–424 (2004). https://doi.org/10.1016/j.omega.2004.01.006

Gefen, D., Karahanna, E., Straub, D.W.: Trust and TAM in online shopping: an integrated model. MIS Q. **27**(1), 51–90 (2003)

Wang, Q., Zheng, C., Zhou, G.: An empirical study on the relationship between B2C website design factors and initial trust. J. Manag. **6**(4), 495–501 (2009)

Hu, L., Bentler, P.M.: Cutoff criteria for fit indexes in covariance structure analysis: conventional criteria versus new alternatives. Struct. Equ. Model. **6**(1), 1–55 (1999)

Raykov, T.: Estimation of composite reliability for congeneric measures. Appl. Psychol. Meas. **21**(2), 173–184 (1997)

Influence of HNB Product Packaging Health Warning Design on Risk Perception Based on Eye Tracking

Lili Sun[1], Lizhong Hu[1], Feng Zheng[1], Yue Sun[2], Huai Cao[2], and Lei Wu[2(✉)]

[1] Anhui Key Laboratory of Tobacco Chemistry, Anhui Tobacco Industrial Co., Ltd., Hefei 230088, People's Republic of China
[2] School of Mechanical Science and Engineering, Huazhong University of Science and Technology, Wuhan 430074, People's Republic of China
lei.wu@hust.edu.cn

Abstract. This paper reports on an experimental psychology study in the field of HNB packaging design, which used to measure the influence of health warning design on consumer's risk perception. Based on eye tracking method, we conducted an experimental design. The independent variables were the presentation form of the health warning design (text warning, picture warning). The dependent variable included the eye movement data and subjective scores. A total of 68 subjects participated in the experiment. The main finding of this study were as follows: (1) the presentation form of the health warning design significant affects the consumer' visual attention; (2) picture warning has stronger visual impact than text warning which easier to stimulate the user's pupil diameter; (3) the presentation form of the health warning design significant affects the consumer' risk perception. Furthermore, the research results provide an approach of using eye-tracking evaluation method in the relevant consumer products packaging design field.

Keywords: Health warning · Eye tracking · Risk perception · Packaging design

1 Introduction

With the implementation of the WHO framework convention on tobacco control, especially the gradual expansion of smoking bans in public places around the world, global tobacco control actions continue to advance [1]. The tobacco epidemic is one of the most serious public health problems in the world. The current tobacco epidemic causes more than 5 million deaths each year. If effective tobacco control measures not taken, the annual death will exceed 8 million by 2030. China has more than 300 million smokers and more than one million deaths per year from smoking-related diseases [2]. Therefore, tobacco control has become an important issue of public health in China.

Nowadays, HNB product (Heat-not-burn) have become an important replacement product to traditional cigarette, because it can bring the same taste as real cigarettes while reducing the harm to the human body. Various studies have shown that its safety

© Springer Nature Switzerland AG 2021
V. G. Duffy (Ed.): HCII 2021, LNCS 12778, pp. 390–402, 2021.
https://doi.org/10.1007/978-3-030-77820-0_29

is higher than traditional cigarettes. The advantage of HNB product are as follows: ①
No need to burn, greatly reducing the harmful components produced by combustion,
and less harmful than traditional cigarettes; ② No second-hand smoke is produced, and
it is not harmful to the public environments; ③ High safety, avoiding the open flame
of traditional cigarettes. Research from the Royal College of Medicine in the UK has
been committed the impact of HNB product on the human body is significantly lower
than that of traditional cigarettes. In terms of emissions, HNB product account for 5% of
traditional cigarettes. From the perspective of cytotoxicity, HNB product are only 14%
of traditional cigarettes.

Smoking behavior and motivation are complex and influenced by many environmental and situational factors. For products that are potentially harmful to consumers,
warnings labels on packaging are important tools that be used in public health policies
[3, 4]. Such warnings and disclosure of information can inform consumers of the risks
and potential dangers associated with product use. Public health researchers believe
that warning labels are part of the education process, which aims to provide consumers
with information to influence their attitudes, intentions and behaviors. Many countries
in the world have enacted laws to regulate the tobacco packaging design. For example,
The United States, Australia and European Union have printed serialization of warning
pictures on cigarette packaging and introduced tobacco plain packaging. For tobacco
use, key policy issues include informing consumers of the risks of smoking, trying to
persuade smokers to reduce smoking behavior. However, in this paper, an experiment
carried out by using the eye tracking technology, in order to explore the influence of
consumer's visual attention and risk perception of the health warning in different HNB
product packaging design.

2 Literature Review

In recent of research literature on eye movement evaluation of consumer packaging
design, Li (2019) proved through eye movement tests that the position of the product
on the shelf, the shelf area occupied and the color of the packaging have a greater
impact on visual attention. Product packaging located in the upper part of the shelf,
occupying a relatively large area and forming a strong color contrast with the surrounding
products is easy to be noticed [5]. Zhang (2019) extracted key design elements that
affect consumer emotions in product packaging design through eye movement indicators,
obtains consumers' perceptual image evaluation through semantic difference method
[6]. Cheng (2016) analyzed the perceptual factors in packaging design with Kansei
engineering methods, understands user's psychological perceptions [7]. Zhang (2018)
perfected the design and optimization of ceramic packaging containers for food by
applying the concepts of Kansei engineering and Kano model [8]. Zhao (2009) studied
the potential value of eye tracking in packaging design evaluation [9].

The current research based on eye tracking in the field of cigarette packaging design
was as follows. Sillero (2021) examined how cigarette pack features affected visual attention and self-reported avoidance of and reactance to warnings [10]. Zhu (2015) studied
the cognition of smoking group to different tobacco warning label, and compared the
warning effectiveness with different warning label [11]. Byrne (2018) examined whether

patterns of visual attention to graphic warning labels on images of cigarette packs predict key outcomes associated with warning label effectiveness [12]. Ranney (2019) used eye tracking method to test the effectiveness of messages about the harmful chemicals in cigarettes smoke among adult smokers. Find out that anti-smoking messages, containing chemical information, can successfully increase negative attitudes toward smoking cigarettes and potentially encourage quitting [13]. Londerée (2018) examined the relationship between adolescent attentional bias and willingness to try flavored e-cigarettes. The result showed that flavored e-cigarette marketing attracts the attention of adolescents, increases their willingness to try flavored e-cigarette products [14]. Nonnemaker (2018) used eye-tracking to examine how little cigar and cigarillo (LCC) pack features influence adults' (aged 18–34) visual attention to warning labels [15]. From the related research, that eye tracking technology provides a scientific and objective basis for the users' visual attention to packaging design. However, there are not enough eye tracking evaluation studies on the risk perception of the health warning design of HNB product packaging.

3   Experiment Method

3.1   Definition

In order to confirm the following hypotheses, we designed an experimental psychology study. In this paper, we measure consumers' visual attention and risk perception using eye-tracking data (objective metric) combined with a subjective questionnaire (subjective metric). The independent variables were the presentation form of the health warning design (text warning, picture warning). The dependent variable included the participants' eye movement data (AOI time to first fixation, AOI first fixation duration, AOI total fixation duration, AOI the second fixation time, pupil diameter). The subjective scores collected by the five-point Likert scale questionnaire. This paper use three subjective indicators to measure the risk perception: 1) perceived significance of warning design (significance); 2) perceive the severity of smoking hazards (severity); 3) reduce the willingness to smoking (reduce smoking). The control variable is the brand type.

3.2   Hypothesis

The main hypothesis of this study are as follows:

H1: The presentation form of the health warning design (text warning, picture warning) affects the consumer' visual attention.
H2: The presentation form of the health warning design (text warning, picture warning) affects the consumer' risk perception.

3.3   Stimuli

The packaging design of "TOOP" HNB product in Anhui Tobacco Industrial from different countries adopted (Including six countries: China, Japan, Korea, Thailand, Russia and France). The packaging of China and Japan belong to the form of text warning, and the packaging of Korea, Russia, Thailand, and France is belong to the form of picture warning. As shown in Fig. 1.

| 中国 China | 日本 Japan | 韩国 Korea | 泰国 Thailand | 俄罗斯 Russia | 法国 France |

Fig. 1. Six form of the health warning design in the experiment

3.4 Equipment and Environment

The Tobii X300 desktop eye tracker manufacture from Sweden used in this experiment (300 Hz, 23-inch screen size, 16: 9 screen resolution, 1920*1080 pixels). The eye tracking experiment carried out in a quiet and undisturbed indoor laboratory. The participants sat in front of the eye tracker with their eyes facing the center of the screen and the distance between the eyes and the screen was about 40 cm–50 cm. Desk and monitor position and height fixed. The chair was adjustment to fit participant's natural angles of elbow and knee. Participants instructed to switch off their mobile phones to reduce possible distractions. As shown in Fig. 2.

Fig. 2. The participant in the experiment and the environment

3.5 Participants

A total of 68 participants randomly selected to participate in this experiment. Male subjects accounted for 77.94% of the study, female subjects accounted for the remaining 22.06%. The age distribution is 20–30 years old, 30–40 years old and over 40 years old, accounting for 42.65%, 35.29%, and 22.06% respectively. On the smoking status, there are 38 smokers, accounting for 55.88%, and 30 non-smokers, accounting for 44.12% of the total number. All participants had normal or corrected-to-normal color vision. None of the participants had prior eye surgeries or eye problems such as "droopy" eyelids. The specific groups shown in Table 1.

Table 1. The categories of the 68 effective participants in this experiment

Gender	Male		Female
	53 people (77.94%)		15 people (22.06%)
Age	20–30 years old	30–40 years old	Over 40 years old
	29 people (42.65%)	24 people (35.29%)	15 people (22.06%)
Smoking status	Smoker		Non-smoker
	38 people (55.88%)		30 people (44.12%)

3.6 Procedure

Before the experiment began, participants asked to read an introduction of the experiment requirements and then sign the "experimental consent". Next, they read a short manual about the experiment stimuli to insure they were able to understand and solve the given task. When the participant was ready, we started the eye-tracking experiment. We designed a within-subjects study design with 68 participants. All participants were involved in the six eye-tracking task (China, Japan, Korea, Thailand, Russia and France). Each picture of HNB product packaging design randomly presented, allowing users to observe freely in 10 s, and collect participants' eye movement data. Data gather by the eye tracker analyzed using Ergo Lab 3.0. After the tasks were finished, participants completed the subjective evaluation questionnaire. Finally, 68 participants completed all the 408 tasks (68 participants * 6 tasks).

4 Experiment Results

4.1 Heat Map and Gaze Plot Visualization

Firstly, the participants' attention behavior visually displayed through qualitative analysis visualization, such as heat map and gaze plot. By using different colors to display the number of gaze points of the subject. Red indicates that the fixation duration is longer; green indicates the fixation duration is the shorter. It can help researchers understand which visual elements of packaging design are most concerned or easily ignored. Gaze plot can record the coordinates and sequence of eye movements, which can help the researcher explore the pattern of the participants' eye movement. The health warning design area of the text warning type is more distracted, while the logo area attracts longer and more concentrated attention. The health warning design area of the picture warning type attracts most of the participants' attention with large pictures, thereby increasing the heat intensity, as shown in Fig. 3.

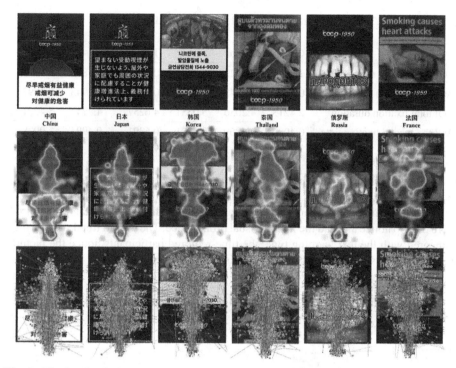

Fig. 3. The first line is the experimental stimuli; the second line is the heat map visualization; the third line is the gaze plot visualization.

4.2   Eye Tracking Data in AOI

The experimental materials divided into two types of health warning designs. The warning in China and Japan are belong to text warning types, and the Korea, Thailand, Russia and France are picture warning types. We calculated the average value of eye tracking data (AOI time to first fixation, AOI first fixation duration, AOI total fixation duration, AOI the second fixation time) when 68 participants observe the health warning design of HNB product packaging.

The specific numerical distribution is as follows: (1) AOI time to first fixation (China = 1.58 s, Japan = 0.56 s, Korea = 0.37 s, Thailand = 0.32 s, Russia = 0.59 s, France = 0.30 s). (2) AOI first fixation duration (China = 0.19 s, Japan = 0.19 s, Korea = 0.44 s, Thailand = 0.42 s, Russia = 0.19 s, France = 0.39 s). (3) AOI total fixation duration (China = 2.42 s, Japan = 4.21 s, Korea = 5.04 s, Thailand = 4.63 s, Russia = 4.87 s, France = 5.43 s). (4) AOI the second fixation time (China = 0.40 s, Japan = 0.49 s, Korea = 0.59 s, Thailand = 0.64 s, Russia = 0.50 s, France = 1.09 s), as shown in Table 2.

AOI Time to First Fixation: The time from the start of the stimulus to the first time the participant looked at the AOI. The data showed that the AOI time to first fixation of France packaging is the shortest, followed by Thailand packaging, Korea packaging, Japan packaging and Russia packaging. China packaging has the longest AOI time to

Table 2. Eye tracking data of health warning design AOI (s)

	China	Japan	Korea	Thailand	Russia	France
AOI time to first fixation	1.5825	0.5622	0.3700	0.3219	0.5878	0.3010
AOI first fixation duration	0.1881	0.1943	0.4359	0.4207	0.1943	0.3897
AOI total fixation duration	2.4213	4.2050	5.0351	4.6257	4.8743	5.4281
AOI the second fixation time	0.4000	0.4869	0.5871	0.6391	0.4994	1.0938

first fixation. The result showed that the average time from the start of the stimulation to the first time the participants looked at the France packaging was the shortest, which quickly attracted the participants' visual attention, while the China packaging required more time to notice and had the lowest visual prominence. The overall trend showed that compared with the text warning type, the time-required participants notice the picture warning type is shorter, and obtain higher visibility, as shown in Fig. 4.

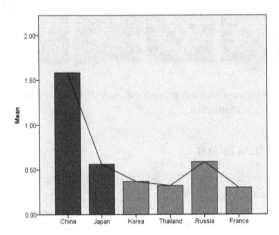

Fig. 4. AOI time to first fixation of health warning design (s)

AOI First Fixation Duration: The duration of the participants' first fixation point in the area of interest. The data showed that the AOI first fixation duration of Korea packaging is the longest, followed by Thailand packaging, France packaging, Russia packaging and Japan packaging. China packaging has the shortest AOI first fixation duration. This showed that the participants have the longest average duration of their first visual focus when observing Korea packaging, and its first user engagement is the largest, while the first user engagements of China packaging, Japan packaging are significantly smaller. The overall trend showed that compared with the text warning type, the participants observe the picture warning type is longer, and can generate greater visual interest, as shown in Fig. 5.

AOI Total Fixation Duration: The total time of the participants in all fixation points in the area of interest. The data trend showed that the AOI total fixation duration of France

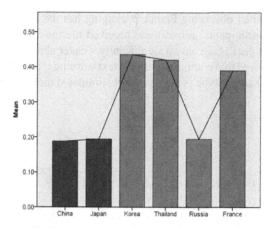

Fig. 5. AOI first fixation duration of health warning design (s)

packaging is the longest, followed by Korea packaging, Russia packaging, Thailand packaging and Japan packaging. China packaging has the shortest AOI total fixation duration. This showed that the participants have the longest time of all their visual attention when observing France packaging, which is the most attractive, while China packaging and Japan packaging are significantly less attractive. The overall data showed that compared with the text warning, the participants observe the picture warning type is longer, and it is easier to attract the user's visual attention, as shown in Fig. 6.

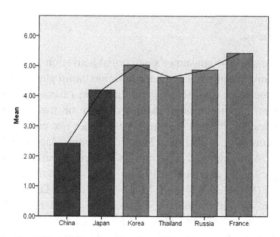

Fig. 6. AOI total fixation duration of health warning design (s)

AOI The Second Fixation Time: The time of the second fixation in the area of interest. That is the duration of the second fixation point. The data trend showed that the AOI the second fixation time of France packaging is the longest, followed by Thailand packaging, Korea packaging, Russia packaging and Japan packaging. China packaging has the shortest AOI the second fixation time. This showed that the second focus point of the participants when observing France packaging has the longest duration, which has stimulated the participants' interest and received the most attention, while China packaging and Japan packaging have a significantly weaker ability to stimulate interest. The overall trend showed that compared with the text warning type, when the participants observe the picture warning type is longer, and it stimulated more participants' interest, as shown in Fig. 7.

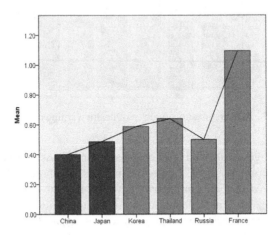

Fig. 7. AOI the second fixation time of health warning design (s)

4.3 Pupil Diameter

Pupil Diameter represents the consumer's emotional activation level, contains the average pupil diameter, minimum pupil diameter, and maximum pupil diameter. This paper calculated the average value of different pupil diameters (average pupil diameter, minimum pupil diameter, maximum pupil diameter) when 68 participants observe HNB product packaging design. The text warning type includes two countries, China packaging (Mean = 3.08 mm, Min = 2.52 mm, Max = 3.47 mm); Japan packaging (Mean = 3.20 mm, Min = 2.56 mm, Max = 3.58 mm). The picture warning type includes four countries: Korea packaging (Mean = 3.19 mm, Min = 2.58 mm, Max = 3.55 mm); Thailand packaging (Mean = 3.24 mm, Min = 2.57 mm, Max = 3.63 mm); Russia packaging (Mean = 3.09 mm, Min = 2.54 mm, Max = 3.51 mm); France packaging (Mean = 3.23 mm, Min = 2.61 mm, Max = 3.63 mm), as shown in Table 3.

The data trend showed that the average pupil diameter of Thailand packaging is the largest, followed by France packaging, Japan packaging, Korea packaging, Russia packaging and China packaging. It indicates that compared with the text warning type, the average pupil diameter when the participants observe the picture warning type is larger. Studies have shown that changes in pupil diameter closely related to consumers' emotional activation. Since warning picture has stronger visual impact than text warning, it is easier to stimulate the user's pupil diameter, as shown in Fig. 8.

Table 3. The average value of different pupil diameters (mm)

	China	Japan	Korea	Thailand	Russia	France
Average pupil diameter	3.0768	3.2046	3.1868	3.2365	3.0910	3.2349
Minimum pupil diameter	2.5199	2.5575	2.5807	2.5738	2.5372	2.6104
Maximum pupil diameter	3.4699	3.5825	3.5534	3.6256	3.5078	3.6328

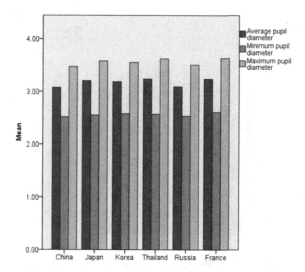

Fig. 8. Different pupil diameters of health warning design (mm)

4.4 Subjective Evaluation

Finally, we calculated the average values of the subjective evaluation perceived by 68 participants. The data showed that the average of subjective evaluation is: (1) the text warning type includes two countries, China packaging (significance = 3.59, severity = 3.32, reduce smoking = 2.94); Japan packaging (significance = 3.25, severity = 3.00, reduce smoking = 2.69). (2) The picture warning type includes four countries, Korea packaging (significance = 4.21, severity = 4.25, reduce smoking = 4.09); Thailand packaging (significance = 4.16, severity = 4.38, reduce smoking = 4.18); Russia packaging (significance = 3.96, severity = 4.09, reduce smoking = 3.99); France packaging (significance = 3.62, severity = 3.68, reduce smoking = 3.59).

The data trend showed that the picture warning design of HNB product packaging design has stronger significance (3.99 points), severity (4.1 points) and reduce smoking (3.96 points). The text warning design of HNB product packaging design has lower significance (3.42 points), severity (3.16 points) and reduce smoking (2.82 points). The result showed that compared with the text warning type, the warning design perceived by the participants through the picture warning type are more significant and the severity of smoking hazards, and for consumers to change their smoking attitudes and reduce their willingness to smoke, as shown in Table 4, Fig. 9.

Table 4. The average value of subjective evaluation (point)

	China	Japan	Korea	Thailand	Russia	France
Significance	3.5882	3.2500	4.2059	4.1618	3.9559	3.6176
Severity	3.3235	3.0000	4.2500	4.3824	4.0882	3.6765
Reduce smoking	2.9412	2.6912	4.0882	4.1765	3.9853	3.5882

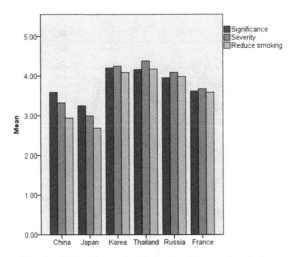

Fig. 9. Subjective evaluation of health warning design

5 Conclusion

Traditional user testing methods and performance measurements may indicate that the user has a problem or obstacle, but do not explain the "problem of why" or reveal the implicit cognitive process. Researchers in the data age can make design decisions based on data analysis. The development of quantitative data collection such as eye tracking has changed the way researchers think and the research perspective of experience design. Based on eye tracking method, we conducted an experimental design. The independent variables were the presentation form of the health warning design (text warning, picture warning). The dependent variable included the eye movement data and subjective scores. A total of 68 subjects participated in the experiment. The main findings of this study were as follows:

(1) The presentation form of the health warning design significant affects the consumer' visual attention. The AOI time to first fixation is shorter and higher visibility for picture warning than text warning. The AOI first fixation duration is longer, and can generate more first user engagements for picture warning than text warning. The AOI total fixation duration of picture warning is longer than text warning, and it is easier to attract the user's visual attention. The AOI the second fixation time is

longer in picture warning, and it stimulated more participants' interest for picture warning than text warning.

(2) The picture warning has stronger visual impact than text warning. The picture warning is easier to stimulate the user's pupil diameter.

(3) The presentation form of the health warning design significant affects the consumer' risk perception. Picture warning allows participants to feel the significant and the severity of smoking hazards more than text warning and it is easier for consumers to change their smoking attitudes and reduce their willingness to smoke.

HNB product packaging regulations are constantly being strictly in the world. This research could help academia to evaluate consumers' risk perceptions of the health warning design and the mechanism of their psychological impact on consumers. However, this study still has some limitations: (1) 77.94% of the participants were male, so the feedback to female users may need to be further research; (2) the study based on the eye tracking and Likert scale method. Future research may include other biofeedback measures, such as EEG and other physiological signal. Although this study has its limitations, we hope that it can serve as a basis for the future research.

Acknowledgments. The research supported by research on quantification analysis technology of eye tracking in user experience of HNB product (project number: 202034000034009). Lili Sun & Lizhong Hu contributed equally to this work and considered co-first authors.

References

1. World Health Organization: WHO report on the global tobacco epidemic, 2008: the MPOWER package. World Health Organization (2008)
2. China reported health hazards of smoking. http://www.gov.cn/jrzg/2012-05/31/content_2149 305.htm. Accessed 31 May 2012
3. Bettman, J.R., Payne, J.W., Staelin, R.: Cognitive considerations in designing effective labels for presenting risk information. J. Public Policy Mark. **5**(1), 1–28 (1986)
4. Martin, I.: Consumer response to warnings and other types. Handbook of Marketing and Society, p. 335 (2000)
5. Li, D.: Research on visual attention of product packaging on shelves based on eye movement measurement technology. J. Beijing Inf. Sci. Technol. Univ. **34**(03), 79–83 (2019)
6. Zhang, Y., Hou, Y., Li, H.: Analysis of packaging design elements based on eye tracking technology and quantitation theory. Food Mach. **35**(04), 113–119 (2019)
7. Cheng, C.: A feasibility study of kansei engineering in packaging design. Packag. Eng. **37**(04), 14–17 (2016)
8. Zhang, Y.: Design of ceramic containers products for food packaging based on kansei engineering. Food Mach. **34**(07), 115–120 (2018)
9. Zhao, W.: The function of research on measuring eye movement in the value evaluation of packaging design. Art Des. **09**, 102–103 (2009)
10. Sillero-Rejon, C., et. al.: Avoidance of tobacco health warnings? An eye-tracking approach. Addiction **116**(1), 126–138 (2021)
11. Zhu, G., Wu, Y.: The eye-tracking of cigarette warning label design. Packag. Eng. **36**(06), 97–99+104 (2015)

12. Byrne, S., Kalaji, M., Niederdeppe, J.: Does visual attention to graphic warning labels on cigarette packs predict key outcomes among youth and low-income smokers? Tobacco Regul. Sci. **4**(6), 18–37 (2018)
13. Ranney, L.M., Kowitt, S.D., Queen, T.L., Jarman, K.L., Goldstein, A.O.: An eye tracking study of anti-smoking messages on toxic chemicals in cigarettes. Int. J. Environ. Res. Public Health **16**(22), 4435 (2019)
14. Londerée, A.M., Roberts, M.E., Wewers, M.E., Peters, E., Ferketich, A.K., Wagner, D.D.: Adolescent attentional bias toward real-world flavored e-cigarette marketing. Tobacco Regul. Sci. **4**(6), 57–65 (2018)
15. Nonnemaker, J.M., et al.: Adults' visual attention to little cigar and cigarillo package warning labels and effect on recall and risk perceptions. Tobacco Regul. Sci. **4**(6), 47–56 (2018)

The Influence of the Aesthetic Design of Taobao APP on Users' Emotional Experience

Yimeng Zhang, Yang Zhang, and Jiaojiao Gao[✉]

School of Economics and Management, Anhui Polytechnic University, Beijing Central Road. 8, Wuhu 241000, China

Abstract. On the basis of previous researchers' impact of image aesthetics design on user purchasing behavior, this article uses classic aesthetics, performance aesthetics, S-Q-R and other theories from the perspective of user emotional experience to classify products into search and experience types, and analyze its influence mechanism on user emotional experience and purchase decision in different forms. This article summarizes the questionnaire based on the related theories of APP aesthetic design and user emotional experience in human factors engineering, determine the independent variables (different types of aesthetic design: symmetrical simple, symmetrical complex, asymmetrical simple, asymmetrical complex) and dependent variables (user's emotional experience and purchase decision), and the questionnaire survey divides Taobao APP interface design into four types: symmetrical simple, symmetrical complex, asymmetrical simple, and asymmetrical complex, and discusses using repeated measures two-factor analysis of variance. Finally, it is concluded that the asymmetric design of search products can make users have greater desire to buy, and the asymmetric and complex design of experience products can make users have greater desire to buy. The research results of this paper are the perfection and supplement of APP emotional design and human factors engineering theory and methods. The application of research results is of great significance for guiding APP design, improving APP user experience and enhancing APP competitiveness.

Keywords: Taobao APP aesthetics design · Expressive aesthestics · User emotional experience · Purchase decision

1 Introduction

As of June 2020, the number of monthly active users of my country's mobile Internet has reached 1.155 billion, and the monthly active users of Taobao Tmall mobile reached 742 million, an increase of 119 million compared with last year. In the past ten years, with the increasing number of online shopping users, various shopping apps have appeared one after another. As the influential Taobao APP shopping software, if you want Taobao online stores to continue to attract consumers under fierce market competition, interface design is very important, and aesthetic design is an important part of interface design. It allows users to resonate emotionally when they first see the app, and improves users'

© Springer Nature Switzerland AG 2021
V. G. Duffy (Ed.): HCII 2021, LNCS 12778, pp. 403–414, 2021.
https://doi.org/10.1007/978-3-030-77820-0_30

purchasing decisions on Taobao. Based on the actual situation, this paper uses questionnaires to get the influence of different types of aesthetic design on the user's emotional experience and purchase decision.

Han Fangfang [1] pointed out that aesthetics is getting more and more attention in web design. Through questionnaire and observation methods, it is concluded that the classic aesthetics of product pictures are negatively related to consumers' arousal, and performance aesthetics is positively related to consumers' arousal; classic aesthetics and performance aesthetics can improve consumers Comparing with the pictures of functional products, the experience-based product pictures are more awakening to customers, and the functional products pay more attention to customers, Yan Huimin [2] experimental results show that the interface layout is a palace-like frame, and the interface design with high brightness, saturation and light background has the highest evaluation. Bhandari [3] proposed the influence of visual aesthetics on user evaluation. The conclusion is that the underlying reasons for users to choose certain applications are applications based on aesthetic evaluation and "emotional" responses. The downside is that different categories bring different design types, and it is not absolutely certain which emotions are at work; Huang Li [4] fully considered the user experience in the process of APP interface design. Wang Lei and Guo Hang [5] showed that APP interface design has a greater impact on user emotional experience.

At present, the research in this area is difficult to achieve the aesthetic design expected by users. Few researchers compare symmetry and asymmetry in classic aesthetics. The simplicity and complexity in performance aesthetics are compared, and many researchers have only proposed certain ideas, but they have not proposed specific methods to improve user emotional experience and purchasing decisions.

2   Method

2.1   Research Design

For this research, first, the purpose of the questionnaire survey is to understand the impact of different types of aesthetics (classic aesthetics, performance aesthetics) of Taobao APP interface on user emotions and purchasing decisions.

Independent variable: Different types of aesthetic design (symmetrical simple, symmetrical complex, asymmetrical simple, asymmetrical complex), Dependent variable: user's emotional experience, purchase decision.

The survey content is based on the assumption of certain price, quality and other conditions, users need to buy two types of products: search-type products and experience-type products (the photos of the products have been placed, and each is divided into four types of aesthetic design, including symmetrical simple, symmetrical complex, asymmetrical simple, non-Symmetrical and complex). The questionnaire includes a total of 8 pictures, four of which are shown in the figure below (Fig. 1):

The purpose of this design is to ensure that users really need to buy the product, and to exclude the influence of other factors such as price and quality. Investigate people's judgments on classic aesthetics and performance aesthetics, and if the judgment is the same as the answer expected in your mind, the subsequent investigation is meaningful;

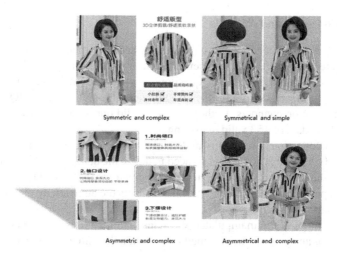

Fig. 1. Four different types of pictures

Then investigate the relationship between the four aesthetic designs of each type of product and user emotions and purchasing decisions.

2.2 Participants

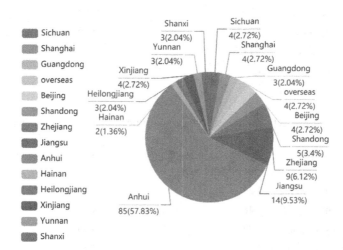

Fig. 2. Geographical distribution of the questionnaire

In Fig. 2, It is known that Anhui Province has the largest number of people completing the questionnaire, with a rate of 57.52%; Hainan Province has the smallest number of people completing the questionnaire, with a rate of 1.31%.

2.3 Data Collection and Analysis

First, Investigate people's judgments on symmetry and asymmetry, simple and complex, and investigate the impact of the aesthetic design of pictures on users' emotional experience and purchasing decisions; The questionnaire uses the "Wenjuanxing" website as a research platform, and distributes the questionnaire through WeChat, QQ, Weibo and other communication channels. In the end, 12 invalid questionnaires were eliminated. We analyzed the data of 153 valid questionnaires.

After data collection, a reliability and validity analysis is performed and it is found that Alpha = 0.981 > 0.8, so there is no need to delete the data. The value of the correlation between the revised item and the total is far greater than 0.3, and the questionnaire data can also pass the validity test well, which reflects the authenticity and reliability of the questionnaire.

The verification of the manipulated variables, and then uses the repeated measurement two-factor analysis of variance method to obtain the influence of different types of aesthetic designs on user emotions and purchasing decisions.

For experiential products and search products, users' judgments on symmetry and asymmetry, as well as simplicity and complexity:

Table 1. Experiential products -symmetrical and asymmetrical, simple and complex judgments

Aesthetic design type	Average score for symmetry and asymmetry	Simple and complex average score
Symmetrical and simple	3.61	4.97
Symmetrical and complex	3.84	3.96
Asymmetrical simplicity	4.24	4.58
Asymmetric and complex	4.39	3.86

Table 2. Search products -symmetrical and asymmetrical, simple and complex judgments

Aesthetic design type	Average score for symmetry and asymmetry	Simple and complex average score
Symmetrical and simple	4.24	5.06
Symmetrical and complex	4.48	4.16
Asymmetrical simplicity	4.73	4.99
Asymmetric and complex	4.48	4.18

The average score of symmetrical and asymmetrical, simple and complex judgments varies from 1 to 7. The larger the number, the more it shows that it is consistent with the default answer in your mind. In Table 1 and Table 2, it can be seen that the numbers are all greater than 3.5. It is learned that users' symmetrical and asymmetrical, simple and complex judgments of experiential products and Search products conform to their own assumptions. Therefore, it is meaningful to study the influence mechanism of website aesthetics design on purchase decision.

3 Result

3.1 Emotional Experience

The influence of experiential product and search-type product aesthetic design on emotional experience is divided into the influence on happiness, relaxation, fun, and pleasure, as follows:

For experiential product, after the within-subject effect test and analysis, the P value of classical aesthetics (F value is 1.862 and the error df value is 152) is 0.174, and the P value of performance aesthetics (F value is 6.222 and the error df value is 152) is 0.014, both The P value of the interaction effect (F value is 2.24, and the error df value is 152) is 0.137.

It is found that only the p-value of expressive aesthetics is $0.014 < 0.05$, so expressive aesthetics has a significant impact on the user's happy emotion. Because the performance aesthetics has a significant impact on the user's happy emotion. So there are the following studies:

In the comparison of simple and complex aesthetic design to happy emotions, it is found that the simple average value of performance aesthetics is 3.163, and the average value of complex performance aesthetics is 3.288. Therefore, complex designs in performance aesthetics make people feel more happy than simple designs.

After the within-subject effect test and analysis, the P value of classical aesthetics (F value is 6.055, the error df value is 152) is 0.015, and the P value of performance aesthetics (F value is 5.074, the error df value is 152) is 0.026, two The P value of the interaction effect (F value is 4.456 and the error df value is 152) is 0.036. It is found that the P value of the three is less than 0.05, so the three have a significant impact on the user's emotion-easy. So there are the following studies:

In the comparison of symmetrical and asymmetrical aesthetic design to relaxed emotions, it is found that the average value of symmetry in classic aesthetics is 3.271, and the average value of asymmetry in classic aesthetics is 3.386. Therefore, in the classic aesthetics, asymmetrical design is more relaxing than symmetrical design.

In the comparison of simple and complex aesthetic design to relaxed emotions, it is found that the simple average value of performance aesthetics is 3.268, and the average value of complex performance aesthetics is 3.389. Therefore, in the performance aesthetics, a complex design is more relaxing than a simple design.

In Fig. 3, it can be seen that a simple asymmetric design will make users feel more relaxed than a simple symmetrical design. Compared with a complex asymmetric design, the difference between a complex symmetrical design and a complex asymmetrical design on the user's ease of emotion is not different. Big. When the symmetrical design is gradually converted to asymmetrical design, the user's ease of emotion is gradually increasing.

After the within-subject effect test and analysis, the P value of classical aesthetics (F value is 16.820, df value of error is 152) is 0.000, and the P value of performance

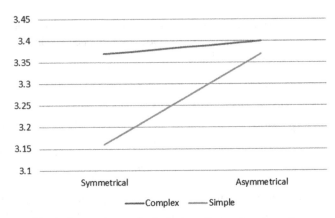

Fig. 3. Interactive aesthetic design affects relaxed emotions

aesthetics (F value is 10.536, df value of error is 152) is 0.001. The P value of the interaction effect between the two (F value is 0.005, error df value is 152) is 0.945. It is found that the P value of both classic aesthetics and performance aesthetics is less than 0.05, and the P value of the interaction effect between the two is greater than 0.05.

Therefore, the classic aesthetics and performance aesthetics have a significant impact on the user's emotion-interesting, and the interactive effects of the two have no significant impact on the user's emotion-interesting. So there are the following studies:

In the comparison of symmetrical and asymmetrical aesthetic design to interesting emotions, it is found that the average value of symmetry in classic aesthetics is 2.997, and the average average value of asymmetry in classic aesthetics is 3.222. Therefore, the asymmetrical design in the classic aesthetics makes people feel more interesting than the symmetrical design.

In the simple and complex aesthetic design compares interesting emotions, it is found that the simple average value of performance aesthetics is 3.010, and the average value of complex performance aesthetics is 3.190. Therefore, in the performance aesthetics, a complex design is more interesting than a simple design.

After the within-subject effect test and analysis, the P value of classical aesthetics (F value is 7.110, the error df value is 152) is 0.008, and the P value of performance aesthetics (F value is 3.103, the error df value is 152) is 0.08, The P value of the interaction effect between the two (F value is 0.063 and the error df value is 152) is 0.803. It is found that only the p-value of classic aesthetics is less than 0.05, so classic aesthetics has a significant impact on user emotion-pleasure; performance aesthetics and the interactive effects of the two have no significant impact on user emotion-pleasure. Therefore, which of the simple and complex aesthetic designs is more pleasant to the user.

In the comparison of symmetrical and asymmetrical aesthetic design to pleasure emotions, the average value of symmetry in classic aesthetics is 3.167, and the average value of asymmetry in classic aesthetics is 3.304. Therefore, asymmetrical design is more pleasant than symmetrical design in classic aesthetics.

For search products, after an analysis of within-subject effects, the P value of classical aesthetics (F value is 455.057, error df value is 152) is 0.000, and the P value of performance aesthetics (F value is 450.803, error df value is 152) is 0.000, The P value of the interaction effect between the two (F value is 450.387 and the error df value is 152) is 0.000.

It is found that the P value of the three is less than 0.05, so the three have a significant impact on the user's emotion-happiness. So there are the following studies:

In the comparison of simple and complex aesthetic design to happiness, the simple average value of performance aesthetics is 3.598, and the average value of complex performance aesthetics is 41.797. Therefore, a complex design in the performance aesthetics will make users feel happier than a simple design.

In the comparison of symmetrical and asymmetrical aesthetic design to happiness, it is found that the average value of symmetry in classic aesthetics is 41.810, and the average value of asymmetry in classic aesthetics is 3.585. Therefore, symmetrical design in classic aesthetics will make users feel happier than asymmetrical design.

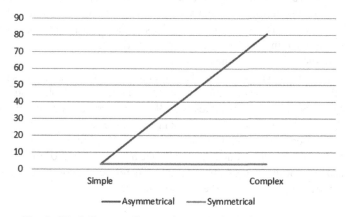

Fig. 4. The influence of interactive aesthetic design on happiness

In Fig. 4, there is no difference between asymmetric and simple design and asymmetric and complex design on the impact of user happiness. Symmetrical and complex design makes users feel happier than symmetrical and simple design. Under the premise of simple design, Symmetrical and asymmetrical design is irrelevant to the user's happy emotions. Only under the premise of symmetry, the user's sense of happiness will increase when the user changes from simple to complex.

After the within-subject effect test and analysis, the P value of classical aesthetics (F value is 0.095, the error df value is 152) is 0.759, and the P value of performance aesthetics (F value is 0.899, the error df value is 152) is 0.344, The P value of the two interaction effects (F value is 0.483, error df value is 152) is 0.488. Because the P values of the three are greater than 0.05, all three have no significant impact on the user's emotion-relaxed.

After the within-subject effect test and analysis, the P value of classical aesthetics (F value is 0.726, error df value is 152) is 0.396, and the P value of performance aesthetics (F value is 0.000, error df value is 152) is 1, The P value of the two interaction effects (F value is 0.027, the error df value is 152) is 0.869. Because the P values of the three are greater than 0.05, all three have no significant impact on the user's emotion-interesting.

After the within-subject effect test and analysis, the P value of classical aesthetics (F value is 0.530, the error df value is 152) is 0.468, and the P value of performance aesthetics (F value is 0.08, the error df value is 152) is 0.778, The P value of the two interaction effects (F value is 0.029, and the error df value is 152) is 0.864. Because the P values of the three are greater than 0.05, all three have no significant influence on the user's emotion-pleasure.

3.2 Perceived Attractiveness

For experiential products, after the within-subject effect test and analysis, the P value of classical aesthetics (F value is 29.895, the error df value is 152) is 0.000, and the P value of performance aesthetics (F value is 23.474, the error df value is 152) is 0.000, The P value of the interaction effect between the two (F value is 9.411 and the error df value is 152) is 0.003. It is found that the P values of the three are less than 0.05, so the three have a significant impact on the user's perceived attractiveness.

So there are the following studies:

In the comparison of symmetrical and asymmetrical aesthetic design to perception, it is found that the average value of symmetry in classic aesthetics is 3.003, and the average value of asymmetry in classic aesthetics is 3.294. Therefore, asymmetrical designs are more attractive than symmetrical designs in classic aesthetics.

In the comparison of perception between simple and complex aesthetic design, it is found that the simple average value in performance aesthetics is 3.003, and the complex average value in performance aesthetics is 3.294. Therefore, the complex design is more attractive than the simple design in the performance aesthetics.

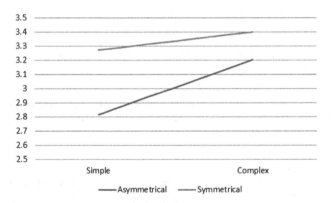

Fig. 5. The impact of interactive aesthetic design on perception

In Fig. 5, it is found that a symmetrical and complex design gives users greater perceptual attractiveness than a symmetrical and simple design. Asymmetrical and complex designs and asymmetrical and simple designs do not have much difference in perception of attractiveness to users. In the transition from simple design to complex design, the perceived attractiveness of users is increasing.

For search products, after an analysis of within-subject effects, the P value of classical aesthetics (F value is 1.209, df value of error is 152) is 0.273, and the P value of performance aesthetics (F value is 1.227, df value of error is 152) is 0.273, The P value of the two interaction effects (F value is 0.362, the error df value is 152) is 0.548. Because the P values of the three are greater than 0.05, all three have no significant influence on the user's perceived attractiveness.

3.3 Purchasing Decision

The influence of search-type product and search product aesthetics design on decision-making is divided into two types: the influence on meeting purchase requirements and the influence on willingness to purchase, as follows:

For experiential products, after the within-subject effect test and analysis, the P value of classical aesthetics (F value is 37.214, the error df value is 152) is 0.000, and the P value of performance aesthetics (F value is 30.495, the error df value is 152) is 0.000, The P value of the interaction effect between the two (F value is 9.076 and the error df value is 152) is 0.003. It is found that the P value of the three is less than 0.05, so the three have a significant impact on the user's purchase decision-meeting the purchase requirements. So there are the following studies:

In the comparison of simple and complex to meet purchase requirements, it is found that the simple average value of performance aesthetics is 2.807, and the average value of complex performance aesthetics is 3.137. Therefore, the complex design in the performance aesthetics will make people feel that the product is more in line with their purchase requirements than the simple design.

In the comparison of symmetrical and asymmetrical aesthetic design to meet purchase requirements, it is found that the average value of symmetry in classic aesthetics is 2.807, and the average value of asymmetry in classic aesthetics is 3.137. Therefore, in the classic aesthetics, asymmetrical design makes people feel that the product is more in line with their purchase requirements than symmetrical design.

In Fig. 6, users feel that the symmetrical and complex design is more in line with their purchase requirements than the symmetrical and simple design, and the asymmetrical and complex design is more in line with their purchase requirements than the asymmetrical and simple design. In the transition from simple design to complex design, users feel that products meet their purchase requirements are increasing.

After the within-subject effect test and analysis, the P value of classic aesthetics (F value is 26.892, the error df value is 152) is 0.000, and the P value of performance aesthetics (F value is 20.970, the error df value is 152) is 0.000, The P value of the two interaction effects (F value is 5.156, and the error df value is 152) is 0.025.

It is found that the P values of the three are less than 0.05, so the three have a significant impact on the user's purchase decision-willingness to purchase. So there are the following studies:

In the comparison of willingness to buy between symmetric and asymmetric pairs, it is found that the average value of symmetry in classic aesthetics is 2.814, and the average value of asymmetry in classic aesthetics is 3.114. Therefore, in the classic aesthetics,

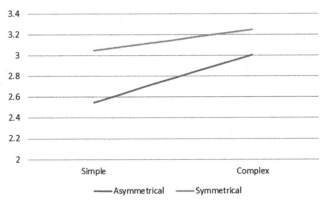

Fig. 6. The impact of interactive aesthetic design on meeting purchase requirements

asymmetrical design will make people more willing to buy the product than symmetrical design.

In the comparison of simple and complex aesthetic design to willingness to buy, it is found that the simple average value of performance aesthetics is 2.837, and the average value of complex performance aesthetics is 3.092. Therefore, a complex design in the performance aesthetics will make users more willing to buy the product than a simple design.

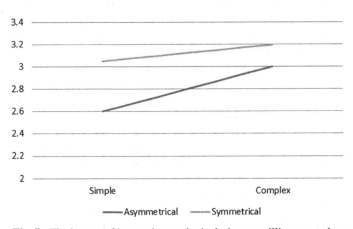

Fig. 7. The impact of interactive aesthetic design on willingness to buy

In Fig. 7, it is found that symmetrical and complex design brings users greater shopping desire than symmetrical and simple design, and asymmetrical and complex design brings users greater shopping desire than asymmetrical and simple design. There is a gradual shift from simple to complex, and the user's purchase decision-willingness to buy is also increasing.

For search product, after the within-subject effect test and analysis, the P value of classical aesthetics (F value is 3.478, the error df value is 152) is 0.064, and the P value of performance aesthetics (F value is 0.823, the error df value is 152) is 0.366, The P value of the interaction effect between the two (F value is 0.006, error df value is 152) is 0.937.

Because the P values of the three are greater than 0.05, all three have no significant influence on the user's purchase decision-meeting the purchase requirements.

After the within-subject effect test and analysis, the P value of classical aesthetics (F value is 6.178, the error df value is 152) is 0.014, and the P value of performance aesthetics (F value is 2.702, the error df value is 152) is 0.102, The P value of the two interaction effects (F value is 0.436, the error df value is 152) is 0.510. Because the P value of the performance aesthetics and the interaction between the two is greater than 0.05, and the P value of the classic aesthetics is less than 0.05, the modern aesthetics and the interaction effect of the two have no significant impact on the user's purchase decision-willingness to buy. Classic aesthetics has no significant impact on the user's purchase decision- Willingness to buy has a significant impact. So there are the following studies:

In the comparison of symmetrical and asymmetrical aesthetic design to willingness to buy, it is found that the average value of symmetry in classic aesthetics is 3.327, and the average value of asymmetry in classic aesthetics is 3.441. Therefore, in the classic aesthetics, asymmetrical design can make users have greater shopping desires than symmetrical design.

4   Conclusions and Limitations

Through the research of the aesthetic design of Taobao APP on user emotional experience, it is found that there is a connection between aesthetic design and user emotion and purchase decision:

1. For experiential products, users prefer asymmetrical and complex designs, asymmetrical designs make users' emotions more pleasant, asymmetrical and complex designs make users more perceptually attractive, Asymmetrical and complex designs will also Increase users' purchasing decisions;
2. For search products, symmetrical and complex designs will also feel happier, and asymmetrical designs will give users greater desire to buy.
3. Aesthetic design has different emotional experiences and purchasing decisions for different people.

The shortcomings of this research are: the content of the research only contains a small part of the classic aesthetics and performance aesthetics. It only studies symmetrical design and asymmetrical design, simple design and complex design. If time is sufficient, we will study classic aesthetics and aesthetics. Show other aspects of the content to make the research content more complete. Aesthetic design is very important to the interface design of Taobao APP, and its research results provide an important reference basis for the interface design of Taobao APP.

Acknowledgments. The authors are genuinely pleased to extend gratitude to Professor Yaqin Cao for her valuable comments. This work is supported by the National College Students Innovation Training Program (Grant no. 201910363060), the National Natural Science Foundation of China (Grant No. 71701003, 71801002, 71802002), Ministry of Education Industry-University Cooperation Collaborative Education Project (Grant no. 201901024006), and the Key Project for Natural Science Fund of Colleges in Anhui Province (Grant no. KJ2017A108).

References

1. Han, F.: The Influence of Product Image Aesthetics on Customer Purchasing Behavior in the Context of Mobile E-Commerce-Based on Eye Movement Data Analysis. Zhejiang University of Technology, Zhejiang (2017)
2. Huimin, Y., Junfeng, W., Wenjun, W.: Analysis and evaluation of eye movement experiments on the interface design of shopping app. Ind Des Res **00**, 06–09 (2018)
3. Upasna, B., Klarissa, C., Tillmann, N.: Understanding the impact of perceived visual aesthetics on user evaluations: an emotional perspective. America: National University of Singapore, Singapore (2018)
4. Li, H.: Discussion on APP interface design based on user experience. Technol. Wind **63**(07), 1–4 (2019)
5. Lei, W., Hang, G.: Visual interaction in the interface design of publishing apps. Technol. Publ. **03**, 02–03 (2019)
6. Ce, J., Luode, C., Lihua, D., Shichun, Z.: Research on the application of visual communication in university website design. Comput. Inf. Technol. **06**, 1–6 (2018)
7. Wenjia, Z.: Research on User Experience Evaluation of Yihaodian Online Supermarket Website. South China University of Technology, Guangzhou (2015)
8. Qiuyun, Z.: Point-and-click reading method-a new method of website user experience evaluation. Art Design (Theory) **12**, 1–8 (2019)
9. Mei, C., Fei, G., Jingfeng, Z.: Application of CSS3 in improving website user experience. Comput. Knowl. Technol. **23**, 1–6 (2015)
10. Li, P.: Research on the redesign of Fashion.de portal based on user experience. Shanghai: East China University of Science and Technology (2010)
11. Xue, C., Meiyu, Z.: Analysis of interface design factors based on user experience. Design **01**, 01–04 (2019)
12. Yaping, Z.: Research and analysis on the interface design of smart table lamp APP. Popular Literature Art **115**(24), 1–6 (2018)
13. Ping, C., Yanru, F.: Mobile UI interface design based on real estate. Digit. Technol. Appl. **05**, 1–5 (2019)
14. Min, Z., Dai, L.: Research on the application of color in the interface design of preschool children's APP. Design **06**, 6–12 (2019)
15. Sheng, Z., Yingbing, G., Jing, Y., Liang, D.: Research on the art design of news app interface——taking "the paper" as an example. News Front **18**, 2–9 (2018)
16. Meng, G., Hui, Z.: Design and implementation of the sun doctor APP interface. Western Leather **01**, 03–06 (2019)
17. Massis, B.: The user experience(UX)in libraries. America: Columbus State Community College, Columbus, Ohio, USA (2018)

Research on Chinese Traditional Garden Immersive Aesthetic Experience in the Era of Artificial Intelligence

Lili Zhang[✉]

School of Art, Shandong Jianzhu University, No. 1000, Fengming Road, Licheng District, Jinan 250101, Shandong, China

Abstract. Artificial intelligence is the greatest opportunity ever faced by mankind and is now permeated every aspect of our lives and is changing our future. Chinese traditional garden is a comprehensive art hall of literary beauty, philosophical beauty, painting beauty, architectural beauty, plant beauty and so on, and it is the carrier that carries the most concentrated oriental style, which preserves the unique "life imprint" of the Chinese nation and embodies the survival wisdom and life art accumulated by the Chinese cultural elite. In the era of artificial intelligence, the research and expression of immersive experience in traditional Chinese gardens is very important.

Keywords: Traditional Chinese gardens · Immersive · Aesthetic · Experience

1 Introduction

Once the term "immersive experience" was born, it was quickly applied in various fields, making people's senses detached from the real world and pleasant and satisfying in the current situation. The threshold for the immersion experience is rising, and in this day and age, simple scenic tours, flat exhibitions, or traditional performances are becoming increasingly difficult to satisfy the audience. The exhibition, exhibition and scenic environment of traditional Chinese gardens urgently need to "seek new, change and upgrade", inject intelligent elements into the garden space, and make cultural consumers get a richer aesthetic experience through the "all-immersive" sensory feast.

Many places have joined the immersive experience, quickly become a popular net red card, which can be seen the value of the immersive experience. At present, China has become a large spending power for leisure and entertainment activities, as a comprehensive art hall of Chinese traditional garden "flow body IP" immersive experience prospects can be spent. There is no shortage of precedents: Disneyland, for example, has brought real entertainment to users through immersive experiences, as well as huge economic and brand benefits for Disney. In 2019, Disney's Q3 media networking business generated revenue of $6.713 billion, compared with $5.534 billion a year earlier; Among them, parks and resorts accounted for more than 30% of total revenue, and increased by 3% year-on-year. This reflects the business value and prospects of an immersive experience.

© Springer Nature Switzerland AG 2021
V. G. Duffy (Ed.): HCII 2021, LNCS 12778, pp. 415–427, 2021.
https://doi.org/10.1007/978-3-030-77820-0_31

Also such as Beijing SKP Immersive Shopping Center" shopping mall in November 14–24, 2019 held an anniversary event, during which SKP single-store sales reached 1.01 billion yuan a day, in the context of the global new crown epidemic, China's epidemic prevention and control of the normal maintain, for all Chinese enterprises to create a unique business environment. Under such circumstances, Beijing SKP will maintain double-digit growth for the whole of 2020 and expects full-year results of about 17.5 billion yuan. In 2019, Beijing SKP single-store sales achieved 15.2 billion yuan, sales output per square meter of single-store ranking the world's first, single-store sales output of the world's second.

Compared with the industrial revolution that began in the 18th century, the now ubiquitous artificial intelligence has gone far beyond the economic field and is moving forward in the field of upper-level construction. People's lives, learning, education, etc. are integrated into the intelligent ecological system; the operation, management and Internet of Things, cloud computing, big data, blockchain are closely linked; people live in intelligent communities and smart cities where artificial intelligence is everywhere, fully enjoy the convenience of intelligent medical care, smart home, intelligent transportation, intelligent travel; even in the face of natural disasters, people rely on modern communication technology, smartphones, drone monitoring, GPS positioning, life detector robots and other intelligent tools. There is no doubt that artificial intelligence has opened up an unprecedented new era in human society, an era of social productivity development that is completely different from the industrial revolution.

Throughout the history of garden development, the purpose of gardens of any era is to serve people, and its form and style depend on the way of life, cultural orientation and economic and technological level of people in this era. Chinese gardens are unique in the world garden art, not only because of its extremely high ornamental value and material wealth, but also because it transcends the basic needs of housing, embodies the Chinese's ideological pursuit and values, creates a good ecological environment, the formation of a pleasant living space. It is good at discovering beauty in the daily life environment, creating beauty and feeling beauty, emphasizing the unity of life and aesthetic characteristics, full of ecological wisdom. However, as a valuable world cultural heritage, Chinese traditional gardens need to adapt to the era of artificial intelligence with a new look, not only to retain the essence of traditional Chinese culture, but also to enable young people in the A-I era to feel the charm of traditional culture. It's not enough to do this by relying solely on unchanging visits, exhibitions, and displays, and to rely on the "immersive experience" of artificial intelligence to showcase the beauty of the garden.

"Immersive experience" and VR, virtual reality are the hot words of the day "high-tech". In fact, almost everyone has had a similar experience. Such as KTV, the lighting and surround sound, it is easy to let people into the "singing" atmosphere; Fantasy movies, realistic images call out, the audience feel the same way, creating a wonderful and shocking view…Under the environment of artificial intelligence, we take the traditional Chinese garden as the center, let the experience process revolve around the aesthetic theme, use digital media means to create immersive scenic spots, theatres, exhibitions, and feel the charm of "immersive" culture. For example, take 360-degree holographic ultra-high-definition laser projection equipment and VR realistic virtual reality technology, reproduce the traditional garden space holographic video image works, with different themes and experience scenes, the garden life scene restored, visitors into the exhibition area as if walking into the garden house of the literary Gauss, you can hear the conversation of the people in the park, a total of bird flukes, rain banana, fish watching, not happy. Bring the traditional culture, which seems to be "qu Gao and the widow", closer to the audience and create a "immersive experience" of traditional Chinese gardens and a new "national tide".

2 Pay Attention to the "Scripted" Immersive Experience and Construct the "Narrative Space" of Traditional Chinese Gardens

Immersive, the Xinhua Dictionary interprets it as: "Soak, immerse in water". Multi-figurativeness is completely in a certain realm or ideological activity, focused on something". In the French dictionary Le Petit Robert, it is defined as "the act of immersing the body in a liquid" and "the act of finding oneself in it without direct contact with its surroundings". Today, "immersion" means staying in an unknown situation for a certain amount of time. This is actually a process in which individuals actively or passively integrate into it, inextricably linked to the surrounding environment. In this process, the individual is driven by the outside world at the same time as self-driven. The whole body is involved in the situation also experienced a change of consciousness and loss. It's like playing a role in a play and connecting with other individuals in your surroundings. Immersive art is the art of immersing oneself in an unexpected effect and sensory interaction. By activating the perception in our bodies, we further explore our bodies.

In recent years, there is no shortage of artists and experts and scholars on the study of immersive art. For example, artist Miguel Chevalier argues that "immersion is the central concept [1] of digital art" and Philippe Baudelot and Thierry Giannarelli argue that "immersive art is aesthetic creation, and they create or rebuild the world with all their senses" [2].

So what is "narrative space"? The term narratologies was proposed by the French critic Grammaire du decameron in The Ten-Day Talk in 1969. It is an important concept in the field of literature, which emphasizes the relationship between the expression, content structure, form and meaning of the text, and is then introduced into many artistic fields. In the narrative design expression of space environment and architecture, the narrative structure is connected with the spatial structure, so that it produces the spatial order of inner logic and meaning. Through time, the narrative main line and clues, behavior patterns and narrative cultural symbols are spatially expressed, emphasizing the communication of the narrator's thoughts through the medium, establishing a certain connection between time and space, and creating an immersive, resonant space and environment. Narrative design is like directing a play, a film, the behavior of the whole scene, the environment and events in full control, which requires that in addition to the necessary functions, characters, but also have enough wonderful theme, script and plot, in order to attract and move the viewer.

As a form of attention to the world, aesthetic behavior connects people with objects. The space constructed by immersive art subverts the sense of time and space and the traditional aesthetic experience, and greatly broadens the aesthetic dimension. From the point of view of artistic viewing, it can arouse people's deep perception in an environment with aesthetic experience. Like Beijing SKP-S, this new, futurist, sci-fi immersive three-story commercial space tells the story of a "100th anniversary of the successful migration of mankind to Mars" through space design. The theme of "Digital-Analog - Not Coming" creates a "sci-fi world"-like shopping scene (Fig. 1).

Fig. 1. SKP-S's entrance to "Mars" space

Here, like Earth's human entrance to Mars, it presents "the reverie of human migration to Mars" and tells the story of a "human landing on Mars".

The first creation is "Future Farm" in collaboration with SKP X Gentle Monster, on the left hand side is a simulated sheep ring, a group of sheep with fake real sheep vividly presented in a traditional sheep ring, lamb nose lips pink, belly uniform ups and downs, regular breathing, each sheep has its own different delicate expression and movement, occasionally make a cry, auspiciously eat grass, only next to the robot arm to remind the audience that they are a group of machine bionic sheep. On the right hand side is the mechanical sheep area. The sense of conflict between the two regions foreshadows an upcoming dialogue between reality and the future. Step by step to guide customers to immersive interpretation (Fig. 2, Fig. 3).

SKP-S's digital use of digital technology to create a retail experience scene, completely refresh people's awareness of department stores, modern retail, and even immersive experience scene, but also for the "scripted" immersive experience narrative space provides a textbook case.

Chinese traditional garden itself is the perfect cultural and artistic space, carrying the Chinese cultural elite group's concept of life, such as the "Garden of the Million Garden"

Fig. 2. SKP-S "Future Farm" and bionic sheep

Fig. 3. Deconstructed mechanical sheep

known as the Chinese Royal Garden Yuanmingyuan, once furnished with countless bronze, ceramics, jade and other artistic treasures and a large number of precious books; The existing 40-view view of Yuanmingyuan and poems can be seen (Figs. 4, 5 and 6).

There are also Suzhou private home forest famous park lion forest, according to ancient records, the lion forest temple has been renamed Bodhi authentic temple, The Temple of Saint En. At the end of the Yuan, the monks were like disciples of the Zen Master for the residences they had built. The name of the garden is the meaning of Leo in the Buddhist scriptures. In the garden, the fake mountain meanders and is interesting

Fig. 4. Scenes taken by foreign photographers before Yuanmingyuan was burned down

Fig. 5. The forty-view view of Yuanmingyuan is in full light

to the water. Lion Forest's fake mountain is the only remaining garden fake mountain representative in Chinese classical garden-making technology. It has great historical value as well as artistic value. Lion Park false mountain through the simulation of human body, animals, Buddha statues, will be a variety of Buddhist stories in the mountains, to achieve the purpose of rendering the Buddhist atmosphere, this kind of unrecosted practice is very consistent with China's ancient advocacy of the concept of "the one of heaven and man". Garden Zen is full of meaning, but also in Jiangnan garden is extremely rare temple garden (Fig. 7).

Such as the above existing Chinese traditional garden cases are numerous, each garden has a unique history and story, the use of "scripted", "narrative space" to create a method, so that the viewer immersed in the unique story of the garden, scenes, in the garden's cultural interpretation and aesthetic experience will be qualitatively enhanced.

Fig. 6. Yuanmingyuan is bright 3D recovery map

Fig. 7. Lion Lin Shengjing

3 Highlight the Immersive Experience of "Science and Technology" and Give Full Play to the Advantages of "Flow Body IP" in Traditional Chinese Gardens

The fusion of space, narrative and scene constitutes the best immersive experience. The addition of IP operations will make immersive projects more thematic. The traffic from the famous IP will help the immersive experience "Green Cloud Up". The so-called IP, in fact, is the cultural accumulation to a certain level after the output of the essence, with a complete world view, values, have their own vitality. Can be called IP, such as the United States Disney, Marvel, World of Warcraft, Lord of the Rings; The focus is not just on IP themes, but on the thousands of fans who stand behind IP and their spending power.

The Wizarding World of Harry Potter, located at Universal Studios Japan, is a classic example of the reality of film and television and game IP. The Wizarding World of Harry Potter is the place where fans around the world get stuck. It consists of Hogwarts Castle, The Village of Hogsmod and taboo forests, as if crossing into the wizarding world of Harry Potter. Among them, Harry Potter's Taboo Tour project, using 4K holographic technology, allows visitors to hover over Hogwarts at a rapid pace, accompanied by a gorgeous lighting experience of a stimulating flying experience. And in "The Duke of Honey" there are countless boxes with wands, you can buy the wand used by any of the characters in "Harry Potter", you can also experience the "magic wand selection wizard" classic scene, attracting a large number of tourists (Fig. 8).

Fig. 8. The Wizarding World of Harry Potter at Universal Studios Japan

And the world's first VR theme park, The Void, whose surreal extreme VR experience is known as "the strongest entertainment facility on the surface". The Void uses VR technology to blend with architecture for the best experience of gaming, with director Spielberg praising "Woah, that was a great adventure! This is a wonderful adventure!".

The Void captures the user's motion trajectory all over the body, and the planks and stones touched in reality can be key props in the virtual world; And its "redirect walk" will deceive your motion senses, in the virtual world you may have gone through several bends, but in reality still take a straight line. The Void Technology and the adventure of an immersive VR experience allows everyone who comes to experience it to marvel at the most (Fig. 9).

Fig. 9. The Void high-tech theme park VR virtual experience

For a city, a large theme park has a strong pull effect on the city economy. In recent years, the Great Wall, Temple of Heaven, Summer Palace, these ancient historical buildings after thousands of years of "shake-up", to a younger and more fashionable image appeared in front of people, the original appears to be "high and widowed" traditional culture close to the audience, so that cultural relics "high" and not "cold", grounding gas, human touch, not old-fashioned, new enough, the cultural charm in the ancient history immersed in the heart.

Chinese traditional garden is a comprehensive art hall of cultural beauty, philosophical beauty, painting beauty, architectural beauty, plant beauty and so on, bearing the most concentrated and elegant carrier of oriental style, it preserves the unique 'life imprint' of the Chinese nation, reflecting the survival wisdom and life art accumulated by the Chinese cultural elite [3]. The connotation of Chinese traditional gardens in China and the United States is rich and diverse, and the garden space created by them embodies the characteristics of harmonious unity between the living environment and the natural ecological environment. It can be said that "advocating nature, the pursuit of the beauty of heaven, the expression of natural landscape interest, the pursuit of things I blend, things I have the same mood beauty is the connotation of China's traditional garden ecological view" [4]. Gathers the beauty of a full natural ecology. Green plant space has also gained new vitality under the support of science and technology and art. For example, at the Desert Botanical Garden in Phoenix, Arizona, artist Klip Collective incorporates projection and music into the desert botanical garden landscape, breaking the boundaries between people and plants and making them instantly alive, creating an immersive tour of the desert botanical gardens (Fig. 10).

Fig. 10. Desert botanical garden in Phoenix, Arizona, USA

As a world-renowned high-quality IP, in the garden space implanted "science and technology sense" immersive experience, play the traditional Chinese garden "flow body IP" advantage is the future direction of development. The young cultural consumers of the future are unique, aesthetically diverse, like to explore, like to express themselves, and IP immersive experience is precisely to meet this point.

4 Solidified "Perceived" Immersive Art, the Discovery and Re-design of the Aesthetic Experience of Traditional Chinese Gardens

People are more accustomed to feeling the real things in front of them, this feeling does not need any auxiliary conditions, is naturally produced. However, perception is deeper than sensation, and it usually occurs after a mental or physical response and is the accumulation of deep emotional experiences. So can people's perception and understanding of the world around them be acquired in the process of aesthetic experience? As one of the forms of attention to the world, aesthetic behavior connects people with objects, and its support for satisfaction falls within the category of perception. From the point of view of artistic viewing, immersive experience subverts the aesthetic cognition of time, space and tradition, and the aesthetic dimension is greatly increased, thus triggering profound perception.

Aesthetic experience belongs to a specific way of thinking in immersive art. Because it returns to the direct relationship between the body and the world, people pay more attention to the perceived world, thus triggering the visitor's experience of space. Created by the Japanese team TeamLab, "Flower Dance Forest and Future Paradise" is the use of new media technology to place people in the illusion of light, shadow, sound composition of the space, from hearing, vision, smell, touch to feel an immersive interactive experience. Participants can interact with the elements in the exhibit, experience different scenes, and create their own "world" (Fig. 11).

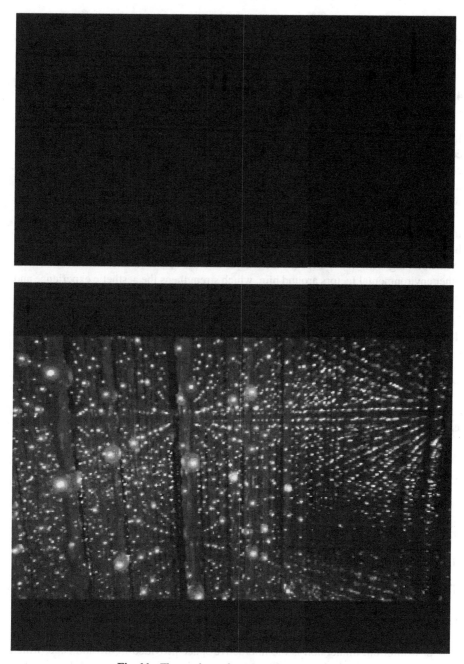

Fig. 11. Flower dance forest and future paradise

Man is part of nature, "and any living space can evolve through interaction and evolution". If immersive experiences emphasize perception, further reveal people's interactions with their surroundings, their coexistence with others, and their interactions.

4.1 Build a Delicate Relationship with the World by Creating an Immersive Art Space in Traditional Chinese Gardens

In the garden, an immersive installation is adopted to bring the viewer into focus and connect his surroundings with his or her emotional changes, resonating with them to complete the work together, which is a place of spatial experience. We can imagine that in this, from the cultural background to the landscape of the garden, to the grass and wood, like a picturesque display of the beauty of the garden, the work of creation. Being in it, the most subtle movements will affect the whole landscape. Everyone is an artist involved in life, creation, and perception through external devices. As a result, people's bodies have become involved in the garden world, opening the door to perception and synchronizing with it. As a result, the viewer is more sensitive to the connection with other environmental factors around him, which strengthens the aesthetic experience and increases happiness.

4.2 Explore the Three Key Points of Creating an "Immersive" Space in Traditional Chinese Gardens

Location - subject - Process is the three main factors that make up the immersion mode.

Location - Where, this is the first question of "immersion". It should be a huge environment that can envelope the audience, or a real environment (natural landscape, exhibition halls, theatres, etc.), or a virtual world.

The subject - who, refers to the audience in the scene, more precisely, should be the "subject", because it can be the human body. Or by digital technology to create virtual characters, the innate of human beings. It can interact with people's bodies through virtual devices.

Process - How, it's an experience of immersive processes that should be as natural as possible and not interrupted.

4.3 Classification of Chinese Traditional Garden Immersive Aesthetic Experience

The way of immersion can be broadly divided into three categories in the field of art:

(1) **True way to immerse yourself.** Immerse yourself in real-world environments such as immersive exhibitions, cinemas, theatres, etc. In the field of art, such as theatre or exhibition, immersion is the interactive space provided to the audience, which involves the physical, psychological and emotional participation of the object in the physical environment, directly by its environment to activate the main body's attention.

(2) **Virtual immersion.** Virtual characters are immersed in virtual environments, such as virtual reality. With technology and virtual devices, visitors are immersed in

virtual environments created by digital technology and re-question the relationship between perceived objects and the environment. This kind of immersion has certain ability of expansion, because it breaks the space and time limit, presents the things that are not seen by people, and stimulates people's imagination.

(3) **The immersive way of combining reality with virtuality.** Such as holographic technology, augmented reality. This immersion is somewhere between the first two immersion experiences, and it enhances the virtual immersion in the real world. For example, in 2010, the Japanese virtual idol first sound future 3D holographic projection form concert.

To sum up, in the traditional Chinese garden to create immersive space art, "immersive experience" gives people a different sensory stimulation from traditional media, greatly improve the aesthetic experience of the viewer, with great prospects for development.

5   Conclusion

An artificial intelligence study wrote in such a literary stroke: "If time were to go back 500 years, how would you tell the world of today to the people of the time?" At that time, Gopani had just published the theory of the sun, Galileo was throwing iron balls at the Leaning Tower of Pisa, and Wu Cheng-en was writing "The Travel of the West" with a brush. We seem to have entered an immersive era of "all things can be immersed", the long history of Chinese civilization, prosperous cultural works never lack of mellow "good wine", "immersive experience" is such a "good-looking bottle", it can be written in ancient books, displayed in the vast land of the heritage are alive, really close to our lives, become our cultural life and spiritual world of an oasis.

References

1. Marc, V.: 100 notes for the digital art. The Editions of the Immaterial, p. 139 (2015)
2. Ana-S, B., Bernard, A.: Manifesto of the Immersive Arts, p. 52. Nancy University Press (2014)
3. Cao, L.: Elements of Chinese culture – gardens. In: Feng, T., Yao, W. (eds.) p. 2–3
4. Wang, Q., Bow, W., Liu, J.: A brief discussion of the ecological view of Chinese classical gardens. J. Northwest For. Coll. **3** (2007)

Author Index

Printed in the United States
by Baker & Taylor Publisher Services